OUR ITALIAN SURNAMES

OUR ITALIAN SURNAMES

By

JOSEPH G. FUCILLA

Baltimore
GENEALOGICAL PUBLISHING CO., INC.
1987

Originally published: Evanston, Illinois 1949
Reprinted by Genealogical Publishing Co., Inc.
Baltimore, Maryland 1987
Copyright © 1949 by Joseph G. Fucilla
All Rights Reserved
Library of Congress Catalogue Card Number 87-80144
International Standard Book Number 0-8063-1187-8
Made in the United States of America

Affectionately dedicated to my wife

REBA ANN

CONTENTS

CONTENTS

PREFACE

As far as we know no comprehensive treatment on Italian surnames has as yet appeared in print. Indeed, the only study that concerns the various classes and subdivisions of Italian last names is a sketch by G. Flechia, "Di Alcuni Criteri per l'Originazzione de' Cognomi Italiani" in *Atti della R. Accademia dei Lincei*, serie terza, vol. II, 1877-78, which is now inaccessible to most people. Fairly full discussions of a more circumscribed character are D. Olivieri, *Cognomi della Venezia Euganea*. Genève, 1923, and E. Lorenzi, "Osservazioni Etimologiche sui Cognomi Ladini," *Archivio per l'Alto Adige*, II-III, 1907-08, which discuss regional names; A. Bongioanni, *Nomi e Cognomi*. Saggio di Ricerche Etimologiche e Storiche. Torino, 1928, which discusses patronymics; and M. Orlando, "Raccorciature dei Nomi e Cognomi," *Italia Dialettale*, VIII, IX, 1932-33, which treats of the pet name type of surname.

The aim of the present volume is to fill the lacunae which have existed until now by the presentation of a reasonably complete and detailed account of Italian surnames. While we have, naturally, availed ourselves of the studies just cited and other investigations, (See Appendices I-II) the bulk of our materials and many of our statements and conclusions are new due to the fact that we have made such extensive use of primary sources of information—numerous city and telephone directories, *annuari, calendari, almanacchi,* author lists, Crollalanza's *Dizionario Storico Blasonico* . . . etc. etc.

As the subject is an unusually complicated one we have, in the interest of unity and simplification, dealt with each surname under one of the classes to which it might belong, but have reserved a place in the footnotes for other explanations. This means that instead of making hordes of irritating cross-references we have preferred to repeat information wherever and whenever it has seemed necessary or desirable. Each chapter is thus a unit unto itself. We might also have saved space by limiting our surname citations to root-words. But to have done so would have deprived the reader of the understanding and enjoyment of one of the most characteristic features of Italian names, their abundant use of suffixes which give them such a rich and attractive coloring.

We are keenly aware of the fact that there are many surnames that do not really signify what they superficially imply. The wear and tear of time upon names has caused many a corruption; new and entirely different meanings have come to replace the forgotten originals. In such cases it is frequently impossible to separate the spurious from the genuine terms. We also confess that we may inadvertently have given a number of mistaken interpretations directly chargeable to us. The great quantity of names cited has made this inevitable. Neither has it been possible for us to get behind the scenes in order to watch our surnames come into being and have all the pertinent information on how and why they were originally conferred. This means that except for the patronymics and place names, the real origins of the bulk of individual names are shrouded in the deepest mystery. Fortunately, we have some knowledge of the formation of nicknames, which can be of invaluable assistance, and we have the surnames themselves which, by virtue of their meanings, can be grouped in a definite class or sub-class, thereby permitting the drawing of certain inferences. We have likewise been materially aided in our listings and interpretations by names in other languages and studies devoted to them. Though we can make no claim of furnishing positive proof, we can, thanks to this knowledge, offer a series of hypotheses which may be employed as clues in obtaining the answers we are seeking.

With reference to surnames susceptible of more than one interpretation we are naturally confronted by origins that have both stronger and weaker probabilities. In such cases, first preference should generally be given to a font-name or a place-name source if there be one. Yet the acquisition of a surname, as has already been hinted, is dependent upon so many different and widely divergent factors that we must all admit that for some individuals the lesser probability may, on occasion, prove to be the correct source and the stronger probability the wrong one. A certain amount of receptiveness is necessary. As to the dialect names we know that they are apt to wander into adjoining provinces but not very far beyond. Thus a dialect term from the North would rarely be applicable to a man from the South particularly if his parents or grandparents hail from a rural community. But if a family is known to have come from a large urban center or near one any section of Italy might plausibly furnish the source of the name. Numerous investigations of a local character are necessary before this complicated question can be solved to any degree of satisfaction.

We have, finally, tried to avoid being excessively erudite so as to bring the contents of this book within the easy range of the average reader. This attempt at popularization includes translations or explanations of the surnames cited so as to make it possible for those knowing no Italian at all to share with those who are conversant with the language any enjoyment or information which this study may be capable of conveying.

Thanks are due to the Graduate School of Northwestern University which, by means of several small grants, has enabled me to locate and use a considerable amount of valuable material available in our Mid-Western and Eastern Libraries.

OUR ITALIAN SURNAMES

Chapter I

GIVEN NAMES

All of us have at one time or another asked ourselves the question—What are the reasons that have led parents to give their children the names that they bear? A brief examination of the subject reveals that most of us are namesakes, that is, we are named after one of our parents, a relative, a friend, a saint, a ruler, a famous individual, a well-known character in fiction. The motives that prompt this type of naming are love, respect, devotion, admiration. As ties of blood are stronger than the others they naturally play the dominant role in name-repetition. If it were possible for us to have access to our family tree we should discover identical names used by our forefathers for generations, even centuries. Delving into the past in this connection would make us realize more and more that the love-respect motivation has been re-enforced by obligatory naming imposed by tradition. Indeed, we find that in the late Middle Ages custom had pretty much frozen the order of the names to be conferred upon the offspring, particularly the male issue. This was approximately as follows: the first born bore the name of its paternal grandfather, the second that of its maternal grandfather, the third that of its father, the fourth the name of its paternal great grandfather. Remaining children took the names of the paternal and maternal grand uncles in alternation. If the oldest child had received a votive name in place of that of its paternal grandfather, the second child took the name of its father instead of that of its maternal grandfather. If the father died before the birth of his child it was customary for it to assume the deceased parent's name. Should the names of the relatives be identical they could either be omitted or repeated.[1] In the latter case pet name variants of the identical name were employed for distinction. Giulio Cesare Croce, a sixteenth century Bolognese, in his famous poem, *Bertoldo, Bertoldino e Cacasenno,* still popular in prosified form, shows how this problem was solved in Italy when he had Bertoldo say somewhat satirically: "I am from Bertagnana; my name is *Bertoldo. Bertolazzo* is my father's name, or was his name, for he has laid down his earthly burdens, a man of much renown among us. *Bertin, Bertuzzo*

---

[1] See F. Gabotto, "L'Elemento Storico nelle *Chansons de Geste* e la Questione delle loro Origini." *Bollettino Storico Bibliografico Subalpino,* XXVI, 1924, 19, and G. Volpi, "Uno Squardo all' Onomastica Fiorentina." *Rivista d'Italia,* VI, 2, 1903, 109-21.

and *Bertolino* were my grandsires." [2] Though the sway of this rigid tradition has now largely been broken, it still prevails in modified form in a surprising number of families. In many sections of Italy the taking of the grandparents' name on the part of the grandchildren continues to be a well-nigh universal custom and many of us here in the United States are living examples of this practice. In Catholic countries votive names are now conferred with less and less frequency. The calendar of the saints is, however, a popular repertoire from which names are chosen. For instance, if a child is born on a certain day, let us say the 24th of June, he may be given the name of John because St. John's day falls at this time. Of course, the saint is expected to watch over the individual named in his honor throughout the duration of his life. Even more often saints' names are given without reference to the calendar, particularly those of the great saints, such as Joseph, Peter, Paul, John, James, Francis, Dominic, Anthony, Nicolas, Mary, Elizabeth, Anna. Often, too, the saint's name chosen coincides with that of the patron saint of a town or city, or one held in particular reverence in a certain section. In Italy Battista is popular in Genoa, Bonaventura in Bagnoreggio, Berardo in Teramo, Vitaliano in Catanzaro, Gennaro in Naples, Rosalia in Palermo, etc. In Spain, where the cult of the Virgin is especially strong, about three fourths of the girls are called Mary either directly or indirectly through the use of one of the numerous designations of the Virgin, such as Mercedes, Dolores, Carmen, Amparo, Encarnación, Luz, Concepción (Concha, Conchita), Rosario, Consuelo, Pilar, referring to María de las Mercedes, de los Dolores etc. Mary (Our Virgin) of Mercy, Sorrows, etc. Southern Italy, which for a long period was under Spanish rule, has followed this tradition in its Assuntas, Immacolatas, Annunziatas, Rosarias, Carmelas, Concettas, Addoloratas. Consolata is popular in the Turin section, while Consiglio is widely used in Central Italy. In the lower portion of the peninsula the cult is further reflected in the re-appearance of some of these indirect names in masculinized form—Rosario, Concetto, Carmine, Carmelo, Nunzio, and, at Messina, Letterio, Litterio, from the Madonna della Lettera. Apparently it is Italy that has contributed the curious custom of using Maria as the second member of a man's name. It happens to have been

---

[2] Cf. the original

> Di Bertagnana io son; Bertoldo ho nome
> E Bertolazzo il mio padre si chiama,
> O si chiamò, che le terrene some
> Depose, uomo tra noi di molta fama.
> Bertin, Bertuzzo, e Bertolino furo
> Gli avi . . .
>
>   Canto I, xxiv

Consult also our chapter on Pet Names.

owned by a considerable number of distinguished individuals—Matteo Maria Boiardo, Galeazzo Maria Sforza, Francesco Maria della Rovere, Francesco Maria Molza, Giovan Maria Cecchi in the Renaissance; Carlo Maria Maggi, Giovanni Maria Mazzucchelli, Giuseppe Maria Crespi in the eighteenth century; and Fausto Maria Martini in present-day Italy. In other countries the vogue of this practice seems to begin in the eighteenth century. In Spain it has been claimed by such well-known writers as the Conde de Noroña, Samaniego, Blanco-White and Pereda. In Germany we have Rainer Maria Rilke and Karl Maria von Weber. In France there is Victor Marie Hugo, Alphonse Marie Louise de Lamartine, and, with Mary as a first name, Marie François Arouet, the real name of Voltaire, and the poet, Marie Joseph Chénier. Jean Marie is a favorite combination in French-speaking territory, where, incidentally, Joseph is frequently added to girls' names. In order to counter-balance this seemingly all-pervading cult of the Virgin the Spaniards have adopted the custom of naming many of their male children Jesús or Salvador. The popularity of Salvatore in Southern Italy may, perhaps, be due to Spanish influence. Until a few years ago the name Jesús was very common in Mexico, but since, due to an anti-clerical government, I understand that its application has been forbidden by law. Even among Spanish women it is not at all unusual to meet with a Jesusa or a Salvadora.

One of the most universal forms of hero-worship is the use of names of rulers—emperors, kings, queens, princes, and presidents—as sources of given names. Friedrich Charles, Franz Joseph, Wilhelm Friedrich, Marie Antoinette, Maria Theresa, Marie Louise, testify to the German and French regard for their princes. From England come the Georges, Edwards, Victorias; from Scandanavia the Olafs, Eriks, Gustavs and Christians; from Hungary the Stephens and Arpads; from Russia the Ivans, Vladimirs, Alexes and Peters; from Poland the Casimirs and Ladislauses; and from Italy Vittorio Emanueles, Amadeos, Umbertos, Elenas, Margheritas, Yolandas and Mafaldas. All over the United States one encounters hordes of Abraham Lincolns, Theodore Roosevelts, Herbert Hoovers, Woodrow Wilsons etc., but more often it is the last name of such men that are perpetuated as can be seen in the legions of Jeffersons, Madisons, Monroes, Grants, Clevelands etc. Much less widespread but increasing rapidly within the past fifty years are hero-worship names of honored scientists like Edison, Newton and Marconi; of generals like Sherman, Sheridan, Lee and Garibaldi; writers like Milton and Dante; artists like Michelangelo; and even movie stars like Gloria Swanson and Rudolph Valentino whose given names now account for many of our Glorias and our Rudolphs.

Characters we admire in legend or in fiction have furnished their quotas: Lancelot, Tristam, Gawain from the Arthurian Romances; Armida from Tasso's *Jerusalem Delivered;* Orlando, Roland, Rinaldo, from Ariosto's *Orlando Furioso;* Beatrice from Dante's ideal in *Vita Nuova* and in the *Divina Commedia;* Laura from Petrarch's *Canzoniere;* Margaret from Goethe's *Faust;* Portia from Shakespeare's *Merchant of Venice;* Pamela from Richardson's famous novel; Aida, Tosca and Eleonora from well-known Verdi operas; Norma from the *Norma* of Bellini.

Most of the other given names can be grouped under the heading of significative names. They are probably the oldest type of appellation. Among the savages and barbarians the name reveals some aspect of the bearer's personality. In the civilized world the considerable attention given by the Hebrews to this matter is abundantly attested to by the Bible. Everyone will remember the famous words of Jesus in *Matthew* XVI, 19: "And I say unto thee, that thou art Peter and upon this rock I will build my church." In the *Book of Ruth*, I, 20, the widow Naomi exclaims: "Call me not Naomi (cheerfulness), call me Mara (bitterness) for the Almighty has dealt bitterly with me." And again in *Samuel*, I, XXV, 25, we find: "for as his name is, so is he, Nabal (fool) is his name and folly is with him." Ancient Greek names, especially the metaphorical ones, had clear-cut meanings: Pericles, very illustrious; Demosthenes, strength of the people. A mere glance at any list of Roman cognomina will reveal the heavy role played by names with signification: Faustus, Severus, Calvus, Paulus, Taurinus, Probus, Victor, etc. Germanic names from the sixth to the twelfth centuries predominantly consisted of two parts or themes. Friederich, for instance, is composed of Fried, peace, and—rich, rule; Hildebrant of—hilde, war and -brant, sword. There were a certain number of themes that were always initial like Adal, noble and Theod, people, tribe; and others that were always final, -mundo, protection. In many cases the themes were interchangeable: Friede, for example, could be used as a front theme—Friede-rich or Ferdi-nand, or as a back theme Goda-fried, Wil-fried. There is now some doubt as to whether the compounds were originally bestowed upon offspring for the sake of their significance,[3] but, at any rate, the meaning of the individual theme is generally clear enough.

Today we can all easily see the meaning of such abstractions as Constance, Grace, Hope, and the so-called fancy names, Rose, Lily, Hazel, Emerald, Pearl, May, June. Also, thanks to the considerable

---

[3] See H. Bradley, *The Story of the Goths from the Earliest Times to the End of the Gothic Dominions in Spain*, New York, London, 1888, 368.

amount of information currently appearing in books,[4] periodicals
and newspapers on the subject of names most of us have become or
are rapidly becoming name-meaning conscious. This tendency will
inevitably bring about a reduction in the vogue of such popular and
time-honored names as Cecilia (Latin), blind; Gladys (Welsh
through Latin Claudia), lame; Priscilla (Latin), ancient; Sylvia
(Latin), woods; George (Greek), farmer; Lloyd (Celtic), grey;
Spencer (English), steward; Thomas (Semitic), twin. Perhaps we
shall likewise witness a diminishing of the Peters (Greek), stone;
Pauls (Latin), little; and many of the names of the apostles and
prophets.

Some names, by virtue of their sound alone, are capable of arous-
ing in us certain images, aesthetic sensations, and may even be suggestive of the character or the physical make-up of an individual.
When one of the greatest men of the Renaissance, Leon Battista
Alberti,[5] led a sort of revolt to substitute beautiful names for ugly
ones, he was thinking of the sound of names as well as their meanings. This is an echo of Plato in his "Cratylus" where he insists that
persons should have happy, harmonious and attractive names. It is
said that the great novelist, Balzac, was so fascinated by the sound-
meaning of names that the name not only preceded his story but
even evoked it. Of course, the extent to which such names allure or
displease us is a subjective matter that varies with the imagination
of each person. Expressing their reactions to names, students at
Columbia University in a test given recently have judged persons
named Richard as handsome, Herman as stupid, Rex as athletic,
Claude as sissified, Barbara as charming.[6] An anonymous writer
gives us his own personalized picture of the sound-effect of names.
"Julia and Delia have a sedate and studious sound. Susan is bustlingly
domestic, Martha and Sarah are suitable for presidents of Woman's
Auxiliaries and Benevolent Societies, Sophia suits a belle and Augusta
a chairman of committees. Caroline plays a swift game of tennis
and is a daring horsewoman . . . Emily is intensely dutiful and
daughterly . . . Jane, I fear is a minx. Mabel is a gambolling and
caroting character indelibly girlish . . . Jessie, too, is perennially
youthful. Olivia and Isabella belong to the parlor . . . Lucy is un-
worldly, romantic, rather distinguished, preferably to be met by

[4] One of the most popular books on first names in English is E. Weekley,
Jack and Jill, London, 1939. A similar book in Italian is G. Fumagalli, *Piccolo
Dizionario dei Nomi Propri Italiani di Persone*, Genova, 1901.

[5] See *Opere Volgari*, II, Firenze, 1844, 170-71.

[6] See T. G. Brown, "Names Can Hurt Me," *Wilson Library Bulletin*, April,
1943, 637.

the moonlight." [7] It is recorded that a man called Leroy considered his name so effeminate that he blushed whenever he mentioned it.[8] But it is the names of Percy, Cecil, Reginald and Algernon that more than any of the others carry with them the implication of effeminacy in the United States. The well known critic, Percy Hammond, has this to say about the name he boldly assumed in place of the harmless Hunter, his real first name. "The Percy, handicapped by the jinx of his piffling appellation, is barred by that deformity from all achievement and from any privileges. The Williams and Fredericks and even the Cyrils may wear spats and monocles, but the Percys may not do so and be safe from sneers. They may not sing tenor with impunity as the Georges and Josephs do; and if a Percy is graceful at dancing or etiquet, contemptuous aspersion is his only reward. . . . If Abraham Lincoln had been christened Percy Lincoln the Negroes might be yet in chains. . . ." [9] Phonetic symbolism of a different sort is occasionally employed when several children in the same family are given alliterative names, that is, names having the same initial letter. This procedure appears to be most frequently used in connection with the naming of twins and supertwins [10] many of whom also bear rhyming names.[11] First names that partially or completely duplicate the spelling of the cognomina reflect a similar custom. Italians have persistently employed this device from the Middle Ages to the present as we can see in Malatesta de' Malatesti, Galileo Galilei, Speron Speroni, Aleardo Aleardi etc. Perhaps the quaintest duplication of this sort on record is a member of a noble Veronese family who lived in the early fifteenth century. His name was Occhio di Cane degli Occhi di Cane, literally Dog eye, Dog eyes. Finally, writers and actors have for a long time taken advantage of phonetic symbolism in order to accentuate their popularity by adopting carefully selected pseudonyms, and now movie stars are employing it abundantly so that their names may continue to glow brightly on the neon signs.

There are names that receive new interpretations through accidental orthographical similarities to other words or other fancied

[7] See an article in *Scribner's Magazine*, LIX, 1913, 139-40, captioned "Maria to the Fore." There is a jesting undertone in all of these interpretations.

[8] Given by C. P. Oberndorf, "Reactions to Personal Names," *Psychoanalytical Review*, V, 1918, 48.

[9] See D. Avery, "The Man Who Dared Call Himself Percy." *Chicago Sunday Tribune*, March 12, 1944.

[10] See an article in *Life*, March 6, 1944, entitled "Super-Twins." Mention is made here of Johann Ambrosius and Johann Christoph, musical twins, the first being the father of the famous Sebastian Bach, the Caspar quadruplets of Passaic, N. J., known as Francis, Frank, Felix, Ferdinand, and the Baget quads of Galveston called Jeraldine, Joan, Jean, Janet.

[11] For instance, Wayne and Blayne, Ivan and Malvin, Richard and Willard.

correspondence. In the Middle Ages people deliberately read a meaning into names and saw in them a relationship between them and the bearer, for "names are the consequences of things," "nomina sunt consequentia rerum." [12] Dante readers are well acquainted with this strange belief.[13] Nowadays, to many people, Reuben automatically recalls rube and Ignatz nuts; Italian Cecca and Checca, pet forms of Francesca, a gossip and magpie.[14] Benedict may in some cases evoke the shady figure of Benedict Arnold; Abbondio, the faint-hearted character of the curate in Manzoni's *Promessi Sposi*, etc. A psychoanalyst reports that a misguided human being called Crystal was so obsessed by the contrast between his name and his behavior that he would often repeat in anguish: "My name is Crystal and I should be pure." [15] Similar inherent feelings of weakness are also apt to cause re-actions against great names like Salomon, Hector, George Washington, etc.

In their zeal to transform themselves into replicas of the men of the Latin and Greek classical periods, the Humanists adopted many classical names. The tendency was still in progress when Ariosto wrote in his Seventh Satire:

> The apostle or saint's name given to you by your parents
> when they made you a genuine Christian through baptism,
> you now change into Cosmico and Pomponio. Others alter
> Pietro into Pierio and Giovanni into Giano and Giovian.[16]

In the Italian provinces of Lazio and Umbria in particular, old Latin names abound—Ascanio, Catullo, Cesare, Livio, Pompeo, Pomponio, Remo, Romolo, Tarquinio, Virgilio. They seem to tell us by im-

---

[12] Dante, *Vita Nuova*, XIII.

[13] For instance, in *Vita Nuova* II in dealing with the relationship between Beatrice and beatitudo; in *Vita Nuova*, XXIV, where he links Giovanna and the nickname Primavera; in the *Divine Comedy*, *Purgatorio*, XIII, 109, *Purgatorio*, XVI, 140, *Paradiso*, XII, 67-70, 79-81 in connection with Sapia, Gaia, St. Dominic and his parents.

[14] The influence of sound upon the naming of animals can be seen in the following anecdote. A stableman had in his charge a horse Ajax. The name did not seem to have any special significance for him and when another horse was added to the stable he promptly rose to the occasion and christened him Bjax.

[15] See Oberndorf, *op. cit.*

[16] Cf. the original Italian

> Il nome che di Apostolo ti denno
> O d'alcun santo i padri, quando
> Cristiano d'acqua e non d'altro ti fenno,
> In Cosmico, in Pomponio vai mutando.
> Altri Pietro in Pierio, altri Giovanni
> In Giano o Giovian va riconciando.

plication that their owners are descendants of the ancient Romans. The Puritans with their preference for Old Testament names and such as directly expressed their religious sentiments; the makers of the French Revolution with their excessive favoring of names of Greek and Roman republican heroes; American adoption during the last century of the names of the great men of the early days of our Republic;[17] the German Nazis' elimination of Jewish names and use of pure Teutonic appellatives,[18] all attempt to recreate by means of these types of names a state of mind, a mood, calling forth a cultural era, a race, a primitive religious spirit, nationalism. They might be labelled evocative names.

It is in Italy perhaps more than any other nation that a person may be identified as a native of a definite section of the country or even of a particular province through his given name. For example, Calogero, Basilio, Nunzio, Rosalia are typical Sicilian names. Santo, Pasquale, Natale, Biagio, Rosario, Rocco, Gennaro, Alfonso, Serafino, Gelsomina, Filomena belong to the South. Aldo, Arrigo, Nella, Oreste, Corrado, Gustavo, Romualdo, Melchiorre, Dino, Edmondo, Renato, Cherubino are, on the other hand, characteristic of Central and Northern Italy. A curious group of names also characteristic of these same regions are the number names— Primo, Secondo, Quinto, Sesto, Settimio, Ottavio, Decio.[19] There is likewise a group of given names which exist in two forms or spellings, one of them typical of the South and the other typical of the North of Italy. Thus we have Peppe in the South and Beppo in the North; Nicola in the South and Niccolò in the North; Angelo, Gabriele, Raffaele in the South and Agnolo, Gabriello and Raffaello in the North.

In the United States the first generation Italians tend to maintain their old world traditions in naming, but as they become more and more a part of the American environment there is a certain amount of name-changing which reflects the new habits and customs that prevail in this country. The second and third generations of Italo-Americans are much more iconoclastic in this respect frequently allowing the dominant non-Italian surroundings in which they live to dictate names such as Edith, Ethel, Phyllis, Hilda, Patricia, Donald, Gary, Harvey, Leroy, Russell and Spencer which are virtually non-

[17] See A. R. Schlesinger, "Patriotism Names the Baby," *New England Quarterly*, XIV, 1941, 611-18.

[18] The London *Times*, August 8, 1939, notes that the *National-zeitung* stresses names for German children taken from German history, tradition and legend—Siegfried, Dietrich, Otto, Heinrich, Gudrun, Gertrude.

[19] See more detailed discussion in section on Number Names under Miscellaneous Types of Surnames.

existent in the land of their forefathers.[20] Italian names for which there are no popular English equivalents in the community often suffer changes in order to be made to sound or to appear like the English names in general currency. This analogical application results in an amphibolous product which means one thing to Italians and another to non-Italians. Agata, for instance, is transformed into Agnes, Carmine into Herman, Fanina (from Stefanina) into Fanny, Gaetano into Guy, Melina (from Carmelina) into Milly, Natale into Ned, Raffaele into Ralph, Rosario into Ross, Salvatore into Sam or Sol etc. Where no similar English name appears to be readily available the Italian name may be replaced by a completely new and different name. Thus Vincenzo and Pasquale re-appear throughout this country in the strange guise of James (Jimmy) and Charles (Charlie).[21] These changes echo an innate desire on the part of Italo-Americans to tone down or to erase what seems to them to be an unassimilable trait, a desire to be like the others with whom they associate.

---

[20] In like manner their Jewish neighbors choose the names of Irving, Sidney, Milton.

[21] However, there is a growing tendency among the younger generation to make use of the direct equivalents, Vincent and Pascal, for Vincenzo and Pasquale. In some instances, through the influence of analogy, Pasquale has become Patsy. Cf. also Don from Dominic and Jerry from Jerome.

Chapter II

THE EVOLUTION OF ITALIAN SURNAMES

A surname or family name may be defined as an identification tag which has legal status and is transmitted by the male members of a family from generation to generation. It is a comparatively recent phenomenon.

Among the Hebrews only one name used to be employed, but during the Greek and Roman dominations a second temporary name was adopted for individuals, such as Paul of Tarsus, Mary Magdalen (from Magdala). Officially, the adult Athenian Greeks bore three names—a given name, the name of the father in the genitive case and the name of his dime or gens—Demosthenes Demosthenous Paianieus, Demosthenes, son of Demosthenes of the dime of Paianieus. In ordinary life, however, the single name prevailed. It might be followed by the father's name if further identification was necessary. To the single praenomen which was employed in the early days of Rome, a gens-name was later added, which was derived from the founder of the family tree and was passed on to his descendants. An Aulus of the gens Fabia would be designated as Aulus Fabius, the -ius being one of the common suffixes used to express this relationship. As the members of the gentes became more and more numerous they broke up into separate families and assumed cognomina in addition to their gens names, for example, Cajus Fabius Vibulanus. In 45 B.C., in consequence of the lex Iulia municipalis, census takers were called to register the cognomina together with the other names. These cognomina continued to grow in importance and were commonly used alone as legal names in the third and fourth centuries.[1]

Christianity with its institution of a single baptismal name and the one-name system of the Germanic tribes who were soon to become the masters of Western Europe, eventually caused the collapse of the whole Roman name system. Nevertheless, the Germans made compensation for the lack of second names by expressing relationship or descent through the frequent use of the principles of alliteration, variation and repetition. Alliteration, the oldest of these devices consists here of the repetition of the initial sound of the

---

[1] See A. Dauzat, *Les Noms de Personnes*, Paris, 1928; O. Marucchi, *Epigrafia Cristiana*, Milano, 1910; E. Sandys, *Latin Epigraphy*, Cambridge, 1919, for further information on this subject.

ancestor's name if it was a consonant, or, if beginning with a vowel sound, the same or any other vowel would be employed to indicate descent, since the rule was that any vowel alliterates with another vowel. Examples: Sigemund, Switried; Oeuric, Octa, Ormenric. Variation involves the replacement of one of the two themes or parts. There may be a front variation—Garibald, Faroald, Romuald, or an end variation—Aripert, Arichis, Ariold. Repetition is the use of identically the same name by other descendants. There were, in addition, a number of single theme names that were used by the Germanic tribes, especially the Lombards. Some occurred independently like Penda; others were shortened forms like Cutha for Cuthwulf etc. In such cases descent was indicated by the use of a patronymical suffix -ingo, -engo, Bruningo, Brunengo.[2]

Meanwhile, a new name system, the hereditary surname universally in vogue today, was slowly taking root. Probably the first place where it was instituted was among the patricians of Venice in the tenth or eleventh centuries. But it took eight hundred years and more to mold it into an all-pervasive institution. As recently as the opening of the last century there were a number of families in Trieste that did not have any hereditary names, while on the island of Elba they were just beginning to appear.[3] In Norway and Sweden, in the mountainous districts of Wales and Scotland, in Turkey, and among the German Jews the adoption of fixed cognomina has been very recent.[4] Even now, though it is difficult to detect them, new names are still being created among which are, without a doubt, the Italian names Ferrovia (railroad) and Telegramma (telegram). But despite all this, not long after the Venetian patricians had started the vogue, wherever the shackling bonds of feudalism and oligarchy were broken or were relaxed these modern last names were quick to establish themselves. They stand as tokens of the triumph of the individual over his environment. Hence it is that we find that many of them took permanent root in Central and Northern Italy during the democratic Commune period and in Venice after the creation of the Grand Council, but in Southern Italy where anti-democratic feudalistic conditions continued to persist they were much tardier in asserting themselves.

[2] Very useful on this subject is H. B. Woolf, *The Old Germanic Principles of Name Giving*. Baltimore, 1939.

[3] Noted by E. Salverte, *Les Noms d'Hommes de Peuples et de Lieux*, Paris, 1824, I, 300-01.

[4] Due to complications created by an increased population the Jews of Germany and Austria (who in the 18th and part of the 19th century persisted in clinging to their one-name system) were forced by government appointed committees to accept surnames that the latter chose to impose on them such as Himmelblau, heaven blue; Rubenstein, ruby stone; Bernstein, amber; Hirsch, stag; Löwe, lion, etc.

PATRONYMICS

The pattern serving as a basis for fixed Italian surnames was originally that of universally existing forms—expressions of paternity such as Giovanni d'Alberto, that is, Giovanni, son of Alberto, Giovanni di Lucia, Giovanni, son of Lucia, Giovanni di Pietro d'Alberto, Giovanni, son of Pietro and grandson of Alberto, or Giovanni di Pietro di Paolo d'Alberto, Giovanni, son of Peter, grandson of Paolo and great grandson of Alberto.[5] If Giovanni had a son by the name of Leonardo the expression of paternity in Leonardo's case would automatically change to Leonardo di Giovanni. Alteration, as can be surmised, took place with each new generation. When the simple d'Alberto or any other combination of preposition and first name was carried in the same family for several generations it could crystallize into a surname and in the course of time actually did so. This is the type that eventually has prevailed in Southern Italy and most of Europe. Incidentally, the preposition di, de, d' came to be omitted in a great many cases making it possible for Alberto and other names to become adjectives which remained masculine in form if linked to a male owner or assumed a feminine form if linked to a female possessor, for example, Alberto, Alberta.

In some instances, however, both father and grandfather's name were frozen into a single compound connected by a particle, such as Coladangelo, Coldebella, Ciccodicola, Ciccodicorato, Iadiccicco, Giandinoto, Tanidiorio, Tannidinardo, Pietrodangelo, Zandigiacomo, Vandibella. These surnames are not now very abundant, to be sure, but when we add to them numerous compounds like Colangelo, Pietrangelo etc., many of which must originally have contained a preposition, we can reach the relatively safe conclusion that the type has had a fairly vigorous and continued existence. It is interesting to note that all over Italy one still hears with frequency reference to persons in terms of a father-grandfather relationship. The Renaissance custom, by the way, of using a parent's first name with a fixed last name which we see in such groups as Giuliano di Giambattista Gondi, Antonio di Giovanni Berardi, is not quite the same thing we have been talking about. It has continued to be employed

---

[5] In the Renaissance there was a tendency to carry the series to still further extremes. The owner of one of the manuscripts of A. Pucci's *Contrasto delle Donne* identifies himself as Francesco di Bastiano di Filippo di Ghuidetto di Jachopo di Lando di Jacopo di Manello di Lando di Messer Tommaso Ghuidetti. (See A. Pace's edition, Menasha, 1944, 25.) The chronicler, Galeotto Cei, signs as Galeotto di Giovambatista di Galeotto di Francesco di Filippo di Salvestro di Francesco di Ceo di Ceo di Bonacorso di Bernardino di Aliotto di Troncapane de' Cei, while Bonaccorso Pitti, another chronicler, introduces himself as Bonaccorso di Neri di Bonaccorso di Maffeo di Bonsignore d'un altro Bonsignore de' Pitti.

especially in firm names such as Lodovico di Giovanni Bortolotti, Tipografo e Libraio. Notable because of its uniqueness is the name of the Doni-Dati family of Florence showing a parent-great-grandparent relationship in a continued state of preservation. One of the founders of the family was Filippo di Dono di Lapo di Dato, prior of the city between 1365 and 1369, hence the name Doni-Dati.

In a large part of Central and Northern Italy the development of the singular surname went one step further. When our hypothetical d'Alberto family acquired power in its home town or city through politics, commerce, war or otherwise it became known as degli Alberti, of the Alberts (plural). This started in the age of the Communes when family units controlled all phases of communal life.[6] For a long period, however, at least until the sixteenth century and perhaps later, it was customary for the family from these regions to be referred to in the plural, degli Alberti, while the individual members of the family were designated as d'Alberto.[7] In due time the singular surname disappeared and the plural with or without the preposition remained to refer to both family and individual. In the case of the first type, d'Alberto, it is an individual who gave his name to a family; in the case of the second type, degli Alberti, it is the family that has given its name to the individual members.

As to whether Tuscan names in -i are plurals or genitives there is still some controversy due to the existence of a profusion of Latin genitive names in the notarial documents of the Middle Ages.[8] But whatever their source most of them were undoubtedly interpreted as plurals by the common people. Compare de' Medici, dei Buondelmonti, dei Cavalcanti etc.

It also appears that many of the names in -i that arose in the agricultural sections of Northern Italy go back to rural settlements

---

[6] Some idea of the power of these families in mediaeval Florence can be gained from Villani's *Chronicle* in the English translation by R. E. Selfe and P. H. Wicksteed, London, 1906.

[7] Bandello in his *Novelle*, though he is not always consistent, preserves this distinction. In Novella XVII, Part One, Loschi is used for the family unit and Losco for the individual member, and in Novella XXXIV, Part II, the same distinction is made between Frescobaldi and Frescobaldo. See also Ariosto: *Orlando Furioso*, esp. canto 46.

[8] Among those who accept the genitive derivation of Tuscan names are B. Bianchi in "La Declinazione nei Nomi di luogo della Toscana," *Archivio Glottologico Italiano*, X, 1886-88, 337-38, who is supported by B. Migliorini in *Dal Nome Proprio al Nome Comune*, Genève, 1927, 37. Among those opposing it and holding that the -i is a plural are A. Gaudenzi, "Storia del Cognome a Bologna nel Secolo XIII," *Bullettino dell'Istituto Storico Italiano*, No. 19, 1898, and G. D. Serra, "Per la Storia del Cognome Italiano. Cognomi Canavesani (Piemonte) di Forma Collettiva in -aglia, -ata, -ato," *Dacoromania*, III, 1922-23, 523-49.

controlled by family units. Since the farm colony was communal property the plural of the name of the head of the family first occupying it was frequently used both to identify the place and to express collective ownership. The combined family and place name was later applied to individual family members.[9]

A surprisingly large number of -i plural names were translated at different times into Latin ablatives of the second declension— de Albertis, de Franchis, de Horatiis, de Paolis, de Robertis, de Silvestris, etc.[10] Here, too, the de is sometimes dropped. A few appear as ablatives of the third declension—de Lionibus, de Maioribus etc. Compare also the title names de Comitibus, de Regibus.

Another way of expressing family units surnominally is through the word figli, sons, descendants, expressed through Fili, Fi, prefixed to font names. The plural prefix differs, therefore, from a similar type common in Irish names involving Fitz, from French fils, son, in the singular, for example, Fitzpatrick, Fitzgerald. It is interesting to note that Firidolfi, Filipietri, Figiovanni are of Florentine origin.[11] The few remaining examples of this type, practically all that are in existence, are Fibonacci, Fifanti, Fighinaldi, Filangieri, Finardi, Firoffini, Fittipoldi, Fimognari (literally, descendants of the millers). The Neapolitan Figliomarini reverts to the Latin type, for example, Marci filius, with figlio in the singular and the name of the parent in the genitive case. Gianfigliazzi, Gianni dei figli d'Azzo, John of the sons of Azzo, is a unique extant instance of a form that must have been fairly common during the Middle Ages.

Casa is a synonym for family (cf. casato, family-surname). Only a few surnames have survived which employ the word—Cadamosto, Casaburi, Casalaina, Casamassimo, Casorsi, Casurso, Casamicciola, Casapieri. The eighteenth century writer, Giuseppe Manno, in a note printed in an edition of Bonaccorso Pitti's *Cronica* (Bologna, 1905, 154), plausibly adds to our list the Pisan name Casassi, which he says comes from cas'Azzi, i.e. Casa degli Azzi. Cassazza, Casassa may be the same cognomen with its plural ending singularized to agree with casa. The use of the word casa in this sense still survives in Lombardy where one frequently hears the noble families referred

---

[9] See Serra *op. cit.* The author also notes that in Piedmont the breaking up of the family as an economic unit caused the individual to be recognized as the paterfamilias of the small groups, a tendency which is reflected by the change of the plural into the singular.

[10] For the most part the -is names represent font names, but occasionally they come from other sources, Canalis, Fabris, Ferraris, Grandis, de Magistris, de Piccollelis, Sopranis.

[11] Given as such by S. Ammirato: *Delle Famiglie Nobili Napoletane*, Firenze, 1680, 15.

to as Casa Busca, Casa Taverna, etc., or hears the familiar greeting: Oh, Casa Pennuti, come vala? how is the Pennuti family.[12]

The Germanic patronymic -engo, -ingo continues to live in a score or more Central and Northern Italian names—Lambertenghi, Martinenghi, Gualenghi, Marcolenghi, Lotteringhi, Mazzinghi, Tosinghi. The singular Brunengo, Gallenga, Orengo generally indicates place name origin, but the plural may also point to the same provenience—Martinengo = Martinenghi. Some names in -ini were originally terminated in -engo, -ingo. For example, the old Corte Rodolenga at Lucca is now called Corte Orlandini, while at Verona Mussolengo becomes Mussolini.[13] The descendants of Orso were called Orsini in Rome, which would seem to point back to this Germanic pattern. But Italian -ino could also give the same meaning independently since it refers to appurtenance or resemblance, which we see in words like canino, canine, Fiorentino, Florentine, serpentino, serpentine.

Surnames in -eschi usually indicate descent, but sometimes they mean party, retainers, followers. A few from this relatively numerous group are Baldeschi, Brunelleschi, Monaldeschi, Vanneschi. The common Roumanian -escu presumably has the same origin— Adamescu, Antonescu, Georgescu, Petrescu, etc. The last name Palleschi very likely refers to a follower of the Medici and point to the palle, balls, on their coat of arms. It is curious to note that the Popoleschi, a Florentine family, used to be called Tornaquinci, but changed its name in order to gain the sympathy of the people.

Only seldom has the ending -esi, -ensi, denoting descent, been adopted as a surname—Carbonesi, Marcellesi, Cavalensi, Barbensi. However, it should be noted that -ese is a typical adjectival place suffix as is made evident by such names as Pergolesi, Calabrese, Veronese, Milanesi, Maltese, Ascolese, Genovese.

Another popular collective surnominal suffix is -ato, or -atto and its variant -uto, -utto. It is found for the most part in Northern Italy. There are several possible explanations for this ending: the Lombard place-name suffix -ate (Brunate-Brunati, Arconate-Arconati); -ato used with nouns to indicate collectivity—senato, ducato, marchesato, principato etc.; the genitive -atis (ati) as in Tomati, Cosmati; the use of -atos in Greek last names, e.g. Evangelatos, Alexatos; and -ato denoting an inhabitant of a place, e.g. Sanseverinati, Cesenati. Whatever the source there are quite a number of last names with this suffix—Cenzatti (Vincenzo), Giulianati, Marti-

[12] See F. Cherubini. *Vocabolario Milanese-Italiano*, I. Milano, 1839, 244.

[13] Consult E. Gamillscheg, "Romania Germanica," *Grundriss der Germanischen Philologie* 11/2, 1935, 70-71.

nati, Pompeati, Ruffinati, Turati (Ventura), Strinati (Silvestrino). Its variant -uto, -utto is more infrequent. Cf. Francescuti, Battistuta, Belluto, Berruto, Biasutti and Valeruto.

The Greek patronymic -antis (cf. Georgantis) has probably given Nicolante, Nunziante, Olivanto, Paolanto, Peranto, Petranto, Puccianti (from Jacopo), Primanti, Fiorante, Giuliante, Albertanti, Violante, Baldante and some other last names, but the most abundant models for names of this sort must have been the Romances of Chivalry with their many -ante names in their Italian forms—Bramante, Agolante, Sacripante, etc.[14]

One might normally be led to expect that the impact of Humanism would be strong enough to bring about the revival of the Latin gens name form with its typical suffix in -ius. There are, to be sure, a number of surnames having -io, the Italianized version of -ius, but they offer us only a handful of patronymics—Agnisio, D'Addamio, di Primio, Filippio, Galvagno, Genario, Iacobuzio, Nestorio, Salvagno, Silvagno.[15] However, we cannot be too certain that the -io is a suffix equivalent to -ius in all cases. For example, in Tuscany the morphological epithesis of -o was once fairly common.[16] Besides, we must reckon with the analogical influence of such names as Gervasio, Aurelio, Ambrosio, Apollonio etc.

The ending -ich of the Istrian peninsula also seems to have a patronymical meaning—Alessich, Bacich, Brunich, Michalich, Perassich, Ulianich.

Obertaglia and Bertinaglia are rare collectives from Oberto and Bertino. The suffix -aglia is, however, more common in place names —Boscaglia, woodland, Casaglia, group of houses. Nor are the -anza surname collectives much more abundant—Bertanza, Baldanza, Celanza.[17]

METRONYMICS

Although the bulk of personal last names are patronymics in that they are taken from parents or grandparents on the male side of the family, there is also a very considerable number of metronymics

---

[14] See section on the Romances of Chivalry in Chapter on Miscellaneous Names. Some pet forms produced by these -ante names are Lanti, Lantini, Mantelli, Mantellini. Cf. also Amante for the derivation of the last two. At times -ante may be a variant of -ando. Cf. Ferrante from Ferdinando.

[15] The -io ending appears also in a number of trade and ecclesiastical names —Arcario, Ballesterio, Barberio, Capitanio, Ferrario, Fornario, Molinario, Sartorio, Loiaconio, Presbiterio as well as in Bovio, Falconio, Anglesio, Pavesio, Molinio and a few other names.

[16] See B. Bianchi, "La Declinazione nei Nomi di Luogo della Toscana," *Archivio Glottologico Italiano*, X, 1886-88, 405-06. Cf. also novembrio, settembrio in Old Vincentino.

[17] Perhaps from Cello deriving from Dominicello. See G. D. Serra, *op. cit.*

furnished by parents or grandparents on the distaff side. In some cases an ancestress' name reveals illegitimacy, but in many others the metronymic may have different explanations. For instance, widows' children often assumed the mother's name or their names referred to her as we can discern from Della Vedova, La Cattiva, widow's child. Lengthy absence on the husband's part due to military service or other employment naturally led to the children being identified through their mother's rather than their father's name. Again where there were two or more persons in the same locality with the identical first name and surname the mother's name might be resorted to for the sake of distinguishing between them. Occasionally, too, when the woman's personality was markedly stronger than that of her mate, or when she belonged to a higher social stratum the same thing might happen. In fact there are cases on record which show the assumption of the wife's name might begin with the mate himself. Villani tells us in his *Chronicle* [18] that a Biscomini married a Tosa, heiress of her family, and took on her name, della Tosa, later changed to Tosinghi. Filippo Scolari, who lived in the fourteenth century was called Pippo d'Ozora after his marriage to Barbara d'Ozora.

We have already alluded to the practice of transforming surnames into adjectives in vogue in certain sections of Italy. Wherever this custom prevailed a Giovanna Alberti would be designated by her neighbors as Giovanna Alberta, which, during the formative period of the surnames might have been transmitted as Alberta (a false metronymic, of course) to her descendants for the same reasons and under the same conditions that have favored the creation of other metronymics. It is interesting to note here that Leonardo's famous Mona Lisa is also called La Gioconda after her father, Francesco del Giocondo. Conversely, adjectivization in connection with men can change a surnominal Alberta (metronymic) into Alberto (a false patronymic) and apparently pure female names like Concetta, Maddalena, Margarita, Caterina into Concetto, Maddaleno, Margarito, Caterino. It is just as likely, nevertheless, that these masculinized female names were at one time also given to males as font names. Further complications have risen from the tendency in Northern and Central Italy to make most surnames end in the plural -i. Compare Buonarroti from Buonarrota, Malatesti from Malatesta. Metronymical cognomina like Alberta, Pietra, Michelina, Faustina, Teresa, under such conditions, become Alberti, Pietri, Michelini, Faustini, Teresi. It is thus impossible to distinguish them from the patronymics. This has created the mistaken widespread illusion that female surnames are more abundant in the South than elsewhere.

---

[18] *Op. cit.*, 10.

GREEK, ROMAN, GERMANIC AND HEBREW
PATRONYMICAL NAMES

About 650 B.C. Ligurians, Illyrians, Umbrians, Etruscans, Sabini, Latini, Greeks and Carthaginians occupied the various parts of Italy. They were all sooner or later assimilated by Rome. After the fall of the Roman Empire a number of Germanic peoples including the Lombards, Franks and Normans overran the peninsula. They, too, were assimilated by their environment, and, with the others, have through centuries of cross-breeding fused into a fairly close-knit ethnical group now called the Italians.[19] Yet despite fusion traces still remain particularly in the guise of place names that carry us back to one or another of the stocks just mentioned. However, from the standpoint of personal surnames a virtual monopoly is enjoyed only by three of the groups—Greeks, Romans and Germans. Their names eventually spread all over the country and, from time to time, through invasion, immigration, cultural tradition and religion, received reenforcements and accretions. A large mass of personal surnames was later adopted from an outside group, the Hebrews.

GREEK AND ROMAN NAMES

Some Greek names with an apparently classical background are Agamenone, Anacreonte and its reduction Creonti, Achillini, Alessandri, Diomedi, d'Esopo, Ercole, Ettori, Tesei, Solone; others showing the influence of Christianity are Agabiti, Alessio, Basilio, Cosimo, Erasimi, Eusebio, Giorgi, de Nicola, Sebastiani, Stefani, Teodori. The same two tendencies are discernible in Roman names, the classical in such cognomina as d'Anchise, Antinori, Augusto, Cesari, Cincinnati, di Domizio, d'Ortensi, Enea, Manili, Marcotulli, Sallusti, Seneca, and the ecclesiastical in Agostini, Bonifazio, Clementi, Chimenti, Celestini, de Gennaro, Lorenzi, Marcelli, Patrizi, Prosperi, Vittorini. These are only a few samples taken at random from the hundreds that might have been cited.

GERMANIC NAMES

The conquering Lombards and Franks abandoned their native tongue and accepted the language of the higher Latin civilization with which they had come into contact. But they retained for hundreds of years the Teutonic names they had originally brought into the territories they occupied, and succeeded in imposing them upon the people over whom they ruled. As late as 1266, a year

---

[19] For an excellent account of the history of Italy, see L. Salvatorelli, *A Concise History of Italy*, New York, 1940.

after Dante's birth, the majority of the first names in the city of Milan were of the Germanic type.[20] And about the same time they show up in considerable strength as far south as Palermo.[21] Particularly in Central and Northern Italy the surnames that began to become fixed in the late Middle Ages reflect the prevailing Germanic tradition. Had they become fixed subsequently, let us say in the Renaissance period or during the Counter-Reformation, when the fashion of given names had undergone a change, the results would have been much different. Nonetheless, we must not fail to emphasize the fact that the Germanic group had, in the meantime, managed to supply saints in large numbers, so that even when the tradition had petered out its influence was able to go on indirectly for a long time. It should, therefore, not occasion any great surprise to point out that the number of Germanic personal last names is equal to that of either the Greek, the Roman or Hebrew groups. Only a suggestion of their abundance can be given at this point. Many can be recognized by their end-themes: -ardo in Bellardi, Berardi, Boccardi, Contardi, Gherardi, Girardi, Eduardi, Gottardi, Leonardi, Mainardi, Riccardi, Ricciardi, Rizzardi, Viscardi, etc.; -aldo in Ansaldi, Garibaldi, Grimaldi, Maraldi, Marcoaldi, Monaldi, Rambaldi, Rinaldi, Sinibaldi, Teobaldi; its Lombard variant -oldo in Arcimboldi, Mazzoldi, Rinoldi, Tiboldi; its Piedmontese variant -audo in Baudi, Ballaudi, Einaudi, Gribaudi, Pacciaudi, Rinaudi; and its Central and Southern Italian variant -allo in Ramallo, Ranallo; -berto, -perto in Alberti, Aliperti, Cuniberti, Faperti, Garimberti, Gualperti, Gualberti, Ghiberti, Giliberti; -iero-i, -eri in Arnieri, Ghisleri, Gualtieri, Guarnieri, Mainieri, Sighieri; -olfo, -ulfo in Agilufo, Arnolfini, Bistolfi, Gandolfo, Grandolfo, Landolfi, Mondolfi, Ridolfi; -manno, -mano in Germano, Alamanno, Bermanno, Riccomanni, Russomanno and Cusmano, Gusumanno, Sicilian through Spanish Guzmán; -mondo in Arimondi, Baiamonti, Edmondi, Gismondi, Raimondi, Rimondini, Sismondi. A few others of the well-known or popular surnames that derive from Germanic sources are -Abba, Adimari, Albizi, Altrocchi, Annichini, Arado, Arrighi, Azzolini, Bodoni, Bottoni, Bosi, Boselli, Donizzetti, Ermini, Gandi, Gandini, Ghedini, Ghiselli, Goldoni, Gosellini, Maddaloni, Maruccelli, Moriconi, Occhi, Occhini, Panzacchi, Patari, Penco, Rabizzani,

[20] See list in A. Ratti, "A Milano nel 1266," *Memorie del R. Istituto Lombardo di Scienze.* Classe di Lettere e Scienze Morali. Ser 3, vol. XXI, 1899-1907.

[21] Consult list in R. Starabba, "Miscellanea. Catalogo Ragionato di un Protocollo del Notaio Adamo de Citella del'Anno XII d'Indizione, 1298-99," *Archivio Storico Siciliano,* n.s. Anno XIII, 1888.

Ramponi, Sandicchi, Videmari, and a few Tasso, Turichi, Turchi, Torchi and Verdi.[22]

HEBREW NAMES

Hebrew surnames are drawn entirely from the Bible as might be expected. It goes without saying that those borrowed from the pages of the New Testament are as numerous as they are obvious. On the other hand, those furnished by the Old Testament are quite limited, very much so, if we are to count only the full forms such as Abele, Abello, Adami, Adamoli, Adamolli, Abrami, Beniamino, Caino, Danielli, Davite, Davitti, Giobbe, Ioppi, Racheli, Salomoni, Salamoni, Sansoni, Sassoni, Saulle. But are these directly allusive to personages in the older book? Some unquestionably are; others may be connected with saints who themselves are namesakes of the holy ancients.[23] Figurative meanings have helped to re-enforce the vogue of a few others—Abele, a well-bred young man (Calabrese), Beniamino, favorite, Caino, treacherous, Giobbe, long-suffering, Salomone, wise, Sansone, strong. Offhand, I should say that quite a few of the full forms point to comparatively recent surnames. They can be flanked by a group of pet name variants which, by virtue of being loppings, tend to prove that they are chronologically earlier— Bramo, Bramini (from Abramo), Cabei (from Maccabeo), Dami, Dametti, Damerini (from Adamo), Lacchini (from Malachia), Mini, Minotti, Minucci, Monelli, Monetti, Monini (from Salomone), Sacco, Sacchetti (from Isacco), Saia (from Isaia, Osaia), Vidi, Vidoni, Vitti, Vitelli (from Davide).[24] These more than the complete

---

[22] These names of Germanic provenience can be checked through E. Förstemann, *Altdeutches Namenbuch*. Erster Band. Personnennamen. 2d ed. Bonn, 1901, pp. 11, 66, 61, 99, 137, 734, 221, 321, 329, 418, 474, 594, 637, 649, 664, 613, 1112, 1106, 1117, 1172, 246, 228, 243, 1199, 1244, 1297, 1571, 405, 435, 1558. Many additional names of possible Germanic derivation will be referred to in other chapters. A few of the names cited bear, as one might expect, the competition of other homographs—Bottoni from bottone, button and possibly Giaco-BOTTO, Bosi, Boselli from AmBrOSIO, Occhi, Occhini from occhio, eye, oca, goose, Rampone, a flower, Tasso, badger, Turchi, Turk, Verdi, green. Those who want still more examples can find them in A. Bongioanni, *Nomi e Cognomi* . . . Torino, 1928, and O. Olivieri, *Cognomi della Venezia Euganea*. Genève, 1923.

[23] This statement can be verified by consulting any list of saints' names. One of the most accessible is F. G. Holweck. *A Biographical Dictionary of Saints*. St. Louis, 1924.

[24] Other possible explanations of the above are damerino, dandy, Mino, Minotto, Minuccio from Giacomo, Carmine or any name in -no, -ne, monello, urchin, Monello, Monetto, Monino from Simone, Sacco, coat, bag, and Sacco from the Germanic (cf. Förstemann, *op. cit.*, 1287), saia, serge, doublet, Vidi, Vidoni variants of Guido, Guidone, Vito, Vitone and GioVITO. Vitello is, of course, the common term for calf. It may be added that Davitu is Calabrese for David. Sassone, incidentally, may refer to Saxon, or come from sasso, stone, rock.

forms may point to the influence of the mediaeval mystery plays that once enjoyed such a tremendous popularity.

DECEPTIVE PATRONYMICS AND METRONYMICS

Since we have just hinted that some Old Testament surnames may not be true patronymics in that they do not start with legal first names, but rather with nicknames, it will be well for us to further expand the suggestion. These are, of course, by no means the only ones to lose their status as proper nouns by becoming common nouns. Almost any font name can, in fact, undergo a similar change in meaning. The alterations may be linked to interpretations of personal appellations ultimately furnished by written sources—Ercole, giant, powerhouse; Maddalena, repentant sinner; Lazzaro, beggar; Marfisa (last name Marfisi), Bolognese for an ugly woman, or they may be linked to folk interpretations of font names that have become excessively diffused in certain localities. Frequently their inordinate vogue has set up a re-action which has given them a depreciative nuance. To this class belong names like Agnese (Bolognese), Bernardo (Modenese), Bertoldo, Cipriano (Calabrese), Lorenzo (Tuscan nencio), Marcantonio [25] (Pavese), Pandolfo (Venetian), Pantalone, Pasquale (Milanese), Peppe (Romagnuolo), Teodoro (Friulano todaro), Domenico (Lucchese menno), all of which mean fool. Martino (Castro de'Volsci and Amaseno) refers to a thief, Michelaccio and Antonio (Modenese tugnon) to idlers, Tofano (from Cristofano, Romano and Marchigiano) to an uncouth person. As euphemisms they can be made to serve admirably as polite insults which wound without putting too much salt on the hurt.[26]

Abundantly scattered all over the globe are place names attributable to the original proprietor or person in charge of a holding. With thousands of other place names they are employed as cognomina. Hence both metaphorical and topographical types are in many case indistinguishable from genuine patronymics even though the odds heavily favor derivation from ancestral sources.

ORDER OF TYPES OF SURNAMES

The earliest of the fixed surnames stem predominantly from personal names. They were soon joined by nicknames usually those denoting moral or physical attributes, Rosso, red; Nasuto, large nose; Lodestro, skilful; Rozzo, uncouth (direct); Gallina, chicken = timid; Cicala, grasshopper = chatterer; Volpe, fox = cunning;

---

[25] Marcantonio is in Bolognese a tall, heavy-set individual.

[26] An excellent discussion of the proper noun employed as a common noun can be found in B. Migliorini, *Dal Nome Proprio al Nome Comune*, Genève, 1927.

Pesce, fish = good swimmer = simpleton (metaphorical), or names from roles in pageants or performances—Farisei, pharasee; Faraone, Pharoh; Magnani, locksmith; Notaro, notary; Baroni, baron; Urso, bear; Oca, goose; Vecchia, old woman.

Names from heraldic devices were also assumed at an early date. But these are difficult to trace because a coat of arms can represent many things—four-footed beasts, birds, fish, the human form and its parts, plants, celestial phenomena, etc. Moreover, devices are often pictorial reproductions of surnames already in existence. Some surnames are, nevertheless, quaint enough to make us feel reasonably certain that they are taken from the coats of arms which pictorialize them, such as (1) Novespade, nine swords; (2) Mezzavacca, half cow; (3) Capo d'Asino, donkey head; (4) Cascapera, pears falling from a tree.[27]

Shortly afterwards came the place-name surnames, originally employed with personal names such as Giovanni d'Alberto da Milano. Then, due to the operation of the law of minimum effort the name was shortened in many instances to Giovanni da Milano, Milano, or Milani instead of Giovanni d'Alberto or Alberti. Anyone who peruses a list of the names of the great men of the late Middle Ages and Renaissance will note at once how strongly this custom was entrenched. A few samples are Jacopone da Todi, Francesco d'Assisi, Cino da Pistoia, Giacomo da Lentino, Leonardo d'Arezzo, Raffaello d'Urbino. These names were, for the most part, used to refer to persons who no longer resided in their native towns. In contrast, landholders, feudal or otherwise, assumed the names of their holdings—Ruggiero, conte di Sanseverino became Ruggiero da Sanseverino, Sanseverino, etc. Small spot names like Cippolaro, onion patch; Quaglieri, quail haunt; Chiesa, church; Molino, mill; seem to have sprung up later. Others of the same group are names from the shop or inn signs. They are quite varied like Sole, sun; Corona, crown; Biscia, snake; Cavallino, horse; Crocetta, cross; Sant'Antonio, St. Anthony, etc., but, unfortunately, they face the easy competition of identical names that have come into being in various ways. However, color adjectives attached to substantives tend to betray an inn or shop sign origin of some of them such as Concadori, golden conch; Coppadoro, golden cup; Candori, golden dog; Canerossi, red dog; Gallodoro, golden rooster;

[27] Nos. 1 and 2 are names of Bolognese nobility, 3 the name of a Veronese noble family and 4 the name of a noble family from Velletri. They are listed by G. B. Crollalanza in his *Dizionario Storico Blasonico delle Famiglie Nobili e Notabili Italiane*, Pisa, 1886-88. For detailed information on armorial devices see also G. C. Rothery, *ABC of Heraldry*, Philadelphia, G. W. Jacobs, n.d.

Gallorosso, red rooster; Cattabianchi, white cat; Gattorosso, red cat; Gambadoro, golden leg (bootery); Pomodoro, golden apple.[28]

Titular names—Conte, count; Cardinale, cardinal, followed suit, and lastly came professional and trade names. In this last connection, as one writer puts it, their tardiness in becoming acclimated is due to the clear and precise meaning of such a name which works against its transformation into a proper name, and to the fact that where there are other persons carrying on the same trade or profession the name can hardly become the characteristic mark of any one of them.[29] But as trade or titular nicknames with metaphorical implications or resulting from parts played by individuals in pageants, some could have become surnames at a fairly early stage. Incidentally, one of the most striking features of the Italian trade name is the double form that it assumes, the direct trade name appellative—Carradore, Carrieri, carter; Cestaro, basket maker; Cappellari, hatter; Lanaro, woolman; Gallinaro, poulterer; or the indirect trade name through the use of the name of the article or product made, raised or sold—Carri, Cesti, Cappelli, Lana, Gallina. If these are genuine indirect trade names, and some of them are, it is likely that they were first put to use as appositives most frequently appearing as quello dai (dei) carri, quello dalle (delle) ceste, quello dai (dei) cappelli, quello dalla (della) lana, quello dalle (delle) galline,[30] whenever these tradesmen were referred to. It is probable that the next step in connection with these men's descendants consisted in alluding to them as Giovanni, Alberto, figlio

---

[28] Though there have been a number of revivals of the custom, Italian inn and shop signs are nowhere as numerous as they were several centuries ago. In 1385 Gian Galeazzo Visconti issued a decree making it compulsory for innkeepers of the city and dioceses of Bergamo to publicly expose the sign of their business. For curious information on the subject see L. Angelini, "Insegne d'Osteria Bergamasche." *Rivista di Bergamo*, IX, 1931, 290-99. One of the above mentioned names Coppadoro has a figurative meaning, excellent person.

[29] This is the opinion of A. Gaudenzi in his "Storia del Cognome a Bologna nel Secolo XIII," *Bullettino dell' Istituto Storico Italiano*, No. 19, 1898, 71. It will be difficult to find complete agreement on the order of the origin of surnames. For instance, B. Migliorini in *Dal Nome Proprio al Nome Comune*, Genève, 1927, gives the following order: Patronymics, social condition, esp. trade and professional titles, place names, nicknames indicative of moral or physical characteristics, and, finally other nicknames.

[30] B. Boerio's *Dizionario del Dialetto Veneziano*, Venezia, 1829, 475-76, gives the most complete list of this type of indirect trade name. A few examples are quel da aghi, needler; quel dai drapi, draper; quel dai guanti, glover; quel da le barete, hatter; quel da l'ogio, oil dealer; quel dal tabaco, tobacconist. The same list re-appears, of course, in the second edition, Venezia, 1856.

di quello dei carri, son of the man of the carts, etc. Then came the elimination of the middle section giving Giovanni, Alberto delli Carri (an existing surname). Finally, when the surname reached the one-word stage it began to function as a masculine or feminine adjective, or as an -i ending plural like any other surname. In many instances, too, the materials and instruments used in carrying on a trade became nicknames and later surnames. Thus names like della Sega, saw; and Martelli, hammer; might be given to carpenters; Tenaglia, pincers, to a blacksmith; della Barca, Barca, boat, to a fisherman, etc.[31] It is noteworthy that the dictionaries still give a few instrument words with this double meaning like cornetta, bugle and bugler; tamburro, drum and drummer; trombetta, trumpet and trumpeter. Also compare stendardo, standard and standard bearer. There is no valid reason, therefore, why a similar equation should not exist between the trade and the place where one plies his trade, which would tend to make synonymous a del Molino with Molinaro (an of the mill with miller) and a del Forno with Fornaro (an of the baker's shop with baker.) If this is true, it should also follow that a shop sign or wares on display when applied to a person could be interpreted in one direction as a spot (address) name and in another as the equivalent of a trade or occupation. Not the best example, but sufficiently good to illustrate our point, is the name Pigna given to a well-known Renaissance personage, G. B. Nicolucci, because of the pigna or jar which was the sign of his father's apothecary shop. Object names could also originate from the common practice of crying the wares.

CHANGE OF SURNAME

During the French Revolution it was ruled that no individual could have any other name or names except as stated on the birth certificate. Similar conditions prevailed in the past in England as we can easily deduce from a half-humorous, self-serious byword: "If human beings had a voice no one would be a *Bugg* by choice." But time was when surnames were frequently changed, particularly in Italy from the Middle Ages to the seventeenth century. This lack of stability is a strong indication that definitive crystallization has been the work of centuries rather than that of a few generations.

We know that all through rural Italy today and to a lesser extent in the populated centers each family has, in addition to its legal surname, a nickname which, though not absolutely fixed is transmitted to it from one generation to another. Various circumstances

---

[31] A. Gaudenzi, *op. cit.* 71, points out that in thirteenth century Bologna this type of indirect trade name was more popular than the direct. A Florentine example is the famous organist Francesco Landino who is frequently referred to as Francesco degli Organi.

have given rise to this custom, but probably the most common cause of it has been the existence of a large number of identical surnames in one locality, which has contributed in making it difficult to distinguish one family from another without employing some kind of sobriquet.[32] Continued usage then brings about the obsolescence of the original cognomen and in many cases results in gaining legal status for the nickname. Of course, these eke-name family names ultimately go back to an individual ancestor. They are a global phenomenon that needs no further comment. The average Italian's attitude towards the one which he owns has always been marked by a good-natured acceptance of the same much like that of the old Romans. If we were to examine documents from the tenth century on through the Renaissance we should at once be struck by the great frequency with which the nickname is added to the surname as auxiliary information. We would notice, too, that even the most influential personages have followed this procedure and that many of contracting parties have signed the documents with their nicknames alone.[33] In Florence during the Middle

---

[32] Sub voce sopranome, G. Finamore in his *Vocabolario dell' Uso Abruzzese,* Lanciano, 1880, writes: "Ne' piccoli comuni, le famiglie dello stesso casato, perchè numerosissime, quasi tribù, e mal si distinguerebbero a nominarle col solo cognome, portano per lo più un sopranome; ed è ben raro che in ciò non si riveli il genio furbesco o la scurrilità o la disposizione satirica di chi l'applica." "In small towns families with the same surnames, because they are so numerous, almost tribes, thus making it difficult to distinguish between them, usually bear a nickname; and it is rare if in this matter we do not see an outcropping of the roguish character, scurrility or satirical disposition of those who apply it." Finamore, however, places too much emphasis on the abusive first cause of these names. His view is not borne out by two of the few published lists dealing with the sopranomi: B. D. Benussi, in his *Storia Documentata di Rovigo,* Trieste, 1888, 359, and G. Longa, "Vocabolario Bormino," in *Studi Romanzi,* IX, 1912, 330-32. Compare Finamore's statement with one previously made by L. Cibrario in "Dell' Origine dei Cognomi," (*Opuscoli Storici e Letterari,* Milano, 1835, 91-92) which reads as follows: ". . . nelle terre alquanto distanti dalle città capitali appena si trova qualche famiglia che non abbia oltre ai nomi d'agnazione qualche sopranome; ed avrà esiandio osservato (addressed to Cav. Giuseppe Manno) che rade volte que' che lo portano se ne mostran gravati. La qual cosa procede sia dall' esser umano ingegno per sua natura bugiardo, sia dall' utilità che il terzo nome arreca in luoghi dove moltissime sono le famiglie dal medesimo ceppo derivate." . . . "in regions somewhat removed from the important cities there is hardly any family that does not have a nickname in addition to a surname; and you probably have observed that rarely are those bearing one offended by it. This is due to the fact that the human mind is mendacious by nature or to the utility which a third name has in places where are many families with the same name."

[33] This statement may be confirmed in L. Chiappelli, "I Nomi di Donna in Pistoia dall' Alto Medioevo al Secolo XIII," *Bullettino Storico Pistoiese,* XXII, 1920, 8, 10-11.

Ages and Renaissance nicknames virtually amounted to a mania.[34] For the most part such names are coinages accepted as the result of their being employed by friends and relatives, but often the necessity for differentiation between families has caused individuals, more especially those who had acquired some prestige in their communities, not only to confer new surnames upon themselves but also to label themselves with any other cognomen that might please their whims. Villani in his *Chronicle* of medieval Florence records that the Scali and Palermini were offshoots of the Garucci, that the Adimari came from the Cosi, the Tieri from the Catellini, the Foraboschi from the Ormanni, etc. When the Garucci and the del Nero found that there were other families in the city possessing their names they changed them to Aldobrandini. After the death of Count Martini of Genoa in the thirteenth century the Fieschi separated into a number of different branches. One line kept the name of Fieschi while others were called Scorza, Ravaschieri, Della Torre, Casanova, Secchi, Bianchi, Cogorno and Pinelli.[35] It will be remembered that when the Romans faced the problem of more precise identification they solved it not by substitution but by tacking a cognomen on to their gens name.

Because of the unpopularity of their owners certain names have now and then acquired a bad odor. Livy tells us that the tyranny of Marcus Capitolinus forced the gens to eliminate the name of Marcus from its nomen list. Similarly members of the Albizi family which had become hateful to the Florentine republic traded their name for Alessandri.

Names can also at times be changed by decree. In Genoa after

---

[34] B. Varchi in his *Storia Fiorentina*, Vol. I, Libro II, Firenze, 1843, 114-15, writes: "Conciosiacosachè Piero d'Alamanno Salviati, giovane sopra la nobilità molto ricco e di grandissimo parentado s'era insieme con Giuliano di Francesco fatto come capo d'una moltitudine di giovani non meno abili che animosi, tra i quali i principali erano Alamanno d'Antonio de' Pazzi, Dante di Guido da Castiglione, Francesco Spinelli, Giuliano di Giovambatista Gondi chiamato per sopranome secondo il *costume di Firenze* l'Omaccino, Antonio di Giovanni Berardi cognominato l'Imbarazza, Batista di Tommaso del Bene nominato il Bogio, Niccolò di Giovanni Macchiavelli appellato il Chiurlo, Giovambatista di Lorenzo Giacomini detto il Piattellino, Giovamfrancesco altrimenti detto il Morticino degli Antinori e molti altri." "Inasmuch as Piero d'Alamanno Salviati, a young and very wealthy noble from a very influential family had, together with Giuliano di Francesco made himself head of a group of young men no less able and audacious, chief among whom were Alamanno d'Antonio de' Pazzi, Dante di Guido da Castiglione, Francesco Spinelli, Giuliano di Giovambatista Gondi nicknamed *according to the custom of Florence*, the dwarf, Antonio di Giovanni Berardi eke-named, the confuser, Batista di Tommaso del Bene, called Bogia, Niccolo di Giovanni Macchiavelli named curlew or simpleton, Giovambatista di Lorenzo called saucer (?), Giovamfrancesco alias Corpse degli Antinori and many others."

[35] See E. Celesia, *The Conspiracy of Gianluigi Fieschi*, London, 1866, 6.

the revolution of 1528 all the families that had any political rights were obliged by law to merge with the twenty principal families. When the law was revoked some of them returned to their original cognomen as in the case of Giulio Cibò who re-adopted the former family name of Sale.[36] In the former Italia Irredenta there had been many an Italian family that had been forced to Germanize or Slavicize its surname. After this territory was redeemed in World War No. I, a law (April 7, 1927) directed the people to re-take their original or supposedly original Italian names. Obituaries in the Trieste dailies which I saw in 1938 made it clear that a number of non-Italian Triestini, possibly as the result of the working of this decree, owned official Italian names and unofficial non-Italian names.[37] Several hundred years previously, in France in 1539, a governmental edict was put into effect for the purpose of assimilating the foreign names that had become so abundant in that country. Among the Italians caught by the ordinance was a descendant of the Florentine publishers, Giunti, who became a well-known playwright under the Gallicized name of Larivey. For centuries there have, of course, been thousands of non-Italians who upon living in Italy either adapted their names to their new linguistic environment or were receptive to their Italianization. Thus the famous soldier of fortune John Hawkwood (15th century) operated as Giovanni Acuto, while Walter of the Mill, Archbishop of Palermo in the twelfth century, was known as Gualterio Offamilio. The Sicilian family of Bicchetto claims descent from Thomas à Becket, the Roman Braschi from the Swedish Brasck, the Calabrese Grillo from Garifilo Grill, count of the Holy Roman Empire, the Ferraguti of Ferrara from the Ferragut of Scotland, etc., etc.

Partial changes or alterations in spelling like the above were also common in purely Italian names. When the Buondelmonti joined the people's party they became Montebuoni. Men of the sixteenth century like Alessandro Braccesi, Bartolomeo Vitelleschi, Adriano Castellense were also called Bracci, de' Vitellesi, and Castelli respectively. The thirteenth century Annibaldi were also known as Arnobaldi and Annibaldeschi. The fifteenth centruy sculptor Vittore Camelio is likewise listed under Gambello. The family of Pope XXIII used both Coscia and Cossa as a surname.

Caravaggio, the painter, is known by the surname of Merisi and

[36] Noted by E. Salverte, *Les Noms d'Hommes de Peuples et de Lieux*, I, Paris, 1824, 275.

[37] In many cases changes have been voluntary, resulting from a natural desire to be assimilated by the Italian-speaking majority as pointed out in *Le Nazioni Unite* (New York) for June 1, 1945. Some changes cited are Siderini for Snideric, Tiani for Tianic, Giorgi for Jurkoxic, Neri for Cerne, Bevilacqua for Vodopivec.

Amerighi; Politian discarded the family name of Ambrogini or Cini in favor of Poliziano from Montepulciano. In the Cinquecento a member of the house of the Rucellai who had been called Cenni became Bencivenni upon being given a title of nobility. This affords some proof of the fact that many an individual has actually had or has even now two surnames, a local surname, frequently in the form of a pet name, and an official surname. A contemporary instance is Mr. Negronida who is called Nida by his Piedmontese friends and acquaintances.

But this is after all only a small part of the whole story. While hundreds of names have retained their dialectical forms, thousands of others have become completely or partially Tuscanized. Indeed, the tendency towards Tuscanization is one of the most impressive phenomena with respect to both first and last names. We can only refer here to a few of the changes which take place when a dialectical names assumes an official or Tuscan dress. The simplified double consonants of Northern Italian (cf. Giani) usually double again when Tuscanized (cf. Gianni), while the sonorized intervocalic consonants unvoice once more (cf. Nadal = Natale). The final vowels which in the upper regions tend to fall (for example, Lodovich) are replaced (as in Lodovico). The Siculo-Calabrian final vowel -u (cf. Marzu), becomes -o (cf. Marzo). The Neapolitan ending -iello (cf. Cariello) and -illo and -iddu (cf. Carillo, Cariddu) in vogue in other parts of Southern Italy all become -ello [38] (cf. Carello).

REGIONALISM IN LAST NAMES

Wherever these modern surnames arose in Italy they tended to adapt themselves to the patterns that prevailed in the immediate vicinity. In Central Italy, Emilia or Lombardy nine out of ten have assumed the -i ending. In Piedmont, Liguria and Venetia the -i and the -o, -a endings are fairly well divided. The -o, -a prevail in the South. But since the -i terminant is generally regarded as the most official of the types it is gradually changing the other terminations to -i.

There are likewise other spellings or forms of names that make it possible to guess approximately where their center of radiation is located. Some of these have already been considered in our discussion of patronymics. Surnames containing the preposition de plus article are apt to be Central or Northern Italian, especially Tuscan—Dell' Acqua, Della Casa, Della Fonte, Dell' Orto. The use of the article with first names of women in these same regions is

[38] For further differences between Tuscan and other dialects see M. A. Pei, *The Italian Language*, New York, 1941, 154-61, and G. Bertoni, *Italia Dialettale*, Milano, 1916.

reflected in Della Giovanna, Della Margarita, Della Valentina, Della Lena (della Maddalena). Names preceded by da plus article seem to come from Northern Italy—Dalle Carceri, Dalla Vedova, Dall'Ongaro, Dall' Agata, Dalla Cola, Dalla Giacoma.

In some parts of Southern Italy the preposition is dropped but the article is preserved as in La Calendola, La Francia, La Grega, La Licata, La Maestra, La Rocca, La Russa; Lo Bianco, Lo Frasso, Lo Sasso, Lo Sacco, Lo Verde. In Sicily this type as well as a small group of names prefixed by Li,—Li Gotti, Li Rocchi, Li Castri, Li Sferi—indicate that the source of the surname is a place name.[39]

Most of the names that start with the prefix In- or Im- hail from Palermo and vicinity where there is a widespread tendency to add an n or m to the preposition di, usually before a gutteral or a dental sound.[40] In writing the sound appears as In or Im. Cf. Imbergamo, Imburgia, Impollonia; Incalcaterri, Incandela, Incardona (from Spanish Cardona), Incontrera (from Spanish Contreras), Ingargiola, etc.[41] A few names in In, Im are of Germanic origin and are to be found in Northern Italy—Incani, Imazio, Inghilleri.[42]

Some names beginning with s plus consonant are also dialectical. The Friuli section is rich in words of this type, but they are also found elsewhere. Cf. Sbarbaro, Ligurian from Barbara. Surnames like Scarlo (Carlo), Schiarini (Chiarini), Spedracci (Pedracci), Schimenti (Clementi), Spetroni (Petroni), Spolidoro (Polidoro), are, consequently, very likely Northern Italian. However, these should be distinguished from names of Germanic origin employed in the same localities like Scamberti, Scardovelli, Scarselli, Scateni, Schicchi, Scherillo.[43]

Last names ending in -acco often represent a geographical place of Celtic origin. They are located in Piedmont and Friuli-Vidracco, Turiacco. In Lombardy and other northern Italian sections the suffix is written -ago (cf. Cornaghi, Gonzaghi), while in Venetia it is -igo (cf. Barbarigo, Gradenigo, Mocenigo). -Asco originally Ligurian, is found in Piedmont and Liguria. Cf. surnames like Binaschi, Bagnasco. -Ate is a Lombard place name suffix to be seen in last names like Arconati, Gallarate, etc. Surnames in -emi are Arab place names localized in Sicily: cf. Buscemi, Niscemi, Salemi. A large part of those in -à are of Greek derivation and predominate

[39] See C. Avolio, "Saggio di Toponomastica Siciliana," *Archivio Glottologico Italiano*, Supplemento, Sesta Dispenza, 1898.

[40] See G. Pitrè, "Grammatica delle Parlate e del Dialetto Siciliano," in *Fiabe, Novelle e Racconti Popolari Siciliani*, I, Palermo, 1895, CC.

[41] Ingrassia, however, is from Spanish Engracia.

[42] See E. Förstemann, *Altedeutsches Namenbuch*. Erste Band. Personennamen. 2d ed. Bonn, 1901, 960, 952, 960.

[43] See E. Förstemann, *op. cit.* 1304, 1305, 1306, 1307.

in Sicily and Calabria: cf. Giaracà, Scinà, Cariddà. Others in -è are Sicilian: cf. Mulè, Scirè, but a few may be Piedmontese from -acco, cf. Sezzè, Agliè. The numerous place names in -iano, i, -ano, i [44] represent the holding of Romans and subsequent proprietors who gave the sites the gens or family names.[45] They are not always readily distinguishable from real patronymics like Fabiano, Feliciano, Graziano, Marciano, Sebastiano, Florestano, and geographical adjectives of the type Napoletano, Veneziano, Capuano. Furthermore, they can be considered regional only to the extent that they are not apt to be from Sicily which has very few such place names.[46] Least Tuscanized of all Italian names are those hailing from Sardinia. Many can be identified by their -u ending, Madau, shepherd, Nieddu, black, Pau, pole, Ruju, red, Soru, whey.

[44] The -ano termination is a genuine suffix, but the -i of iano is actually a constitutive part of the gens name. Cf. Fabianus from Fabius.

[45] All these place names were first employed with fundus, campus, ager, casa, villa, turris and other nouns and then reduced to one word.

[46] See C. Avolio, "Di Alcuni Sostantivi Locali in Siciliano." *Archivio Storico Siciliano*, n.s. anno XIII, 1888, 380. Those who desire to find the location of an individual place name in -iano, -ano can do so by consulting A. Amati, *Dizionario Corografico dell' Italia*. Milano, Vallardi, 8 v.; *Nuovissimo Dizionario Postelegrafonico*, New York, 1940; G. Flechia, *Nomi Locali del Napolitano Derivati da Gentilizi Italici*. Reprinted from *Atti della Accademia delle Scienze di Torino*, Vol. X; S. Pieri, "Toponomastica delle Valli del Serchio e della Lima," *Archivio Glottologico Italiano*, Supplemento, Quinta Dispensa, 1898, and other studies or lists devoted to place names.

Chapter III

PET NAMES

The Italian language is extraordinarily rich in suffixes which give a peculiar flavor and meaning to the nouns and adjectives to which they are attached.[1] They are used with first names to indicate size, age, physical and moral qualities, affection, pity, etc., and have for the most part developed inside the family circle. Some of the most common diminutives are -uccio, -uzzo, -usso; -occio, -ozzo; -ino; -ello, -iello, -illo; -arello, -erello; -arino; -cello, -cillo; -cino; -icino; -olo, -ollo; -ulo, -ullo; -etto; -otto; itto. The augmentatives are -one and -cione. A few examples of names that employ them are the following: Carluccio, Mattiuzzo, Mattiusso, Martoccio, Andreozzo, Luigino, Beltramello, Marcarello, Marcherello, Marcarino, Antonicello, Leoncillo, Simoncino, Lupicino, Adamolo, Adamollo, Vitulo, Vitullo, Lorenzetto, Cesarotto and Iannitto. Augmentative examples are Bernardone, Ugoccione. -Accio, azzo, -aso, -asso in such names as Donataccio, Robertazzo, Giacomaso, Giacomasso, look like pejoratives, but we suspect that in many cases the idea of depreciation was not originally implied in the suffix. Today pejoratives are frequently used jocosely to express endearment. One scholar sees in names of Germanic derivation with -acio, -accio a patronymic application.[2] Other less common suffixes come from Celtic and Germanic sources: -ucco, -occo, -acco (cf. Bertucco, Bertocco, Bertacco), -ico, -izzo, -isso, -isio (cf. Perico, Perizzo, Perisso, Perisio). Just what they stood for is not absolutely certain.[3] Compound diminutives are popular: -ino + etto in Guglielminetto, -ino + -ello in Albertinello, -occio + ello, -uccio + ello, -uzzo + -ello, -uzzo + -iello in Petroccello, Petruccello, Petruzzello, Petruzziello, -uccio + -illo in Marcuccillo. In Albertonino and Marconcino we have augmentative-diminutive combination, -one + -ino

---

[1] Those who wish to learn more about Italian suffixes will do well to consult V. Luciani, "Augmentatives, Diminutives and Pejoratives in Italian." *Italica*, XX, 1943, 17-29.

[2] Namely, B. Bianchi in "La Declinazione nei Nomi di Luogo in Toscana." *Archivio Glottologico Italiano*, X, 1886-88, 350.

[3] For a number of -ico names it is, naturally, possible to posit the influence of the common Spanish diminutive. Incidentally, even the -one ending may not always indicate an augmentative. Cf. Carlone, Ugone, Ganelone, used in Italo-French Romances of Chivalry and their imitations, which derive their forms from Old French accusatives.

and -one + -cino. In Lucaccino, Antognazzino, Martinazzolo it is the suffix -accio and its variant -azzo that combine with the diminutives -ino and -olo. These combinations are reversed in Petroccione, Petruccione, Gianninaccio. When we consider that most of the above suffixes or suffix combinations can be tacked on to almost any given name and through it re-appear in a surname, we can obtain some conception of the great variety which results therefrom.

However, the use of suffixes does not stop with the full forms of the font names. They are just as often employed with the short or pet forms of the same. But first let us consider how these reduced versions are made up, for once you know the principles underlying Italian name-shortening a huge collection of names that may hitherto have been meaningless acquires significance. By far the most typical and popular method is apheresis, the dropping of the first part of a word—Antonio = Togno, Nicola = Cola,[4] Teodoro = Doro,[5] Salvatore = Tore, Toro,[6] Liborio = Borio, Serafino = Fino,[7] Enrico-Arrigo = Rico, Rigo,[8] Tommaso = Maso,[9] Raimondo = Mondo,[10] Alberto = Berto.[11]

Another popular method of forming pet names is through syncope, that is taking letters out from the middle of a word. By this means we get Betto[12] from Benedetto, Bardo from Bernardo or Berardo,[13] Buto from Benvenuto, Borso from Bonaccorso, Tacco[14] from Talacco, Meo[15] from Matteo or Mazzeo or Amedeo, Dato[16] from Donato, Gardo[17] from Gerardo, Lenzo from Lorenzo, Mele[18] from Manuele.

A third group consists of names abbreviated twice, once by

---

[4] Less common Agricola also gives Cola.

[5] Cf. Doro from Isidoro, Eliodoro, Polidoro, Ristoro, etc.

[6] Cf. Tore, Toro from Ettore, Vittore, Amatore, etc., and Genoese Toro from Cristoforo.

[7] Any name in -fo will yield the same results: Ruffino, Rodolfo, Guelfo, Astolfo, etc.

[8] Cf. Rico, Rigo from Federico, Federigo, Americo, Amerigo, etc.

[9] Cf. Maso, Masso from DalMAS(S)O, GiacoMAS(S)O.

[10] Cf. Mondo from Edmondo, Sigismondo, etc.

[11] Cf. Berto from Umberto, Cuniberto, Filiberto, Giberto, Lamberto, etc.

[12] Through apheresis Betto could also be derived from ElizaBETTO, JacoBETTO, etc.

[13] Again through apheresis and substitution of a b for a p Bardo might come from Pardo, Leopardo.

[14] Cf. Eustachio, BerTACCO, Germanic TACCO (See E. Förstemann, Altdeutsches Namenbuch. Erster Band. Personennamen. 2d ed. Bonn.

[15] Cf. also Meo from BartoloMEO and Pisan Tomeo = Tommaso.

[16] Cf. Dato from DioDATO.

[17] Cf. Gardo from EdGARDO.

[18] Cf. Mele from MichELE.

apheresis and again by syncope. This causes Alberico to produce Berico and then Bico,[19] Niccolaio to produce *Colaio and then Caio,[20] Nicolosa, Colosa and then Cosa,[21] Bencivenni, Civenni and then Cenni, Angiolotto, *Giolotto and then Giotto.[22]

Some names are shortened through apocope, that is, the dropping of the last part of the name. For example, Bartolomeo is reduced to Bartolo, Baldovino to Baldo,[23] Barnaba to Barna,[24] Riccardo to Ricca,[25] Bencivengo to Benci, Gabriele to Gabrio, Guicciardo to Guiccio. Though it was a common pet name type in Italy before the year one thousand its vogue has been weakened by the rise in popularity of other pet name types. Incidentally, the apocopated name form used so often as a vocative today—Giusè for Giuseppe, Francì for Francisco, etc.—differs from it by always ending in an accented vowel. This vocative form has had little effect on the production of last names.

Still another group uses apheresis with regressive assimilation giving Memmo from Lelmo from Guglielmo, Momo from Lamo from Girolamo, Dando from Nando from Ferdinando, Totto from Lotto [26] from Angelotto, Nencio from Lencio from Lorenzo.

Now let us repeat these five groups this time adding suffixes to the pet names already cited. From Antonio we have Ton(n)i and Tonietto, Tonini, Tonnoni, Tonoli,[27] Tognarelli, Tognola, Tognetti, Tognotto. From Nicola = Cola we get Colello, Col(l)etti, Colini, Col(l)azzo, Colacci, Colozza, Colocci, Coluzzi, Colona. From Teodoro = Doro, Dorini; from Salvatore = Tore, Torini, Toretti, Torelli; from Liborio = Borio, Borini, Borelli, Boretti; from Serafino = Fino, Finelli, Finetti, Finotti, Finocchi;[28] from Enrico-Arrigo = Rico-Rigo, Righetti, Righini, Rigoni, Ricotta,[29] Rigotti, Rigucci; from Tommaso = Maso-Masso, Masini, Masetti, Masone, Masotti, Masucci; from Raimondo = Mondo, Mondelli, Mondini, Mondoni, Mondola; from Roberto = Berto, Bertone, Bertelli, Bertacci, Bertaccini, Bertotto, Bertozzi, Bertuzzi, Bertoncelli.

In the second or syncopated group we get from Benedetto =

[19] Cf. Bico and Vico which could come from Lodovico.

[20] Cf. Latin Gaius as well as Caio, Caia from Genoese Maccaio (Maccario and Zaccaia (Zaccaria). Asterisks indicate hypothetical forms.

[21] Cf. COSimA and BonaCOSA from Bonaccorsa.

[22] Luigi, Lancillotto, Ambrogio and other names could lead to Giotto.

[23] Cf. GariBALDO, AnniBALDO, etc.

[24] Cf. Barna from Barnardo variant of Bernardo.

[25] Through doubling of the internal consonant, common in Southern Italy, Ricca could be reproduced from Enrica, etc.

[26] Cf. CarLOTTO.

[27] This and some other forms could come from Ottone.

[28] Finocchio is a term for fennel.

[29] Cf. ricotta, cheese of whey.

Betto, Bettazzi, Betassi, Bettarelli, Bettelli, Bettini, Betussi, Bettacchi, Bettinelli, Betteloni, Bettoloni; from Bernardo = Bardo, Bardelli, Bardellini, Bardone, Barducci, Barduzzo; from Benvenuto = Buto, Buttini; from Bonaccorso = Corso, Corsini, Corsetti, Corselli; from Talacco = Tacco, Tacchini, Taccoli; from Donato = Dato, Dattino, Dattoli; from Matteo = Meo, Meocci, Meucci, Meoli; from Gerardo = Gardo, Gardini; from Lorenzo = Lenzo, Lenzini, Lenzoni; from Manuele = Mele, Meletto, Melino, Melone.[30]

In the third syncope apheresis group we get from Alberico = Bico, Bighetti, Bighini, Bigotti;[31] from Niccolaio = Caio, Caioli, Cajazzo;[32] from Bencivenni = Cenni, Cennini; from Nicolosa = Cosa, Cosetti, Cosini, Cos(s)azza; from Angiolotto = Giotti, Giottini, Giottonini.

In the fourth or apocopated group we obtain from Bartolomeo — Bartolo, Bartolini, Bartolotti, Bartolucci, Bartolone, Bartolozzi, Bartolussi, Bartolaccelli; from Barnaba = Barna, Barnetti; from Riccardo = Ricca, Ricchetti, Ricasoli; from Guicciardo = Guiccio, Guiccioni, Guiccioli.

The fifth or apheresis-regressive assimilation group contributes through Guglielmo = Memmo, Memo, Memola; through Girolamo = Momo, Momolito; through Angelotto = Totto, Tottola; through Lorenzo = Nencio, Nencini, Nencioni.[33]

[20] Melo = Carmelo could furnish the last three names of this group.

[31] Bigotto is also bigot.

[32] Cajazzo is also a magpie, figuratively a chatterer (Neapolitan), a lazy fellow (Vastese cajasse), a simpleton (Calabrese), a place name—Caiazzo.

[33] More competing homographs in the five groups just taken up can be obtained through the names mentioned in Notes 4 to 27. By far the best study on pet names is that of M. Orlando, "Raccorciature di Nomi e Cognomi," *Italia Dialettale*, VIII, 1932, 1-54 and IX, 1933, 65-135. Other useful lists can be found in G. Fumagalli, *Piccolo Dizionario dei Nomi Propri Italiani di Persona*, Genova, 1901. E. Ferrari, *Vocabolario de'Nomi Propri Sustantivi Tanto d'Uomini che di Femmine*, Bologna, 1827-28, 2v. A. Bongioanni, *Nomi e Cognomi . . .* Torino, 1928. Shorter lists appear in L. G. Blanc, *Grammatik der Italienischen Sprache*, Halle, 1844. G. Piccolo, "Vezzeggiativi Italiani di Persona." *Zeitschrift für Romanische Philologie*, L, 553-556. S. Raccuglia, "Saggio di uno Studio sui Nomi di Persona Usati in Sicilia," *Archivio per lo Studio delle Tradizioni Popolari*, XVIII, 1899, 49-54. G. B. Grassi-Previtera, "Nomi Propri e Loro Vezzeggiativi Usati a Partinico (Sicily)," *Studi Glottologici Italiani*, VIII, 1928. Dialect dictionaries that give lists of pet names are the following: G. Biundi, *Dizionario Siciliano Italiano*, Palermo, 1857. G. Casaccio, *Vocabolario Genovese Italiano*, Genova, 1851. P. Contarini, *Dizionario Tascabile delle Voci e Frasi Particolari del Dialetto Veneziano*, Venezia, 1850. R. d'Ambra, *Vocabolario Napoletano*, Napoli, 1873. G. Ferraro, *Glossario Monferrino*, Torino, 1889. G. Longa, "Vocabolario Bormino" in *Studi Romanzi*, IX, 1902. U. Mortillaro, *Nuovo Dizionario Siciliano-Italiano*, Palermo, 1881. G. Nazari, *Dizionario Vicentino-Italiano*, Oderzo, 1876. P.F.B., *Vocabolario Tascabile Genovese-Italiano*, Genova, 1873. B. Samarani, *Vocabolario Cremasco-Italiano*, Crema, 1852.

Since the pet name, specifically the full name plus suffixes, and its reduced equivalent plus suffixes unquestionably furnish us with the largest and most typical block of Italian surnames, we hope that we are not overtaxing the patience of our readers in reserving special treatment for the most wide-spread of pet surnames deriving from Francesco, Domenico, Giacomo, Giovanni and Pietro. The multiplicity of the different forms each of these names can assume will, at least, prove startling to those who peruse the lists for the first time.

THE FRANCESCO TRIBE

Full Forms

Francesco, Francisco, Franseco, de Francisci, de Franciscis

Variant Forms

Franco,[34] de Franchis, Lo Franco, Franci, Franso, Franzo

Full Forms with Suffixes

Franceschilli, Franceschiello, Franceschetti, Franceschini, France-schinis, Francesconi, Fransecone, Franchella, Franchetti, Franchino, Franchitti, Francone, Francoli, Francolino,[35] Francino, Francioli, Francione, Franciotto, Francello, Francillo, Frangello, Fragino, Franscioni, Frangione, Franchioni, Franscella, Franscilla, Fransinelli, Fransoni, Franzini, Franzetto, Franzitti, Franzona, Franzotta, Franzelini,[36] Franzolin, Franzonello, Franzonetti

Short Forms: Apheresis
Models followed by derivative shortening

FranCESCO — Cesco, Ceschini
FranCISCO — Cisco
* FranSISCA [37] — Sisca
FranceSCHELLO — Schellini
FrancesSCHETTO — Schetti, Schettini
FranceSCHINO — Schini,[38] Schinelli, Schinetti, Schinone
FranceSCOTTO — Scotto, Scottini, Scotton [39]

---

[34] Franco can come from Francesco through Franceschino according to M. Orlando, *op. cit.* It also means frank, bold. Cf. Lanfranco.

[35] Cf. francolin, partridge, and finch (Bormino dialect).

[36] Franzelin seems to be a dialectical word for finch.

[37] Starred forms here and elsewhere mean that the terms have not been found as last names. The words that follow, however, are all genuine cognomina.

[38] Cf. Piedmontese schin-zecchino, sequin.

[39] Occasionally from Scot.

FrancesCHELLO, FranCHELLO — Chella, Chellotti, Chellini, Chilussi, Cheleni, Ghelli

FrancesCHINO, FranCHINO — Chini, Chines, Chinetti, Chinotti, Ghini, Chinozzi, Ghinossi, Ghinetti

FrancesCOCCIO, FranCOCCIO — Cocci [40]

FrancesCONI, FranCONI — Coni, Conelli, Concini, Gonella, Gonnella, Gonetta [41]

FrancesCOTTO, FranCOTTO — Cotta,[42] Cottini, Cottazzi, Cottoni, Cottarelli, Cottirelli

FrancesCOZZI, FranCOZZI — Cozzi,[43] Cozzetti, Cozzoli, Cozzolini, Gozzi, Gozzini, Cozzola

FrancesCUCCIO, FranCUCCIO — Cuccia, Cuccinotti, Cucinelli, Cucciniello, Cuccetta, Guccioni, Gussoni,[44] Gucci, Guccerelli

FrancesCUZZO, FranCUZZO — Cuzzi, Cuzzetti, Cuzzone,[45] Cuzzella, Guzzi, Guzzini, Guzzoni [46]

FranZINO — Zini

FranZETTO — Zetto

FranZOTTO — Zotti, Zottoli

FranZOLA — Zola, Zolla,[47] Zolini

FranZONA — Zona

FranCINO — Cino, Cinelli

FranCIOTTO — Ciotto, Giotto, Giottini, Giottonini

FranCESCO-CESCO, CECCO — Cecchi, Ceccarini, Ceccaroni, Ceccherelli, Ceccherini, Cecchetelli, Cecchile?, Ceccoli, Cec(c)olin, Cec(c)oni, Cec(c)orella, Ceccucci, Ceccuzzi

FranCESCO - CESCO - CECCO - CHECCO — Checchi, Checchia, Checo, Chieco, Checchetelli, Chec(c)ucci, Checcacci, del Checcolo

---

[40] Coccia is a regular Southern Italian word for head. In Cremonese a coccio is a coachman.

[41] Cf. the Southern Italian place name Conetta from ikon, image. Gonnella also means a skirt. See Object Names.

[42] Cotta may be another object name meaning gown, long coat, mail coat. Cf. the old Roman name Cotta, and the Germanic Cotta (see Förstemann, op. cit. 659.

[43] Cozzo is one of the words for summit; in Neapolitan cuozzo is a harsh impolite fellow; cozza in Calabrese is an oyster.

[44] In Marchigiano a cuccia is a weasel. Gussoni may be related to Germanic Gusso (see Förstemann, op. cit. 713).

[45] Some of the cozzo meanings may apply to cuzzo. However, a cuzzone can be interpreted as a broker, or Venetian cuzzon, rascal.

[46] Guzzini (Gozzini) is in some cases aguzzino, convict keeper, rascal.

[47] Zola, Roveretano for crow and Barese for jug, have a thin chance as surname sources. One meaning of zolla is clod.

FranCISCO-CISCO-CICCO — Cicco, Ciccarelli, Cic(c)atella, Cic-chetto, Ciccherone, Cicchelli, Cicchillo, Cicchini, Cicchinelli, Cicchitello, Cicchitti, Ciccolella, Cic(c)colini, Ciccolo, Cicculi, Ciccone, Cicconetti, Cic(c)otti, Ciccottini, Cicullo, Cic(c)u-rillo [48]

FranCISCO-CISCO-CICCO-CICCIO — Cicci, Cic(c)ella, Cic(c)-etti, Cicciarelli, Cicciotti, Cicirello, Ciccione [49]

FranCISCO-CISCO-CICCO-CHICCO — Chicco, Chiccone, Chi-cotti, Chicarelli, Chiccorino, Chiechio

* FranSCISCIO — Sciuscietto

Syncopated Forms

These come from FRAncesCO, FRancESCO, FRansISCO, FRANceSchINO and produce Frascarelli, Fraschella, Fraschetti, Fraschini, Frascone;[50] Freschi, Freschini, di Frisco, Friscune, Fran-schini [51]

THE DOMINIC TRIBE

Domenico, Dominico, Domico — Menchi, Minchi, Mengarino, Men-gorini, Mengrino,[52] Mencherini, Meco, Mechi, Mecacci, Meche-rini, Mecocci, Meconi, Mecozzi, Mico, Micocci, Michetti, Mic-chini, Micone, Micotti, Micola [53]

* Domenicocci — Menicocci, Cocci

---

[47] Checca and Cecca meaning magpie compete to a certain extent.

[48] Some of the Cicco names (and perhaps also some of the Cecco names) may be outcroppings of Longobard Ciccus, Cicus. See B. Bianchi, "La Declina-zione nei Nomi di Luogo della Toscana," *Archivio Glottologico Italiano*, X, 1886-88, 310-11.

[49] Southern Italians differentiate between Cicco and Ciccio by applying the first to ordinary folk and the second to children of nobles and artisans. Cf. Ciccia Genoese for Battista and Cice pet form for Felice and Beatrice.

[50] Not impossible as a nickname surname is frasca, flirt.

[51] Aside from the homographs given in the preceding footnotes, the differ-ent forms of Francesco coincide at various stages with pet forms of Pasca, Domenico, Rocco, Marco, Amico, Arrigo, Enrico, Americo, Luca, Pacifico, Vincenzo, Marzo, Costanzo, Lattanzio, Terenzio, Maurizio, Tizio, Prudenza, Providenza, Gioacchino, Malachia, Zorzo (Giorgio), Angelo and the dialectical Anzolo, Simone, Luigi, Pacino, Lancilotto, Ambrogio, Sergio, Lucia and others. On the basis of what he has learned about pet name formation the reader can make his own deductions. Many of the Francesco forms given here are also listed in A. Bongioanni, *Nomi e Cognomi* . . . Torino, 1928. Inci-dentally, the name Schettini, cited above may be explained through Schettino, province of Catania.

[52] Mengarino, Mengrino may be a medicinal plant, gromwell.

[53] Cf. Micol, wife of David. Miccola in Avellinese is a lentil.

Domenichelli, Dominichelli — Menichelli, Menichiello, Menichillo, Minichelli, Menghiella, Minghelli, Chelli, Ghelli, Chellotti, Chellini

Domenichetti, Domeneghetti, Dominichetti — Menichetti, Menchetto, Menchella, Meneghetto, Menghetti, Minghetti, Ghetti [54]

Domenichini, Dominichini — Menichini, Menghini, Menegheni,[55] Minichini,[56] Chini, Chinetti, Chinotti, Chinozzi, Ghini, Ghinetti, Ghinozzi, Ghinosi Ghinossi

Domenicone — Meniconi, Miniconi, Mengoni, Coni,[57] Conino, Concini, Conelli, Gonelli, Gonnella, Gonetta

Domenicacci — Menicacci, Mencacci, Mencaccini, Cacci, Caccini, Gaggia,[58] Gaggiotti

Domenicucci — Menicucci, Menegucci, Minigucci, Cucci, Gucci, Cuccioli,[59] Cuccetta, Gucci, Guccioni, Gussoni, Guccerelli

* Domenicotti, Dominigotti — Mencotti, Mengotti, Mingotti, Mincotti, Cotti, Gotti, Gottini, Cottone, Cotazzi, Cottarelli, Cottirelli

* Domenicozzi — Minicozzi, Mingozzi, Mengozzi, Cozzi, Cozzone, Gozzi, Gozzini, Gozzoli

* Domenicuzzi — Meneguzzi, Meniguzzi, Minguzzi, Cuzzi, Guzzi, Guzzini, Cuzzone, Guzzoni, Cuzzella, Guzzula

* Domenicazzi — Menegazzi, Mengazzi, Mengazzini, Mingazzini, Cazza, Cazzola, Gazza, Gazzola [60]

* Domenichezzo — Menghezzi, Ghezzi [61]

* Domenicola — Mengoli, Mengula

* Domenicarelli — Mengarelli, Carelli, Garelli

* Domenicarini — Mencarini, Mengarini, Garini

Domenici, Dominici, Domicelli — Minneci, Mencini, Mencitto, Minciotti, Ciotto, Giotti, Giottini, Giottonini, Micci, Micciotti, Micciarelli, Miciola [62]

Domini, Dominelli, Dominetti, Dumini (Venetian), Minelli
Menis, Menazzi, Menini, Menoni, Menotti, Minotti, Menozzi, Minozzi, Minocchi, Minucci, Minutelli (Venetian-Friulano),

---

[54] A ghetta is a gaiter, hose and Ghetto, the Jewish Quarter.

[55] A Meneghin in Milanese is a servant loaned out for Sunday work.

[56] Germanic forms Minnico, Minco are in existence. Cf. Förstemann, *op. cit.* 1125.

[57] Cf. the Sicilian first name Cono.

[58] Gaggia is also magpie, acacia.

[59] A cucciolo is also a lap dog, ninny.

[60] A gazza is likewise a magpie.

[61] Ghezzo also means dark, a black crow, a lizard (Milanese). Cf. Germanic Sighezzo.

[62] A miccio is also an ass, stubborn person.

Minnunni, Minoletti; Menno,[63] Mennonna (Lucchese)
Bechi, Bechelli, Becchetti, Becchini,[64] Beghini, Becherini, Becheroni, Becherucci (all Tuscan)[65]

THE JAMES TRIBE

Giacomo — Como, Comarelli,[66] Cumo

* Giacomaccio — Macci, Maccioni [67]

Giacomasso — Maso, Masini, Masoni, Massoli, Masolesso(?), Massotti, Massucci [68]

Giacomazzo — Comazzi, Mazzo, Mazzoni, Mazzini, Mazzarella, Mazzerella, Mazzitelli, Mazzola, Mazzolini, Mazzucca, Mazzucchelli, Mazzucchetti, Mazollo [69]

Giacomelli — Comel, Comelli, Comellini, Cumella, Mello, Mellone, Melone [70]

Giacometti — di Giacomettino, Cometti, Metti, Metino

Giacomini — Comini, Cominetti, Cuminetti, Cominazzi, Cominotti, Comincioli, Cominoli, Minetti, Minotti, Minucci, Minoletti

* Giacomitti — Mittino [71]

* Giacomizzi — Comizzoli, Mizzi

* Giacomocci — Moccia, Mocciola, Mocello, Mocerelli, Mocerini, Moggio [72]

* Giacomolo — Comola, Comolli, Comoletto, Mola, Moleti, Molossi [73]

---

[63] Menno is also a beardless fellow, while menna is a nipple—see Anatomical Names.

[64] Cf. becco, goat, beco, earthworm, becchini, grave digger, sexton, bicchiere, glass, bcher, becher (Northern Italian), butcher.

[65] Homographs coinciding with the above include short forms of Francesco, Michele (Mico), Caro, Ungaro, Zaccaria, Maccario, Giacomo, Tommaso, Carmine, Anselmo, Guglielmo, Filomena as well as the short forms of other names noted under Note 51. For pet names of Dominic I follow and expand the long list given by G. Flechia, "Di Alcuni Criteri per l'Originazione de' Cognomi Italiani." *Atti della Reggia Accademia dei Lincei*, Anno CCLXXV, 1877-78, serie terza, Vol. II, 609-22.

[66] Cf. the geographical Como and comarella (dialectical) godmother, midwife.

[67] In some dialects a maccia is a thicket.

[68] The Masso names are also connected with stony ground, boulder.

[69] Some of the Mazzo names also refer to club. In Genoese Mazzo = Maggio. Mazzone can be, in addition, interpreted variously as a fish, an old ox, a slow moving person (Calabrese), a cattle field (Neapolitan); mazzino (Sannio) as a corpulent fellow; mazzucca as a sort of hammer, a stubborn person and, in Venetian, head; mazzarella as gnat (Calabrese).

[70] Cf. the word for melon.

[71] The pet form of Margherita in Sicilian is Mita.

[72] Cf. moscerino, gnat and mogio, sleepy, dull.

[73] A mola is a grindstone; moleta in Bergamascan and Bresciano a grinder and a molosso a mastiff.

Giacomoni — Monelli, Monetti, Moneta,[74] Monini
* Giacomosso — Mosso, Mossolini, Mosotti, Mossini [75]
* Giacomotto — Motto, Mottini, Mottinelli, Mottola [76]
Giacomozzo — Mozzi, Mozzini, Mozzetti, Mozzarelli, Mozzoni [77]
* Giacomucci — Mucci, Muccillo, Muccino, Muceli, Mucerina [78]
* Giacomusci — Muscio, Musciarelli [79]
* Giacomussi — Musso, Mussettini, Mussone, Mussilli, Mussotti, Mussetti, Mussolini, Muselli, Musulillo [80]
Giacomuzzo — Muzzi, Muzzarelli, Muzzarini, Muzzini, Muzzillo, Muzzolo, Muzzullo, Muzzone, Muzzonini [81]

The Giacop(p)o-Iacop(p)o Branch

Giacoppo — Copo, Coppa [82]
Giacop(p)ello —Copello, Coppelli, Pellini [83]
Giacopini — Coppini, Pini, Pinelli, Pinetti, Pinocci, Pinotti, Pinerella, Pinolini [84]
Giacoppoli — Coppoli, Coppolillo, Copolino, Coppolla, Pollo, Pollini [85]
Giacopone — Giacoponelli, Ponelli
* Jacoparino — Parini, Paretto, Parelli, Parrini,[86] Parrelli
* Jacoperino —Perini, Rini, Rinetti, Rinelli, Rinucci, Rinuccini
Iacopetti — Peto, Petti, Pettinelli, Petterino, Petorella, Pettoello [87]
* Iacopaccio — Copaci, Pacelli, Pacetti, Pacini, Pacinotti, Pacioni, Pacciotti

---

[74] A monello is likewise an urchin and moneta a coin.

[75] Perhaps these words can also be related to gnat.

[76] It may be that we are here dealing with names indicating a dumb person. Cf. Romagnuolo mott.

[77] Mozzo can also mean stable boy, maimed, and mozzone (Neapolitan) pigmy.

[78] In Modenese a mucina is a cat. Cf. Mocerino with moscerino.

[79] Muscia is one of the popular words for cat, while muscio also stands for flabby, slow.

[80] Muso, Musso also mean snout. P. Aebischer in "L'Origine et l'Air de dispersion du Prénom Médiéval Italien Muntius." *Archivum Romanicum*, XVII, 1933, 279-88, would trace most of these musso-words, including Mussolini, to Muntius.

[81] See Note 77.

[82] The word for cup is coppa.

[83] In Abruzzese pelline signifies dim-sightedness. Cf. AmPELLINO.

[84] Pino will be easily recognized as pine. See Botanical Names.

[85] A coppola is also a cap and pollo a pullet. Pollo is likewise a variant of Polo, Paolo and can come from Southern Italian Leopollo, that is, Leopoldo,

[86] Cf. Sicilian parrino, priest, godfather, and Gasparrino, Gasparrello, the best sources of these names.

[87] Poor alternative choices are petto, breast, pettinello, comb, and for Petterino, Peter, Italian-Swiss for Peter.

* Iacopassi — Copassi, Pasini, Passotti, Passetti, Paselli, Pasolini, Passeroni, Passerone [88]

* Iacopazzo — Pazzo, Pazzini [89]

Iacopini

* Iacopozzo — Copozza, Copozio, Pozzetti, Pozzoli, Pozzolini, Pozzonelli, Pozzone, Pozilli [90]

* Iacopotto — Coppotelli, Pottino, Pottoni, Potoni [91]

* Iacopucci — Puccio, Puccetti, Puccini, Puccillo, Puccinelli, Pucciarelli, Pucciarini, Puccioni [92]

* Iacopussi — Pussini

* Iacopuzzo — Puzio, Puzzo, Puzzinelli, Puzzone [93]

The branch of Giacobbe, Giacobbo, Giacubbo, Iacobbe, Iacobbo

Giacobbo — Cobo, Cobetto, Cobello, Cobioni, Gobbo, Gobbetti [94]

* Giacobaccio — Bacci, Baccelli, Baccetti, Baccini, Baccioni, Bacciotti [95]

Giacobazzi — Bazzo, Bazzini, Bazzoni, Bazzetta [96]

Giacobillo — Billo [97]

Giacobbini — Bini, Binelli,[98] Binetti, Binozzi, Binazzi

* Giacobbocci — Boccia, Boccioni, Bocciarelli, Boccini [99]

Giacobono — Boni, Bonelli, Bonetti, Bonini

* Giacoboscio — Boscia, Boscioni [100]

* Giacobos(s)i — Bossi, Bossetti, Boselli [101]

[88] Passerino, Passerone are words for sparrow.

[89] Pazzo, insane, should not be excluded as a surnominal possibility. Bazzo is a variant form; see below. Cf. bazza, chin.

[90] Some of these names may refer to pozzo, well or pozzol (Northern Italian) terrace. Also cf. the place name Pozzuoli.

[91] Cf. Germanic Potho, Potoni in Förstemann, *op. cit.* 30. Both potta and pota (Bergamascan-Modenese) are syncopated forms of podestà.

[92] Agnonese pucce is a donkey and is also applied to children.

[93] Puzzo is also a word for well. Puzzone can mean a fly, or in Parmigiano, a polecat. Oscillation between voiced and unvoiced consonants would make Puzzo a variant of Buzzo.

[94] Cf. gobbo, gobbetto, hunchback.

[95] Baccio can come from Bartolomeaccio (Tuscan) or Cremasco Bacio for Battista. A baccello is rated as a simpleton, while a baccina is sometimes a cow.

[96] Cf. Germanic Bazzo in Förstemann, *op. cit.* 253, bazza meaning prominent chin and Genoese bazetta, slender child.

[97] Billo is a pet form of Camillo.

[98] Binello is a term for twin.

[99] Boccia is a ball, crystal bottle and, metaphorically, a thick nose. A boccin in Piedmontese is a calf. In Val di Serchio Bocci, Bocciarelli are place names from boccio, thorny shrub.

[100] Cf. preceding note.

[101] Cf. the botanical name bosso, box-tree. Both Boso and Bosso could come through Amb(r)osio. Cf. also Bosa in Förstemann, *op. cit.* 329.

* Giacobotto — Bottini, Bottinelli, Bottoni, Botticelli, Bottazzi [102]

* Giacobozzi — Bozzi, Bozzelli, Bozzetti, Bozzoli, Bozzini, Bozzolini, Bozzoni, Bozzarello [103]

Giacobuzzi — Buzzi, Buzzetta, Buzziconi, Buzzolini, Buzzoni, Buzelli [104]

Giacubbo — Cuba, Cubito, Cubinelli, Cubbino, Cuboni, Cubucci

* Iacobarino — Barinetti

Iacobassi — Bassi, Bassetti, Bassini [105]

Iacobelli, Iacobellis — Cobelli, Belli, Bellelli, Belletti, Bellini, de Bellis, Belloni, Bellucci, Bellusci, Belluzzi [106]

* Iacoberino — Berino [107]

Iacobetto — Betti, Bettazzi, Bettini, Bettinelli, Bettolo, Bettoloni, Bettoni, Bettucci, Betuzzi, Betussi, Bettarelli [108]

Iacobini

* Iacobollo — Bolla, Bollini, Bolletti, Bolino [109]

Iacobone

Iacobucci — Bucci, Buccino, Bucella, Bucciarelli [110]

* Iacobuscio — Buscio, Buscini, Busciarelli [111]

* Iacobus(s)o — Busetto, Busso, Bussone, Busoni [112]

The * Giacovo-Iacovo Branch

Giacovelli, Giacovetti

di Iagovo

Iacovolo

Iacovaccio — Covazzi, Vaccini [113]

Iacovazzi

Iacovelli, Iacoviello — Covelli, Govella, Coelli, Coviello

* Iacoverello — Coverelli

---

[102] Botta normally means a tub, fat, person (tubby). Cf. bottaccio, bottazzo, Florentine, thrush. Bottone, button, is, of course, a very weak competitor.

[103] Cf. Germanic Bozo, Förstemann, op. cit. 330. Calabrese vozza, goitre, could give bozza as a variant. In Piacentino bozzarel is a person of small stature.

[104] Cf. Germanic Buz, Förstemann, op. cit. 331. In Sicilian a buzzu is a small fat man, sometimes malformed, while buzzetta is from buxetum, boxwood.

[105] Naturally, basso means small, short. Giacobassi is a variant.

[106] Some of these names are what they seem, e.g., bello, beautiful.

[107] Cf. Germanic Berin, Förstemann, op. cit. 258.

[108] If from the Bassanese, Betussi could derive from the word meaning robin.

[109] In Aretino bolla is a term for chicken.

[110] Buccio might also come from Boezio, Boezuccio. The name Buccio was popularly applied to Rainaldo di Popleto, 14th century. See A. Capasso, Le Fonti della Storia delle Provincie Napoletane dal 568 al 1502. Napoli, 1902, 122.

[111] See Buscio names. Busciarello is a place name in Val di Serchio.

[112] See Bosso names. A buson in Romagnuolo is a sort of Don Juan.

[113] Covazzi and several names listed below could refer to covo, lair. As for Vaccini, it, like Baccini, might be traced to cow.

Iacovetta
Iacovino — Covino, Govini, Vino [114]
Iacovoni — Covone, Govoni, Covolini
* Iacovotto — Covotti, Di Votto
* Iacovullo— Vullo
Iacovozzo — Vozzo, Vozzella, Vozzarella [115]
* Iacovuccio — Vucciarello [116]
Iacofi, Siacovelli

> The * Iacabo, * Iabaca, * Iacapo, * Iacama, * Iakmen,
> * Iakmey, * Giakimu, * Gican, * Iaccian Branches [117]

* Iacabo —Iacabacci, Iacabella, Iacabucci, Cabella,[118] Cabotto, Ca-
boni, Gabo,[119] Gabotti
* Iabaca — Baca, Bacca, Baccarelli, Bagarelli, Vacca, Vaccarelli,
Bacchi [120]
* Iacava — Cavazza, Gavazzi, Cavazzoni, Cavello, Caviello, Cavina,
Gavini, Cavolini, Cavozzi, Gavozzi, Cavoto, Gavotta, Iacavone,
Gavoni, Cavaretta [121]
* Iacapo — Capaccio, Capaccioli, Capasso, Capelli, Capini, Capettini,
Capone, Capuccia, Capozzi [122]
* Iacama — Cameli, Cammelli, Cametti, Caminetti, Caminit(t)i,
Camino, Cammiso, Camisa, Camolli, Camoscio, Camozzi, Ca-
mosso, Camusso, Camoletto, Camerini [123]

---

[114] As a nickname surname Vino could be interpreted for what it appears to be, vino, wine. Cf. also BaldoVINO.

[115] In Calabrese, as we have already noted, a vozza is a goitre.

[116] Cf. Busciarelli.

[117] Most of these odd-looking forms of Giacomo are current in various parts of the Italian speaking regions: Iabaca in Saracena, prov. of Cosenza, Iacava in Lucania, Iacama in Puglia, Campania and Sicily, Iakmen in Bardi, prov. of Piacenza, Iakmey in Emilia, Giakimo in the prov. of Rome, Giacan, Iaccian in Italian Switzerland. See Vol. I, Karte 83 of the Jaberg and Jud Linguistic Atlas. On the strength of these I have added the forms Iacaba, Iacapo.

[118] Could be a combination of Iaco and Bella. See Compound Names.

[119] Gabo is a Ladin form of Giacomo and is listed in E. Lorenzi, "Osserva-zioni Etimologiche sui Cognomi Ladini." *Archivio per l'Alto Adige*, III, 1907. This tends to confirm *Iacapa.

[120] Competition arises from Germanic Bac(c)a, Baga (Förstemann, *op. cit.* 231) and words for cow, cowherder and silkworm.

[121] Some of these terms might be connected with cava, quarry, Cavo, from capo, may also play a part. But Cavaretta may be related to goat, locust and Cavoto, to Piedmontese gavot, goitre, or Romagnuolo gavott, hypocrite.

[122] All these terms recall capo, head. Cf. capoccia, farm overseer, and cavazza, Tarantino for mullet.

[123] In Cremonese Camel stands for Camillo. Cam(m)ello is the everyday word for camel; Caminit(t)i is also a resident of Camini in Calabria and through an attempt at Tuscanization might give Caminetti; Cammisa is a word for shirt; Camoscio, Camozzo, Camosso, Camusso, mean chamois, pug nose, and Camerini, a native of Camerino.

* Iakmen — Cheminelli, Menna, Menoni, Menotti, Menini, Mennella, Menola
* Iakmey — Comei
* Giakimu — Chiminelli
* Giacan — Cano, Canello, Canelotto, Canini, Canet(t)o, Canottoli, Cancello [124]
* Iaccian — Cian, Ciani, Cianelli [125]

The Ciacco, Giaco, Iaco and Zacco Branches

Giachi,[126] Giaccarini, Giacchello, Giacchetti, Ghetti, Giacoletti, Coletti, Giacolla, Giacolone, Giacalone, Colona, Colonelli, Giac-(c)one, Coni, Giacotti, Cotti, Cottini, Chiacchini, Giachinotti, Chini, Chinelli etc.
Iaccacci, Cacci, Caccini, Cacciotti; Iaccarino; Iacchino; Iacoli, Iacollo, Iacoletti, Iacolucci; Iacone, Iaconello, Conelli, Gonella, Gonnella; Iacotti; Iacozzo, Cozza, Cozzolini, Cozzone, Cozzini; Iacuzzi; Iacuzzio, Cuzzi, Cuzzone; Iacucci, Cucci, Cuccinelli [127]
Zacco — Zacchetti, Zacchini, Zaccherini, Zaccheroni, Zaccone, Zago, Zagoma, Zagone [128]

The Ciapo Branch

* Ciapo — Ciappa, Ciappone, Ciappini, Ciaparelli, Ciapusso, Chiapusso,[129] Chiapazzo, Chiapelli, Chiappini, Chiapone

The Iapico-* Giappico Branch

Iapicchino — Picchoti, Pighini [130]
Giappichelli

---

[124] Cane, the term for dog, can compete here as well as canneto, cane field, and cancello, gate.

[125] Cf. Cian(n)i from Gian(n)i, Ciano from Feliciano, Marciano, etc., cian (Trentino), dog, ciano, fleur de lis, batchelor's button, ciano, ill bred person, ciano Southern Italian for plain, piano.

[126] A poor competitor is giacco, jacket. As for the other derivatives, a colonel in Cadore is a strip of land, though colonello may mean colonel in the military sense. Both it and Colona can come from NiCOLONE, NiCOLONA. See Francesco and Dominic section with their footnotes for homographs.

[127] See Francesco and Dominic sections with their footnotes for homographs.

[128] Friulano Izach (Isaac) as well as an apocopated form of Zaccaria can give all of these forms. A zacchera in Bresciano and Bergamascan is an importunate man; a zacon in Bresciano a large coat; zago in Venetian a cleric. In Neapolitan a zaccaro is a child and a zacchero a squat individual. Zaccherone in Tuscan is a dirty person, from zacchera, splash of mud.

[129] Ciappa means slate or fish market in Genoese. It can be related to chiappa, buttocks. In Bresciano a ciapì is a comely child. A ciapusso, if from Piedmontese, is a poor artisan and if from Genoese an old clothes man. Originally the term meant carpenter.

[130] Cf. Bicco, Picco (Förstemann, op. cit. 302), pica, magpie and picchio, woodpecker.

The Papo and Lapo Branches

Papi, Papini, Papotti, Paparino, Paparella [131]
Lapi, Lapini, Lapaccini, Lappoli, Laparelli, Lapponi [132]

Syncopated Strays

GIAcoMo gives Giamo,[133] GIAcoMETTO, Giametti, Chiametti, GIAoMITTO and IAcoMITTO, Giamitti, and Iamitti, GIAco-MELLO, Giammelli, GIAcoMUSSO, Giamusso, GIAcoMUZ-ZO, Giamuzzi, GIAcoMONA, Giammona, GIacoMOSSO, Giosso, GIAcoPESSO, Giapessi, GIAcoPPONE, Giapponi, GIacUBBONE, Giubboni, GIacUBBINO, Giubbini, GIAco-PASSO, Giapasso, IAcoPELLO, Iap(p)elli, IAcoVAZZO, Ia-vazzo.[134]

THE JOHN TRIBE

Giovanni Branch

Giovanni — Vanni, Nanni, Nannini, Nanuccio, Nannuzzi, Nanna-relli, Nannariello, Nannizzi.[135] Giovannazzi. Giovannilli. Gio-vannini-Giovanninetti, Vannini, Ninni, Ninnoli, Ninotti. Gio-vanetti — Vannetti, Netti.[136] Giovanitti — Nitti, Nita.[137] Gio-

---

[131] Cf. Papo, Papa (Förstemann, *op. cit.* 223), and the word papa, Pope. Paparino and Paparella are also words for goose. Note that both Papo and Lapo are Tuscan forms of Giacopo.

[132] We may here, in some cases, be dealing with agglutinated forms: Lapini from LA GiusepPINA, etc.; Lappoli from La Pola (Paola); Laparelli from LA GasPARELLA, Lapponi from LA JacoPONE, etc. Láppola also means burdock.

[133] Cf. Spanish Jaime.

[134] At various stages our pet names for James meet with competition from homographs deriving from pet forms of other names, viz.: Tommaso, Damaso, Dalmazzo, Carmelo, Girolamo, Remo, Carmine, Giovanni, Martino, Stefano, Anna, Simone, Salomone, Ampellio, Giuseppe, Filippo, Crispino, Pipino, Prospero, Gaspare, Caterina, Marino, Guarino, Elizabetta, Benedetto (Betto), Cherubino, Tobia, Bono, Tiberio, Libero, Baldovino, Salvino, Acuzio, etc. Bino and derivatives could come from BernardINO as well as CheruBINO. For the benefit of those who might be inclined to be skeptical regarding some of the above mentioned pet variants we shall note here that E. Ferrari, *Vocabolario de' Nomi Propri Sustantive* . . . 2 vol. Bologna, 1827-28; L. G. Blanc, *Grammatik der Italienischen Sprache*, Halle, 1844, 164-66; and R. d'Ambra, *Vocabolario Napoletano*, Napoli, 1873, all give the following forms of Giacomo, Iacopo, Giacobbo—Ciapo, Ciaccio, Iaco, Lapo, Coppo, Pino, Perino, Rino, Comino, Buccio, Puccio, Muzzo, Minuccio, Nozzo, Baccio, Paccio, Bongioanni, *op. cit.* adds Comello, Conello, Mizzo, Musso, and Gobbo.

[135] Ferdinando, Marianna, Anna all give Nanno. Cf. also nannu, grand-father, and nano, pigmy.

[136] Netti could come from Venetian Beneto from Benedetto.

[137] Nittu is a Sicilian pet form for Benedetto.

vannizio. * Giovanoccio — Nocelli, Noccioli.[138] Giovannola—-
Noli,[139] Nolli. Giovannoni — Noni.[140] * Giovannotti — Notti,
Noto, Nottola.[141] * Giovannozzo — Vanozzi, Nozza, Nozzoli,
Nozzolini. * Giovannucci — Vannucci, Vanucchi, Vanuccini,
Nucci, Nuccitelli, Nucciotti.[142] * Giovanusso — Nussi. Gioan-
neti. Svanetti, Svanini (Bolognese)

Gianni, Ianni, Zan(n)i Branch

Gianni, Cianni, Ciani, Cian.[143] * Gianaccio — Gianaccini, Nacci.
Giannarello — Narelli. Giannalone. Gianassi, Gianasi — Nassi,
Nasi.[144] Gianazzo. Giannecchini. Giannerini — Nerini. Gia-
nessi. Gianeti — Gianettini. Giannini, Gianinotti, Gianinacci,
Gianninazzi. Giannico — Nico, Nicchia, Nicchini.[145] Gianilli,
Cianelli. Gianocca — Nocchi.[146] Giannola, Gianoli — Gianolini,
Giannuli, Giannullo. Giannoni — Giannoncelli. Giannotti. Gian-
(n)ucci, Gianuzzi — Nuzzi, Nuzzetti, Nuzzarelli

Ianni; Ianelli, Ianiello, Ianniello; Iannacchino; Iannacone; Iannazzi,
Iannazzone; Iannacito; Iannetti; Iannico; Iannitello; Iannitti;
Iannocioni; Iannocconi; Ianizzi; Iannone; Ianuccelli, Ianussi,
Iannuzzi, Iannuzzelli

Zan(n)i, Zan(n)etti, Zan(n)ini, Zan(n)oli, Zan(n)olli, Zanolini,
Zaniolo, Zanoncelli, Zanotti, Zannotti, Zan(n)oni, Zanetello,
Zanoletti, Zanuccoli, Zanussi

Strays

de Ioanna, Iavanucci, Zuanazzi [147]

---

[138] Cf. noce, nut. See Botanical Names.

[139] Cf. the place names Nola, Campania and Noli, Liguria. Through the
Spanish Nola could come from Manola.

[140] Cf. Nono, Northern Italian for nonno, grandfather, and nono, ninth. See
Kinship Names and section on Number Names in the miscellaneous name group.

[141] Noto is a town in Sicily and Nottola may be a bat.

[142] Cf. nuce, dialectical for nut.

[143] See Note 125.

[144] IgNASIO, AtaNASIO compete here as well as naso, nose.

[145] Nico is Romagnuolo and Venetian for Nicola. Cf. also Spanish Iñigo
(Innico) and Germanic Niko (Förstemann, op. cit. 1156).

[146] In Neapolitan a nocco is a tassel, tuft of hair. In Central Italy nocco is
also a nut.

[147] Other font names supplying homographs through their pet forms are
Ivano, Stefano, Antonio, Petronio, Leone, Bruno, Marino, Guarino, Feliciano,
Luciano, Marciano, Gennaro, Raineri, Maineri, Domenico, Veronico.

THE PETER TRIBE

Pedro Branch

* Pedro — Pedrazzi, Pedrazzini, Pedrazzoli. Pedretti. Pedrini, Pedrinelli, Pedrizoli, Pedrocchi, Drocchi. Pedroli. Pedroni, Pedroncelli. Pedrotti, Pedrottini. Pedrozzi

P(i)etro Branch

Pietri, Petracci, Petracco, Petraccone, Petracchini. Patrasso.[148] * Petrazzi, Trazzi. Petrella, Petriello, Petrelluzzi. Petrettini. Petricca. Petricelli. Petriccini. Petriccioni, Cioni,[149] Cionini. Petriconi. Petrillo, Trillo, Trillini. Petrina. Petrizzi, Petrizzelli, Trizzello, Trizzino. Petroccello. Petrocchi, Trocchi, Troccoli.[150] Petroccini, Troccino. Petrolli. Petronacci. Petrongelli. Petroni, Troni.[151] Petroselli. Peteroti, Petrotta, Trotta.[152] Petrozzi, Petrozzini, Trozzi.[153] Petrucco, Patrucco, Petrucchini, Trucco.[154] Petrullo, Trulli.[155] *Petruscello, Truscello. * Petrusso, Trussa. Petruzzo, Petruzzio, Petruzzelli, Petruzziello, Truzzilini, Truzzolino. Petrugelli. Petuzzo, Tuzzo, Tuzzolino [156] (Sicilian). Pietrucci. Spedracci, Spedroni

The Piero-Pierro, Pero-Perro Branch

Pieri, Pierro. Pieraccini, Raccio. Pieralli, Ralli. Pierattelli. Pieretti, Pierettini. Pierini, Rini, Rinelli, Rinetti, Rinucci,[157] Rinuccini. Pierotti, Rotti, Rota, Rotella, Rotellini.[158] Pierizzi. Pierozzi,

---

[148] Patrasso might also have a religious provenience or come from a place name, Patras, Greece.

[149] Cioni could be obtained from Mauricio, Clarice, etc.

[150] Trocchi could come from tarocco or Romagnuolo trocc, a ball game. Troccola in Neapolitan is a rattle used during Holy Week.

[151] For several of these names compare Petronio. Troni could come from Mitro, Metro plus augmentatives, Venetian tron meaning a political office (tribunus) or the dialectical term for thunder, trono.

[152] In Bolognese Trotta stands for Catarinotta or stammerer; in Milanese for a fast walker. In Neapolitan trotta is a trout.

[153] Derivatives of Mitro and Metro also compete here.

[154] A trucco is also a kind of ball game. See above.

[155] In Agnonese a trulle is a rather fleshy individual. Both it and a common term for simpleton derive from citrullo (citriolo) cucumber. Cf. also trullo, a pre-Roman type of house found at Alberobello and other parts of Puglia.

[156] We get these forms due to the disappearance of the r. Cf. also Bogio for Brogio (Ambrogio), Dea from Drea (Andrea). It is not improbable that the same explanation can be used for some of the Petitto, Petillo, Petella, Petaccia, Petazzi, Pedicini.

[157] For these names and others following compare short forms plus suffixes -ino, -etto, -otto of Gaspare, Prospero, Marino, Caterina, Jacopo, etc.

[158] Cf. rotella, round shield.

Rozzi,[159] Rozzini, Rozzetti, Rozzolini. Pieruccio, Peri, Perri, Peeri. Peracca, Peracchino, Peracchio, Peracchione, Racca, Peras(s)i, Perazzi, Perazzelli, Perazzini.[160] Razza, Razzetta, Razzolini.[161] Percella. Perchetti. Per(r)elli. Peresio, Perissini, Perissinotto. Peretti. Pericoli.[162] Perini, Perinelli, Perinetti, Perincioli, Peronotti. Per(r)igo.[163] Perillio, Perillo. Perriconi. Per(r)otti, Perottoni. Perozzi. Persella. Perucca, Perucchini, Rucco, Ruccoli. Perrucci. Peruzzi,[164] Ruzzini. Perisi.[165] Prinetti, Proci, Proto,[166] Prozzo, Prozillo, Prucci,[167] Prusso (Piedmontese). Peyretti, Peyron, Peyronel, Peiroli. Pei [168] (Genoese). Preto, Pretti

The Pir(r)o Branch

Piro, Pirri, Piraccioli, Pirelli, Prini, Pirioli, Pirocchi, Pirola, Pirolini, Pirona, Pirrone, Pir(r)otti, Pirazzi, Pirazzini, Pirazzoli, Pirozzi, Pirozzolo [169]

The Pitro Branch

Pitrasso, Pitrelli, Pitrillo, Pitricone, Pitini, Pitoni, Pitta, Pittarella, Pittoli [170]

---

[159] Cf. also rozzo in the sense of uncouth.

[160] Some competition may be expected from Germanic Bera (Förstemann, op. cit. 260) and pera, pear, for quite a few names in this group.

[161] Less formidable rivals are razza (Cogorno, Liguria) for black berry, Sicilian for charlock or rockcress, Modenese for dogrose, and razza meaning skate or ray. See Botanical and Fish Names.

[162] Pericolo, of course, means danger. In Calabrese a periculu is a convolvulus.

[163] Not to be eliminated as a source is Perico, Perigo used in (Reggio Emilia) Tuscany, Sicily to indicate the St. Johnswort.

[164] It will be recalled that the famous Florentine family of the Peruzzi were also called della Pera, referring to pear.

[165] Perisi might also be a variant of Parise.

[166] Cf. St. Proto.

[167] These Pr-names are due to the drop of the unaccented e.

[168] Competing words are PomPEO, and the terms for foot and pear.

[169] In a few cases Pirro, Pyrrhus, may be the source of these names. So might piro, variant of pero. Most of the names of this type are probably Romagnuolo.

[170] If the r can disappear in the case of Petro (see Note 156), it can also do so in the case of Pitro. Orlando (op. cit.) thinks, for example, that Sicilian Piti comes from Pitiddu through Pitriddu. Therefore, we cannot go too far astray in putting these names in the Peter tribe. However, cf. Germanic Pito (Förstemann, op. cit. 301), and pitta, a term for fritter, pita, pitta, pittone, Northern Italian for turkey and chicken. It should be added that some of the apparent Peter-tribe names may derive from place names. Cf. Perrillo (Benevento), Perrona (Asti), Petrazzi (Firenze), Petrella (Arezzo, Pesaro), Petrizzi (Catanzaro).

Chapter IV

KINSHIP NAMES

Sensitiveness about ties of blood is mainly responsible for the vogue of names of kinship. We can imagine neighbors joining with members of one's family in applying a term of relationship to an individual particularly if such a person is in the habit of making an exaggerated use of the word. Avoli, Avetta, Di Nonno, Nonna, Nona,[1] Nanni, Nannini, Nannarella,[2] Tatananno, Tatarone, Tataranno,[3] and occasionally Grande, Grandi[4] (cf. Biellese grant) are grandpa and grandma, but at the same time names that are commonly employed to designate old people or those who are infirm. Barbetti[5] (if Piedmontese barbet) alludes to great uncle, while Barbi is from the Northern Italian word meaning uncle. Other words that express this relationship are Barbano, Lo Zio, del Zio, and Romagnuolo Zei.[6] Like grandpa uncle is also frequently used everywhere with reference to elderly persons. Aunt is expressed by Lalli (if Genoese), Magni[7] (if Piedmontese), Meda[8] (if Tridentino). Drawn

[1] The name Avolio appears in the romances of chivalry. Cf. also avolio, ivory. Nona might also come from nona, ninth, that is, ninth child. See section on Number Names in chapter on Miscellaneous Names. Nona could likewise derive from AnNONA, GiovanNONA, Parmigiano BerNONA = Bernardona. Nonna, Nonno might be related to St. Nonna, Nonno.

[2] Nanno and derivatives are generally more apt to go back to Nanno, pet forms of Ferdinando, Giovanni, Marianna (Neapolitan).

[3] If Calabrese, Tataranno is equivalent to Carnevale who, at the end of the Lenten period appears in the role of an old man.

[4] It is unnecessary to add that the usual meaning of grande is large, tall.

[5] Barbetti is also obviously connected with beard, thin beard, Germanic Barbo, and with balbo, stammerer, through the substitution of an r for an l. The same explanations would apply to Barbi.

[6] Competition comes from Zeo, short form of Mazzeo, Zebedeo and zei (Romagnuolo, Bresciano) meaning lily. Though Ziella may also go back to aunt, zia, it can also be related to GraZIELLA, MarZIELLA, etc.

[7] If Sicilian, Lalli may be from Eulalia, or if Bergamascan from lallo, dullard. Since the name Carlomagno exists as a font name and surname we may think of Magni as a reduction of the same. But compare also St. Magnus and Magna = Alemagna.

[8] Otherwise Meda could be interpreted as stemming from DioMEDA.

from father are Cremonese Paderi, Baccani [9] (if Genoese), Babini,[10] Tata, Tatarello [11] (both Southern Italian), Siri [12] (Lecce and Taranto). In Abruzzese sire means grandfather while siru in Calabrese signifies father in compounds like Sirangelo. Perhaps we should add here the Graeco-Calabrese term for head of a household, Codespoti, its translation Capodicasa, its aphetic forms Despoto, Spoto and Spotti, and the Abruzzese Maiuri, terms usually synonymous with father or grandfather. Maiuri, along with Maggiore, Maiorello also means eldest son. In contrast to Minori, junior, it can likewise mean senior, in the same way that Vecchio and derivatives, that is, senior, contrast with Giovane, Novello, junior. Mother contributes Matre, Madre, Mammaccia, Mammina, Mammarella, Caramadre (literally, mother dear) while brother offers Frati, Fratetti, Frattini, Fradelletti, Fraticelli, Bonfratelli, Germano,[13] and Carnelli (Romagnuolo slang). Sister appears to survive in Sorelli and Sorini.[14] Gemini, Gemelli,[15] Bessoni [16] (Piedmontese), Binelli [17] (also Piedmontese). Jomelli, Jemolo (Sicilian jemmulu) refer to twins, and Ternullo to a member of a group of triplets. Moglia, Mogliera, Sposa mean wife; Marito, Maritello, Bommarito, husband; Consorte, Consortini, Sposini, husband or wife. Closely associated with these are Sposato, Casato, Maritato, Zito, Lo Sito, Zitello,[18] the rare Ammogliati, married man; Zitella, Citella, married woman;

[9] Genoese baccan stands for both father and head, chief. Otherwise cf. baccano, hubbub, Piedmontese bacan, rascal and, in the Comelico dialect of Cadore, baccan, small real estate holder.

[10] Cf. Germanic Babin cited by E. Förstemann, *Altdeutsches Namenbuch*. Erster Band. Personennamen. 2d ed. Bonn, 1900, 224, and Romagnuolo baben, child.

[11] In Trieste and Venice tata is a term for child while in Liguria a tatta is the husband of a midwife.

[12] For further information see discussion by P. Aebischer, "Un Mot Normande dans les Dialectes des Pouilles, sire, père." *Archivum Romanicum*, XXII, 1938, 357-63.

[13] Sometimes a germano is a cousin.

[14] Padre, madre, s(u)ora, frate might occasionally refer to names from religious sources. Marino Patrigno, foster father, was a notary at Aquileia in 1303.

[15] Cf. St. Gemino and Northern Italian gema = gemma, gem.

[16] A bessone could be obtained through Romagnuolo bessa, snake plus suffix, or, better, through the font name Obesso, variant of Obizzo plus suffix.

[17] Cf. the short forms Binello from CheruBINO, GiacoBINO, etc.

[18] For Zito, Lo Sito, Zitello, -a, cf. St. Zita and MazZITELLA from Mazzo. The surnames Femmina, Femminella, Mascolo, female, male, may also have been terms to denote wife or husband. Cf. French femme. However, Femminella is also possible from Eufemia.

Dalla Vedova, Vedovati, Veroli (Neapolitan), Cattivo,[19] La Cattiva, Cattivelli, widower, widow; Nubile, marriageable girl. Figlio, Figliola, Figliuolo, Figliolini, Belfiglio, Bonfigli, Bonfiglietti, Bonfioli, Carofiglio all indicate son or daughter. Here more than elsewhere, perhaps, belong some of the numerous names for child, Fanciulli, Fanciullacci, Fanciullini, Fante, Bonfante, Fancelli, Fancellotti, Fancillotti, Fantetti, Fantini, Ragazzi, Ragazzini, Regazzi, Regazzoni, Bambino, Bimbi, Bimboni, Creatura (Calabrese); Piccolo, small, with its derivatives and variants; Marmocchi, Garzoni, Garzonetti, Carocci, Carucci (from caro, dear); Redi (from erede, heir); Cherubini, cherub; Angelo, angel; Tosi, Caruso, Carosi, shorn, cropped; various epithets drawn from the vegetable and animal kingdom like Ravanello, radish; Cece, chick pea; Piccioni, pigeon; Agnelli, lamb; Topini, mouse.[20] Fiastri (Cremonese) and Configliacci signify stepson. Besides Maggiore and Minore, eldest and youngest son, there is Mezzanini, second child, perhaps Minimi,[21] Caronia[22] (Valle Anzasca) youngest, and Marni,[23] youngest child of very old parents. Cugino, Gugino[24] mean cousin, Nepote, Nevi (Piedmontese), Nievo, Negoda (Trivigiano), Nesi[25] (Piedmontese and Ligurian), Nezzino, Nezzo (Venetian and Vincentino nezza), hark back to nephew, niece or grandchild.[26] Madonna[27] is often employed as mother in law in Northern Italy while the Veronese Messeri comes from father in law. Genero, Generini (Bresciano), Zenerini, Zenero,[28] Zendrini[29] (Tridentino zendro) refer to son in law and Nora, Norelli[30] to daughter in law. La Cognata, Cognato are brother and

---

[19] Cattivo is otherwise captive, bad man. As to Veroli, cf. the place name in Lazio and Piedmont, Germanic Verro, Vera (Förstemann, *op. cit.* 1555-56 plus the ending -olo, and the word for small pox, verola = vaiolo.

[20] For these and other terms meaning child see I. Pauli, *Enfant, Garçon, Fille dans les Langues Romanes*, Lund, 1919, and chapters on Botanical, Animal and Anatomical Names.

[21] At times a minimo is a monk of the order of St. Francis of Paola.

[22] Literally carrion.

[23] In Parmigiano marna is a type of rich soil and in the dialect of Como a laggard.

[24] Cugino, Gugino could spring from any name in -co. Cf. MarCUCCINO.

[25] Nese is a normal reduction of Agnese or Ginesio. In Romagnuolo nes signifies nose.

[26] Malnipote is the name borne by a noble Cremonese family.

[27] Madonna, lady, has frequently been used as a font name.

[28] Competing Bresciano terms are Zener = Gennaro, and zeneer, juniper.

[29] This is more usually from Alessandro which in Venetian is Zendrin.

[30] Also regular reduction of Eleonora, Leonora.

sister in law. We also have Parenti, Parentini,[31] Parentuccelli from the generic term parent, relative. Finally, we note Commare, Comari,[32] Comparini, Comparetti, Patrini, Parrino, Parini, Perini [33] (Piedmontese), Guazzo (Veronese guaso), Patini (Castro de' Volsci), Santoli, Guidazzio (Lombard) all meaning god father, god mother as well as god son, god daughter.

[31] Parenti may stem from the Roman Parentes. Cf. Parenti, a Calabrese place name.

[32] The same words can mean midwife in Venetian, Friulano and Sicilian. A good source is also Dagomaro which exists as a last name, Dagomari.

[33] Parrino is also everyday Sicilian for priest, but it and Parini, Perini could stem from Gaspare, and Parini, Perini also from Jacopo.

We may now compare kinship names in French, English and German with those already mentioned by quoting from R. Mowat, *Les Noms Familiers chez les Romains*. Extrait des *Mémoires de la Société de Linguistique de Paris*. Paris, 1871, 3-4. "En France, les noms de famille qui répondent a ceux que je viens de rappeler (i.e. Roman names) sont assez répandus: Lancestre; Ulysse Parent; Lepère; Maman; Loncle; Belloncle; Belletante; Beltente; Neveu; Lenepveu; Niepce; Lefils; Petitfils; Enfant; Lenfant; Enfantin; Belenfant; Bonenfant; Malenfant; Ainé; Laisnè; Cadet, Frère; Frèret; Frèron; Frèrot; Lefrère; Petitfrère; Soeur; Bru; Labrut; Victor Cousin; Cousineau; Cousinet; Cousinot; Beaucousin; Maucousin; Marié; Lemarié; Gendre; Legendre; Gendret; Gendrin; Gendron; Beaugendre; Maugendre; Beaupère; Beaufils; Fillastre; Malfilatre; Beaufrère; Père-et-Mère, nom d'un militaire au 15 bataillon de chasseurs.

Comparez-encore nos noms propres bas breton; Le Car, le parent; Le Ni, le neveu; Quenderf, cousin; Le Guéver, le gendre; Guével, jumeau; Le Deun, le beau fils; Le Douaren, Ledouarain, le petit fils; L'Ozach, le marié; L'Intaon, le veuf; L'Emizivat, Limizivat, l'orphelin; penher, chief héritier, fils unique; Le Henaff, l'ainé; Le Iaouer, le cadet; Le Tad, le père; Tadic, petit père. En Angleterre on recontre les noms; Parent; Fathers; Uncle; Uncles; Brother; Farebrother, contracté de father-brother, mot dont on se sert en Ecosse pour designer l'oncle maternel; Cousin; Cousins; Daughters; Girl; Boy; Kinsman; Husband; Younghusband; Widow; Widows; Wife; Bride; Ward; et chez nos voisins d'Allemagne; Ahn; Vater, Altvater; Kindervater; Altmütter; Mütterlein; Bruder; Brüder; Brüderlein; Vetter; Vetterlein; Vetterling; Trautvetter; Schweig; Schwieger; Schwager; Tochtermann; Süstermann; Systermans et Schwister, noms de familles établis a Paris; Eidam; Ehemann; Kind; Sohn; Einenckel; Wittwer; Mutterlose; Ohme, Oehmichen, etc." For additions and few corrections on the English side consult also E. Weekley, *Surnames*, London, 1936, 3rd edition, 243-51, and C. W. Bardsley, *A Dictionary of English and Welsh Surnames*, London, 1901, 33.

Chapter V

COMPOUND NAMES

One of the most curious groups of compound cognomina are the theophorous names, that is, names containing a divine element. Such appellatives have been common among the Semitic people. In the Old Testament the many names containing El, God, or Ja (Ja, Je, Iah, etc.), Jehovah, are of this type. Compare Elisua, God is salvation; Isaiah, salvation of Jehovah. In Christian communities they were once, and to a small extent still are, first names. Among these are Diotisalvi, Salvidio, God save you; Diotajuti, God help you; Aiutamicristo, so help me Jesus; Diotiguardi, Guardidei, God watch over you; Diotallevi, God nurse you: forms which are frequently contracted into Salvi, Duti, Dardi, Guardi, Allevi. Mantegna is short for Dio ti mantegna, God preserve you, while Bonaiuti seems to be coined from Diotajuti. Others are Sperandeo, hope in God; Laudadio, praise God; Amidei, Amedei, Amodei, Amaridio, Maradeo, love God; Credidio, believe in God; Servadei, serve God; Graziadei, thanks be to God; Rogadeo, pray to God; Piacquadio, it pleased God; Diotifeci, shortened to Feci, God made you; Diodati, shortened to Dati, and Donadio, given by and to God.[1] Donato may be taken as a variant of Donadio, and Omodeo, Ondidei, man of God, and Servidio, Servindio, servant of God, as variants of Servadei. In Salvanima, save your soul, we see a link with Diotisalvi. Perhaps the most striking of the theophorous names is Chirieleison (= Kyrie eleison, Greek words meaning Lord have mercy on us, used in the Mass, etc). Among its owners is Domenico Chirieleison, general in charge of the open city of Rome during World War II.

Constructed from a compound with a subjunctive like some of the above are the good augury names Bentivenga, Bentivegna, Bencivenga, may good befall you or us.

Specimen of imperatival compounds that were formerly used as first names are Arrivabene, arrive well, another way of saying Benvenuto (also apparently synonymous with Bonaggiunta, Giunta, Giuntoli and Buonarroti); Acquistapace, often reduced to Pace, gain peace (cf. English Makepeace), Crescimbeni, Salimbene, grow in prosperity; Menapace, bring peace, the name of a contemporary Ticinese writer; Nascimbene, Nascimpace, to be born for good, for

---

[1] Diodato may be compared with Jonathan, gift of Jehovah and with Nathaniel and Theodore, gift of God.

peace; Vivimpace, live in peace; Penzabene, think well; Torna-
bene, Tornabuoni, be good; Tornaquinci, come hither.
Odd among the odd is Accorramboni, Accorimboni, said to come from
accorri uomo buono, hasten good man.[2] It is possible that Accoroni
is a shrinkage of the same.

Other imperative combinations seem to be substitutions for
occupational names. Sometimes they have a contemptuous or
humorous connotation. Tagliapietra is a stonecutter or sculptor.
Paccasassi (i.e. spaccassassi) and Schiappapietra, stone breaker, stone
splitter, may be synonyms. Tagliacarne, cut meat, is a meat cutter
or butcher, while a beef, goat or lamb butcher appears to be implied
in Tagliabue, Massabò, Scannabecchi, Scannapieco. Tagliatela, cut
the cloth, and Tagliasacchi, cut sacks, coats, recall tailors.[3] Batti-
ferri,[4] Maccaferri, Acicaferro, beat iron; Tagliaferro, cut iron;
Rompiferro, Spezzaferro, break iron; Scaldaferri, Brusaferri, heat
iron; Guastaferro, waste iron; point in the direction of a smith.[5]
Pisacreta and Fracacreta, beat, break clay, signalize a potter. Mena-
boi, Pungibuoi, Tirabò indicate people engaged in handling oxen,[6]
Pistamiglio, grind grain, a miller; Maccafava, grind bean, bean
grinder; Portalegni, carry wood, a woodseller; Cargasacchi, load
sacks, a porter; Scardapane, warm bread, a baker; Scopacasa,
sweephouse, a house servant. Faconti,[7] cast accounts, appears to be
an accountant; Falimmagini, make images, an image maker; Facaccio, make cheese, a cheese maker; Falecalze, make hose, a hosier;
Fassoldati, be soldier, and Falaguerra, make war, speak for themselves. Segafeni, mow forage; Zappalorti, hoe garden, Zappavigna,
hoe farm, refer to agricultural workers. A Battilana, beat wool, is
a wool carder; a Battiloro, beat gold, a gold beater; and a Battistrada, beat path, an outrider. A Mazzacane, kill dog, is in some
localities the official dog killer.[8] Beccamorto, body snatcher, is a
common term for a grave digger.

There is another group of compound imperatives involving the

---

[2] For similar names in English see E. Weekley, *Jack and Jill*, London, 1939,
117-18.

[3] A Mariano Particappa, cut cape, lived during the Renaissance.

[4] Battiferro is likewise steel for striking a light.

[5] It is interesting to note that the coat of arms of the Brusaferri of Velletri
pictorializes the name with a smithy. With Tagliaferro, turned into English
Tolliver, compare German Eisenhauer, Eisenhower. In Pugliese, a spezzaferro
is a hawfinch.

[6] Zaccaria Tosabecchi, goat (sheep) shearer, was a 13th century condottiero.

[7] It is possible that Faconti is nothing more than a variant of the font-name
Facundo.

[8] See Bird chapter for other meanings of mazzacane. In Calabrese the term
means an indolent person.

words canta, brucia, brusa, caccia, cazza, mazza; sing burn, hunt, kill plus an animal name. Here derivation may be either from nicknames or place names. Compare Caccialupi, hunt wolf; Cacciabue, hunt ox; Cantagallo,[9] Cantagallina, Cantalupo, sing rooster, chicken, wolf; Brusaporci, burn pig, Brusasorci, burn rat; Ammazzalorso, Mazzalorso, Mazzalovo, Mazzabue, Mazzagalli, Mazzapica, kill bear, wolf, ox, rooster, magpie. Scorcialupi, flay wolf, and Squarcialupi, rend wolf, probably belong to this list.[10]

Most of the remaining imperative compounds are nicknames of miscellaneous provenience—Basadona, Basacomadri, kiss woman; Battipede, stamp foot; Beccaluva, peck grapes; Beccafico,[11] peck fig; Beccafava, peck bean; Beccalosso, pick bone; Rudilosso, gnaw bone; Bevilacqua, Bevivino, drink water, drink wine; names for teetotalers and heavy drinkers; Buttacavoli, Buttafava, Buttafiori, Buttipaglia, throw cabbage, beans, flowers, straw. Caccialanza, thrust spear; Crollalanza, shake spear (cf. Shakespeare); Cantabene, sing well; Cantavespri, sing vespers; Cantamessa, Cantalamessa, sing mass; Cappisanti, deceive saint, a canting fellow;[12] Cenatiempo, eat on time; Cocilovo, cook the egg, (but compare French Cachelouve, English Catchlove, wolf haunt), Donatuti, give to all; Fapoco, do little (cf. Doolittle); Fateinanzi, come forward; Ferragalli, catch rooster; Fumagalli (from afumica gallo) smoke rooster; Ferragatti, catch cat; Ferracane, catch dog; Fragapane, Fregapane, Frangipane, Amaccapane, break bread. The Roman Frangipani, incidentally, earned the appellation of bread breakers from having distributed bread during a great famine. There are also Grattapettini, scrape comb; Guardabasso, Guardabascio, Mirangiuso, look down, an astute person; Guardalabene,[13] look at her well; Guastalegname, waste wood; Guastapaglia,[14] waste straw; Ingannamorte, deceive death; Lascialfare, let him do it; Lavacapi,[15] wash head; Ligabue, tie ox; Mangiben, eat well; Mangiaspesso, eat often; Mangiacapra,[16] eat goat; Magnacervi, eat deer; Mangiacavallo, eat horse; Mangia-

[9] In the Trentino dialect al canta gal means day break, and might be extended to refer to an early riser.

[10] For more examples see an interesting article by P. Skok, "Die Verbalcomposition in der Romanischen Toponomastik," *Beihefte zur Zeitschrift für Romanische Philologie*, XXVII, Heft, 1911, 1-56.

[11] A beccaluva is also a kind of thrush and a beccafico a figpecker. Perhaps beccafava is also a bird.

[12] Cappasanti is the name of a Vicentino family altered from Gabbasanti.

[13] Wardapass is Pugliese, Lucanese for a snake. Guardalabene is Italo-Albanian.

[14] Guastadisegni, spoil plan, is the real or assumed name of the author of *Lo Stato Giuridico ed Economico degli Impiegati Civili*, Roma, 1936.

[15] As a noun lavacapo means reprimand, scolding.

[16] A mangiacapra in Milanese is a sharper.

troie, eat sow; Mangigalli, eat rooster; Mangiatordi, eat thrush; Mangiafico,[17] Mangiameli, Mangiarancie, eat fig, apples, oranges; Mangialardo, Pappalardo, terms for hypocrite, simpleton; Mangiapane, bread eater, lazy fellow; Mangiaracina and possibly Mangiaregina, eat root; Mangiarapa, eat turnip; Mangiaspicca, eat corn ear; Mangiaterra, eat earth; Mazzamuto, kill deaf, probably said of a noisy fellow, Mazzamici,[18] kill friend; Mettifuoco, Apicciafuoco, Piccifuoco, set fire; Moccafighe, eat fig; Mozzapiede,[19] cut foot, name of an Aquilano family now extinct; Parlapiano, speak softly; Parlagreco, speak Greek; i.e. unintelligibly; Passalacqua,[20] pass water; Passafiume, pass stream; Passavanti, Passananti, pass on; Passacantando, pass singing; Passafaro, pass beacon; Passamonti, pass hills; Passavalli, pass vales; Pelagatti, skin cat, which has the figurative meaning of dead beat, cheater; Pelagallo,[21] pluck rooster; Pigialovo, catch wolf; Pialorsi, catch bear; Pintamura, paint walls, painter; Prendibene, take well; Prendiparte, take part, meddler; Prendilacqua,[22] take water; Sartalamacchia, Saltalamacchia, jump thicket; Scaccianoce,[23] crack nut; Scannagatta, kill cat; Scannatopi, kill rat; Sceppaquercia, rend oak; Schifalacqua, shun water; Sconciagioco, spoil play; Scozzafava, shell bean; Seccafico, dry fig; Spaccamela, break apple; Spezzamolin, break mill; Squarciapino, break pine; Stracciabende, tear mourning veil; Strazzabosco, tear woods; Strazzacappa, tear cape; Tagliamonti, cut mountain; Taglianetti,[24] cut clean; Tagliafico, cut fig tree; Taglialavoro, cut work; Tagliazucchi, cut gourd; Tirrinnanzi, go on; Tornincasa, return home; Vinciprova, win contest; Voltatorni,[25] turn and come back.

In Italian Renaissance comedies we find braggarts or bullies bearing compound appellatives like Frangipietra, break stone in Pasqualigo's *Fedele;* Spezzaferro, break iron, in Calmo's *La Spagnuola,*

[17] Mangiafico may be a variant form of beccafico.

[18] Some of the fairly common Mangias and Mazzas may well be reductions of any of the above compounds.

[19] Mozzachiodi, cut nails, was a mid-16th century Spezzino name. See M. Ruffini, "Onomastica Lunigianese. Cognomi Spezzini fra il 1558 e il 1650," *Memorie della Accademia Lunigianese di Scienze, Giovanni Capellini,* XVI, 1935, 15.

[20] Passalacqua is a Piedmontese place name. In Calabrese the word means butterfly.

[21] Cf. with pelagallo the word pelapollo, chicken-hearted, ninny.

[22] Pungileone which looks like goad lion is very likely an alteration of Ponce de León.

[23] Scaccianoce is also a bird, the nuthatch.

[24] Taglianetto is also the name of a plant, the hyoseris radiata. Cf. (I)talianetto.

[25] Volgicapo, turn your head, was the name of an old Italian writer.

Vinciguerra, win war, in Borghini's *Amante Furioso;* Lanfranco Cacciadiavoli, hunt devil, in Cecchi's *Martello.* Similar interpretations, at least in some instances, apply to current surnames like Spezzaferro, Spezzacatena, break chain; Piccapietra, Paccasassi, break stone; Pestalozzi, Fracalossi, Scaccialossi, crush bone; Spaccanasi, break nose; Mangialomin, eat men; Brusomini, scorch men; Buttafuoco,[26] spit fire; Cacciaguerra, Vinciguerra, Finiguerra, hunt, win and end war; Caccianemici, hunt enemies; Cacciamali, hunt (expel) evil; Tagliagamba, Taglilegamme, cut legs; Tagliabrazzi, cut arms. One of the three malefactors in a fifteenth century *Rappresentazione di S. Antonio* is, in fact, called Tagliagambe.[27] Venedico Caccianemico, hunt enemy, it will be recalled, appears in Dante's *Inferno,* which suggests that many of these compounded imperatives have been handed down from the Middle Ages. In quite a number from this epoch there lurks an unmentionable coarseness.[28] Happily most of them have found a safe refuge in oblivion.

Numerous compounds formed by adjectives plus nouns and nouns plus adjectives are treated in the chapter on Anatomical Names. A few of them with bella, bel, that have not been listed there are Amorebello, Amoribello, Bellamore, beautiful love; Bellanima, beautiful soul; Belfiore, Bellafiori, beautiful flower; Bellarosa,[29] beautiful rose; Bellavita,[30] beautiful life. It goes without saying that the terms compounded with bello may be, and for the most part are, first names. Additional compounds with buono, bono are Bomparola, good word; Bonadonna,[31] good woman; Bonafede, good faith; Bonagente, good people; Bonalumi, good light?; Buonamico, good friend; Bonapace, good peace; Bonauguro, good augury; Bonavita, good life; Bonavoglia,[32] good will; Buonavolta, good

---

[26] Romagnuolo batr e fogh alludes to a thin, emaciated person.

[27] The other two malefactors in this *Rappresentazione* are Carapello and Scaramuccia (skirmish). They also survive as surnames.

[28] See G. Flechia, "Di Alcuni Criteri per l'Originazione dei Cognomi Italiani," *Atti dell'Accademia dei Lincei,* III, 2, Scienze Morali, 1877-78; G. Gaudenzi, "Storia del Cognome a Bologna nel Secolo XIII," in *Bullettino dell'Istituto Storico Italiano,* No. 19, 1898; C. Poma, "Fallaci Apparenze in Connomi Italiani," *Archivio Glottologico Italiano,* XVIII, 1918, 353-54.

C. Poma, *Il Composto Verbale nell'Onomastica Italiana,* Torino, 1910, which I have been unable to consult, very likely contains further examples of verb-compounds.

[29] It is curious to note that in Romagnuolo roguery slang bellarosa means guitar. Incidentally, a belfiore in Tuscan is a chrysanthemum.

[30] In Anconitano, the dialect of Pitgliano and perhaps others bellavita means sans overcoat. In Venetian belavita refers to shapeliness. Cf. Bella + font name Vita.

[31] The word for midwife in Genoese is bonadonna.

[32] A bonavoglia is also a loiterer and a medical intern.

return, another variant of Benvenuto; Bonavolontà, goodwill; Bonconsiglio, good counsel; Bonconti, good count; Boncompagni, good companion; Boncore, good heart; Buoncristiano, good Christian; Bonvassallo, good vassal; Buonfidanze, good faith; Buonguadagni, good gain; Buonincontro, Buonscontro, good meeting; Bonfratelli, good brother; Bonfigli, Bonfiglietti, Bonfioli, Bongarzoni, good child (cf. English Goodchild, French Bonfils, German Gutkind); Bommarito, Bonmarito, good husband; Buoninsegna, good sign; Bonomo, Bonomone, Bonomelli, Bonometti, good man, also a simpleton, good-natured fellow; Bonomini,[33] good men; Buonopera, good deed; Buonpane, good bread; Buonpastore, good shepherd; Buonpensiere, good thought; Buonricovero, good refuge; Buonristoro, good comfort; Borromei, good pilgrim, Buonsangue, good blood; Bonsaver, Buonsenso and Buontalento, good sense; Buonservizi, good service; Buonsignore,[34] good lord; Buonsolazzi, good solace; Bonsustegni, good support, protection; Bontempo, Bontempone, Bontempelli, good time; Bonvalori, good courage; Bonvicino, Bommicino (Calabrese), good neighbor; Buonviaggio, bon voyage. We are told that the family name of St. Bonaventura was Fidenza; his font name was Giovanni. At the age of four he became dangerously ill causing his pious mother to appeal on her knees to St. Francis that he pray for her son. The great saint's prayers were granted and the mother overjoyed by the turn of events cried out "o buona ventura!" "Oh, good fortune!" after which the name of Bonaventura supplanted that of Giovanni Fidenza.[35] Incidentally, most of the above re-appear in the guise of contractions—Amico, Amore, Parola, Volta, Compagni, Pagni, Consiglio, Core, Cristiano, Fante, Fidanza, Guadagni, Guadagnoli, Incontri, Scontri, Contri, Insegna, Inzinga (Sicilian), Omini, Pane, Pastore, Pensieri, Ristori, Sangui, Sensi, Signori, Sollazzo, Sostegni, Talenti, Valori, Vicini, Bontura, Turi, etc.

Buono is sometimes used with occupational names as in Bonclerici, good cleric; Bonferraro, good smith. More often it is prefixed to font names—Bombardo (i.e. buon Bernardo, Berardo), Bonoguidi, Bommartini, Bonarigo, Buonandrei, Boncardo (buon Riccardo), Bongerolami, Bongiordano, Bonciani, Bongioanni, Bongiovanni, Bonzani, Buommattei, Bonvito, Buonsaro (buon Baldassare, Rosario). Buono may also be affixed to font names—Guidoboni, Riccobono, Rigobon (from Arrigo), Ottoboni, Antonibon, Pietrobono. Such names were popular among the West Frankians and Langobards and have presumably been transmitted to us largely

---

[33] Bonomini were well-known Florentine city officials in the Middle Ages.

[34] Buonsignore is often a variant of monsignore.

[35] See G. Belèze, Dictionnaire des Noms de Baptême, Paris, 1863, 70.

through them. Originally the affix did not mean good as it did later, but was merely one of the two themes employed by the Germans to form their names.[36] Their vogue may also have contributed to the growth of a newer type of compound, a font name making use of an affixed bello instead of bono such as Colabelli, Lucabello, Perbellini, Petrobelli, Riccobelli, Spinabelli. But these might be explained, too, by the use of Bello as a font name or coinages based on the model Isabella, Lucibello.

A few compounds containing malo may have arisen from contrasts with the buono group. Compare Malanima, bad soul, with Bonanima, good soul; Malomo, bad man, with Bonomo, good man; Malfante, bad child, with Bonfante, Bonfantini, good child; Malquore, bad heart, with Boncore, good heart; Malvicini, bad neighbor, with Bonvicino, good neighbor; Maluccelli, bad little bird, bad little one, with Bonuccelli, good little bird, good little one; Maltempo, bad weather, with Bontempo, good weather. Conversely, Bonerba, good grass, seems to come from a contrast with Malerba, bad grass, weed, annoying person; Bonaspina, good thorn, from Malaspina, bad thorn; Bonatesta, good head, from Malatesta, bad head. Other examples are Malantuono, bad Anthony; Malaguerra, bad war; Malacarne, Malpeli, Malpezzo, Malafarina, Malavita, Maffatore, synonyms of rogue, knave, evil-doer; and Malvezzi, bad habit.[37] There is a noble Bolognese family that curiously enough continues to carry on both the name of Bonconsigli and its foil Malconsigli.[38]

Font names compounded with titular designations are particularly rich and varied. Mastro, master, is a general appellative for a notary, a teacher or an artisan, especially the head of a workshop. It is used with almost any first name—Mastroandrea, Mastrangelo, Mastrogiuseppe, Mastroippolito, Mastromarini, Mastrominico, Mastronardi, Mastropasquà, Mastroroberti, Mastrosimone, Mastrototaro, Mastrovalerio. Occasionally dialectical influences change mastro to mast as in Mastandrea, Mastantuono, to marro as in Marronicola, or to misto as in Mistorigo. Ser indicating a notary was once quite popular, but it is now practically restricted to Serfilippo, Sergia-

---

[36] For a short discussion of Germanic dithematic names see chapter on Given Names.

[37] Malavita, one of the apparent rogue names, is in the Etna region nothing more than a black horehound. A Giovanni di Malorespectu, ill-respect, lived in the thirteenth century. See C. Minieri-Ricci, "Memorie della Guerra di Sicilia negli Anni 1282, 1283, 1284, Tratte dai Registri Angioini dell'Archivio di Stato di Napoli," *Archivio per le Provincie Napoletane*, I, 1876, 506.

[38] Given by G. B. Crollalanza, *Dizionario Storico Blasonico delle Famiglie Nobili e Notabili Italiane*, Pisa, 1888, II.

comi, Sergianni, Sermartelli, Sernicola, Serristori and Serandrei.[39] On the other hand, font names compounded with notaro, likewise a notary, are fairly widespread: Notardonato, Notardonado, Notarnicola, de Notaristefani, Notarangelo, which is abridged to Tarangeli and Tarangioli. Giudiceandrea, judge Andrew, Giudicepietro, judge Peter, and Contegiacomo, Conteguidi, Contughi, Contalberti, count James, Guido, Hugo, Albert, are unique in these categories. Presti, Southern Italian for prete, priest, shows up with Prestifilippo, Prestigiacomo, Prestianni,[40] Prestipino (Giuseppino, Filippino, Jacopino etc.). Pre is used for priest in the Venetian section and from it have come Precarlo, Premarco, Premarin, Pressanto. Papa can mean priest, too—Papandrea, Papaianni, Papapietro, Papatodero (all Southern Italian forms), but in Calabrese papa in the same combinations can also refer to uncle.[41] Siri in Sirianni and Sirimarco has the meaning of father, as does tata in Tatangelo, Tatafiore, Tatasciore. Don is usually an ecclesiastical title, but throughout Southern Italy, especially Sicily, it is a term of respect. Surnames containing it are Donnangelo, Donnantuoni, Donnorso, Donzorzi, Dompieri, Donvito. Donnamaria is one of the very few feminine title-names. It should not be forgotten that the lower clergy in the Greek Catholic church, which used to flourish in the South but is now extinct, was allowed to marry. For monks, fra, brother, is used in Frantonio, Frabasile, Fraccaroli, Fradistefano, Fraggiorgi, Frallonardo, Frappoli, while frate, a full form, may be seen in Fratangelo, Fratarcangeli, Fratepietro, Fratinardo, Fraterrigo. This is paralleled by the employment of abate, abbott, abbé, in Abatemarco, Abatecola, Abatescianni, Abateminnici, and by monaco, monk, employed as the second member of the compound in Colamonico, Pietromonaco, Iamonico. Deacon, jacono, is linked with Giovanni in Jaconianni. These names, too, are apt to be Southern Italian.

Likewise numerous are number-compounds which refer either to nicknames or place names—Mezzacappa, half cape; Mezzalama, half blade; Mezzamici, half friend; Mezzofanti, half soldier (cf. English Halfknight); Mezzoconti, half count; Mezzadonna, half woman; dwarf, Mezzasalma, half load; Mezzoprete, half priest; Mezzavacca, half cow; Tricase, three houses; Trecroci, three crosses; Tredente, three tooth, trident; Trepiedi, tripod; Trecapelli, three hairs; Tribastuni, three (of) spades; Trepiccione, three pigeon;

---

[39] Among the confalonieri of Lucca in the 15th century were Serantoni, Sergiusti and Serlunardi. See *R. Archivio di Stato di Lucca*, 1907. Further older ser-names are Sermini, Sercambi, Serarcangeli.

[40] It would not be fantastic to suppose that Prestianni can be related to the famous Prester John.

[41] See Alessio, *Saggio di Toponomastica Calabrese*. Firenze, 1939, under papa.

Quattrocchi,[42] four eyes; Quattrorecchi, four ears; Quattrocciocchi, four locks; Quattrimani, four hands; Quattrohuomini, four men; Quadrupani, four loaves; Cinquemani,[43] five hands; Settepani,[44] seven loaves; Settanni, seven years; Settecase, seven houses; Settecastelli, seven castles; Novespade, nine swords; Trentanni, thirty years; Trentalance, thirty lances; Trentacoste,[45] thirty ribs; Trentacapilli,[46] thirty hairs; Centanni, hundred years, also part of a toast; Centomani, hundred hands; Centofanti, hundred soldiers; Centomiglia, hundred miles; Centolanze, hundred lances; Millanni, one thousand years, likewise part of a toast; and Millomini, one thousand men, the name of a Genoese family.[47]

From a wealth of adjective-plus-noun sanctuary surnames (originally spot names) we can only give a sampling: Santangelo, Sandonato, Sanfilippo, Santa Caterina, Santarosa, Sannicandro, San Romano, Sanvitale, Sammartino, Zampieri.

Except in those words used with titles, numerals and saints' names the prefixed adjective plus noun is of rare occurrence. These names we shall lump into a miscellaneous group, namely, Biancamano, white hand; Caramadre, dear mother; Caravita,[48] dear life; Dolciamore, sweet love; Falsaperla,[49] false pearl; Gentilcore, gentle heart; Massimbeni, reduced to Simbeni and del Bene, greatest good; Cortopasso, Piccolpasso, Parvupasso,[50] short step; Pocaterra, little land, (cf. German Anacker); Pocorroba, little goods; Poveromo, poor man; Senzamici, without friends; Senzamalizia, without malice; Senzanome, without name; Senzarasone, without reason; Senzatimore, without fear (cf. French Sanscrainte and German Sorgenfrei); Sozzinfante, shameless child; Tuttolomondo, Tuttoilmondo, all the world; Verasaluce, true light.

The affixed adjective is found rather frequently in compounds. It is used to describe a physical attribute of a person by a certain given name: Giangrande, Big John; Giangrasso, Fat John; Giarusso,

---

[42] Jocularly quattrocchi is used to refer to spectacles or to a man with spectacles. Cf. also parlare a quattr'occhi, to speak in private, and quattrocchi, a dialectical word signifying plover.

[43] Cinquevie, five roads, is the name of a now extinct Piedmontese family.

[44] One can't help being reminded of the Biblical miracle of the seven loaves and fishes (Matthew, XV).

[45] Also the name of an aquatic bird.

[46] Cf. Greek Triantafilous, a word for rose, and the name of a valley near Pizzo di Calabria.

[47] See also Coin names under Miscellaneous Names and C. Poma, "Numeri come Cognomi." *Archivio Glottologico Italiano*, XVIII, 1918, 345-52.

[48] Cf. with this the Sicilian word caravita meaning caraway.

[49] A Guglielmo Ficomaturo, ripe fig, was a 13th century condottiero.

[50] Parvupasso can be found as a Piedmontese place name.

Iarussi, Red John; Ciccotosto, Stubborn Frank.[51] It likewise appears in quite a number of place names, for example, Acquafredda, cold water; Fiumefreddo, cold stream; Campolongo, long field; Collalto, Montalto, high hill; Fontanabuona, good spring; Terranova, new land; Torregrossa, big tower; Vallunga, long vale. Some other instances are Caparotta, broken head, Capracotta,[52] roast goat; Sanguedolce, sweet, gentle, blood; Mentesano, sound mind; Spadavecchia, old sword and Paternostro, Patenostro, our father, which may be of religious derivation, but is also connected with pratum, meadow, as a Sicilian place name.[53]

Compounds formed from an adverb plus a past participle may come from first names: Benamato, well beloved; Beninato, Bennato, well-born; Benemerito, well merited, man of merit; Bencrisciuto, well reared; Benveduto, well liked; Bentrovati, with its shortened form Trovato, well found; Benvenuti, welcome; Bonaccolti, well received; Bonavolta and its pet name variant Volta, well returned; Bonbissuto, Bomvissuto, well lived; Carotenuto, held dear. Or they may procede from nicknames—Bellufatto, Bonfatto, well formed; Malfatto, malformed; Maltagliati, ill cut, shaped; Malvisto, Malveduto, disliked; Malvestito, ill dressed; Malnato, ill born, wicked. Benvogliente and Benedicenti are two of the rare names formed from an adverbial linking to a present participle, while in Pocobelli, unbeautiful, we have an adverb and an adjective.

Combinations of two nouns are found chiefly in personal surnames and place name surnames. By far the most popular of the double font names consist of the union of Giovanni, Pietro, Nicola and another given name. From Peter we get Perantoni, Pergiovanni, Petricola, Pierangioli, Pierfederico, Pierleoni, Piermei (Pietro Bartolomeo or Amedeo), Pietrangeli, Pietromarchi, Pietropaolo, etc.; from Giovanni we get Giandrea (Giannandrea), Giammaria, Giamberardini, Giancamilli, Giancarli, Giancola, Giammatteo, Giampieri, Giampuzzi (Gian Iacopuzzi, Filippuzzi, Giuseppuzzi), Giallorenzi, Iannantonio, Iannicola, Iannfiorelli, Zandonati, Zammarchi, Zampieri. From Nicola come Colandrea, Colangeli, Colantoni, Colabattista, Colacicchi (Nicola Francesco), Colagiacomo, Colajanni, Colapietro, Colasanti. Of the less frequent doublets the following are an illustration: Aloisantoni, Amicagnioli, Angelsanto, Bartolomasi (Bartolomeo Tommaso), Ceccopiero (Francesco Piero), Cicconardi (Francesco Leonardo), Guidantoni, Giorgianni, Marcotulio,

[51] For other examples see Anatomical Names. Add Giarraputo, which seems to stand for Gian-rapito, kidnapped John.

[52] Capracotta appears as an Abruzzese place name.

[53] See C. Avolio, Saggio di Toponomastica Siciliana." *Archivio Glottologico Italiano, Supplemento,* Sesta dispensa, 1898, 91.

Marinpietro, Meomartini (Bartolomeo Martino), Michelangioli, Nannipieri (Giovanni or Ferdinando Piero), Nantista (Giovambattista), Piomaria, Polfranceschi, Pasqualangelo and its shorter forms Scalangelo, Scarangelo, Titomanlio, Vittorangeli. Occasionally a first name, especially Giovanni, joins a nickname in such odd combinations as Giambarbieri, John Barber; Giamporcari, John Hogherd; Jacapraro, John Goatherd; Giammarinaro, John Sailor; Giancipoli, John Onion; Zambeccari, John Butcher; Ciambecchini, John Sexton; Giangobbi, John Hunchback; Gianguercio, John Squint Eyed; Gianbarese, John of Bari; Gialombardo, John Lombard; Giangreco, Gianturco, John Turk; Zanovello, John Junior; Zantedeschi, John German; Colasurdo, Nick Deaf; Colurso, Nick Bear; Colavolpe, Nick Fox; Colavecchio, Old Nick; Francomagaro, Frank Sorcerer.[54] All these show the nickname in apposition to the font name. Gianformaggio, John Cheeseman; Giansiracusa, John of Syracuse; Giannitrapani, John of Trapani, are interesting examples showing the omission of del after Gian in the first case and of di in the last two.[55] The same phenomenon is illustrated in the combination of two nouns in many of the Italian place names such as Montalbano, Montefiore, Monteleone, Montessori, Montoro, and others too numerous and obvious to cite. Compare also Pontecorvo, Casasanto.

A double adverb is found in the Sicilian name Poidomani with the apparent literal meaning of after tomorrow, but this has been traced back to a place name Poidomani in the province of Modica which, in turn, is connected with the word demesne.[56] Carassai, very dear and Piampiano, very slowly, are other examples.

We shall conclude with a handful of queer names like Accavallo, on horseback; Agnusdei, lamb of God; Bellenetto, pretty clean; Benessere, well being; Bentivoglio, I love you; Boccadifuoco, fire mouth; Caponinsacco, head in a sack; Capocefalo, head (Latin) and head (Greek); Capusotto,[57] head down; Carnesale,[58] meat and salt; Cordiferro, iron heart; Corforati, pierced heart (probably belonging to heraldry); Corleo, Corleone, Cordileone, lion heart; Forteguerra, Fortiguerra, strong in war; Gesumaria, Jesus Mary, a speech mannerism or a double font name; Lucenteforte, shining

---

[54] Andrea Giasoldati, John Soldier, was a vicar at Bologna in the 15th century. For other examples see Anatomical Names.

[55] Another of the rare names of this sort is Paolo Pizabeccari, who lived in Modena in the 16th century. Here Piza is probably Opizza, a first name, while beccaro is a butcher.

[56] Cf. C. Avolio, *op. cit.* 104.

[57] Capusotto is also a Pitigliano place name.

[58] Carnesale may be Teramano carnassale, a term for a masked person, or old Vicentino carnassale, carnival.

strong; Materdomine, mother of God; Mirallegro, I am glad; Nidobeato, blessed nest; Nonmai, nevermore; Nontigiova,[59] it does not avail you; Pennimpede, feathers on feet or wingfooted; Pochintesta, little in the head; Portincasa, bring home; Santesano, hail and hearty; Semperboni, always good; Sonaccorso, I have come; Spadafora,[60] drawn sword, Neapolitan for a quarrelsome fellow. Mivanto seems to stand for I boast.[61] Finfino, very thin, fine; Triatria, three by three, may also be speech mannerisms, though they may derive from SeraFINO di SeraFINO and Ntria Ntria, Sicilian for Andrea d'Andrea. Rotiroti looks like roll and roll but it may also be explained as an abbreviated Buonarroti Buonarroti. The Venetian Dondon,[62] looking like ding dong, was originally Doni, so that here, too, we have a duplicated last name Doni Doni.

[59] Nontigiova, Nonmai and Mivanto may be last names derived from mottos.

[60] Spadafora is also a Sicilian place name.

[61] Apparently so interpreted by M. Ruffini in "Onomastica Lunigianese Cognomi Spezzini fra il 1558 e il 1650. "*Memorie dell'Accademia di Scienze, Giovanni Capellini*, XVI, 1935, 15.

[62] An Alberto Pertempo, on time, was a notary in Venice, 1398-1421. Antoniotto Usodimare, sea bear, was a Genoese navigator, b. 1415. The name was carried for at least a century longer in Italy since we find a Bernardo Usodimare-Granello, scribe of an arch-episcopal court, 1527. Later the family seems to have transferred its residence to Spain-Murcia. A Carmela Chiarchiari, very clear, or from Chiara di Chiara, is author of *Fedra di Seneca*, Palermo, 1929. Giuntotardi, late arrival, was the name of the teacher of the well-known 18th century Spanish writer, Tomás de Iriarte.

Chapter VI

DESIRABLE AND UNDESIRABLE QUALITIES

THE DESIRABLE ONES

Some of the surnames indicating desirable qualities come from first names that once represented the joys and hopes of parents on the occasion of a new arrival in the family, precisely as quite a number do today. Names like Amatus, Amicus, Benigna, Clemens, Felix, Fortuna, Gloriosus, Honoratus, Justus, Jocundus, Laetus, Mansuetus, Nobilis, Prudens, appear plentifully in Roman times as shown by the inscriptions.[1] These and others like them became crystallized in saints' names, thus providing an additional prolific explanation for their origin. A few are nicknames.

Cognomina betokening gladness are Allegretti,[2] Allegria, Allegri, Alliegro, Allegranti, Allegranza, Allegrezza, Aspettati, Contento, Contentini, de Felice, Festa, Festino, Festivolo, Lieto, Sorriso, Gaudioso, Gaudio, Gioia, Giocondo, Gioiuso,[3] Delizia, Letizia, Glorioso, Solazzi, Saporito, D'Ilario, Larini,[4] Laretti, Loffaro (Calabrese). Others pointing towards kindliness, courtesy, good nature are Aggarbati, genteel; Amabile, amiable; Amante, lover; Amico, Amici, friend; Amore, love; Amorevole, lovable; Amoruso, loving; Benevoli, benevolent; Benigni, kindly; Buono, Bono and derivatives, good; Bontade, goodness; Bravo, Bravetti,[5] good, honest, courageous; Clementi, Chimenti, Clemenza, Clemenzia, gracious, mild; Cortese,[6] Cortesini, Galante,[7] courteous; Fiuccia, trust; Canoscenti, grateful; Fedele, faithful; Generosi, Gerosi,[8] Liberale, generous; Premuroso, solicitous; Grazioso, polite, gracious; Soave,

---

[1] Many more could have been added from the *Corpus Inscriptionum Latinorum*, Berlin, 1863 ff. Handy lists are given by L. H. Dean, *A Study of the Cognomina of Soldiers in the Roman Legions*, Princeton, 1916.

[2] An allegretto often alludes to a drinker. In Rome the term means a watercress.

[3] Cf. the place name Gioiosa Jonica in Calabria.

[4] Larini, Laretti, are, of course, pet forms of Ilario. Cf. Larino place name in Abruzzi-Molise.

[5] Sometimes a ruffian, bandit.

[6] Cf. Spanish Cortés.

[7] Galante is also gallant, lady's man.

[8] This reduction is confirmed by the Milanese geros, affable. Another meaning of the word, probably connected with cera, face, is jovial.

Gentile, Mansueto, Mascioli (Romano, Marchigiano), gentle; Modesti, Modestini, modest; Nobile, noble; Onesti, honest; Onorato, honorable; Tranquilli, peaceful; Pace,[9] peace; Pacifico, Pacione, easy-going; Riposati, calm; Pacera, peace maker; Paziente, patient; Pazienza, patience; Dolce, kind, sweet; Piozzi (from Pio), Pietoso, pious; Placido, placid; Consolatore, comforter; Pulito, Pulido, genteel, refined, clean; Quieto, quiet; Santo, saint. Names indicative of courage and strength are Ardito, Audaci, bold; Forte, strong; Gagliardo,[10] vigorous; Impavido, fearless; Sforza,[11] fierce; Poderoso, Possenti, powerful; Pro, Prodi, Perodi, Parodi,[12] Valente, Valorosa, valiant; Virili, virile; Stoico, stoical; Tenace, tenacious. Cognomina suggesting cleverness, good sense, skill and intelligence are Acuto, Scaltrito,[13] Astuto, Avveduto, Accorti, Ingegno, sharp; Esperto, Spierto,[14] Navigato, clever; Svegliato, Vigilante, Vegliante, alert; Prudenti, prudent; Diligenti, diligent; Sollecito, quick, attentive; Assennato, sensible; Senno, good sense; Serio, serious, sober; Providenti, Providenzi and the pet forms Denti, Densi, Denzi, provident; Savio, Saggio, wise, learned; Talenti,[15] talent. Cristiano, Christian, in Tarantino and Sicilian means a clever, judicious person. Liveliness is implied in Pronto, Snelli, Veloce, Scalabrini,[16] (Valle Anzasca); wittiness in Buffo, Buffa,[17] Buffone, Faceto,[18] Spiritoso and Pagliaccio. Purity, faithfulness, finds a place in Casti,[19] Lo Casto, chaste; Virtuoso, virtuous; Purificato, purified; Candido, candid, pure; Leale, loyal; Ricordati, remembered; hope of future fame in Celebre, Celebrini, celebrated; Famoso,[20] famous; Distinti, distinguished; Maestoso, majestic; Signorile, seignorial; Trionfante, triumphant; Venerato, venerated; praise in Lodato,[21] Laudato, Mira-

---

[9] Some Paces were once Bonapace. Pace may also be a translation of Greek Irene, which means peace.

[10] Cf. Spanish Gallardo and the word for an old dance, gagliarda.

[11] Mutio Attendolo, founder of the Sforza family, was so nicknamed on account of his fierceness in battle.

[12] Perodi, Parodi would, of course, be the result of epenthesis.

[13] Often in a derogatory sense.

[14] Cf. AnSPERTO. In Calabrese spiertu also means fugitive, homeless.

[15] Usually a reduction of Buontalento.

[16] In Tuscan an astute individual.

[17] Buffa is a toad in Reggio Calabrese and Sicilian; it also means a hood covering the head and face.

[18] Bonifacio reduced to Facio plus the addition of the suffix -eto may yield Faceto.

[19] Cf. GioCASTA.

[20] Also has a depreciative meaning; notorious.

[21] Either Dato from DonATO or DioDATO with the prefixed article, lo, could produce Lodato.

bile, Ammirato, Adorato, adored; Amato, loved. The three cardinal virtues are represented in Fedi, faith; Bonafede, good faith; Speranza, hope; Carità, charity. Another abstract surname is Verità, truth. A few more desirable qualities are pictured in Ardenti, ardent; Favorito, favorite; Innamorato, Morati, Amatore, lover; Fortunato, fortunate; Faustini, Avventurato, lucky; Sparagna, economical; Faticati (Calabrese), industrious; Fulgenti, Fulgenzio, bright, shining; Illuminati, enlightened; Desiderato, Desiderio, desired. Garbo looks as if it might come from garbo, grace, pleasing manners.[22]

THE UNDESIRABLE ONES

Undesirable characteristics in the guise of surnames have for the most part started out as nicknames. As such they are apt to reveal to the point of exaggeration the knavery, abusiveness, carping proclivities and jest of the original conferrers. They are word-pictures that resemble the reflections that come to us through a distortion mirror. Their numbers show that their owners have been good-naturedly receptive towards them. Cognomina from words connoting bully or rogue are Malandrino, Malandra,[23] Landri, Frabotta (cf. Calabrese, Romano, Marchigiano frabutto), Balossi [24] (Northern Italian), rogue; Manigoldo,[25] villanous ruffian; Loperfido, Perfidi, perfidious; Perversi, perverse; Ribaldo,[26] ribald; Fieri, Feroci, fierce; Imbiso (possibly from Calabrese 'mpiso), gallow bird; Malo, bad; Crudo, Crudeli, Marvasi, Tinto (Southern Italian), Barbaro,[27] barbarous; Pericolosi,[28] dangerous; Terribile, Terribilini, terrible; Salvatico, Salvaggio, Selvaggi,[29] Spaventa, Paventa, frightener; Temerario and Francone,[30] rash; Tiranno, Tiranetto, tyrant; Despoto,[31] despot. More inocuous bullies of the bragadoccio, noise-

---

[22] But the Florentine del Garbo is related to lana del Garbo, garbo wool from Algarvia, a district in Portugal. The textile gave the name to a street in Florence and from it it was first assumed as a surname by the famous doctors, Dino and Tommaso who lived in it. See *Statuti Sanesi*, III, Bologna, 1877, 424-25.

[23] In Valle Anzasca a malandra is an idler. If Calabrese, landra is merely dogbane.

[24] In Venetian a baloso is a good-for-nothing.

[25] Also hangman, but compare the Germanic first name Mangold.

[26] In most cases the source is GaRIBALDO.

[27] Also a masculine form of Barbara, and a horse, barb.

[28] Pericoloso can be formed from a combination of Pero (Piero) plus Coloso from Nicoloso. Cf. also Pericoli from Pero plus Cola (Nicola).

[29] Often used as a first name. The fictional warrior Guidone Selvaggio may have had some influence.

[30] More acceptable as the augmentative form of Franco.

[31] Usually from Codespoto, head of a household.

making brand are Smargiassi, Fanfarra, Fraccassi, Fraccassini, Fanfalone, Baioni,[32] (Cremonese bajon), Faloppa, Trambusti, Terremoto [33] (literally, earthquake). Though they are susceptible of other meanings we place here several of the terms for devil—Maligno, Lucifero, Cifariello (Southern Italian), Ciferri, Cioci (Abruzzese), Ciappini (Pavese), Pinto [34] (Calabrese); the term for ogress, Laorca, De Orchis and the terms for sorcerer Streghi, Ariola, Magaro (Southern Italian). Saccenti [35] and Saputi are wiseacres. Malizia, Mordaci, Vendetta,[36] Mascagni describe spiteful persons; Tizzone [37] a fire brand, mischief maker; Falso, Falsetti or Finti, one who is deceitful; Favaloro (Sicilian), Ciaffone (Abruzzese), a cheat; Piglione, a grabber; Frugoni,[38] a rummager, ransacker. A Fusco [39] (Sicilian-Calabrese) is an anti-social fellow; a Pesante, unless related to Bisanto, Byzantine, is an annoyer and a Baccieri (Sicilian-Calabrese 'mpaccieri), a meddler. In Bergamascan Zaccherini, Zaccheroni [40] could be interpreted as Importuni, importunates. Impronto seems to point in the same direction. Hot-brained people are known as Furibondo, Furiosi, furious; Furia, fury; Rabbiosi, wrathful; Ragghianti, literally brayer; Raggia,[41] hydrophobia; Ghignoni, bold faced, sneering; Chizzoli, Chizzolini [42] (Modenese chizza), an irascible person. Facilla,[43] Favilla, spark; Fiamma, Svampa, flame; Dal Foco, Focolino,[44] Incendio, fire; Focoso, fiery, may also relate to choleric people. The jealous are designated by Gelosi,[45] Ielosi. Those who are obstinate and querulous receive

[32] Baione might refer to a color, bay, and to a horse. See Animal Names.

[33] We also have the surname Maramotti which looks like a sea-movement produced by an earthquake, but the source is probably marmotto, marmot.

[34] This and some other terms are frequently applied to children. As to Ciappini a good source of the name is Ciapo from Giacomo.

[35] For Ariola cf. ariola, birdsfoot trefoil. In the Middle Ages saccente meant wise. Cf. Salomone il saccente, Salomon the wise.

[36] The Romagnuolo term for Benedetto is Vandett. Vendetta could, therefore, be a variant.

[37] Another meaning of the word is black.

[38] In Pavese a cart or wagon. Cf. furgone, ammunition wagon. Piglione can, incidentally, hail from PomPILIO plus -ONE.

[39] Also means dark.

[40] Both could come from Zaccheria, Isacco) (Izacco), Tuscan zaccherone, from zacchera, splash of mud, is a dirty person.

[41] Possibly related to Orazia.

[42] Chizzola in Cremonese is a fritter.

[43] Can be linked to Bonifacia through BoniFACILLA.

[44] There is a St. Phocas, Foca.

[45] Another guess would be AnGELOS(S)O.

appellatives like Ostinato,[46] Storto,[47] Stortiglione, Scazzuso (Southern Italian) and Mogni [48] (Bolognese); the gossips as Ciarloni,[49] Ciarlante, Parlatore, Catani [50] (Castro de' Volsci) a talkative woman; gadabouts as Gironi, Girelli, Errante,[51] Annarino (Sicilian), Ciraulo, Ciraolo;[52] eccentrics and insane people as Pazzi, Pacciotti,[53] Matto, Mattone, Mattarella, Mattina,[54] Cretinelli,[55], Strambi,[56] Capriccio, Bizzarri, Bizzarrini, Falotico, Fantastici, Fantasia, Scapati; idlers and good-timers as Poltrone, Potrone, Sciampagna, literally drinker of champagne; the haughty as Superbi, Boriosi, Fumoso, Orgogliosi, Argogliosi; dandies or Don Juans as Moscardino,[57] Damerini,[58a] Possumato, Incatasciato (Sicilian), Busoni (Romagnuolo); the greedy and covetous as Avido, Avarello,[58] Taccagni, Pitocco, Pitocchelli, Betocchi;[59] the whimperers as Cianciosi; timid souls as Paura, fear; Tremarelli, trembler; Coardi,[60] coward; a nasty fellow

---

[46] Agostino can give Ostino which, with the addition of the suffix -ato (common in the Venetian section) gives Ostinato.

[47] Storto can also mean bandy-legged, squint-eyed. In Venetian the term means a wafer.

[48] In Parmigiano a mogna is a seller of boiled chestnuts.

[49] Might be a variant of Ciarlo from Carlo. Cf. French Charles.

[50] Parlatore could be an orator. In parts of Southern Italy Gaetano is Gatano, of which Catano might be a variant.

[51] Girone recalls Girone il Cortese, hero of one of the romances of chivalry. A girello is also a weathercock, fickle person, turncoat. Both Girone and Girelli may likewise be reproduced from a pet form of Girolamo plus an augmentative or diminutive. Ciro, Cyrus, through a change of c to g, is an extremely important contender. Errante brings to mind cavaliere errante, knight errant.

[52] Also a Mountebank.

[53] Cf. JacoPAZZO, JacoPACCIO, and Germanic Pazzo.

[54] All of these names could derive from Mattia (Matthias) and Mato from Amato by means of the doubling of the internal consonant, a common phenomenon.

[55] Derivatives of Policreto and even Anacleto might give this name.

[56] Strambo like storto is also squint-eyed, bandy-legged. Cf. the famous Latin name Strabo. In Palermo at the end of the thirteenth century lived a Gino Rabbuffati, deranged. See R. Starabba, "Miscellanea . . . *Archivio Storico Siciliano*, n.s. XIII, 1888, 84.

[57] Might be a Germanic name, Moscardo.

[58] Cf. Alvarello.

[58a] Could easily come from Adamo.

[59] If we may consider -occo as a suffix good claimants would be Germanic Bito, Beto. See E. Förstemann, *Altdeutches Namenbuch*, Erster Band. Personennamen. Bonn, 1900, 301. In this case we would have an unvoicing of the initial consonant. Bongioanni, *Nomi e Cognomi*. Torino, 1928, derives Pitocco from Agapito.

[60] The name was originally Codardi. As for Tremarelli, it could mean aspen if from the Carnian region.

as Cacchione.[61] The wretched, poor and miserable are recalled by Infelise, Afflitto, Malenconcio, Tribolati,[62] unhappy; La Mesta, sad; Tenebruso, gloomy; Meschino, Meschinelli,[63] wretched; Povero and Scarso, poor; Nudo, Gnudi, naked;[64] the wearisome by Stanco, Stancato, Affaticati, Affranti; the ailing by Malato,[65] Marotta [66] (Genoese), Scarmato, Calato, Fiocco, Debolini, and by Calvario, literally, calvary; Podragosi, gouty person; Tignosini,[67] scabby; Rogna, Rognetta, itch; Sogliuzzo (Southern Italian) hiccough. Individuals or families who have suffered mishaps are designated as Infortunio, Patuto, Scaduto; Cadavero, corpse; one who has suffered physically or mentally as Risanato, cured; Scampato, Salvato and Risalvato, saved. Other names alluding to mishaps are Scorticati, flayed; Mazzato, killed; Percossi, beaten; Potuto, overcome; Peropato, Perrupato (Calabrese), a person who has fallen from a cliff; Muzzicato, Morso, La Morsa, bitten; Fuggiti, runaway, escaped; Spirsi, Persa, Perduto,[68] lost; Profughi, refugee; Fascinato, Affatato, bewitched; Traditi, betrayed; Gabbato, deceived; Scorpati and Innocenti, innocent; Racchiuso, confined; Cacciato, Scacciati, Discacciati, ejected, exiled. A lethargic fellow is a Lomuscio or Tardone.[69] The results of some foolish action crop out in Norante, Stupidetti, Semplici, Locchi, Babione, Mangione, Baggiani, Baccelli,[70] Bazzani, Bazzanelli, Gagliuffii, Tangheroni, Badalone, Taccarello (Tarantino from taccaro, club), Cimadomo,[71] Ciam-

---

[61] Literally, the worm of the bee. But compare cacciune, caccione, dog.

[62] Could be from tribolo, bramble. The added -ato would make it bramble field.

[63] As an additional source we recall Guerin Meschino, a hero of the romances of chivalry.

[64] Nudo, Gnudi are not necessarily indicative of wretchedness, nor are such last names as Straccioni, Stracciati, Strazza, Strazzolini, Pellizzone (Calabrese), Bracalone (Abruzzese), all meaning a person in frayed or tattered clothes. This is also true of Piediscalzo, Scalzo, barefoot. Bongioanni, op. cit. suggests under Bene that Gnudi might come from Benvenuto. The same observation holds for Nudo. Silence may or may not be golden, but we have, at any rate, the surname Silenzi.

[65] Might mean apple orchard, malus, plus the collective suffix -ato.

[66] Cf. Aldemaro and other names in -maro. Marotta is usually Southern Italian.

[67] A tignoso from Palermo might be a tarantula. Elsewhere in Sicily the word indicates an upstart, or a small or worthless fellow. In Calabrese a tignusu is an irascible individual.

[68] Perduto also means a lost soul, rascal.

[69] Possible from Gottardo.

[70] Both Battista and Bartolomeo give the net name Baccio, which, with the addition of the dimunitive become Baccello. Cf. also JacoBACCIO. Baccello is a green bean, pod, the source of the dolt meaning.

[71] The meaning is, of course, acquired antiphrastically.

briello (both Calabrese), Sciocchetti, Attontito, Gnocchi, literally, dumpling, Corbellini,[72] Lanciani,[73] Goggio (Piedmontese), Ciolli (Pavese), Cionci, Brocchi [74] (Modenese), literally, bull's eye, Tallo,[75] Talluto, literally, stalk or stalk-like, Taccone,[76] literally, heel, Tambelloni, literally, brick, Carugno, Carogna, Caronia,[77] literally, carrion, Ciambrone (Abruzzese), literally, a broken, ill-conditioned shoe, Marzocchi,[78] referring to a sculptured or painted lion. The uncouth are labelled Lotosco, Bruschi, Villano, Rustici, Cafone, Tamarro, Zambra (Lucanese), Targione (if Calabrese), Tarallo, Marrabello (from Calabrese marrapiellu), Coticone, Codegone, thick-skinned, terms also applicable to peasants. However, a cafone is quite often a gormandizer, and so are people with such names as Ghiotti, Mangione, Magnoni,[79] Leccardo, Cannaruto (Southern Italian), and Appitito, appetite. Heavy drinkers are known as Ubbriachi, Imbriaco, Briachi, Beoni, Picogna (if Calabrese); a dissolute, frequently an eccentric person, is dubbed Scapigliati.[80] The sloven receive names like Bavuso, Bavoso,[81] driveller; Puzzoso, malodorous; Luridi, Sozza,[82] Cajozza [83] (Reggio Calabrese), untidy; Macchiati, spotted, sutty; Infangati, muddy. A Ridarelli may go back to ridarello, one who is easily provoked to laughter.[84] A Tentoni is perhaps a groper; an Impicciati, one who is embroiled, con-

[72] A second guess towards the explanation of Gnocchi would be Agno + occo either from Agnello or Agnolo. In the Pisan dialect gnocco means anger. For Corbellini, cf. basket, crow, and corbel, Bresciano for sorb tree.

[73] Cf. the town of Lanciano.

[74] Ciolli calls to mind Lucia + olla. In the Iesino dialect a cioncia is an untidy woman. With Brocchi cf. the terms for hedge hog, flask.

[75] Tallo is possible from Cataldo (cf. last name Catallo) and perhaps any name in -to, -ta. Cf. Albertalli.

[76] Very likely from the given name TalACCO. A tacon in Piedmontese is a tatterdemalion.

[77] In Valle Anzasca the last born of children.

[78] It would not be too illogical to assume that Marzocchi is also a derivative of Marzo + occo.

[79] Magno (cf. St. Magnus) and Carlomagno might account for Magnoni and even Mangione. A Giovanni Mangiadori, heavy eater, was a fourteenth century condottiero.

[80] Literally, dishevelled.

[81] Bavuso also means giddy headed. It is likewise a mushroom and a fish, blenny.

[82] There is a St. Sozza.

[83] Niccolaio becomes Colaio and then Caio. Add the suffix -ozza and you obtain the homograph Cajozza. Similarly Cajozza can be reproduced from Genoese MacCAIO (Maccario) and ZacCAIA (Zaccaria).

[84] Paride through its short form Ride plus the suffix -arello leads to Ridarello.

fused. A Bigotti,[85] a Pinzoccheri and possibly a Bizzoccheri is a bigot. Impallomeni, the name of a famous Graeco-Venetian family, means agitated.[86]

But this is only a part of the entire picture. The well-informed reader must already have become aware of the fact that most of the figurative terms alluding to desirable or undesirable characteristics have been omitted. Some can be found scattered in the chapters dealing with animals, vegetables and objects; others in the chapter on Compound Names. As to the attractive or unattractive aspects of physical appearance described figuratively or otherwise, they can be located in the chapter on Anatomical Names.

---

[85] More often a Bigotto goes back to Bico from Alberico.

[86] The sixteenth century Sognatori, dreamer, visionary, may or may not have contained an unfavorable implication.

Chapter VII

BOTANICAL NAMES

FLOWERS

Somewhere in his *Life Thoughts* Henry Ward Beecher has stated: "Flowers are the sweetest things God ever made and forgot to put a soul into." This oblivion has been partially remedied by the humanization of the flowers in the guise of the many people that have been named after them. Their exquisite beauty and delicate aroma have been sufficient to insure their popularity as personal names, but floral symbolism and the attitude of the Christian Church, which has regarded them in general as emblems of goodness, have also operated in their favor. These are the chief reasons why we find Floras, Roses, Lilys, Violas and Violets in almost every community. All of them and many others besides exist in Italian both as first and as last names.

However, these personal surnames merge with groups that have had more prosaic beginnings. One of them, the spot name, takes precedence over all the other sources in the number of contributions that it has made. A large number of the names of this class probably represent elliptical forms, for example, Fiori may be an abbreviated version of Val di Fiori, Campo di Fiori, Monte di Fiori, etc., flower vale, flower field, flower hill. Though the plural ending is logical in this type of surname, the singular is also common due, in part, to the influence of the personal flower name and the tendency to adjectivize the last name in the singular according to the sex or gender of the possessor. The other contributing sources are inn or shop signs, heraldic devices, and the extremely popular love ditties called fiori or stornelli in which the lady-love is called by the flower name.[1]

The generic term flower, appears in the surnames Flori, Florio,

---

[1] See G. Pitrè, *Studi di Poesia Popolare*, I, Palermo, 1872, 55, and L. Bonfigli, "Un Mazzetto di stornelli Genzanesi." *Archivio per lo Studio delle Tradizioni Popolari*, XXIII, 1906-07. The last name Fiordimalva, mallow flower, pretty clearly shows the influence of the stornelli. Fiordispini, thorn flower, may point in the same direction.

Fiori, Fioretti, Fiorini, Fiorelli, Fiorucci, Fioroni.[2] Among the individual members of this botanical category are: lily, giving Giglio, Gigliello; anemone, Anemone; aster, Baccari[4] (if Tuscan); bouncing Bet, Garofalo (if Sicilian), Garofolo (if Lombard), Garofano[5] (if Tuscan); Canterbury Bells, Campanelli[6] (if Trivigiano); celandine, Papagno (if Neapolitan); chrysanthemum, Crisanti, Grisanti (if Neapolitan),[7] Belfiori (if Tuscan); cockscomb, possibly Gelosia,[8] Celosia; cornflower or bachelor's button, possibly Ciano[9] (if Tuscan), Ghirlanda[10] (if Piedmontese), Garofalo (if Veronese); Coventry bells, Campanelli (if from Lugano), Campanini (if Parmigiano); creeping bell flower, Ramponi[11] (if Veronese); crocus, Castagnoli[12] (if Veronese), cyclamen, Azara (if it hails from Sicily, Lecce, Salentino), Baccari (if Bresciano); everlasting Capparelli[13] (if from Val di Chiana), Musco[14] (if Calabrese); field buttercup, Brusi[15] (if Bresciano); fleur de lis Fiordaliso,

---

[2] But these names are not always what they seem to be since they can all stem from the short form of Fioravanti, a hero in the chivalric romance, the *Reali di Francia*, or, if Tuscan, from the short form of Fiordinando, a distortion of Ferdinando, or the Germanic stem Flor (see Förstemann, *Altdeutsches Namenbuch*. Erster Band. Personennamen. Bonn, 1901, 511-12). Fiorello is also a hero of the *Reali di Francia*. If Milanese, Fiorino and Fioroni can refer to figliolino and figliolone, small and large child. In Marchigiano a fioron is a broom rape plant.

[3] Gigliodoro, golden lily, looks like an inn sign or armorial device.

[4] Could easily be a variant of vaccaro, cowherd. The same word is used for daisy.

[5] Garofalo and garofano frequently refer to clove. Locally the same word is also used for bachelor's button.

[6] A campanello and campanino literally mean bell. In Northern Italy the words also apply to belfry. Furthermore, they may be related to campana, metaphorically a deaf person and (in Pavese) a simpleton. Quite a number of plants bear the same names.

[7] Also a common first name.

[8] The literal meaning of the word is jealousy.

[9] Ciano usually comes from LuCIANO, MarCIANO, FeliCIANO or may be a variant of Gianni (John). In Trentino a cian is a dog. Cf. cianu, Calabrese for plain, level land.

[10] Cf. the word for garland.

[11] A rampone also means an iron hook.

[12] Castagnolo may be a petard. See also term for meadow saffron. However, its most obvious connection is with castagna, chestnut.

[13] Capparelli is a caper bush, a kind of mushroom or in Abruzzese an untidy person with wax in his ears.

[14] Musco is musk, moss or a tassel hyacinth.

[15] There is a chance that Brusi may come from Ambrosio, Ambrusio.

Ciano [16] and, if Milanese, Bizzarri;[17] four o'clock, Maraviglia;[18] geranium, Gerani, Grisetti [19] (if Piedmontese); gladiola, Cortelazzo [20] (if Veronese); golden rod, Carazzo [21] (in Matera, Lucania); grape hyacinth, Cipollone [22] (if Tuscan) and Scioli (if Piedmontese); heliotrope, Girasoli, Mirasoli (obsolete), Solari [23] (if Neapolitan); herb Robert or red robin, Gambarossa [24] (if Piedmontese), hyacinth, Giacinti;[25] iris, Spatola, Spatula (if Sicilian); Cortelassi and Cortelazzo (if Veronese); jasmine, Gelsomino; lady's smock, Crescioni [26] (either Tuscan or Neapolitan); love in a mist or devil in a bush, Barbisio [27] (if Piedmontese); marigold, La Calendula, Calendario [28] and Garofano (the last two Abruzzese); meadow saffron, Castagnoli (if from Potenza), mignonette, Campanelli (if from North and Central Italy), Campanini (if from the Romagna, Piedmont or Como regions), and (if Tuscan) possibly Amorini, Morini;[29] narcissus, daffodil or jonquil, Narcisi;[30] paper white narcissus, Campanini (if from Masone, Liguria), Pissotti (if Veronese); pasque flower, Fioroni [31] and Gattinari (in case both are Veronese); peach bells, Campanelli (if Bresciano or Tuscan); periwinkle, Gelsomini (if the origin is Tuscan); pheasant's eye, Papanio and Papagno [32] (if Abruzzese); poppy, Papavero, if Southern Italian, Papagno, if Tuscan Paparini,[33] if Romagnuolo Fioroni;

---

[16] See Note 9.

[17] Cf. bizzarro, bizzarre, fantastic, irascible.

[18] Cf. maraviglia, marvel. It is also a term for lady's slipper.

[19] Cf. grisetto, a gray-haired person, and Germanic Griso.

[20] A cortelazzo is also a chopper or a burweed. See also term for hyacinth.

[21] For Carazzo, cf. Maccario, MacCARAZZO.

[22] A cipollone is also an onion, big head. Sciol in Piedmontese is also an onion.

[23] A solaro may be a garret, attic or a sun-dial place. Solari is a place near Milan. Cf. Spanish surname, Solar.

[24] Gambarossa, if Neapolitan, may stand for gamba grossa, large leg.

[25] Giacinto is a common given name.

[26] Crescioni can be connected with Crescio from Crescenzio and also means a water cress.

[27] A barbisio may be a rush.

[28] Calendario usually means almanac.

[29] Amorini and Morini are just as likely to derive from Amore or from Mauro, Moro, Moor, dark.

[30] Commonly used as a first name.

[31] For Pissotti, cf. Opissotto-Opizzotto, and for Fioroni see Note 2.

[32] Cf. Calabrese papagna, necklace. The Tuscan term papavero also means a good for nothing fellow.

[33] See Bird Names.

primrose, Cucchetti;[34] proboscis flower, Capocelli [35] (if Neapolitan); purse or mountain anemone, Fiocchini [36] (if Piedmontese); rock rose, Razzara [37] (if Ligurian), Scornavacco (if Romano); rose, Rosa, Roselli, Roseto, Rosari;[38] scabious, Forcelli, Forcellini [39] (if Abruzzese); scorpion senna, Strazzabosco; snapdragon, Codebò;[40] snowdrop, Campanelli (if Piedmontese); snowflake, Campanelli (if Veronese); sowbread, Baccara [41] (if Bergamasco); sunflower Mirisole and Sole (if Tuscan), Cirasole; sweet pea, Castracani [42] (if Veronese, Trivigiano); verbena, Forcella, Forcellini (if Abruzzese); violet, Viola, Violetti, Mam(m)ola,[43] Ciocchetti (if Venetian).[44]

---

[34] May be related to cucco or cocco, an egg or favorite or cuckoo. B. Bianchi in "La Declinazione nei Nomi di luogo della Toscana." *Archivio Glottologico Italiano*, X, 1886-88, notes on p. 310, that at Città di Castello, cuccumina was a nickname for a short, fleshy woman. He suggests further that cucco may be used as a sobriquet when anyone as a child persistently asks for an egg or has an egg-shaped head. ". . . abbia avuto il vizio di chiedere spesso il cucco (uovo) o abbia la testa lunga col vertice rotondo." He likewise finds that Cuccoli is a common surname in Tuscany and Cuccuini in Chianti, and that cucco was and is still used as a nickname in Pisa.

[35] Cf. Neapolitan capozziello, a stubborn person.

[36] A fiocco may be a tassel, lock.

[37] Razzara is the name of several plants, smilax, etc.

[38] However, sometimes Rosari may be from Rosario.

[39] Cf. forcella, a fork, a forked piece of land, an earwig.

[40] Literally, bull-head. Cf. Tuscan plant name capo di bue.

[41] For Baccara and Mirisole see other flower names. Sole, of course, means sun and could have contributed the name through being used as an inn sign.

[42] Another meaning of castracane is salsify.

[43] A. Bongioanni, *Nomi e Cognomi*, Torino, 1928, points out under Massimo that it can be shortened to Mamo. If we add suffixes we might arrive at Mam(m)ola. Ciocchetti may likewise be from ciocco, blockhead.

[44] Though somewhat defective and incomplete O. Penzig's *Flora Popolare Italiana*. Genova, 1924, with its thousands of local flora names has been found to be extremely useful for names in the entire botanical section. More limited in its usefulness is G. Flechia, "Nomi Locali d'Italia Derivati dal Nome delle Piante." *Atti della R. Accademia delle Scienze di Torino*, XV, 1879-80, 821-42. Incidentally, Flechia found more than four thousand plant names among the sixty thousand place names in the list that he had consulted. He might have added hundreds of other names if he had had available A. Amati, *Dizionario Corografico dell'Italia*, Milano, Vallardi, n.d. 8 vols. English equivalents have been obtained throughout the chapter from Latin translations given in N. L. Britton and A. Brown, *Illustrated Flora of the United States, Canada and British Possessions*. New York, 1898. 3 vols.

A few floral place names or homographs of the same are Fiore (Piedmont), Fiorino (Liguria), Cerasole (Marche, Emilia, Terra di Lavoro), Cian (Venetia), Ciano (Emilia), Cucchetto (Piedmont), Garofali (Naples), Garofano (Emilia), Mammola (Calabria), Rosa (Venetia, Piedmont, Tuscany), Spatula (Calabria).

THE GARDEN

Popular, too, astonishingly popular, is the catalog of cognomina drawn from individual names of vegetables. Why are these surnames so numerous and varied especially when contrasted with the apparently smaller volume of representation enjoyed by vegetable surnames in England, France and Spain? The question cannot easily be dismissed by the answer that Italy is primarily an agricultural country, since all countries were agricultural until a short time ago. A clue comes to us from Sicily where the farmer was formerly under obligation to grow year in year out and without rotation only a certain type of plant on the piece of land turned over to him for cultivation.[45] The patch had thus the time necessary for it to crystallize into a spot name, after which it was transferred to the grower (sometimes owner) indicating place of residence or occupation. This situation may also have obtained in large sections of continental Italy.

Whether used as a spot name or to denote occupation ellipsis is common in this type of name as in the case of the flower appellatives. A phrase like orto, campo, valle del finocchio, fennel garden, field, valley, is reduced to finocchio. Similarly, a phrase like quello del finocchio, the fennel man, that is, the producer or seller of fennel becomes finocchio. There are, to be sure, a few vegetable surnames that contain the occupational suffix -aro (aio) like Finocchiaro, Cavolaja, Cicciari, Cipollaro, Favaro, Piparo or Peponari, Vizzari and Zuccaro, fennel, cabbage, chickpea, onion, bean, pepper and gourd grower or dealer, but just as the elliptical occupational name is duplicated by an elliptical spot name, so the occupational suffix is duplicated by a collective suffix which gives these same words the meaning of fennel, cabbage, chickpea, onion, bean, pepper and gourd patch.

Leaving out spices and condiments for the moment, let us take up in plant families the other vegetable surnames. The buckwheat family offers us garden sorrel and hence the possible surnames Panevino [46] (Brescia), and Pazienza [47] (Tuscany), either of which could be translated into our herb patience. The carrot family contributes

---

[45] See C. Avolio. "Saggio di Toponomastica Siciliana." *Archivio Glottologico Italiano.* Supplemento. Sesta dispensa, 1898, 74-75.

[46] Panevino is barberry in Belluno and a wood sorrel in Friuli. It may conceivably describe a person taking particular delight in dunking his bread in wine, or (with less likelihood) one who frankly expresses or professes to express his thoughts—dire il pan pane e il vino vino, which, freely translated, means to call a spade a spade.

[47] The face value of the word is patience. Cf. the name of the French saint, St. Patient.

fennel, represented in Italian by Finocchio,[48] Fenoglio, Fenolio (Ventimiglia), Fenoli (Friuli), Carosella [49] (Naples); celery represented by Apio,[50] Pioli, Lacci (Abruzzi); carrot which may have contributed Caroti, Carotti;[51] beet which may have given Sarchi [52] (Modica, Siracusa), Ravi (Finale, Liguria). The chicory family offers us chicory with Cicoria, Cecora (Abruzzi), Cicogna [53] (Sicily), Mazzocchi [54] (Rome), Craveri [55] (Piedmont), Radicci (Genoa); lettuce with Lattuca, Salata (Istria, Verona); endive with Scarola,[56] Mazzocchi (Tuscany), Costetti (Genoa).[57] The goosefoot family furnishes spinach in Italian Spinaci, Spinazzoli.[58] The gourd family supplies the gourd names Zucca, Zucchi, Zucchini, Zucchetti, Zuccola, Zocchi, Zocchini, Cocuzza, Cocuzziello (both Southern Italian), Cossa [59] (Piedmont), and the cucumber surnames —Citroli, Cetrulo, Citrulo. The lily family furnishes the onion

[48] Finocchio could be from Serafino, Adolfo or any name in -fo + the suffix -occhio.

[49] Carosella also refers to a kind of wheat, a carousel, a cart in Northern Italian, a thrush (Lombard), or if it comes from Southern Italian carusiello (Tuscanized into carosello) refers to a clipped head, child.

[50] Apio recalls the Roman Apius. Pioli could come from Pio plus -olo or OlimPIOLO. In Valle Anzasca, a piola is an axe, in Venetian an annoying person, in Piedmontese a nit-wit. It may stand for a peg or stick, an adjunct of melo, melo apiolo, apple, or be a Tuscanization of piulu, Calabrese for owl. In Tarantino a piulo is a petulant man. On the other hand, Lacci may be supplied from the pet form of Carlo, Paolo, etc. plus the suffix -accio.

[51] Carota, Carotti also stem from caro, dear, or from a pet form of Maccario. In Calabrese a carota is a beet.

[52] Sarchio is also a weeding hook.

[53] The most familiar meaning of cicogna is stork. In Calabrese a cicogna signifies head.

[54] A mazzocchio is a tuft of hair, a variety of corn; in Venetian Bresciano and Romagnuolo the knob end of a mace; metaphorically in Venetian and Milanese head; in Bellunese a youngster, and in most of Northern Italy a simpleton.

[55] Craveri may be from caprero, crapraro, goat herd, or from the Slav cravar, herdsman through the Friulano place name Cravero. See F. Musoni, "I Nomi Locali e l'Elemento Slavo in Friuli." *Rivista Geografica Italiana*, IV, 1897.

[56] Scarola is a possible variant form of Carola.

[57] See Note 54 on Mazzocchi. Costetti is more likely from Costanzo, Costantino. See also Anatomical Names.

[58] Spinacci can be reconstructed from Spino through Crispino plus the suffix -accio. In Serrone (Prov. of Rome), a spinaccio nero is a wild plum while a spinaccio bianco is a hawthorn.

[59] Zocchi, Zocchini might come from Marzo + -occo. In Lombard a zocca is an arm in a body of water. Likewise Zucchi, etc. could go back to MarZUCCO, used as a first name in Dante's time. Cf. *Purgatory*, VI. See Anatomical Names for cossa.

names—Cipolla, Cepolla, Cipolletti, Cipollone, Cippollini, Cipulo, Zigoli [60] (Parma), Scioli [61] (Piedmont), Ceva (Friulano), and the asparagus names—Sparacio, Sparraccio, Sparracino, Sparacino.[62] From the mustard family we have the turnip names—Navone,[63] Bordoni [64] (Como), Ravi,[65] Rapuzzi, Ravera, the collective Rabajoli; the radish names Ravanelli, Ravizza, Ravazzini, Ravizzoni (all Northern Italian), Rafanelli, Raia [66] (Catania), and the collectives Ravaglia, Raviglia; the cauliflower names Calafiore, Calafiure, Capozzi [67] (Reggio Emilia), Capuccino (Avellino), Capuzzo (Verona); the cabbage names Cavolo, Cavolini, Verzone, Verzolini and the single broccoli name, Broccoli.[68] From the nightshade family we have the potato, Patatta (Genoa), Patano (Neapolitan); the egg plant Maranzano (Piedmont), Marangiani (Taranto); the tomato Pomodoro;[69] the pepper Pepi,[70] Peparetti, Peverelli, Peveraro, Peverini and the collectives Pepirato, Piperata. From the pea family we obtain Piselli,[71] Pisellini, Pisillo (Southern Italian), pea; Ceci,[72] Cecere, Ciciari, Cicero, Cicerone (Southern Italian), and the collective Cicerale, chickpea; Faggioli, Fasolo, Fasulo,[73] Fasolis, Soraca (perhaps from Calabrese suraca), kidney bean; Fava, Favagrossa, Basani, Bazani (Genoa), Bazzani, Bazzanelli, Scafa, Scaffa and Scafetti (these last three Abruzzese), Vezza, Vezzola, and the

---

[60] Another meaning of zigolo is hawfinch.

[61] The same word in Piedmontese is a grape hyacinth.

[62] These names might well be logical offshoots of Gaspare.

[63] There is a chance that Navone may come from BarNABONE = BarNAVONE.

[64] Bordoni may be from Boldoni possibly through GariBOLDO. Otherwise can be defined as pilgrim's staff.

[65] Some Ravi, Rava are from the Hebrew rabbah. See C. Poma, "Fallaci Apparenze in Cognomi Italiani." *Archivio Glottologico Italiano*, XVIII, 1918, 459.

[66] In Naples a raia is a greenbrier.

[67] Capozzi, Capuzzi are diminutive forms of head, and as Northern Italian terms both can be grouped with cappuccio, cappuzzo, a hood. Dialectical Jacapo could also have produced some of the above just as dialectical Iacava might give us Cavolo, Cavolini.

[68] Broccolo may come from a saint's name, Proculus.

[69] Pomodoro points likewise in the direction of an inn sign, the Pomo d'Oro, golden apple.

[70] Pepe is Northern Italian for Peppe, Giuseppe. Cf. Spanish Pepe pet name form of José.

[71] Piselli, Fava may possibly go back to Germanic first names in some instances. See Förstemann: *op. cit.* 308, 509.

[72] Cece is often a pet form of Cesare (see Ferrari, *Vocabolario de'Nomi Propri Sustantivi* . . . Bologna, 1827) or a Tuscan pet name form of Felice.

[73] Fasolo, Fasula and possibly Faggiuoli can derive from Bonifazio, Bonifacio.

collectives Favale, Favaro [74] and Vizzari (Calabria, Sicily), broad bean; Lenticchia,[75] lentil; Lupino, Lupinetti,[76] lupine. Finally, the thistle family contributes Carcioffo, Caccioffo, and possibly Gobbo [77] (Bergamo, Tuscany), Cardone,[78] Cardei, meaning cardon thistle.

Though we may take it for granted that the grower-dealer and patch meanings have a strong claim on the names just listed, we must not pass over other possibilities. One is the metaphorical significance attached to certain plants. Their inert, inanimate qualities have transformed some of them into favorite appellatives for stupidity—faggiolo, bean, pisello, pea, rapa and navone, turnip, cavolo, cabbage, broccolo, cipolla, onion, citrullo, cucumber, zucca, pumpkin (cf. pumpkin head), carcioffo, artichoke.[79] To these we may add the popular baccello (last name Baccelli),[80] the pod of leguminous plants. A few of the vegetables indicate small individuals or children such as ravanello, rafanello, radish, cece, chickpea (cf. Abruzzese cice), faggiolo (if Bergamascan), pisellu (if Sardinian). To explain the double meaning of several of these words there is, of course, no need to recall at this point that childishness and foolishness are often synonymous terms. In English the head is humorously referred to as a dome, while in Italian it is more realistically dubbed a pumpkin (zucca, cocozza), or onion (cipolla). Moreover, the onion, at least in its augmentative form, cipollone (Vastese), alludes to one in the bloom of health; zucon (Venetian for zucca) is a stubborn person or sleepy head, and pepper, pepe, to an individual with a florid complexion. Cf. Rosso come un pepe, as red as a pepper. Tuscan cece may mean a rascal, a meaning duplicated by Castro de'Volsci pomodoro (pumpadore). In the Irpino dialect a cicerone is a stout man while in Teramano a carciofene denotes a large nose.

[74] In Sicilian a favara is a common term for spring. See C. Avolio, "Di Alcuni Sostantivi Locali in Siciliano." *Archivio Storico Siciliano*, n.s. XIII, 1888, 369.

[75] Lenticchia is sometimes used to indicate small-pox.

[76] Lupini, Lupinetti can, of course, be interpreted as wolf cubs. See Animal Names.

[77] Gobbo is regular for a hunchback though it may come from Cobbo, Giacobbo.

[78] Cardone is possible from any of the various names in -cardo, Riccardo, Biancardo, etc. In Piedmontese a cardon is a Canadian thistle.

[79] With such a full repertoire of vegetable food names, it is surprising not to find among them one of the most common: pastinaca, carrot. Bietolone, beet, is also missing.

[80] In the majority of instances a Baccello is probably from the dialectical shortening of Battista or Baccio from BartolomeACCIO plus a second suffix -ello. Baccelli are also new beans.

SPICES AND CONDIMENTS

Secondary vegetables, spices and condiments, are also frequent as cognomina. Anise, caraway and cumin are confused in the dialects under the term cimino. A Cimini from Tuscany is likely to have drawn his appellation from cumin. If he hails from Calabria he derives his name from caraway and anise, or, if his home is Sicily he will trace it either to cumin or anise. The Sicilians have, in addition, a separate word for caraway, caravita, which has also produced a last name. Lemon balm re-appears in Limoncelli [81] (Val di Chiana). Abruzzese and Calabrese Chiapperi, Chiapparelli recall capers. The chive and the clove are represented by Tuscan Cipollini and Garofani,[82] and the coriander by the Ischian Coliandro,[83] Cogliandro. Garlic surnames are Agli, Aglione,[84] Aglietti, Poreni (Parmigiano poren'na), Scordo and Scordato [85] (Bova, Calabria). Leek surnames are Porretti (Tuscany), Poretti (Piedmont), Porru (Sardinia), while the shallot is represented by Scalogna (Tuscany, Reggio Emilia) and Ceva (Friuli). Those connected with marjorum are Maiorana and Rigani (both common in Calabria and Sicily). The cognomen Mirra may reflect the Tuscan word for myrrh. Parsely is represented by Prezzemolo, Petrosello (Tuscany), Petrosino, Petrusini [86] (Southern Italian), Erbetti [87] (Metaurense); pepper grass by Mostardi (Tuscany); the rosemary by Rosamarina,[88] Ramorini (Milan). Basilico (Tuscany) points back to basil and Zaffarano to saffron. Sage supplies Salvioni (Sicily, Abruzzi), de Salvio (Lecce); sweet bay or laurel Lauro, Allori, Laurini, Lauretti;[89] thyme Peori (Mentone-peori d'azze).[90]

[81] A limunicello in Calabrese is a kind of lemon or bitter sweet apple.

[82] A cipollina is often a green onion and sometimes, and in the dialect of Aquila, Abruzzi, ornitologum narbonese. Garofano may be a carnation, Spanish moss, pot marigold in different parts of Central Italy.

[83] Another meaning for cogliandro in the Neapolitan region is acorn.

[84] It is possible that Agli is connected here with the metaphorical meaning of a very erect person—essere tisu e dirittu cuomu n'agliu as the Calabrese say. Romagnuolo aglion is a lion.

[85] Scordato recalls the words meaning out of tune, forgotten.

[86] It would not be too difficult to link this and the two preceding terms to the given name Pietro.

[87] Erbetti may possibly hail from MinERBETTA =Minervetta.

[88] With the same word compare the compound Rosa Marina.

[89] Lauro and derivatives are frequently used as first names. In the province of Palermo and elsewhere the laurel has been used as an inn or wine shop sign.

[90] Names from other spices and condiments—comfrey, horehound, lavender, pennyroyal, are discussed under the heading of medicinal plants. A few of the vegetable place names or homographs of the same are Aglio (Liguria, Emilia, Lombardy), Aglioni (Abruzzi), Carotta (Lombardy, Trentino), Cipolla (Piedmont), Fasola (Lombardy), Faver (Trentino), Lupina (Prov. of Rome), Zucchetto (Tuscany, Prov. of Bergamo), Zucchini (Bergamo).

CEREALS

Most of the cereal surnames are either spot names or else they refer to a producer-dealer. Wheat offers the largest variety with Frumento, Formento (Ligurian), Calvello,[91] Marzolo,[92] Mazzocchio,[93] Civitelli (these three from Tuscany), Carosello (Naples and Abruzzi), Farrella, Farella [94] (Reggio Emilia), Farruggia (Sicilian), Spelti,[95] and Scavuzzo [96] from the Catania section. Oats are represented by Avena, Vena,[97] Avenale, Avenatti, and Biava, Biavati. Biavaschi refers to wild oats. Barley is represented by Orzo, Ordo (Treviso), Orio [98] (Southern Italian) and Malorzo, probably wild oats; rye by Segali, Secale, Seghi and Seghetti (Liguria); buckwheat by Saraceno,[99] Formentoni and Melegatti (Venetian), Melegari (obsolete melega); bran by Semola, Semmola,[100] Simboli (Sardinia); millet by Migliari, Migliarini, Miglio [101] (Tuscany), Panizzo (Tuscany), Panico,[102] Panicola, Panigarola, Panichetti, Panicale;[103] corn or maize by Miglio (Calabria), Melegari (Lombard melega), Meliconi (Milanese melgon), Zalli (Venetia); sorghum (sorghum vulgare), by Saggini, Sainati (Umbria), Scopa [104] and Migliaccio [105] (Puglia); rice by Risi, Risoli.[106] Hops is limited to the Friulano Cervesato.

[91] Calvello brings to mind the Latin name Calvus, calvo, bald, and may allude to a spot barren of trees and shrubs. See Topographical names.

[92] Marzolo refers to marzo, March. A galletto marzolo is a lively child, a pica marzola is a magpie.

[93] See Note 54.

[94] Farella and possibly Farrella can be obtained from Cristo-FARELLA.

[95] The abruzzese Spoltore may also refer to wheat.

[96] Elsewhere in Sicily a scavuzzu is a snail.

[97] Avena and Vena may be related to the term for bagpipe.

[98] May be connected with Iorio, variant of Giorgio, I believe.

[99] Saraceno, saracen, was common as a first name in the Middle Ages. Metaphorically it means a cruel individual.

[100] Semola is metaphorically used to indicate freckles.

[101] A migliarino may be a kind of thrush. Together with Miglio, Migliarino can come from Emilio.

[102] Panico can be linked with Germanic Panico. See Förstemann, *op. cit.* 244.

[103] Valsuganotto panegale is a tall man, simpleton.

[104] The everyday meaning of the word is broom. But cf. Germanic Scopo (Förstemann, *op. cit.* 1309).

[105] Migliaccio can derive from Emilio, too. Another meaning is black pudding.

[106] Cf. Risi and Risoli with Oderiso, Parise, Maurisio and the Germanic Risi. (Förstemann, *op. cit.* 1279). Some place names very likely derived from cereals are Carosella (Umbria), Civitella (Umbria, Abruzzi, Romagna, Tuscany, Campania), Melegaro (prov. of Pavia), Migliarina (prov. of Arezzo), Saraceno (Calabria).

MEDICINAL PLANTS

Many plants have in one way or another been used for medicinal purposes, a large number of them in the old fashioned family remedies. This factor has undoubtedly contributed to their popularity as surnames. As in the case of other botanical names they can stem from spot names or refer to the growers and sellers of these medicaments. Some of the plants that have furnished cognomina are the balm Melissa [107] (Tuscany); the birthwort Baciocchi [108] (Piedmont); bettony Bettonica and Giavarini (S. Bernardo, Liguria giavara); bistort Bistorti, name of a noble family from Turin; the borage Borasa (Piedmont, Parma), Borrasa (Piacenza); the calamint Calamidda, Calamita [109] (Bova, Calabria); catnip Gattari [110] (obsolete), Mentastro [111] (Ronco, Liguria), Melissa (Como); clary Moscatello [112] (Tuscany); comfrey Carestia [113] (Piedmont); convolvulus jalapa Sciarappa [114] (Sicily); darnell Logli (Tuscany); digitalis Digitale (Tuscany); horehound Mentastro (Lecce), Piola [115] (Val di Chiana-erba apiola), Marubio [116] and Marobio (Tuscany, Verona), Malavita [117] (Sicily); lavender Lavandoli, Nardo [118] (Tuscany), Cadoni (Porto Maurizio, Liguria cadò); the mugwort Matrone (obsolete), the navelwort Bucalossi (Rome); pennyroyal Pulio, Poleo (Calabria and Sicily); rue, Rua, Ruga [119] (Valtellina), Rugatti, Rugari, Rucco, Ruccoli (Naples, Abruzzi), Armelli (Tus-

---

[107] Melissa the good enchantress in Ariosto's *Orlando Furioso* can be remembered here.

[108] A baciocco is a rod or bell clapper, which, in Northern Italian indicates a simpleton and in Bergamascan a little man or child, or in Genoese a dandy.

[109] Usually calamita is a magnet. Also storax if Tuscan.

[110] A gattaro could also be a cat fancier or cat haven.

[111] Mentastro means speedwell in Isoverde, Liguria, horehound in Lecce.

[112] Cf. Moscatello, well known variety of grape.

[113] Cf. Carestia from Eucarestia. Carestia regularly means scarcity, famine. In Sicilian a caristia refers to a nut tree. See C. Avolio, "Saggio di Toponomastica Siciliana." *Archivio Glottologico Italiano.* Supplemento, sesta dispensa, 1898, 82.

[114] In Neapolitan sciarappa means good wine. Cf. also the surname Chiarappa.

[115] See Note 50.

[116] In Venetian a marubio is a surly fellow. Cf. A. Prati, "Etimologie." *Archivio Glottologico Italiano,* XVII, 1910-13, 280-81.

[117] A malavita in Southern Italian is a rogue.

[118] Usually from LeoNARDO, BerNARDO, but the term is also applied to several other plants.

[119] Rua and Ruga also mean street. Cf. the French La Rue. In Monferrino rua is an English oak.

can for wild rue); salsify Castracani;[120] smilax Razza (Porto Maurizio, Liguria), Raia,[121] Raiola (Naples, Catania); spearmint Amenta, Aminta [122] (Sicily); squill Zeoli [123] (Venetia); storax Storace (Tuscany), Calamita [124] (Tuscany); Vetrioli from erba vetriola, a medicinal grass; water cress Acione (Alghero, Sardinia).[125]

FRUITS AND FRUIT TREES

Tree surnames are common in all languages. Since the single tree, the clump, the woods, the grove or forest all constitute ideal identification signs, especially in rural areas, it is no wonder that they have become favorite spot names. In numerous Italian villages fond parents still follow the long-standing tradition of planting a tree upon the birth of a child and regard it as symbol of their offspring.[126] In the case of the fruits we may likewise expect the individual fruit to represent the grower-seller.

The apple family through the medium of the apple gives us Melazzo and Melillo, Mei [127] (Genoa, Venice), Buonamela, Melato, Malato,[128] Maletti, Pomo, Pomati, Pometti, Pumo, Calimari (Bergamo), and perhaps Pioli;[129] through the medium of the pear Pera, del Pero, La Pira, Peretto, Piretto, Pei [130] (Genoa, Alessandria), perhaps an occasional Spadoni [131] (cf. pera spadona-Bologna), Carovelli and Piraino (Calabrese for wild pear); and through the medlar Nespoli and Nesporo. The citrus family contributes Arancio,

[120] Castracani is also a word for sweet pea.

[121] Another meaning of raia is radish.

[122] Aminta is a well known pastoral name.

[123] For an alternative explanation of Zeoli, cf. MazZEOLO.

[124] Calamita likewise means magnet, calamint.

[125] For the medicinal uses of these plants see Holbyn's *Dictionary of Terms Used in Medicine and Collateral Sciences*, 15th ed. London, 1912, and Gould's *Medical Dictionary*, 2d ed. rev. and enl. Philadelphia, 1912. A glance at H. Trimen's *Medicinal Plants*, London, 1880, 4 vols. will at once reveal that almost all plants have medicinal properties.

[126] See *Enciclopedia Italiana*, XIX, 966.

[127] Melazzo and Melillo can be derivatives of Carmelo and Mele of Manuele and Michele. In nine cases out of ten Mei may be expected to come from BartoloMEO, Amedeo, Matteo. In Romagnuolo mei is millet.

[128] Buonamela is more convincing if we look upon Buona Carmela, Michela, Manuela as its source. Malato looks like sickly, but may be the Latin malus plus the collective -ato.

[129] See Note 50. The Calabrese surname Piromalli evidently draws upon the Latin term for apple, pyrus malus.

[130] Some words for pear run the strong competition of Pietro. See chapter on Pet Names. Pei may also come from Pietro as well as PomPEO.

[131] Literally, large sword.

Arangio, Aranzello, Ranzi, Ranzetti,[132] Narangi (Emilia), Marangi (Taranto), Melaragno, Portogallo [133] (Southern Italian), Cedrangolo,[134] Cetrangolo (Naples), Cetrone (Genoa), all referring to the orange; Limoni, Limoncelli,[135] Ponzini [136] (Naples), Peretti (Calabria, Naples), Zagara [137] (Girgenti) referring to the lemon; and La Lumia, lime, Cotugno, quince. The ebony family gives Avolio [138] (Tuscany), a word for persimmon and Dattero and Dattilo [139] (also Tuscany), words for date plum. From the olive family come Olivo, Olivetti,[140] Olivelli, Olivotti, Alia (Graeco-Calabrese). The plum family supplies the plum names Susini, Brogni (Emilia), Brugna and Brugnone (Ancona), Brugnoli, Bruno [141] (Calabria), the cherry names Ciliegi (rare), Ceraso, Cerasotto, Cerasini, Ceresini, (most dialects), Maraschi (Tuscany, Bergamo), Marasci (Belluno), Marasconi (Treviso), Marena (Brescia); the apricot names Albicocchi,[142] Percoco, Armellini [143] (Venice); the peach names Peschi (Tuscany), Persico, Persichetti [144] (Pavia), Persegati (Genoa); the almond Amendola, Amandola, Amendolaro, Mandalari, Cassarelli (Piedmont), Zuccarelli [145] and Sacarelli (Milano). Various kinds of nuts provide Noce, Nocera, Nosera (Piedmont), Nocella, Noselli [146]

[132] Ranza may be a scythe or a scythe-like topographical formation.

[133] Portogallo is, of course, Portugal, as well as orange.

[134] Another meaning of cedrangolo is trefoil.

[135] In Val di Chiana a limoncello is a lemon balm.

[136] Possibly also from the first name Ponzio, Pontius.

[137] In Calabrese a zagara is a citrus bloom.

[138] May be a variant of avorio, ivory. But most likely the name stems from Avolio, one of the four sons of Duke Namo, a personage in the Carolingian romances.

[139] Also the name of a mollusk.

[140] Olivo is easily recognizable as a first name. It can also derive from the color, olive. Olivetti, if Sicilian, may come from a shrub, germander, or if from the town of Pragelato, Piedmont, ulivete, means an alouette, lark.

[141] A susino in Romano and Marchigiano may allude to a small or worthless fellow. With Brogni cf. Calabrese vrogna, pigherder's horn and, by extension, a large nose. Most Brunos are, of course, traceable to St. Bruno or to the color, dark.

[142] Bicocchi, usually a small fortress or castle, may also be considered a reduction of Albicocchi.

[143] Cf. armellino, ermine.

[144] Cf. persico, a perch (fish), and persighet, Pavia, a flower. In Pavese a persigh is also an uncouth person.

[145] Zuccarello is also defined as a small gourd and a mole cricket.

[146] There is a possibility that both Nocella and Nosella can come from Giovanni and other names in n plus vowel: GiovanNOCCELLA, Giovan-NOSELLA, etc.

(Verona), Nocci (Umbria-Roma), Corleto, Carideo (Graeco-Southern Italian), Castagno, Castagnetti, Castagnini, Castagnoli, Castagnaro, Marroni [147] (Tuscany). The fig gives Fichi, Figoni, Bonfichi, Ficalbi, Ficarelli, Naccarato [148] (wild fig grove); the pomegranate Granata, [149] Melograno; the prickly pear perhaps Frittelli [150] (Tuscany); the carob Carubba, Garruba, La Carrubba; the sorb apple Sorbi, Sorbelli. The berry group finds representation in the strawberry with Fragola, Fragala, Frola (Old Vicentino); in the hackberry with the doubtful Bagatti [151] (Tuscany); in the barberry with Panevino, [152] Farinelli [153] (both from the province of Belluno); in the blackberry with Razza, Razzari [154] (Cogorno, Liguria), Morra [155] (Emilia), Barazzotti (Friuli), Roncioni (Novara-roncio); in the mulberry with Gelsi, Mura (Calabria). Finally, the grape gives a number of probable surnames — d'Uva, dell'Uva, Muscarella [156] (Calabria), Moscato, Rosasco (Milano), Lambruschi, Lambruschini, Abruscato [157] (Tuscany), Vajani and, with less likelihood Acerbi, Agresti, [158] Grelli, [159] Guarnacci, [160] Verdesi (Milanese uga verdesa). We shall tag on here the name Angoria, which seems to be from the word watermelon, anguria.

[147] Cf. marrone, dialectical from marro, teacher, master, as well as Abruzzese marrone, sickly.

[148] Cf. Sicilian word naccaru.

[149] Equally as probable from Granata = Granada, or granata, garnet.

[150] The word means fritter and by extension a snub nose.

[151] Bagatt (Cremonese) is the first card in a tarocchi game. In Piedmontese it has the additional meaning of clown.

[152] See Note 46.

[153] In the Iesino a farinello is one who conveys flour from the mill to a home. Figuratively the term means a cruel person (Milan), a bold and forward individual (Piedmont). In Lazio where it means red flour pap for chicks it refers to a voluble person. Cf. the term for the orach weed, farinelo in Venetian. Cristofaro reduced to Faro -inello gives Farinello.

[154] A razzara may be a rock rose while razza may be smilax (Porto Maurizio, Liguria).

[155] Cf. Calabrese murra, how-many-fingers-do-I-hold-up? game.

[156] Another mean of muscarello is gnat.

[157] Abruscato usually means bronzed. In Sicilian it is a field where the dry grass has been burned.

[158] Acerbo also means bitter and agreste rustic.

[159] Grell is a Romagnuolo name for grasshopper. Cf. AlleGRELLO.

[160] A guarnaccia is a long robe, but a better source of Guarnacci is Guarinaccio.

FOREST TREES

Cognomina taken from the acer or maple family are Acierno, Aseri (Reggio Emilia), Azzali [161] (Sicily), Ceriello [162] (Terra di Lavoro), Opello [163] (Mantua opi), referring to the common maple; Pionati [164] (Cuneo-pion), and Aseri (Milano) to the sycamore maple; Conocchi (Naples), Bisceglia [165] (Campobasso), Acinello (Calabria), to the acer neapolitanum. From the beech family come Faggi, Fagione, Faceto, Facello,[166] Fago (Southern Italian), Fazi (Parma), Failla (Naples), Faro [167] (Abruzzi ?), Cerrato, Cerrito, Cerreto,[168] Ceri, Cereto, Cerini [169] (Northern Italian), Zeri (Cuneo), Cerza,[170] Cerzale (Southern Italian), Chercu (Sardinian), Serone (Vicenza) meaning turkey oak; Elci, Lecci, Lezzi (Verona, Romagna) meaning holm oak; Rovere (Tuscany), Revere, Rua (Monferrato) meaning English oak; Piccarelli,[171] a Marchigiano term for live oak; perhaps Legnazzi, a Milanese term for cork oak; Pedalino,[172] a Trivigiano term for quercus pedunculata, and Farnetti [173] (if Lucanese) large leaved oak. Cf. the famous della Quercia.

The black alder of the birch family gives the surnames Alano (Marche), Aldana (Lombardy), Ansano (Avellino, Lecce, Salerno-anzano), Azzano (Calabria), Alini (Avellino), Onola (Verona-ono), Onetti [174] (Chiavari), Lonato,[175] perhaps Insana (Calabrese onsana),

[161] The same word in Sicilian is wild ginger or Jack in the Pulpit.

[162] Ceriello could come from Ruggiero, Berlingiero, etc.

[163] It is possible that opello is metaphorical for simpleton. Cf. incantà com'è on opi.

[164] Cf. Peonati from peony. If Venetian the explanation would be Scipione plus -ati, SciPIONATI.

[165] The most wide-spread meaning of conocchia is distaff. In Neapolitan cunocchia indicates a hill-fort. With Bisceglia cf. Bisceglie, a place name near Bari.

[166] Quite a few of these beechnames can also be explained through a pet form of Bonifacio, Bonifazio.

[167] A faro is also a lighthouse.

[168] These names can be likewise connected with cerro, curl, lock of hair.

[169] More plausible if from Ruggiero, Berlingiero, etc. See Anatomical Names.

[170] Figurately a cerza in Calabrese is a person of influence and a cerzale a tall individual. Cf. saying saldo come una quercia, as robust (strong) as an oak.

[171] Other meanings of piccarello are door-clapper, wandering rogue (cf. Spanish picaro), and woodpecker, from picco.

[172] Can also mean the trunk of a tree, stirrup.

[173] Farnet is likewise Piedmontese for orach, a weed. Also compare Cristo-FARiNETTO.

[174] Cf. LeONETTO, LeONOLA. In the prov. of Rome an onola is a laurel.

[175] It may be that the derivation from Lo(DO)nato is also admissible.

Rondani, Rondanini [176] (Reggio Emilia-rondan). The fact that this tree was used in drying wool has probably increased its popularity both as a spot name and as a fertile source of cognomina. In contrast, names from the green alder, Malossi (Valtellina) and the speckled alder Peluso [177] (Roma) seem to be quite rare. Another member of the family is the white birch which furnishes Bedolla (Valtellina), Bettoli [178] (Novara, Porto Maurizio, Marche, Sondrio), Boletti and Bollettino (from Low Latin booletum), Bredoli (Belluno), Medello (Belluno-medel). Still another relative, the hornbeam gives Carpino, Carpaneto, Carpanelli (Reggio Emilia, Piacenza), Carpanini (Northern Italian). The ironwood tree may give Ostrelli (Tuscany) unless we prefer to derive the name from AgOSTaRELLO.

The box family supplies Bussi, Bossi, Bossolo [179] and perhaps a few Martelli [180] (Reggio Emilia). Names that derive from the dogwood are Cornale (Lucanese, Cremasco), Cornioli [181] (Pavia, Lunigiana), Cornelli (Reggio Emilia), Crugnale (Abruzzi).

The elm family is represented by Olmo, elm; the holly or scrub by Ruschi, Rusconi [182] (Tuscany), Biscaro [183] (Naples) and the linden tree by Tiglio, Tei [184] (Milano).

The ash of the olive family is used in the surnames Frascino (Southern Italian), Frassi, Frassinelli, Lo Frasso, and Orno, Ornato [185] (Abruzzi, Romagna, Belluno), flowering ash.

The palm furnishes Palma, Palmucci.[186] Plane trees appear to be limited to the Sicilian Platania, Patanè.

Quite numerous are the members of the pine family and the surnames derived from them. It will be noted that according to the locality the same name can refer to two or more species. First

---

[176] Cf. the word for swallow.

[177] Peluso normally means hairy.

[178] Competition comes from Betto through Benedetto, from Elisabetta, and from bettola, tavern.

[179] These names might come from JacoBUSSO, JacoBOSSO, or the Germanic Bosi, Förstemann, op. cit. 329.

[180] More fertile sources of the name are Marta and marti, dialectical for Tuesday, plus a diminutive. Martello is also a reduction of MARTinELLO. The term also signifies hammer and has several other meanings.

[181] Nettle in Lunigiana, and beard grass in Piedmont.

[182] Like words are asparagus in Ischia, blackberry and butcher's broom in Naples.

[183] A biscaro in the Naples and Avellino region is taken as a mistletoe.

[184] Tiglio can be from AtTILIO and Tei from MatTEO.

[185] Literally, ornamented, ornament.

[186] Palma most frequently refers to a person born on Palm Sunday.

we have the general terms Pino, Pinelli, Pinedo,[187] Pinari. Pignone in Messina is an Aleppo pine, in the Etna region of Sicily a stone pine, and in Verona a cypress. Pignolone in Novara and Pesaro is a stone pine and in Aquila cluster pine. From the silver fir we obtain Abetti, Avezza, Lavezzi,[188] Lavezzari, Lavezzola, Vezzalli, Pescia and Pezzi[189] (both from Como), and Piolli[190] (Roma), but elsewhere in Lombardy and Piedmont pescia refers to a Norway spruce. So does Pezzi[190] if Venetian or Tuscan. A Bergamascan Pezzi (from pez) could refer to a Scotch pine. From the cedar we get Cedro, Cedraro, Cedroni, Cedarella; from the larch Larice, Arese (if from Veronese ares); from the cypress Cipresso and possibly Cipro,[191] Ciprelli; from the juniper Giuniperi; from the yew tree Tasso, Tassoni,[192] Tassinari.

The tamarisk tree or shrub contributes Tamari[193] (Tuscan and Veronese), Tamaroglio (id.) Brucato, Brucale.

Like the pine the willow family has contributed many surnames. Here, too, the same name may be applied to several species. From the white willow hail Salce, Salice, Salsini, Salgari, Salassa (Novara-salas); from the peach leaved willow Gorra (Piacenza); from the osier willow the debatable Brelli;[194] from the salix incana possibly Mignoni[195] (Avellino); from the salix capraea Gori (Piedmont). The white poplar gives Pioppi, Chioppi, Chiuppo,[196] Popolo,[197] Povolo (the last two Tuscan), Albarella (Catania, Perugia), Brancato (Sicilian from Low Latin blanchia; and the European aspen Popolo (Tuscany), Albarella[198] (Tuscany), Gabba[199] (Liguria), Tremari (Carnia) and perhaps Tremarelli.

[187] Any name ending in -po, Jacopo, Filippo, as well as Giuseppe, can give us Pino, Pinelli, Pinedo.

[188] A lavezzo may be a kind of pot, warming pan.

[189] Pescia is a town in Tuscany while Pezzo may derive from Opezzo, Obizzo.

[190] Cf. Pio, and OlimPIO, SciPIO, as sources.

[191] S. Pieri in "Toponomastica delle Valli del Serchio e della Lima," *Archivio Glottologico Italiano*, Supple. 5a dispensa, 1898, gives Cipri from Cypress, p. 85. Cf. also Cipro, Cyprus.

[192] Tasso likewise means badger and is a first name of Germanic origin. Cf. Förstemann, *op. cit.* 405 and the name TalASSO.

[193] In Friulano a tamar is a cattle inclosure. The same word in Veronese is a false tamarisk.

[194] Brelli seems possible from AlVaRELLO, BoRELLO.

[195] Mignoni is more likely from Erminio, Arminio, etc. For Gorra cf. gorra, Milanese for peasant sap.

[196] Pioppo, chioppu have the figurative meaning of simpleton.

[197] Perhaps Germanic Bobo (Förstemann, *op. cit.* 317) competes here and there.

[198] Albarella can also be related to Alvaro.

[199] Cf. Germanic Gaba, Förstemann, *op. cit.* 561.

SHRUBS

Surnames from common fruit-bearing shrubs have been discussed under fruits. But there are also quite a number of cognomina that come from other varieties of shrubbery. The majority of them are spot names, but occasionally, those that have a pharmaceutical use can indicate a grower or seller. Surnominal contributions appear to have been made by the bramble, Rovati, Baraggia, Baraggioli, Barazzoli; the century plant Spatola, Spatula;[200] the chaste tree Peveraro[201] (Verona); the chokeberry Malanzi (Cuneo); the cotoneaster Nespo (Cuneo), Sorbello[202] (Marche); the elder Sambuco, Sambuga, Sambuccetti; the English hawthorn Cerasoli[203] (Marche); the false tamarisk Bruscato (Calabria), Tamari[204] (Verona); the French honeysuckle Lupinacci (Tuscany); the germander Calamandrea (Tuscany), Scalamandrè (Southern Italian), Mandrea, Scordini (Como); the greenbrier Raia, Raiola[205] (Naples); the heath or heather group Brugari, Patuzzi (Verona patusso), Cornale (Potenza), Azzarello[206] (Vicenza), Grion (Friuli), Coda[207] (Roma), Brucale and Brucani (Novara); the honeysuckle Sugamele, Banderola[208] (Verona), Strazzabosco[209] (Belluno); lavender cotton perhaps Roselli[210] (Potenza); the lilac or mock orange Gelsomino[211] (Tuscany), Pacienza, Pazienza[212] (Tuscany); the loosestrife Cannestrelli[213] (Locarno); the myrtle Mirto, Mirritelli (Tuscany), Mortillaro (Naples), Mortola; the oleander Leandro (Lombardy, Friuli, Umbria, Tuscany); Landri;[214] the privet Oli-

---

[200] Also a plover and, in Sicilian, iris.

[201] Can mean pepper patch, pepper grower.

[202] Cf. sorbello, sorb apple.

[203] More commonly heliotrope, sunflower.

[204] See Note 193.

[205] See Note 121.

[206] The most likely source of the name is Azzo, a given name. Cf. also Sicilian azzareddu, arum.

[207] Another meaning is love-lies-bleeding, a plant. Literally, tail.

[208] Also cattails, a weed. Literally, flag on a vessel, weathercock, and, metaphorically, a fickle person.

[209] Also scorpion senna.

[210] One thinks at once of more common sources, e.g. rose. Piedmontese rosele is a wild poppy.

[211] Also jasmine, bouncing Bet.

[212] Literally, patience, but also another plant, herb patience.

[213] Literally, a basket, and in Veronese, wild buckwheat.

[214] Both Leandro and its variant Landro are apt to be from the font name of Greek origin. We note that landra, from obsolete malandra, is a rascally woman.

vetti [215] (Tuscany), Caravana (Piedmont), Crovaia or Corvaia [216] (Piedmontese crovaja), Cannestrelli (Verona); sloe or buckthorn Brignoli (Piedmont); the spindle tree Fusari [217] (Northern Italian), Frascino [218] (Potenza), Roncaglia [219] (Piedmontese-roncaja), valerian Sarzetti (Piedmont), Nardo [220] (Tuscany) and the yellow sage perhaps Camara, Camera [221] (Tuscany). We close this series with Ginestra, broom plant.

REEDS, FERNS, RUSHES

The vegetation of the swamps reappears in the reed surnames—Canevari,[221] Cannizzaro [222] (Sicily), Cannata, Cannari, Cannataro;[223] in the fern names, the bracken Filicetti [224] (Calabria), Filiciaia, Flechia, Moscaroli (Piedmont); the sago Sagari (Tuscany); the moonwart Argentina [225] (Tuscany); the hart tongue Mula [226] (Tuscany); the shield fern Feleti [227] (Friuli), Paviro (Bologna), Capitelli [228] (Val di Chiana), Quadretti (Reggio Emilia). The horse tail or scouring rush names are reproduced in Barbisio [229] (Parma), Bruschi [230] (Tuscany); the cattails in Uda (Catania), Scialetti [231] and Scialoia (Tuscany-sciala), and perhaps Salami [232] (Verona); the bur-reed in Cortellazzo [233] (Verona).

[215] A name with several different sources.

[216] Literally, a crow haunt.

[217] Also a spindle maker.

[218] Usually an ash tree.

[219] Also a stubble field, or in Milanese (roncaja), vineyard on a plain.

[220] Another multi-meaning word. See index.

[221] Camara can be equivalent to cameriera, maid. Cf. donna da camara. Camera also refers to administrative office in the Papal States.

[221] In the Venetian dialect the words means a taverner.

[222] In Calabrese a cannizzaru is the maker of a drying bed (for chestnuts).

[223] Cannata and Cannataro, if Calabrese, stand for jug, pot or jug maker.

[224] But compare Filice from Felice, Felix.

[225] Another multi-meaning word. See Index.

[226] But more often mula goes back to the word for mule with its metaphorical meaning of stubborn, illegitimate child.

[227] Feleti could easily come from Raffaele.

[228] In Venetian the word refers to a tabernacle. Nipple is another meaning.

[229] Barbisio is also a flower. If Piedmontese, barbis, it refers to a mustache, and, by extension, to a courageous man.

[230] The common meaning of brusco is brusque, coarse. Cf. lambrusco, grape.

[231] Teaming with Scialetti, cattails, as claimant of the surname is Ale-SCIALETTA from Alescio or Alesso. Alescio is Genoese and is perhaps current in other dialects.

[232] Everyone will think of salame, sausage, at this point, and its metaphorical meaning ignoramus.

[233] Literally, big knife, chopper, but the term also means hyacinth, gladiola.

GRASSES

Most of the cognomina stemming from various kinds of grasses are, if genuine, spot names. Among those found as surnames are terms for blue grass, Panigarola (Sarzana), Spigaroli (Piacenza); bog grass Falaschi; dog's tail grass Coetti (Piedmont); grille grass Trebbi (Piedmont); hair grass Nebbia [234] (Como and Naples); holcus or velvet grass Scovetti [235] (Lombardy); quake grass Ballerini [236] (Mortola, Liguria), Pennachietti [237] (Etna), Grilletti [238] (Chiavari); reed bent grass Cannelli [239] (Tuscany), Canneti [240] (Pavia); ribbon grass or gardener's garters Canario and Canarino [241] (Tuscany); spear or needle grass Piumati (Sicilian piuma); Gramegna, Gramigna in Northern Italy is applied to blue grass, dog grass, crab or finger grass, cotton grass, or low spear grass. Malerba is used for reed bent grass, foxtail grass, broom rape, choke vetch or for any weedy plant growing among legumes.[242] The surnames Gramegna, Gramigna and Malerba are drawn from these. Among the clover cognomina are Triboli, Tribolati,[243] referring to the white meliot; Treggiari (Valtellina treggia), to hop clover, and Trifiletti,[244] possibly coming from trifillo, trefoil.

WEEDS

Despite the fact that the word weed has no definite application to any plant or species of plants, we all know that the term is used to refer to troublesome or useless vegetation. Most weed surnames have got their start as spot names.

The amarantus blitum, generally classed as a weed, gives us Bioni (Verona), Bidoni (Pavia), Piumetti (Piedmont). The amarantus retroflexus is similarly classified giving Amaranto, Bidoni (Pavia), Bioni, Pioni, Pionati, Beoni, Peoni [245] (all Veronese). The

[234] Literally, a fog, mist.

[235] Recalls scopa, broom, and, more forcefully, veSCOVETTO, little bishop.

[236] A word of many meanings, See Index.

[237] Literally, plumelet.

[238] Literally, little cricket.

[239] May have some relation to cannella, cinnamon.

[240] Also a cane brake.

[241] Canario, Canarino can be a cane brake, too. Cf. canario, canary.

[242] Metaphorically a malerba is an annoying meddler. Cf. French Malherbe.

[243] Tribolato likewise means afflicted.

[244] But compare the saint's name, Triphilius.

[245] Both Bioni and Pioni could come from SciPIONE or from PIO or OlimPIO, while Beoni, Peoni could come from Peo, Genoese for Peter, or Pompeo, or the word for peony. Cf. beone, drinker.

birdsfoot trefoil may furnish Ariola [246] (Reggio Emilia), Denti [247] (Potenza); the Canadian thistle Cardone [248] (Piedmont), Lattarulo [249] (Lecce); the charlock perhaps Razza [250] (Sicily), Rapaccioli (Roma); the chickweed Pavarini [251] (Istria, Milano, Verona); the choke vetch Malerba [252] (Roma); the coltsfoot Lavazzola (Carnia-lavazz) and possibly Lavagetto (from Piedmontese lavasset); the corncockle Vesci (Novara); the dandelion Pisacane (Piedmont pissacan), Castracani (obsolete); the curled dock Romizi (Tuscany); the dodder Raschi (Nizza Marittima); the dock sorrel Linguadivacca [253] (Belluno); the field bindweed Crescioli [254] (Barletta), Malocchi [255] (Etna), foxtail grass Malerba (Sicily), Baravalle (Piedmont), Mazzucchelli [256] (Lombardy); the horseweed Carestia [257] (Pavia); the hedge bindweed Campanelli [258] (Northern Italian, Naples), Campanini (Northern Italian); lady's thumb Gambarossa [259] (Sarzana) the nettle Orticoni; the orach Farinetti, Farnetti (both Piedmont), Farinelli [260] (Venice); the pellitory Pancaldo [261] (Piedmontese pan caud); the pigweed Farinetti (Pied-

[246] Also soothsayer.

[247] Recalls dente, tooth, and the font names arDENTE, ReDENTE, DefenDENTE.

[248] Also cardoon thistle.

[249] Lattarulo may mean milkman.

[250] Razza is also Sicilian for rock cress, Modenese for dog rose, in Cogorno, Liguria, a term for blackberry. It is also a fish, thornback. Cf. PieRAZZA.

[251] May be related to papara, goose, and paparino (Tuscany) poppy.

[252] See Note 242.

[253] Literally translated the term means cow tongue.

[254] Here Crescio through Crescenzio strongly asserts its rights.

[255] Can be an apple orchard. Cf. place name Malocchio listed by S. Pieri, "Toponomastica delle Valli del Serchio e della Lima," *Archivio Glottologico Italiano, op. cit.*, as well as malocchio, a surly look, evil eye, in Monferrino a heap of rags. Biblical Maloc may offer competition.

[256] See Note 54. This may be considered to be a variant of mazzocchio.

[257] See Note 113.

[258] See Note 6.

[259] Gambarossa in the Mondovi and Bordighiera sectors is a pellitory plant, parietaria officinalis. See Note 24.

[260] The metaphorical meaning of Farinetti, Farnetti is a fool, an extension of the weed meaning. An ideal claimant is CristoFARINETTO, CristoFARINELLO. These terms are repeated below along with Farinacci which, if of Parmigiano origin, is a mushroom with a white or yellow cap or, figuratively, a simpleton. In Milan, the same term is used to indicate a game played with six die.

[261] Pancaldo if translated on the basis of superficial appearances is warm bread. Cf. French last name Painchaud.

mont), Farinelli (Liguria, Lombardy), Farinacci, Porcacchi (both used in Tuscany); the plantain Cucciari, Cucchiari [262] (Vercelli), Quadrelli [263] (Tuscany); the plumed thistle Scannagatti [264] (Cicogna, Liguria); the Russian thistle Saponaro [265] (Sicily), Scerba (Avola, Sicily); the speedwell, Mentastri [266] (Isoverde, Liguria).

MUSHROOMS

Mushroom surnames have the same origin as other plant cognomina. For the most part they represent spot names or a grower, dealer, picker, fancier of a particular variety. Nevertheless, because of the existence of quite a number of homonyms, their contribution to the onomasticon may be regarded as weak or doubtful. The chanterelle may furnish an occasional Cantarella,[267] or a Capogallo (Tuscany). The amanita group through the fly agaric may give Coccola (Brescia), Cocconi [268] (Piacenza), Farinacci [269] (Tuscany, Parma). The lepiota group through the parasol mushroom may supply some Ombrello [270] (Liguria), and Pelliccioni [271] (Tuscany). Outcroppings of the boletus group may be Bollettino [272] (boleto), Bavuso [273] (Calabrese vavusu) and Capparelli [274] (Vastese). A subterranean fungus, the truffle, lurks in Truffi, Truffarelli.

MISCELLANEOUS PLANTS

Among the plants that do not exactly fit into the groupings already dealt with are Fenu (Sardinia), fenugreek; Cottone,[275]

---

[262] Literally, cucciaro, cucchiaro is a spoon.

[263] A homograph is quadrello, dart, arrow.

[264] Literally, stab-cat, a cat killer. In Genoese genista germanica.

[265] Literally, soap-maker, seller. In the Naples region also a flower term for bouncing Bet.

[266] Horehound in the Lecce sector; catnip elsewhere.

[267] A cantarella is also a frog, a Sicilian Arabic place name, a singer. Cf. also Germanic Ganthar (Förstemann, op. cit. 596) and see Insect names.

[268] See Note 34.

[269] See Note 260.

[270] Besides being an unbrella, ombrello is a fish, the umber, in the Trieste section, and in Verona a hellebore.

[271] Otherwise a pelliccione is a big fur coat, or a Tuscanization of Calabrese pellizzune, a tatterdemalion. Cf. also the Novarese place name, Pellicioni, the most likely of the sources.

[272] Also the name of the white birch.

[273] If translated Bavuso (vavuso) means drivel. In Sicily the word has a metaphorical meaning, blusterer.

[274] Capparelli may also stem from a nickname since in the Vastese dialect it denotes an untidy person with wax in his ears.

[275] Cottone may perchance stem from Domenico and Francesco through the addition of the augmentative -one.

Cuttone, Cotugno (Sicily), cotton; Lino, Linari,[276] flax; Canava, Canevino, Caneva, Caneparo, Canevari, Canova, Cannova,[277] Cannavino, hemp; Gratto, Grattini (Veronese), hornwort; Visco, Biscari, Viscari (Naples), mistletoe; Schiavone [278] (Naples), water parsnip; Tagliagambe [279] (Bologna tajagambe), the cyperus monti; and Tabacco, Tabacchini,[280] tobacco.

In conclusion, throughout our dicussion in this chapter we have assumed that the popularity of our botanical surnames has, for the most part, been due to perfectly natural and easily explainable causes—primarily spot names, growers-sellers, and nicknames relating to physical or mental qualities. Hence it is that we find it difficult to accept the opinion ventured by E. Weekley in his *Surnames* (London, 1936, 3rd ed. p. 185) to the effect that "there are a great many surnames taken from the vegetable world which can only be regarded as nicknames created by the mysterious medieval folk-lore of which we unfortunately know so little." As has been noticed numerous surnames of botanical origin are dialectical. It is, therefore, necessary to establish a coincidence between the geographical provenience of the individual or his family and the name that is borne before accepting the plant-source of his cognomen. We need quite a number of investigations on regional surnames of the botanical variety before this subject can satisfactorily be cleared up. Meanwhile investigators will find a good starting point in our discussion.

---

[276] Lino is a regular shortening of CarLINO or any name in -lo. Cf. also, St. Linus. Linaro could come from ApolLINARE or a term for a flax seller.

[277] Caneparo may also allude to a hemp dealer. In Venetian a canevaro is a wine dealer while canova is a wine cellar.

[278] Otherwise a big slave, Slovenian.

[279] Literally, cut-legs.

[280] In the sixteenth century tabacchino meant a woman chaser. In Romagnuolo tabac betokens a young man, and in Lombard a simpleton. The word, curiously enough, was in existence before the discovery of America. See G. Volpi, "D'un Uso Antico della Parola 'Tabacco," *Archivio Storico Italiano,* Anno LXXI, 1913, Vol. II, and E. Richter, "Das Altitalienische Tabacco," *Archivum Romanicum,* XI, 1927.

Chapter VIII

TOPOGRAPHICAL NAMES

We may divide the natural and artificial topographical features that have given rise to Italian surnames into six groups—mineralogical characteristics, the hill and dale, the water and waterside, agrarian peculiarities, buildings, man-made highways and byways. Possible members of the first group are Allabastro, alabaster, Argento,[1] silver; Oro,[2] gold; Piombo, lead; Ferro, iron; Calamita, Calamida,[3] loadstone; Petrario, stone quarry; Marmi, Marmora, marble; Lavagna, Lavagnola, Ciappi[4] (Genoese), slate; Lava, Tufo, Pomice, Pumice; Pipierno,[5] lava; Della Calce, lime; Gessi, Chalk; Salnitro, Salpietro, saltpeter; Carbone,[6] coal; Creta,[7] Cretaro, clay and clay pit; Marni[8] (if Parmigiano) type of rich soil. Due to the commercialization of most of these natural products from the soil the names might occasionally refer to dealers in this kind of merchandise, for example quello del gesso, dealer in chalk, chalker.

In a country as rugged as Italy it is natural to find different types of elevations dotting the map in the guise of place names. Their location has prevented most of them from becoming important population centers, but they have furnished an abundance of surnames. Among them are Montagna, Monti, Montale,[9] Colli,

[1] Argento has probably come into vogue largely through its use as a font name, the feminine form of which is the still popular Argentina.

[2] Oro might also stem from short forms of DiodORO, PolidORO, TeodORO, etc. Both oro and argento could of course likewise refer to blond or grey hair or beard. Cf. Barbadoro.

[3] In the section of Calabria under Greek influence, a calamita is a canneto, cane brake.

[4] Ciapo from Jacopo may supply Ciappi. It is also a Genoese term for a fishery; it can mean buttocks, and Reggio Emiliano (ciappa) a constable.

[5] Cf. the well known place name Piperno, as well as Neapolitan peperna, savory.

[6] Another meaning of carbone is charcoal.

[7] Through rhotacism Creta could be from Anicleta, Policleta.

[8] In some sections Marni would be interpreted as the youngest son of very old parents.

[9] Sometimes montale signifies the most fertile part of a field.

Collina,[10] Poggi, Poggioli,[11] del Poggetto, Timpone (Calabrese), all meaning hill or mountain; Cucchi, Cuccoli,[12] a rounded hill; Bernocchi,[13] Borgna [14] (Italian Swiss), Spalla [15] (Alberobello-spadda), Bricchi, Bricchetti,[16] (Piedmontese), hillock; Costa, Costetti,[17] Greppi, Groppi, Clivio, Chinazzi[18] (Sicilian), hillside; Barbarotta [19] (Valle Anzasca), series of peaks; Cima, Cresta,[20] Cacume, Cozzi,[21] Picco, Pizzo, Pizzoni,[22] Punta, Puntoni, Apice, Ciglio, Gigli,[23] peak; Roccia, Roccella, Rocca,[24] del Balzo, de' Rupi, della Ripa, Abisso, Masso [25] (Pisa), Sasso, Lo Sasso (province of Rome), Sassoni [26] (province of Grosseto), Scheggi, Tecchi [27] (Lucchese), Morra [28] (Serrone, province of Rome), cliff, precipice; della Ratta, Ratti,[29] Scala,[30] Perrone,[31] steep incline; Passo,[32] Malpasso, Varchi, Voca-

[10] We can get Colli, Collina through the doubling of the l in Cola, Nicola. Collo is also a word for neck, a rather unlikely surnominal source.

[11] Broggio from Ambrogio at times becomes Boggio. It may also become Poggio through the substitution of a p for a b. Cf. name Poggio Bracciolini.

[12] Also egg, favorite son, cuckoo.

[13] Cf. Germanic Bernocc. See E. Förstemann, *Altdeutsches Namenbuch*. Erster Band. Personennamen. 2 ed. Bonn, 1900, 270.

[14] Borgno is also a word for blind.

[15] Regularly spalla signifies shoulder.

[16] Cf. words for donkey, ram, Romagnuolo brichett, one-edged sword, Piedmontese brichet, match.

[17] Costanza and Costantino could be reduced to Costa. Also cf. the word for coast, costa, ribs, Spanish Acosta, and Portuguese Da Costa.

[18] Possible likewise from FrancesCHINAZZO, FranCHINAZZO, etc.

[19] Barbarota is also a Piedmontese word for mole cricket.

[20] Good competitors are Crest, Romagnuolo for Cristo, cresta, crest, and tuft of hair.

[21] Any font name ending in -co could produce Cozzi, FrancesCOZZO, etc.

[22] For Picco, cf. Bicco, Picho and see Förstemann, *op. cit.* 249-41. For Pizzo, Pizzoni cf. the name Opizzo, and Pizzo, imperial.

[23] Font names like Virgilio, Pacilio, etc., could give either Ciglio or the variant Giglio. Ciglio is eyebrow, and is also a phonetic variant of giglio meaning lily.

[24] Rocca and perhaps roccia can mean fortress. Cf. given name Rocco.

[25] Masso can come from ToMASSO.

[26] Sasso is literally stone, rock. In addition a sassone can be a Saxon.

[27] Cf. tecchio, big, and tecca, stuttering.

[28] Morra is also Emiliano for mulberry and a dialectical word for the game of the mora.

[29] Cf. Ratto from ConRATTO, i.e. Corrado.

[30] Pascala can be shortened to Scala. The common noun meaning of the word scala is usually stairs, step.

[31] Perrone is easily derivable from Perro, Peter.

[32] Cf. JacoPASSO, FilipPASSO, etc.

tura, Serra, defile; La Motta,[33] Lavini,[34] landslide; Vulcano,[35] volcano. In Italy as elsewhere compounds with monte are noticeably numerous such as Montalbano, Montenegro, Montesanto, Montalto, Monteforte, Monteleone, Summonti, Tramonti, forms that could be reduced to the first or second element of the combination such as Monte or Albano or Leone.[36] Unless it relates to a place name Alpe, dall'Alpi is difficult to explain since the vast mountain system of the Alps is too big and indefinite to have produced a cognomen. Alpino could come from St. Alpino. Montano is, of course, equivalent to del Monte. Hillmen and mountain dwellers are known as Collesi, Collarini, Montagnari.

The dale supplies Valle, Vallini, Vallone,[37] valley; della Piana, del Piano,[38] Chiano, Ciano;[39] plain resident names like Pianesi, Pianigiani, Pianciani, Bassi,[40] low ground, and Vallarini, Vallarelli, dalesmen.

Pertaining either to upland or lowland are Petralia, Petroglio, Petrai, Petroso,[41] Sassi, Sassetti,[42] Massa, Massetti, Massello,[43] Massoglia, Macerata, Masera, Cavagna, Scudellati [44] (Italian Swiss), basket and bowl-like depression; Rango, Ranzi, land curving like a scythe or sickle; Conchetta, round depression; Caverna, Caberna, Grotta, cavern; Fossa,[45] Foppa (Alto Adige), Cavone [46] (Calabrese), Vallone [47] (Calabrese-Sicilian), ditch.

---

[33] GuglielMOTTA, GiroloMOTTA, GiacoMOTTA also have claims on the name.

[34] The font name Lavinia competes here.

[35] In Calabrese a vurcanu is an irascible, eccentric person.

[36] Cf. the name of Benedetto Varchi coming from Montevarchi, and Poliziano coming from Monte Pulciano.

[37] Valle might be a reduction of PerciVALLE. In Sicilian a valluni can mean a brook. Cf. also Vallone, Walloon.

[38] Cf. St.UlPIANO.

[39] Ciano has several other meanings, a fleur de lis, a dog (Tridentino cian), but most likely it comes from short forms of FeliCIANO, MarCIANO, etc., perhaps Giano from Giovanni.

[40] The most obvious meaning of basso is small, short.

[41] Possible from the name Peter, Petros(s)o.

[42] See Note 26.

[43] See Note 25.

[44] In the Alto Adige a masera is a flax steeping place. For Scudellati consult M. Gualzata, "Di alcuni Nomi Locali del Bellinzonese e Locarnese," *Studi di Dialettologia Celto Italiana*, Genève, 1924.

[45] Cf. AnFOSSA, Ligurian, Piedmontese for Alfonsa.

[46] Possible from the dialectical form of Jacobbo, JaCAVO. Another meaning is quarry.

[47] Also wide valley, Walloon.

The water and waterside are represented by Acqua, dell'Acqua, water; Fiumi, del Rio, river; Laghi, lake; Torrente,[48] Canale [49] (Tuscan) brook; Currao, Corrao [50] (Sicilian), Frola [51] (Valle Anzasca), waterfall; Cimarosa (Sicilian), torrent; Bagno, del Bagno, bathing place; Stagno, Guazzo, Bosa, Boselli (if from Piedmontese bosa), Pozzo, Puzzo, Pozzetti, Pozzolini,[52] Cisterni, large or small reservoirs of water; Fontana, Fontanetta, Fontanelli, della Fonte, Malafonte, Sorgente, spring; Gorgo, Gorgone,[53] Gorgolini, whirlpool; Fangarezzi, Zangaro (Calabrese zanga), Fracchia (Marchigiano), mire; Ballarini [54] (if Pavese), quagmire; Pantano, Pantanelli, Tampina, Padula, swamp; Forcella, Forcellini,[55] bifurcation of a river; Raina (Alto Adige), ravine; Riva, Piaggia, Spiaggia, shore; dell'Argine, Ripari, dyke, bank; Scoglio, Scoglietti, reef; Isola,[56] island; Capo,[57] Promontorio, headland; Delle Chiaie, Gera,[58] gravel; Arena, Arina, Rena, Arinella, Sabbia, Sabbioni, sand; Salina,[59] Salinaro, salt bed.

We may begin our treatment of agrarian peculiarities with the popular woodland surnames—Bosco, Boschetti, Boschini, Boscacci, woods, forest. Less diffused terms for the same are Selva,[60] Foresti and the Sicilian Fusari, Scarrone.[61] The thicket contributes Macchia, Ronchetti, Rongetti,[62] Roncari (Low Latin ronchus), Rovetta, Marrone [63] (if Amaseno), and the rare Cespuglio; the fruit grove and

---

[48] Another obvious meaning is torrent. Cf. English Torrens.

[49] Naturally, canal is another meaning.

[50] See C. Avolio, "Saggio di Toponomastica Siciliana," *Archivio Glottologico Italiano*, Supplemento, Sesta dispensa, 1898, 94.

[51] Cf. Romagnuolo froll, gadabout.

[52] All these Pozzo names are possible from Jacopo, etc. See also Förstemann, *op. cit.* 329.

[53] Cf. St. Gorgonio.

[54] Ballerina is also a dancer, a frivolous woman (Bergamascan), a wagtail.

[55] Forcella is literally a fork. It also means earwig.

[56] In some cases Isola may be a variant of Isolda.

[57] A derivation which is just as good if not better is from capo, head, chief.

[58] Gera from RuG(i)ERA, etc., would be even more acceptable.

[59] Rena is also Romagnuolo from Catarena = Catarina, and Reggio Calabrese from Irene. In the case of Salina we may at times have an Italianization of the Spanish Salinas.

[60] Might be a variant of Silvia (cf. French St. Selve), or a Northern Italian variant of Salva in which case we can recall Diotisalvi.

[61] See C. Avolio, *op. cit.* 91, for these two names.

[62] Ronca, bill hook, may be connected with the name. Cf. ronchetta, wild duck.

[63] Other meanings are large chestnut, old animal (Calabrese), mattock.

flower patch Cesareo [64] (Low Latin cisaria), Cesaro,[65] Paradiso,[66] Fiorita,[67] Giardino;[68] the kitchen garden Orto, Ortale,[69] Ortaggio, Verdura, Brolati (Tuscan); the vineyard Vigna;[70] the field or meadow Campo, Campello, Campari, Camparini, Campagna, Prati, Pascoli, Pascolati, Gerbi (Low Latin gerbum), Scerba, Scerbini, Erbaggio, Celli, Agelli, Agro, Mazzone [71] (if Neapolitan), Barasa (Piedmontese), Freschi,[72] Frescura (from Low Latin friscum), Lodeserto. Calvello [73] may refer to a place denuded of trees and shrubs; Balma (Valle Anzasca) to a place protected by cliffs against rains; Cortina (cf. Abruzzese curtine) to a zone of land for cultivation between a vineyard and an open field; Cesa [74] (Lazio) to cultivated hilly land; Cannavino [75] (Lazio) to land cultivated near a river; Maggese to fallow ground or, in Calabrese, to land sown with grain or potatoes, Sciara (Sicilian) to uncultivated volcanic land. Perticari [76] may come from pertica indicating land assigned to soldiers for cultivation. Chiusi [77] and Della Corte, Corti, Curti [78] (cf. Low Latin curtis) seem to describe an enclosed field, a meaning implied in Friulano Braida,[79] Braidotti. Pisciotto is Sicilian for a piece of land.

---

[64] There is a Saint Cesario.

[65] Naturally, Cesare, Caesar, immediately comes to mind as a strong claimant.

[66] It is easy to see a rival in paradiso, Paradise. In Carnia the word indicates a flower.

[67] Also explainable through fiore plus suffix -ita. In Calabrese it is a woman's name Jurita. Cf. Fiorita from Pasqua Fiorita.

[68] Giardino can easily be obtained through a syncopated form of Giardino and through Ricciardino.

[69] In Velletri an ortale is a snake.

[70] Lavinia might shorten into Vigna.

[71] Usually from Dalmazzo, Germanic Matzo or Genoese Mazza = Maggio. A mazzune in Calabrese is an old ox. Cf. also mazzone from mazza, club.

[72] The syncopated form of Francesco gives Fresco.

[73] See G. Raccioppi, "Origini Storiche Investigate nei Nomi Geografici della Basilicata," *Archivio Storico per le Provincie Napoletane*, I, 1876. Calvello is also a variety of wheat.

[74] Cesa can, of course, mean church. Cf. Piedmontese cesa.

[75] Connected with canapa, hemp.

[76] See G. Raccioppi, *op. cit.* A maker of pertiche, poles, would also be called perticaro.

[77] Literally, closed, and hence any kind of enclosure.

[78] In Valle Anzasca a corte is an alpine pasture. Corti, Curti also recall corto, short, and court house.

[79] In Sicilian braida seems to mean any field.

Surnames supplied by buildings of sundry types are Casa, house, with its many suffixes and its compound forms, Dalla Casa, Della Casa, Dalla Ca', Casini, Casella,[80] Casaccio, Casazza, Casassa, Casari, Casarini, Casarotti, Casamento, Casale,[81] Cabianca, Casabianca, white house, Casarossi, red house, Casabassi, low house, Casabona, good house, Casagrandi,[82] great house, Casanova, new house, Casavecchia, old house, Capiccioli, little house, Casalegno, woodhouse, Casapietra, stone house, Cabrusà, burned house, Mezzacasa, half house, Trecase, three houses. Synonyms are Maggione, Manzionna, mansion; Maggioncalda, warm mansion; and Palag(g)i, Palazzi, Palazzolo,[83] sometimes palace but more frequently a seigneurial country home. In its old acceptation Sala meant the same thing. Then, too, there are Castelli, Castelletti, Castellini, castle; Castelnuovo, Castelvecchio, new castle, old castle; and a number of other compound forms. Bicocchi [84] means a castle or a hovel on a hill. Among the modest dwellings are Casupola, Casolari,[85] Chiozza, Capanna, Barracca, Pagliaro, Pagliarini, Pagliai, hut, hovel. Those who resided near religious buildings took the names Chiesa, Cesa, church; Casadio, Casadidio, Casasanto, God's house, saint's house; Tempio, Tempietto, temple; Cap(p)elli, Cap(p)ellini, Cap(p)elletti,[86] chapel; Capitolo, chapter house; Capitello [87] (Venetian), tabernacle; Badia, abbey; Monasteri, Munisteri, monastery; Chiostrelli, Giostrelli, cloister; Cannonica, vicarage; d'Eramo, hermitage. With the exception of Chiesa the other surnames are seldom encountered. However, the most popular surnames referring to religious buildings are those compounded with saints' names—San Giuliano, Santa Caterina, Sammartino, etc., etc.—acquired by individuals through a place name or through proximity of habitation.

Other buildings furnishing names are Botteghi, workshop, wine-

[80] Cf. St. Casina. Cf. also casella meaning dairy.

[81] With reference to Casazza and Casassa we also refer to Giuseppe Menni's interpretation of the Pisan Casassi mentioned in the edition of the *Cronica di Bonaccorso Pitti* (Bologna, 1905, 154). According to him the name comes from cas'Assi, that is, casa degli Azzi. A casale is usually a hamlet, group of houses. The common Casalino would then be a resident of a hamlet.

[82] If it comes through the Bolognese casagrande means nobility.

[83] Palazzolo is likewise an Anconitano term for boat.

[84] Both castello and bicocca can mean fortress.

[85] A casolaro is also a hamlet. Casularu in Calabrese may be a garret for the storage of cheese.

[86] Suffixes added to cappa, cape or cappello, hat, could give identical names. A cappelletto is a Venetian soldier.

[87] Capitelli may be connected with the Val di Chiana word for bulrush, or the word for nipple.

shop; Allogio, d'Albergo, Alberghini,[88] inn; Taverna, Tavernini, Bettola [89] wineshop, Canova, wine cellar, and in Tuscan a government bread shop; Molino,[90] Camugnaro, mill; Paratore [91] (Sicilian), fulling mill; Forno, Fornelli, bakery, oven; Fornaci, Carcara (Calabrese), limekiln; Beccaria, meat market; La Forgia, Fucini,[92] forge, smithy; Casella,[93] dairy; Spedale, Spitali, Spedalotti, hospital; Spizio (ospizio), hospice; La Scola, school; Zecca, mint; Tribunale, Corte,[94] della Ragione, court house; del Carcere, Carcerini, Prigione, Segreti [95] (Bolognese), Griera (Ticinese), prison; Casamatta,[96] soldier's prison; Castri, Forte, Fortezza, Rocca, Roccella,[97] Ramponi (Mantovano), Battifolle, Conocchia [98] (Neapolitan), fortress; La Guardia,[99] outpost; Torre,[100] citadel, tower, dungeon; Caserma, barracks; Magazino, warehouse; Graneri, Granara,[101] granary; Massaria, farm house; Stalla,[102] stall. If Venetian a Sammarco may conceivably point back to a tavern, due to the fact that these places had the emblem of St. Mark on their doors.

Some miscellaneous types of constructions represented in the onomasticon are Tortoreto, Palomaro, Colombara,[103] dove cot; Porcile, Iusillo (Lucanese), pig sty; Caprile, goat pen; Pollari, Gallinaro,[104] chicken coop; Teza (Mantuan) hayloft; Parco, Palco [105] (Neapolitan) Tamari (Friulano), animal pen; Mercati, market place.

---

[88] Albergo from Alberico, Alberigo would be just as plausible.

[89] Short forms of Benedetto, Elisabetta serve as alternative explanations for Bettola.

[90] Cf. RoMOLINO or any name in -mo. A few Molinos may be disguised forms of mulo plus -ino, little mule. Also cf. the Spanish Molinos.

[91] Paratore also means a church upholsterer, decorator.

[92] Fucini might be from a name in -fo, Rodolfuccio ino.

[93] Also a little house.

[94] See Note 78.

[95] Secret is also Bolognese for secretary, i.e. one who keeps a secret.

[96] Casamatta in the dialect of Sannio is a hovel.

[97] These terms also mean cliff. Castro is one of the most popular of Spanish surnames.

[98] A more common meaning for conocchia is distaff.

[99] Guardia is, of course, a regular term for guard.

[100] Calabrese turra is a farmhouse.

[101] Otherwise a grain dealer.

[102] Cf. stalla di pecore, sheepfold, stalla di porci, pigsty. Also cf. CaSTALLA from Castalda.

[103] Also dove fancier. Palomaro may be a diver, palombaro.

[104] Pollaro and gallinaro are also poultry men.

[105] In Calabrese a parcu is an orange grove while in Sicilian it is a sheep pen. Parco is also possible from IpPARCO.

At times even a part of a building may be conspicuous enough to give rise to surnames such as Tinello,[106] servant's hall; Terrazzo, belvedere; Solari,[107] attic; Scala, Scaloni,[108] stairs; La Loggia, terrace, balcony, gallery; Pilastri, pilaster; Colonna, delle Colonne, column; dalla Volta, vault; dall'Arco, arch; Portico, portico; Ruderini, Rovini, Roini [109] (Old Vicentino), ruins; Campanaro,[110] Campanile, Campanini,[111] belfry; Tomba, della Tomba, Sepolcri, Sagrati, Calvario, possibly Avellone, tomb, cemetery; Orioli, Orologi, clock; Girandola,[112] Ventarolo, Ventaloro (Calabrese), weather vane; Steccati, Chiovenda (Pavese ciovenda), stockade; Barriera, barrier; Cantieri, dock yard; Pusterla (Modenese), small gate in city wall; Cancello,[113] Porta, Portelli, door, gate.

Some highway-byway surnames are Via, La Via, Viazzi, Viale, Strada,[114] Stradella, Stradali, del Corso,[115] Traversa, Viafora, Viapiana, Pianvia, Carrera, Rua, Ruga,[116] various types of roads and streets; Piazza, Piazzini, Piazzoni, Piazzoli,[117] Chiazza, square. One of the meanings of Traversari [118] would be one who dwells on a cross road. Scala, Scalina, Scalone [119] may refer also to a stair-like path or road, and Croce,[120] Travia, to a road intersection. Dal Ponte, comes from bridge, and Canale [121] from canal. The existence of the rare Ferrovia, railroad, gives evidence of the fact that new surnames are still being created in Italy.

[106] Cf. MarTINELLO, CostanTINELLO or any name in -to. We exclude from this list Camera, Camerini, Stanza, Salone, room. Of these camera may mean maid (donna di camera); Camerini may be a place name Camerino or come from St. Camerino; stanza is very likely from CoSTANZA and Salone from AsSALONE.

[107] A solaro is also a house with an attic. But cf. Santa Maria del Solario, solaro, place for sun dial, and solaro, heliotrope.

[108] Cf. PaSCALA, PaSCALONE.

[109] Roi, hence roini (if Bergamascan) is a pig. Cf. also eroino, little hero.

[110] Also bell ringer, maker.

[111] Campanino, -a, is a little bell and various kinds of flowers.

[112] A girandola is figuratively a gadabout.

[113] Cf. Sicilian canceddu, a pack saddle horse guider.

[114] Possible also from Spanish Estrada.

[115] Cf. Corso from BonacCORSO.

[116] The Genoese term for rue is rua, and the Valtellina term for the same is ruga. In Monferrino rua is a word for oak.

[117] With our street and square names compare French La Voie, La Rue, La Place.

[118] A traversaro is also the maker of a traversa, skirt.

[119] See Note 108. It should be added that the term can denote a steep incline.

[120] Literally, cross.

[121] Can mean a brook.

Chapter IX

GEOGRAPHICAL NAMES

LOCAL SURNAMES

Local geographical names show to what extent internal emigration has taken place. The provinces or regions are represented by Lombardo, Lombardini, Lombardelli, Piemonte, Piemontese, Marcheggiani, Abruzzi, Abruzzese, Abruzzini, Molise, Basilicata, Puglia, Pugliese, Calabria, Calabrese, Sicilia, Siciliano, Sardo, Tosco, Toscano, Toscanini. The substantive forms Lombardia, Le Marche, Sardegna are either rare or non-existent, while the same can be said of the adjective forms Molisano, Basilicatense. Furthermore, Basilicata, Marcheggiano, Molise, Piemonte, Piemontese are numerically weak when compared to the other provincial names just cited. Why, we do not know. As to the people of Emilia, they are still widely known by the older regional name of Romagnuolo, a frequent surname. Other official province names—Lazio, Liguria, Umbria, Veneto, were introduced too late to be productive of cognomina.

But there were also city states, notably Venice and Genoa. There was Rome, the capital of the Papal States, and Naples, the leading city of the Spanish Southern Italian dominions. With reference to them not only were their ex-residents called Veneziani, Venezia, Genovesi, Genova, Romano, Napolitano, Napoli, but also those who came from almost anywhere within the political spheres of these municipalities. Count Sforza in a recent book, *The Real Italians* (New York, 1942, 1-2) says: "Even today the names of the regions of Italy like Piedmont, Lombardy and Liguria mean little to ordinary people. The villager from Liguria, the region which sweeps down the coast from the French border to Genoa and southward to the mouth of the Magra, would not call himself 'Ligurian' but Genoese or at least he would say that he was from the Genovesato." In general, the same may be said about most of the other important centers of population. This has made it possible, for example, for both the former citizen of Cosenza, or for anyone residing in the northern section of Calabria to call himself Cosenza, Cosentino, or anyone from Catanzaro or its province to call himself Catanzaro or Catanzarito, etc.

Of the two forms employed (1) the preposition plus place name —Da Prato, Di Capua, De Genova or the same place name with the preposition understood—Prato, Capua, Genova and (2) the adjectival form—Capuano, Pratesi, Genovese, the first is not only much older but has a greater vogue. Very often it has virtually no competition from its adjective rival as in the case of Palermo, Messina, Catania, Reggio, Salerno, D'Ancona, Cuneo, Orvieto, Modena, Parma. At other times the adjective competition is weak as in the case of Ferrara versus Ferrarese, Milani, versus Milanesi, Verona versus Veronesi, Perugia versus Perugini, Pescara versus Pescarese. It is strong in the case of Pavia versus Pavese, da Bari versus Barese, Bologna versus Bolognesi, Siena versus Sanesi.[1] But only in a few instances does the adjective clearly predominate over the noun as in Fiorentino versus Firenze, Sorrentino versus Sorrento.

While it is true that many Italian Jews have chosen to assume city surnames, particularly Central and Northern Italian names— D'Ancona, Ascoli, Padoa, Ravenna, Terni, Terracini, Viterbo, Volterra; [like their fellow co-religionists in Germany (Compare Berliner, Hamburger, Frankfurter, Wiener)] it should be made clear that they are by no means the exclusive possessors of these cognomina. Nor does it follow that city surnames denote a one-time nobility. They are enjoyed by both aristocrats and commoners alike.

However, a province or city name does not invariably prove ultimate provenience from either one place or the other. Used metaphorically they can apply to anyone from anywhere. For instance, a Bergamasco in Milanese and Piedmontese is a herdsman; a Calabrese in the Trentino is a crafty fellow, in the Abruzzi a gadabout, in Naples uncouth; a Cerretano (native of Cerreto) is a term used for a seller of trifles; a Genovese is a clever individual; a Lombardo is a shopkeeper in Sicilian and in Genoese a dullard; in Genoese a Napolitano is an idler and in Piedmontese a padoan, Padovano, has the same meaning.[2] In addition, many apparent place name-surnames come from a source most of us would not suspect, the baptismal. It seems that this peculiar custom was quite popular between the eleventh and sixteenth centuries.[3]

Persons having surnames that correspond to the proper names of mountains—Montecatini, Monsanti, Montenero, or a lake—Lagomarsino, or a castle—Castelfranco, owe them to settlements that have sprung up near these spots. We know that two brilliant men of the Renaissance, Politian and Varchi, derived their names from Montepulciano and Montevarchi. The Brunamonti of Trevi get their

---

[1] However, Senise refers to a town in Lucania.

[2] For more information see A. Prati, "Nomi e Sopranomi di Genti Indicanti Qualità e Mestieri," *Archivum Romanicum*, XX, 1936, 201-56.

[3] Very enlightening on this point is P. S. Pasquali, "Note di Onomastica Lunigianese. Nomi Personali Maschili da Nomi di Terre e Paesi di Lunigiana." *Memorie della Accademia Lunigianese di Scienze, Giovanni Capellini*, XVI, 1935, 41-46.

name from Serra Brunamonti while the Castelottieri of Siena are also known as Ottieri, all of which indicates a fair amount of decompounding in connection with these types of names. Thus a Cimini, a Covello, a Giordano, a Tessori may ultimately hail from Montecimini in Lazio, Montecovello in Calabria, Montegiordano in Sicily, Montessori in Tuscany. It is likewise evident that Marsino refers to Lagomarsino, Trasimeni to Lago di Trasimeno and Sugana to Valsugana.

What is true of cognomina from proper names of mountains, lakes, castles, valleys is also true of cognomina from proper names of rivers. Stream surnames like Alaro (Calabria), Aterno and Garigliano (Abruzzi-Campania), Brenta[4] (Trentino-Veneto) are apt to come from localities bearing the river name.

EXOTIC SURNAMES

We have already alluded to a number of patronymic names supplied in large measure by ancient Greek, Roman and German sources. Other national groups coming into Italy in the late Middle Ages and after-times have also left their mark on the onomasticon. Many of the new settlers came in colonies forming linguistic islands in rural areas all over Italy—Albanians in Abruzzi-Molise, Lucania, Calabria and Sicily, Byzantine Greeks in Calabria and Apulia, Serbs in Molise, Germans in Piedmont, Franco-Provençals in Apulia, Catalonians in Alghero, Sardinia. Here they still use the language of the homelands of their ancestors, and some of their last names derive from the languages they habitually speak.[5] Like other islands which have

---

[4] We recall here that the famous name, Brentano, comes from Brenta.

[5] It is now generally held that the language of the ancient Greek colonies in Italy had already disappeared under Roman domination. Modern survivals of this tongue are consequently due to new colonies established during the Byzantine period, 536-1069, and during the Norman period that succeeded it. A good summary of the argument is given by G. de Gregorio in "La Grecità del Dialetto Calabrese." *Zeitschrift für Romanische Philologie*, L, 1930, 696ff. Sicily has also had its quota of neo-Greeks, but they have been assimilated some time ago, in Palermo by the fifteenth century. See V. di Giovanni, "Divisione Etnografica della Popolazione di Palermo." *Archivio Storico Siciliano*, n.s. XIII, 1888, 1-66. We mention a few surnames here in addition to the patronymics already cited and to the province-city names that will be listed later— Carideo, walnut, Colosimo, perfumed, Cefalo, head, Arcudi, bear cub, Lico, wolf, Macrì, long, Pittaro, fritter seller, Rodinò, red, Serrao, fish monger, Sgrò, curly haired, Spano, sparse bearded, bald, Starace, little cross. Studies on Serb, Provençal and Catalonian names are lacking. The following is a handful of possible Italo-Albanian cognomina—Artaro (goldsmith), Comara (if from gomar), donkey, Detaro, sailor, Firari, outlaw, La Rocca (if from larocch), grey, Matise, Matesi (matesi), surveyor, Muscari, Mascari (mushkar), muleteer, Zocco (zogu), the bird. There are many Arabic surnames in Sicily but practically all of them go back to place names. See C. Avolio, "Di Alcuni Sostantivi Locali del Siciliano." *Archivio Storico Siciliano*, n.s. XIII, 1888, 369ff. For further information see *Enciclopedia Italiana*, XIX, 928-32—Dialetti non-italiani.

been absorbed by the surrounding Italian dialects these, too, will be absorbed within a relatively short space of time. On the other hand, those foreigners that settled down in urban areas have been rather quickly assimilated as might be expected. Among the new alien town dwellers Spaniards were once to be found more abundantly than the others due largely to several centuries of Spanish domination over extensive sections of Italy.[6] But men from many other lands also flocked to the populated centers. Venice in its heyday was possibly the most cosmopolitan of all Italian cities with its Germans, Grisons, French, Burgundians, English, Hungarians, Slavs, Greeks, Albanians, Tartars, Turks, Armenians, Persians, Moors, Catalans, Egyptians. As one poet puts it, they came there

> By boat and ferry
> To make their living and never more to leave.[7]

Of the Eternal City it was said in the early eighteenth century that it was neither Italy, nor France, nor Spain but an aggregate of all nations.[8] And what was taking place in Venice and Rome could likewise be seen to a lesser extent in Genoa, Naples, Palermo, Florence, Bologna, Milan and other cities.

Occasionally traces of original foreignness remain linked with the surname in the guise of a general descriptive term like foreigner —Straniero, Straneo, Forestiere, Forese.[9] But these terms likewise apply to Italians who have transferred their residence from one section of Italy to another. Africano, Fricano (African), and Moro [10] (Moor), Negro (negro) and their derivatives may denote aliens and at the same time dark-complexioned, dark-haired indi-

---

[6] Spanish names of the non-geographical variety like Almirante, Ballesteros, Cortés, Diaz, Faconti (Facundo), Fregona, Gaglio (Gallo), Galdoz, Galvez, Garcea, Gonzales, Guerrero, Gusmano, Cusumano, Ingrassia (from Engracia), La Brasca (from Blasca), Lopez, Moreno, Mucciaccia, Muñoz, Mugnoz, Paccecco, Perrez, Posada, Raposa, Romero, Soler, Sanchez (Latinized in many instances to De Sanctis), Sannazzaro (from Salazar), Suarez, Torres, Vigliano (from Villano), Zappata, Scimeni (from Ximena), abound in Southern Italy. Geographical names will be cited a little later.

[7] The nationalities listed are mentioned by B. Dudan in *Il Dominio Veneziano di Levante*, Bologna, 1938, 253-54. From the same book come the verses quoted, which in the original read

> . . . . con navi a burchi
> A far sua vita, e zammai no se parte.

[8] Cf. . . . "Roma non è Italia nè Spagna nè Francia ma un aggregato di tutte le nazioni," in *Il Criticon di Don Lorenzo Gracian*, Cattaneo version, Venezia, 1720, 457.

[9] Modern dictionaries define a forestiere as one who moves from one part of a country to another part, and straniero as one who comes from foreign parts, but they are used synonymously by the common people. In Calabrese both a foreigner and an outsider is a forestieru. Forese also has the meaning of farmer, shepherd.

[10] Cf. St. Mauro.

viduals. More specific are the nation-names along with their corresponding adjectives of nationality such as Albanese, Albanise, Arvanise (Albanian), Algieri, Algerino (Algiers, Algerine); Arabia [11] (Arabia); Armenia [12] (Armenia); Armeni [13] (Armenian); Bisanzio (Byzantium); Bisanti, Bissanti, Pesante (Byzantine); Britanico [14] (British); Inghilterra (England); Inglese, Inghilese (English); Bulgaro, Bulgarini, Bulgarelli, Bulgaretti (Bulgarian); Belgio (Belgium); Boemi [15] (Bohemia, Bohemian); Croatti (Croatian); Egitto (Egypt); Egizio (Egyptian); La Fiandra (Flanders); Fiammingo [16] (Flemming); Francia (France); Francese, Franzese, Franco, Francesco [17] and derivatives (French); Frigia, Frisia (Friesland); Frisone [18] (Frieslander); della Greccia (Greece); Greco, Grego (Greek); d'India (India); de Malta, Malta; Maltese, Maltise (Maltese); Marocco (Morocco), Olandese (Hollander); Palestini (Palestine); Persia [19] (Persia); Persiani (Persian); Polonia [20] (Poland); Polacco [21] (Pole); Portogallo [22] (Portugal); Lusitano, Portoghese (Portuguese); Scotto [23] (Scott); Serbia (Serbia); Schiavo [24] (Slav); Schia-

[11] Cf. St. Arabia. Cirenaica, found in Calabria, is probably a new name given to a foundling born at the time of the Tripolitan War.

[12] Name of a Messinese family founded by a Giorgio Armeno.

[13] Cf. Latin Armenius.

[14] Cf. Latin Britanicus.

[15] In some cases Boemi is a variant of Buemi, place name in Sicily.

[16] Cf. fiammingo = flammingo. Flemmings were apt to be classed as Germans. For example, Heinrich, the musician, who came to Florence from Flanders in 1475 was known as Arrigo Tedesco.

[17] Francesco was common for French in the Renaissance period. The given name also comes from the same word.

[18] Frisi is given by A. Bongioanni, Nomi e Cognomi . . . Torino, 1928, as a derivative of Federico, in which case Frisoni could represent an augmentative form of the word. Canavese and Lombard Fris coming from Felice could also give Frisoni if the suffix were added. Frisone also means draft horse and hawfinch (Parmigiano).

[19] If Sicilian, d'India might well be In plus Ddia, i.e. Dorotea. Perhaps Persia is a feminine form of Perseo with a shift in the accentuation. It is also possible that Persia is a variant of Persica in the Biellese district as C. Poma points out in "Fallaci Apparenze in Cognomi Italiani," Archivio Glottologico Italiano, XVIII, 1918, 358.

[20] In most cases Polonia derives from Apollonia.

[21] Polaco, Venetian for pullet, would be a rarer source.

[22] In Southern Italian a portogallo is an orange.

[23] Possible from FranceSCOTTO, PaSCOTTO. E. Menagio, Le Origini della Lingua Italiana, Geneva, 1685, 313, rates as a fable the Scotch beginnings of the famous Marescotti family said to descend from a Mario Scotto. He suggests a derivative from mare (sea), marisco, maresco. Why not amaresca = amarasca, sour cherry? See Botanical Names.

[24] Schiavo is the regular word for slave. In Neapolitan a schiavone is a water parsnip.

vone, Schiavonetti (Slavonian); Spagna (Spain); Spagnuolo, Spa-
gnoletti, Spagnolini, Espano, Spano [25] (Spaniard); Suizzo (Swiss);
Tedesco, Todesco, Toeschi, Todeschini, Teutonico, Alamanni,
La Magna (German and Germany); Turco, Turconi, Turchetti,[26]
Ottomano, Ottomanelli (Turk); Ungaro, Ungaretti, Ungarelli,
Ongaro (Hungarian); Valacchi (Rumania). Gypsies may be indicated by Zingarelli, Zingaretti, Cincanelli, and Jews by Marrano and
Marano.[27] Of course, the mere fact that a person is a foreigner is
in itself sufficient to label one with his national name. In addition,
speech peculiarities and, in the past much more than nowadays, an
alien's dress, hair-do and even wallet, made him different from the
rest of the community, and thus helped the tendency along.

While the individual in possession of one of the above names has
good reason to assume that his ancestors were originally foreigners,
it is risky to be categorical about the matter. The very same names
may, for instance, also refer to Italians who after a certain sojourn
on foreign soil returned to their homeland and were given the nickname of francese, spagnuolo, tedesco, etc., by their fellow citizens,
a tradition which is still very much alive. It is most current in the
nickname americano.[28] It may be that the last name Brasile can be
traced to a former resident in this New World country.[29]

Again some of these names have acquired a depreciative figurative meaning which may now and then have led to their application
to native Italians. Since the days of the Romans Greco has been
a synonym of astuteness and disloyalty and often connotes a stammerer. A Spagnuolo denotes a haughty person or a dandy.[30] A
Lucchese todesco is a stammerer, and a Neapolitan todisco a tippling
simpleton. A Turco is a cruel, wicked or irreligious man, a meaning
it shares with Saraceno, Saracino, Sarasino and Pagano, Paganini,
Paganelli.[31] Tartaro and Tartarini,[32] on the other hand, are apt to

[25] But in Graeco-Calabrese spano is sparse-bearded, bald.

[26] Turco might come from the Germanic Turicco in some cases.

[27] This derivation is made doubtful by Friulano maran, town square sur-
rounded by houses, by St. Marana and the place name Marano = Merano
(Calabria). In Southern Italy a marrano is a rustic as well as an infidel.

[28] Indianos is the universal term that has been applied by the Spaniards to
their citizens returning from the Western Hemisphere.

[29] It is also possible that the same vegetable dye that gave its name to the
republic also eventually furnished an individual cognomen.

[30] The painter, Giuseppe Maria Crespi (1665-1737) was nicknamed Lo
Spagnuolo because of the extreme elegance of his attire.

[31] Both Saraceno and Pagano were exceedingly common as given names in
the Middle Ages.

[32] In Sicilian tartari was used to denote converted Moslems. See V. di Giovanni, op cit. For additional information on metaphorical national names see
A. Prati, op. cit. The Paduan, Marchigiano and Romano term for simpleton
may or may not be connected with Marocco.

mean barbarian, uncouth. A zingaro is commonly a vagabond and often a rogue.

A few are Italian place names. Compare Africa (Lombardy), Franco (Cosenza), Franca (Alessandria, Perugia), Franchi (Cuneo, Parma), Fiammenga (Perugia), Fiamminga (Mondovi), Fiandra (Como, Lodi), Inglese (Piedmont), Inghilterra (Lombardy), Spagna (Florence, Novara, Pavia, Siena), Turco (Florence, Genoa, Messina), Todesco (Belluno), Todeschino [33] (Brescia).

Finally, adjectives and substantives of nationality or language have frequently been employed as first names. From the sixth to the ninth centuries such names as Alaman, Ostrogotha, Baior, Bulgar, Burgundo, Franco, Friso, Huni, Lanpart, Nortman, Sax, Scot, Svab, Thuring, Wandal [34] were quite common. In the Middle Ages Alamanno, Franco, Francesco, Scotto, Ongaro had a fair degree of currency.

In the names aforementioned foreigners have been identified by the language they have spoken or by the country they have hailed from. But many that came from provinces within these countries have been identified by the name of the province.[35] In a number of cases these newcomers had acquired their provincial surnames in their native lands. French provinces supply Ancolemmo (Angoulême); Angioini, Anzovino (Angevin); Averna [36] (Auvergne); Borgogno, Borgognone (Burgundian); Barbone [37] (Bourbon); Brettoni, Bertoni [38] (Breton); Gironda (Gironde); Girundini (Girondin); Guasco, Guascone (Gascon); Normandi, Normanni (Norman); Piccardi (Piccard); Provenzal, Provensal (Provençal); Savoia (Savoy); Savoiardo (Savoyard). Greece contributes Candia,[39] Candioto, Candiotti (Candia or Crete), Capodocia, Cappadocia (Cappodocia), Cipro,[40] D'Epiro, de Pirro [41] (Epirus), Pirroti (Epi-

[33] See A. Amati, *Dizionario Corografico dell'Italia.* Milano, Vallardi, n.d. and T. Zanardelli, "I Nomi Etnici nella Toponomastica." *Atti della Società Romana di Antropologia,* VIII, 1901-02, 100-13. Zanardelli also includes Borgogna (Crema) and Borgognona (Pavia), listed below.

[34] Noted by E. Lorenzi in his "Osservazioni Etimologiche sui Cognomi Ladini." *Archivio per l'Alto Adige,* II, 1907, 371.

[35] It is, of course, clear that some of these provinces formerly existed as countries, but in order to avoid complications we shall not go into this matter.

[36] Cf. Lake Avernus in Campania.

[37] Also from Germanic Barbo, Latin Balbus, as well as barbone, a big bearded individual and barba, Northern Italian for uncle.

[38] Bertone for Breton is used by Bandello in *Novella* I, 98, but the surname is more apt to be from a font name—Alberto, Roberto, Filiberto, etc.

[39] The surname Candiani is apparently not from Candia but from Candiano near Padua.

[40] Some Cipros can probably trace their names back to cypress tree.

[41] Might be from a font name Pirro, Pyrrus, or Pirro = Pierro.

rote), Lepanto (Lepanto), Macedonia, Macidonia (Macedonia), Rodi (Rhodes), da Schio (Schio), Tracia (Thrace). Spain furnishes Aragona (Aragon), Aragonesi, Ragonesi (Aragonese), Castiglia (Castille), Castellano [42] (Castilian), Catalano (Catalan), Galizia (Galicia), Galliego, Gallego, Galliziani (Gallego), Guadalupa, Maiorca (Mallorca), Navarro, Navarrini,[43] Novarro (Navarre), Basco, Vasco (Basque). Province names from elsewhere are few— from Germany, Bavaria, Baviera, Prussia, Prussiano and perhaps Sassone;[44] from the Low Countries Brabanti (Brabant), Barbantini, inhabitant of Brabant, and an occasional Vallone [45] (Walloon). Morlacchi from morla is an Istrian Rumanian. Like the national names these exotic province surnames do not always indicate that the ancestors of their present owners originally came from other countries. Italians who had resided in these regions might likewise be labelled with such names. For instance, those who had been at Santiago de Compostela on a pilgrimage were at times called Spagnoli and at times Galizia. When the Venetians and the French divided the Greek empire, the islands of the archipelago fell to the former. The island of Stampalia then became the feudal holding of the Quirini, a branch of which took the name of Stampalia. This may now be extinct but it suggests the possibility of the existence of other feudal Veneto-Greek names. There are also Italian place names which duplicate the province names cited, for example, Schio near Venice, and Rodi in Puglia. Besides, some of the same names have gone over into the realm of trade and nicknames and have crystallized as cognomina through them. Compare borgognone, porter (Genoese), catalano, noise maker (Bergamascan), basco (Northern Italian), dullard,[46] guasco, guascone, boaster,[47] morlac (Friulano) and murlocch (Monferrino), uncouth.

Instead of the name of a country or province a more local name, usually one taken from a city, might be employed. From France we have Arlotti,[48] (Arlesien), Avignone (Avignon), Avignonesi (Avignonais), Bellei (Bellay), Bordò (Bordeaux), Brienno or Brienna (Brienne), Caorsi (Cahors), Carcassona (Carcassonne),

---

[42] Castellano with the meaning of chatelain is a more common source of the cognomen.

[43] During the seventeenth century the French in Italy were scornfully called Navarrini.

[44] Sassone can mean big stone, cliff.

[45] Much more common in the sense of wide valley, torrent.

[46] Probably so-called because of their unintelligible language.

[47] The meaning seems to be borrowed from the French.

[48] The name of a noble family from Reggio Emilia claiming to trace its origin to Arles. But cf. arlotto, untidy fellow and, in Bolognese, a glutton.

Celona [49] (Châlons), Chiaramonte, Chiaramonte (Clermont), Limosini (Limousin), Lusignani (Lusignan), Marsiglia (Marseilles), Moriacchi (Mauriac), Parigi, Parigini,[50] (Paris and Parisian), Perpignani (Perpignan), Pontieri [51] (Poitiers), Roccelli [52] (Rochelle), Ronsivalle (Ronseveau), Tarasconi (Tarascon), Toloni (Toulon), Tolosani [53] (Toulousain). From Spain we have Alicante, Magro,[54] in some cases from Almagro, Avila, Balboa, Barcellona, Baroja, Cartagena, Celada, Cordova, Cordovani, Garay, Gayangos, Gibilterra, Giron, Granata, Laguna, Lerda, (Lérida), Mendozzi, Moncada, Olmedo, Pampaloni, Quesada, Ribera, Salinas, Samori, Samorani (Zamora, Zamorano), Santigliana, Seguenza, Siviglia, Sibilia, Sibiglia [55] (Seville), Sibilano, Tangora, Tarragò (Tarragón), Toledo, Ulloa, Valenza, Valenziano, Villareale. From Greece we obtain d'Atene (Athens), Atteniese (Athenian), Accorinti and Corinti (Corinth), and perhaps Parisi from Paros [56] and Patrasso [57] from Patras. Locarno, Losanna, Losanese recall Switzerland; Raguseo, Spalatino, Dalmatia; Vienna, Austria; Durazzo, Albania and Belgrado, Serbia. There are, of course, other Greek and Spanish names appearing as Italian place names which can be counted as possible sources of these and other surnames that we have not mentioned. Moreover, it has always been customary to give women names of famous cities,[58] a fact which has almost certainly brought into being not a few of the above-mentioned cognomina.

[49] There are present-day Celonas. In the late Middle Ages we find established in Italy a Giovanni da Celona, Jean de Châlons.

[50] Competes with the first name Paris.

[51] Pontiero can mean bridge builder, tender.

[52] Cf. roccia, cliff, fortress.

[53] We can arrive at Tolone from BorTOLONE, a first name. Tolosani is even more likely to be of Spanish origin, from Tolón.

[54] Otherwise, the name can be associated with St. Macra, and magro, lean.

[55] C. Poma in a review of a book by A. Trauzzi, *Attraverso l'Onomastica del Medioevo in Italia*, Rocca ɔ. Casciano, 1911-13, in *Archivio Glottologico Italiano*, XVIII, 1918, 388, gives as derivatives Biellese Bilia and Biglia and carries the name back to Marsibilia of the Carolingian epic.

[56] But compare Aparisio, Spanish Aparicio.

[57] May be a theological name, provincial superior. It also means a distinguished citizen (Romagnuolo), a fat man (Teramano), or it may be a variant of Pietro through Petrasso.

[58] Cf. the currently popular girls' names, Florence, Roma. For the Middle Ages see G. D. Serra, "Nomi Personali Femminili Piemontesi da Nomi di Paesi e Città Famose nel Medioevo." *Revistă Filologică* (Cernauti), I. 1927, 85-99.

Chapter X

BIRD NAMES

Practically all the birds that wing under the blue vaults of the beautiful Italian skies, sweet warblers and those of raucous note, along with their less fortunate and more prosaic domesticated brethren, have directly or indirectly conferred their names upon a considerable number of humans living on the Mediterranean boot and its outlying territories. The main sources of these bird names are four—nicknames (direct) and spot names, shop and inn signs, proprietorship (indirect). As it is clear that in many instances it is virtually impossible to trace their origin to a unique cause the owners are privileged to make their own choice in the matter. One illustration will suffice to demonstrate the polygenetic character of bird appellations. Falco or Falcone, hawk or falcon, may refer to a bold or keen-eyed or nimble person; a geographical area such as Falchi near Caserta, Falco, a mountain in the Abruzzi, Falcone, a commune in Sicily, a mountain near Palermo, a cape in Sardinia, Falcone Casina, Falcone Marina near Messina, Monfalcone in Istria;[1] an inn or shop sign which, before the days of street numbers, was identified pictorially by a falcon and referred to as All'Insegna del Falco; or the owner or trainer of a Falcon.

The last three (indirect) sources are of no particular interest and will, therefore, except in a few cases, be understood without further mention, as potential explanations of a number of the names that will be cited. What makes the ornithological terms really attractive is their variety and the metaphorical significance which they embody as nicknames, and it is from this point of view that we intend to examine them. On the other hand, for the sake of completeness and clarification, some interpretations of a miscellaneous nature will be injected into our discussion.

The generic name, bird, exists as a surname in quite a number of variant forms: for example Uccelli, Ulcelli, Uzielli, Uccelletti, Augello, Ausiello, Augelluzzi, Oselli, Oseletti and several abbreviated

---

[1] For these names see A. Amati, *Dizionario Corografico dell'Italia*. Milano, Vallardi, n.d. 8v.

versions like Celloni and Celli.[2] As a sobriquet it usually connotes a simpleton, but sometimes, as evident from the phrase uccello da bosco and uccello vecchio, forest bird and old bird, it means a pilferer or a crafty fellow. In the symbolism of Christian art, which should not be counted out as a possible source of some baptismal names and through them of some surnames, a bird represents the Holy Spirit or the soul of the faithful flying towards its celestial fatherland.

Barnyard fowl and other tame feathered bipeds are represented by Gallina, Gallinetti, Gallinone, Chioccia, Peccia[3] (Metaurense), Biocca (Perugino, Senese), Gallo,[4] Gallone, Galassi[5] (Piedmontese), Gaglione, Galletti, Gallozzi, Galluzzi, Capponi, Caponi[6] (Northern Italian), Pollo,[7] Puddu (Sardinian), Pollac(c)i, Pollini,[8] Pollastro,[9] Pollastrino, Pollastrella, Pulcino, Pollicino, a few Puccini,[10] Puccinelli (if from the Subiaco sector, cf. pucino), all of them chickens either full grown or young. By gallina is meant a chicken-hearted person, a noise maker (schiamazzare come una gallina), or, if Aruzzese, a rambling gossip. Gallo and its derivatives refer to strutters, bullies, lady-killers. A cappone (cf. English Capon) is a person with a hoarse voice, while a pollo and a Romano and Marchigiano pollastrello can mean a ninny. That Gallodoro and Gallorosso were very likely inn signs at one time is discernible from the color adjectives joined to the word gallo.

Duck surnames are Anatra, Anatriella; those for goose are

---

[2] It is not too presumptuous to assume that the double diminutive -uccio + -ello, attachable to all given names, i.e. PaolUCCELLO, PetrUCCELLO, etc., may, at times, have been detached from its root, appearing as Uccello. In Piedmontese an usel is a swallow and in Venetian ocela, ausela, a pigeon. The one-word form of the famous Roman Aulus Gellius, Augellius, may also have been adopted by some of his namesakes. Marcello could furnish us with Celloni, Celli. Cf. cella, wine cellar.

[3] One of the words for paunch is peccia.

[4] Many of the names of the Gallo group and some at least of the Gallina group owe their existence to the famous Saint Gallo. Several dialects supply homographs of Galletti-poppy, corn salad, penny cress, orchid, sweet pea. If from the Parmigiano, gallenna, Gallina can mean a sly fellow.

[5] An Italianized form of Galahad, hero of the Arthurian Romances.

[6] Capone is more convincing if attributable to an anatomical source coming from capo, head, hence big head, a stubborn person. But cf. IaCAPpONE = Iacoppone.

[7] Pollo might come from Apollo or any name in -po like Jacopo, Esopo, Crispo, etc. LeoPOLLO, Leopoldo or, through the gemination of an internal consonant, frequent in Central and Southern Italian, from Paolo through Polo.

[8] In Milanese a pollin is a turkey. Other meanings for pollino are marsh, hen louse.

[9] In Neapolitan the word pollasto means a go-between.

[10] The great majority of the Puccinis are, of course, from Iacopo, Giuseppe, Filippo.

D'Oca, Dall'Oca,[11] Occhelli, Occhini,[12] Papara, Paparini, Pavarini [13] (Romagnuolo pavaren), Paparella, Paparazzo; those for turkey Tacchini, Tacchi,[14] Dindo, Ocio, Polanca (Metaurense), Pita, Pitoni [15] (Friulano pite and piton and Parmigiano piton), Gallotta (Calabrese), all of which may be designations for dullards, but the geese [16] and ducks may also describe slow-moving, awkward fleshy persons. Calabrese applies the word papariare to such people and uses paparu to denote an undersized individual. In the dialect of Avellino a papara is a loitering woman; in Sicilian a papara is a waddler; in Ferrarese a paparot is a fat person. Some rachitic individuals with large hips are often called anitre. Then, too, there is the proverbial phrase: Ha il collo lungo come un papero, his neck is as long as that of a goose, which might cause long-necked people to be given this epithet. Tacchino might also be related to Genoese co' di tacchin, turkey colored, i.e. a very pale fellow. In contrast to this saying are the phrases rosso come un tacchino, as red as a turkey, indicative of a flushed or ruddy complexion, and parere un tacchino quando fa la rota, to look like a strutting turkey, denoting a strutter.

Pavone, Pavona, Paone, Paonetti, Paonessa,[17] peacock and peahen, are universally with proud or conceited beings. From the noun pavone comes the verb pavoneggiare, to strut. In Romagnuolo the word pavoncen (pavoncino) serves to indicate a dandy. If religious symbolism has had a role in the diffusion of peacock, and this it

---

[11] In Sicilian an oca is a person camouflaged as a goose during Carnival celebrations, which suggests that some other bird names may have a like origin. (See G. Pitrè, "Supplemento ai Dizionari Siciliani." *Studi Glottologici Italiani,* VII, 1928.

[12] We may be dealing here with possible anatomical names from occhio, eye.

[13] Paparini, etc., could be taken as derivatives of Papo from Giacomo. If, however, the source be botanical Pavarini would mean chickweed (Istria) and possibly poppy.

[14] Both Oca, Tacchi and Tacchini could descend from the Germanic font names Okka and Tacco (E. Förstemann, *Altdeutsches Namenbuch,* Erster Band. Personnennamen. 2d ed. Bonn, 1900, 1174, 391. The syncopated forms of Talacco, Albertacco and other names in -co might also yield Tacco, and, by the addition of a diminutive, Tacchino. Tacchin in Milanese is a miser. Cf. French taquin.

[15] For Pito, Pitoni cf. AgaPITO, AgaPITONE. Pitta is a chicken in Milanese and pita is a chicken-call in Bergamascan. In Parmigiano a piton is a pigeon and a Milanese pitton is a beggar. Bolla and Billa are Aretino and Sienese names for this fowl, but the surnames Bolli and Billi should be referable to JacoBOLLO, JacoBILLO and Billo, pet name for Camillo.

[16] The Valle Anzasca word ok meaning eccentric, extravagant, might better be connected with allocco, owl, than oca, geese.

[17] Paone can be explained as a derivative of Genoese Gaspao, GasPAONE. Cf. also Paonessa, wrasse, a fish.

surely has, these terms stand for resurrection, a colorful synonym of Renato, René.

Cigno, de Cigna, Lo Cigno, de Zigno, Signa, Cignoni, Zignoni, Zignoli, Cignolini, Cignozzi, Cignarella [18] the translation of which is swan, may apply to a sweet singer,[19] or, perhaps, like goose to long necked people.

Different words denoting dove furnish us with some fairly common surnames—Colombo, Colombini, Colummella, Piccioni, Pizzoni,[20] (Bolognese and Milanese), Pittoni [21] (Parmigiano), Tortora, Tortorella, Palumbo, Palombi, Palummo [22] (if Southern Italian), ring pigeon Fassa [23] (also Southern Italian), wild dove Tironi [24] (if related to Sicilian tiruni). The Latin name for a ring pigeon, torquatus, exists as a font name and cognomen, Torquato, Torquati. These terms signify innocence, inexperience, hence a child. However, in the Tarantino dialect a piccione is a simpleton. The frequency of Colombo may be explained by the fact that it is the symbol of the Holy Spirit, that it is given in honor of the celebrated St. Colomba, and that it is an expression of endearment—love, darling. Colombini, should it hail from the Pavese section, sometimes points to a foundling.

The bird that has a European-wide reputation for garrulousness is the magpie giving in Italian such eke-name surnames as Gazza, Gazzola, Gazzelli, Gazzera, Gaggia,[25] Pica, Taccola,[26] and, though

[18] The aphetic forms of Licinio, Iginio, Virginio, Patrocinio, etc., have swelled the popularity of Cigno and its derivatives. Zignon in Romagnuolo means a tuft of hair or curl. See Anatomical Names.

[19] This song bird belief about the swan is due to the acceptance of Greek and Latin tradition rather than observation. In his *Gli Animali nelle Opere di Virgilio*. Pisa, 1896, p. 10, F. Neri writes: "Il canto dei cigni celebrato da tutti i poeti è pura finzione, emettendo anzi quest'animale un suono sgradevolissimo." i.e. "The Swan song celebrated by all the poets is pure fiction, since this animal emits a very disagreeable sound."

[20] Pizzoni and possibly Piccioni can likewise be easily explained through Opizzo, Opizzone.

[21] Pittoni like Pito, Pitoni may stem from Agapito. See Note 15.

[22] Offering rather feeble competition is the name for a dog or toad fish.

[23] It is possible that Fassa may derive from a dialectical pet form of Bonifazio.

[24] But a tirune in Calabrese is a dormouse.

[25] Some of these names can be traced back to a St. Gaggio (cf. S. Gaggio, a place name near Florence), gaggio, acacia, gaggia, variant of gaccia, a Calabrese word for axe, and gazzella, gazelle. Gazzolo, Gazzelli may be obtained from any name in -go or -co, ArriGAZZOLO, etc.

[26] Pica as well as Taccola could be font names of Germanic origin, but the latter may also signify a chick-pea if Tuscan and burdock if Lombard.

debatable, perhaps some Marzoli,[27] Checa, Cecca and Cajazzo and Cola.[28] The Calabrese saying gridare cumu na pica, to scream like a magpie, makes it plain that the term can be applied to a person with a raucous or strident voice. While in Neapolitan a cajazza is a chatterer, in Vastese a cajasse is a lazy fellow, and in Calabrese a cajazzo is a simpleton. We may add here that the famous name, Malpighi, has the possible meaning of a malicious gossip. Another member of the magpie family is Scaccianoce, nuthatch.

The names of the jackdaw—Cornacchia, Cornacchione, Cornaggia, Gracchi,[29] Gracalone (Central and Southern Italian), Ciaula, Ciavola, Ciola,[30] Ianara, Iannariello, Iannarone[31] (Southern Italian) are also synonymous with a babbler. The bird likewise refers to an antipathetic ill-boding person, while two derivatives gracchiamento, cackling, and gracchiare, cackle, indicate that the ornithological name is also used for grumblers. Pare una cornacchia, he looks (acts) like a daw, is said of a chatterbox with a strident voice. The raven surnames on the other hand, are apt to relate to raven-haired or dark-complexioned or voracious individuals—Corvi, Cuorvo, Corbo, Corbino, Corbizzi, Crovelli, Crobu (Sardinian), Coropi, Corobi[32] (Calabro-Arabic). Because they are customarily dressed in black the raven epithet is applied to priests, but corvo, corvaccio, etc., may denote any person similarly dressed. Readers of Manzoni's *Promessi Sposi* will recall that a black robed notary was greeted by the exclamation "Uh, corvaccio! (Chapter XV). Another blackbird, the merle, supplies Merlo, a few of the Merlinos,[33] Merula, Mierula (Tarantino and Calabrese), and Mirra[34] (Sicilian). The merle sobriquet usually points to shrewd persons, but in Milanese and Piacentino it alludes to a simpleton, in Sicilian to a faint-hearted person (cf. tremari comu un merru, to tremble like a merle) and

---

[27] Cf. the font name Marzolo from marzo, born in March.

[28] Ornithological proof of the origin of these names is weakened by the fact that Checa and Cecca are well known pet forms for Francesca, while Cola and Cajazzo are pet forms of Nicola and Nicolaio, and possibly Genoese MaCAIO (= Maccario), ZacCAIA (=Zaccaria).

[29] Gracchi could come in as a namesake of the famous Roman, Gracchus.

[30] In Calabrese a ciola is a lean chicken and by extension a thin woman. But consider LuCI-OLA, FranCI-OLA.

[31] Iannara (ghiandaia) also has the obvious meaning of an oak woods, or acorn gatherer. Ianara, which in the dialect of Sannio means a witch, must also be taken into account. Also cf. Gennaro and Gianni.

[32] Both Coropi and Corobi are cited by G. Rohlfs in his *Dizionario Dialettale delle Tre Calabrie*, Milano, 1939, p. 26, vol. III.

[33] Merlo can be of Germanic origin, cf. E. Förstemann, *op. cit.* 1102. A goodly number of the Merlinos probably ultimately owe their names to Merlin, the great magician of the Knights of the Round Table.

[34] Another meaning of mirra, is myrrh.

again in Milanese to a long-winded annoying singer (cf. canta come on merlo, he sings like a merle).

Shrewdness is also implied in the names that come from sparrow —Passaro, Passeri, Passarella, Passarini, Passerone, and Passone, Alpine sparrow. One variety is called by the Sicilians passaru sbirru, sly sparrow. As suggested by the Calabrese phrase passaru de campanaru, belfry sparrow, the word can also mean a brazen person, while the phrase cammina come un passaro, he walks like a sparrow indicates that the appellation can be applied to an habitually fast walker. Sobrio come un passaro, as temperate as a sparrow, implies an abstemious individual. The passero solitario is, incidentally, not a sparrow but a thrush. It is used to describe hermit-like human beings. The hedge sparrow, Straparola, name of a famous Renaissance story teller (which may be extinct)[35] should be counted among the singing birds.

We have already mentioned some ornithological names for dullards. Others from this group alluding to the same frailty include the horned owl, Assioli, Sioli,[36] Allocchi, Locchi,[37] (Central and Northern Italian), Ruffolo,[38] Buffa, Buffetti, Buffoni [39] (all four Romano), Facciune and Faccione [40] (Southern Italian), Scuto [41] (Calabrese). The screech owl—Civetta—has given rise to the verb civettare, to flirt. The Calabrese terms for this species, Piula, Pioli,[42] Cuccovillo, may allude to the same characteristic. Sicilians call this bird cuccuni, and the Friulani zus, giving rise, perhaps, to the last

---

[35] One wonders, however, if the current surname Parola, is not a survivor.

[36] If from the Emilia region both Assioli and Sioli point to a restless child, and back of it to a word meaning wasp. See Bertoni, "Per la Storia del Dialetto di Modena." *Archivio Glottologico Italiano*, XVII, 1910-13, 368. However, the existence of the surname DioniSIOLI clearly demonstrates that Dionisio must be regarded as a source.

[37] The Neapolitan word locco, a borrowing from the Spanish loco, also means stupid. In Romagnuolo Locca is Luca as well as Lucca.

[38] The Ruffolos of the Middle Ages may, however, hark back to the Germanic font name Roffuli. See B. Bianchi, "La Declinazione nei Nomi di Luogo nella Toscana." *Archivio Glottologico Italiano*, X, 1886-88, 363. Boccaccio readers will recall Landolfo Ruffolo in *Decameron, Giornata* seconda, IV. Ruffolo, Ruffalo, is a common Calabrese name today. Lorenzo Ruffolo held a high position under Charles of Anjou. He was maestro portolano e procuratore e maestro delle saline di Puglia. See C. Minieri-Ricci, "Memorie della Guerra di Sicilia negli Anni 1282, 1283, 1284." *Archivio Storico per le Provincie Napoletane*, I, 1876, 91, 276.

[39] For buffa compare homographs meaning clown, toad, hood. Another explanation of Buffoni is, obviously, buffoon.

[40] Facciune and Faccione are literally chubby faced. Both could, moreover, be derived from Bonifacio.

[41] Scuto can also be a shield, scudo.

[42] For other meanings of piolo see Botanical Names.

names Cocconi,[43] Zuz, Zuzzi.[44] There is hardly any need of adding that the owl is known to be a bird of ill-omen and that it is connected with unsociable people. It is strange that the commonest of owl terms, gufo, should be extremely rare or non-existent as a surname.

More boobies are indicated by the curlew, Chiurlo, Zurlo, Turlini and Turletti [45] (if from Tarantino turlio), and perhaps Falcinelli,[46] Milanese for green curlew; by the seagull—Gabbiani, Gabiani, Caggiani (Vastese), Gavini [47] (Neapolitan), Pivotto [48] (Piveronese dialect in Piedmont). In Latinized form we find the word seagull in the name of the Renaissance Petrus Alcyonis. Of the Bubola,[49] peewit, a relative of the gull, the Bergamascans say: ignorant come öna böba, as ignorant as a peewit. Pappagallo, Pappalallo, parrot, is a loon, sometimes a person with a hooked nose and at other times a noisy fellow.[50] Stornello, Storni, starling, also point to nincompoops, at least if they come through Marchigiano or Milanese.[51] The cuckoo, too, is a blockhead and may account for some of the Cucchi, Cuccoli, Cucchetti.[52] Inasmuch as follaca, Neapolitan for coot, Fasani, Fasanella, Faggiani,[53] pheasant, if or Romagnuolo origin, and Sicilian Pitarro, from pitarra, prairie hen, refer to ignoramuses like the above, and inasmuch as the English woodcock, snipe, coot and dotterel have the same connotation, it is perhaps not too far-fetched to assume that most of the other gallinaceous and anatinae bird-terms likewise point to dolts. Among these are Ganga,[54] prairie hen; Pantana, Arceri (Southern Italian); Cedrone,[55]

[43] If Central Italian Cocconi may derive from the augmentative of cucco, cocco, favorite, or hoop-shaped peak. See B. Bianchi, op. cit. 310n.

[44] So listed under Giorgio by A. Bongioanni, Nomi e Cognomi, Torino, 1928.

[45] However, Milanese Turlini, Turletti would derive their names from turlo, a lark.

[46] In Tuscan a falcinello is identified as a speckled magpie.

[47] A Parmigiano gabian is a rustic. Gavini, on the other hand, could easily be a font name, Gavino, from St. Gavina. Cf. also the chivalric name Gawain.

[48] There is an obsolete term, pivo, meaning dandy.

[49] This could be a font name of Germanic origin, cf. E. Förstemann, op. cit. 317-18.

[50] Pappagallata in Calabrese signifies bustle, uproar.

[51] But if Bolognese a sturnel means eccentric, roguish, while a storno is usually a black and white horse. In Milanese storno is also a term for deaf.

[52] See Note 43. A cucchetto is also a primrose.

[53] Sometimes faggiano is a pheasantry.

[54] Ganga is tooth and cheek is Calabrese, but cf. the Germanic Kanka, E. Förstemann, op. cit. 597.

[55] Cedrone can mean cedar colored, large cedar, and orange if a variant of cetrone (Genoese). There is a slight chance that Lombard Iozzi may go back to the term for woodgrouse. Nevertheless, cf. Pio, Piozzo, Olimpio, OlimPIOZZO, Mario, MarIOZZO.

black cock grouse; Pernice, Francolino, Marenga,[56] Starni, Sterni, Sternini (Romagnuolo), partridge; the shoveler Cucchiarone [57] (Southern Italian), Palozzi,[58] (Bolognese), Spatula, Spatola [59] (Piedmontese(?)), Foffano (Venetian); sandpiper Ballota [60] (Piedmontese balota); the plover Pettinero, Pettinegro, Mallardi (Irpinese), Capoverde,[61] Testaverde; the garrot Garroti [62] (Piedmontese) and Quattrocchi;[63] the common teal possibly Marzolino [64] (if Neapolitan); the grebe La Morticella [65] (Neapolitan for la morte riale); wild ducks Ronca, Ronga, Ronchetti [66] (Tuscan-Vecchiana) and Rochetti [67] (Mantuan). Figurative interpretations are, however, variable. For example, a partridge can betoken a fleshy person (cf. grasso come una pernice), while the term coot is applied in Tuscan to an individual who lives an obscure, peaceful life, a meaning which may be shared by Folegatti (Milanese), Pulega (Sardinian). Marangone, diver, sometimes identified as a wild crow, has apparently never been grouped with the clodpated birds. The expression has been transferred to mean a human diver (palombaro), but in Sicilian it also means a jack of all trades.[68] Another word for a bird-diver is Venetian Capriola.[69] Neither is the quail, Quaglia, Quaglino, Quagliotto, to be included in this dullard grouping. It is generally thought to be an amorous bird. In Sicilian, Neapolitan

---

[56] The immediate relationship between Franco and Francolino should be clear. For Marenga, cf. Marengo, Northern Italian place name.

[57] Literally, large spoon, ladle.

[58] May, after all, be nothing more than a variant of Paolozzo.

[59] Spatula, Spadula, is also a botanical term meaning amaryllis.

[60] Fofano is a pet form of Cristofano thus gaining precedence as the source of Foffano. In Venetian fofano is a misshapen man. Another meaning of balota in Piedmontese is dotard.

[61] In Abruzzese capeverde means a learned or high ranking monk and, by extension, any learned person. We could also obtain Capoverde from green cape, a place name.

[62] There is a possibility of arriving at Garroti through UnGAROTTO.

[63] The term is also applied to bespectacled individuals. A quattrocchi is also a fish, skate or ray.

[64] Related to the word marzo, March.

[65] A rare name which can also be associated with a young deceased female member of a family.

[66] Ronca usually has the meaning of bill hook.

[67] Cf. rocchetto, reel, spool, and rocchetta, little cliff.

[68] However, marangone also means carpenter, specifically a cartwright. In Parmigiano it is a sand bank.

[69] Cf. capriola, roe, caper. Still another aquatic bird which seems to have furnished a last name is Trentacoste, literally, thirty ribs.

and Calabrese it denotes a stout but comely young woman, but any stout person could be so labelled if we think of the saying: grasso come una quaglia, as fat as a quail. In the land of music and of song it is natural to find song birds conspicuously represented among the surnames. One of the most popular is the lark the species of which are not always clearly distinguished. Allodola and calandra are the two most generally employed terms, contributing with their related forms Allodoli, Allodi,[70] Lodolini, Calandra, Calandrella, Calandrino.[71] In the dialect of Pragelato in Piedmont, we find ulivete connected with French alouette, and this may account for at least a few of the Ulivetti and Olivetti.[72] The Bolognesi accept their calandra as a prattler and not as a singer. Other apparently general lark names are Corridore,[73] and Cucciardo, Gucciardo,[74] from the Naples-Avellino section where the term is applied to a short plump woman. More specifically identified are the meadow lark, Pispoli, (metaphorically also a pretty girl, artful woman), the woodlark Fucetola, Ficedola (Neapolitan fecetola, focetola), Canevello [75] (Friulano-Trentino), Favero (if from Capodistria or vicinity), and Beccafigo, fig-pecker, a name for a subspecies, with its probable variants Mangiafico, Magnafico, Pappafico [76] and the Veronese Figarola.[77] The phrases grasso come un beccafico, and Neapolitan chiatto chiatto com'è una facetola, as plump as a figpecker, tell us that the singing qualities of this bird are secondary to its chubbiness. We also have several probable names taken from the willow lark—Ciarla, Ciarlone [78]

[70] The font name Alodia (cf. St. Alodia) must be reckoned as a source of Allodi.

[71] In Southern Italian a calandrella is also a sandal, in Ferrarese one whose health has been ruined, in the dialect of Velletri a firefly. Calandrino may mean stupid, a name diffused through the medium of a famous Boccaccio story—*Decameron*, Giornata ottava III.

[72] No need, of course, to point out the obvious connection of these words with olive.

[73] Strong claimants are corridore, scout and corridore courser.

[74] In the dialect of Castro de'Volsci the word means stubborn coming from coccia, head.

[75] In the Trentino persons with light blond hair are called canevella, a word meaning hemp.

[76] In Teramano a pappafiche is a very fat, chubby-faced man. Another word for figpecker is bigione perhaps supplying on occasion the last name Bigioni. But compare bigio, grey, and Bigio, Milanese for Luigi.

[77] Cf. figaro, fig seller, grower, fig patch.

[78] In competition with the dialect word for Carlo, and the words for babble, babbler.

(Genoese). Other lark names are Milanese Turlini, Turletti, terms that we have already found linked with the Tarantino curlew. The nightingale furnishes us with our Usignuolo, Rosignuoli, Lisignoli, and Capinera,[79] Capofusco, names for a mock nightingale. The thrush supplies us with song thrushes—Tordo, Tordella, Beccaluva (literally, grape-pecker), and possibly Bottacci, Bottazzi [80] (both Florentine); blackbird thrushes (Malvizzo, Marvizzo; lesser rock thrushes Caroselli [81] and Carossini (should both be Lombard), Fogaroli (Neapolitan); redwing thrushes Grivetta (Piedmontese); and grunling Alpiggiano.[82] The phrase grasso (rotondo) come un tordo, as fat (round) as a thrush, is an everyday term of comparison. Possibly through the vogue of Bertoldo in the popular *Bertoldo, Bertoldino e Cacasenno* story, tordo has acquired the meaning of stupid in Calabrese.[83] On the other hand, a marvizzune is, in the same dialect, a shrewd fellow. The thrush is frequently mentioned in the novels of Grazia Deledda with the implication that in Sardinian it is a symbol of timidity.

Finch names are both numerous and varied—Fringuello, Firringuelle, Firrincieli, Firincillo, Frincillo, Froncillo, Fringello, Fingello, Frungello, Frungillo, Frangili, Franzelini (?), Francolino [84] (if of Bormese and Bergamascan origin), Ponzone, Pinzone,[85] Parra (Graeco-Calabrese); chaffinch; Ciofoletti,[86] Frosone (Tuscan frusone), Frusulone, Frusolono (Neapolitan), Piovana [87] (Piedmontese), bullfinch; Lucherini, Lucarini,[88] Lugaro (Vicentino), bramble finch; Frisone [89] (Venetian, Parmigiano and Bolognese), Spezza-

---

[79] Literally, black head.

[80] Cf. bottaccio, flagon, botta, barrel, toad, gudgeon (Piedmontese) and Bottazzo, Bottaccio not impossible from JacoBOTTAZZO, JacoBOTTACCIO.

[81] Homonyms are a kind of fennel, a tournament, a money box (Calabrese). Caroselli could also come from carosa, carriage, and from caroso, a clipped head. Carossi might even be a variant form of caroso.

[82] Literally, inhabitant of the Alps.

[83] The name Tordo in this case would come from BerTORDO = Bertoldo. In Neapolitan, however, a turdo (from turbidus) is an austere, taciturn person.

[84] See Note 56.

[85] With Ponzone cf. the give name Ponzio. Pinzone could be Spanish.

[86] Ciofoletto is a popular form of Cristofoletto.

[87] Usually piovano means rector, parson. Piovana, also Piedmontese, can mean salamander.

[88] Some Lucherini, Lucarini must come from Luca plus diminutive -arino, -erino.

[89] One of the local pet names for Federico is Friso, hence Frisone. See A. Bongioanni, *Nomi e Cognomi* . . . Torino, 1928. Cf. Lombard and Canavese Fris = Federico. Frisone is also Frisian and draft horse.

ferro [90] (Pugliese), hawfinch; Zigolo,[91] Verdone, Verdune (Sicilian), Verdelli, Cirrinciò, Cirrincione, Cirringione, Cirlingione (all four Sicilian), Calenzuolo, Maggiolino [92] (Calabrese), greenfinch; Cardello, Cardillo, Cardellino, Gardella, Gardellini [93] (Udinese), Calderini (Tuscan), Luvara (Neapolitan), and perhaps Cantilena [94] (Umbrian), gold finch. Barbizzoli (Cuneo barbiza) is a black finch. The exotic canary which has given the infrequent Canario,[95] belongs to the finch family. So does Cardinale (cardinal bird), even though it is true that the ecclesiastical homograph should be regarded as a much more common source of the name. Aside from the generally accepted connotation of canorousness figurative meanings for finch differ. In Calabrese a chaffinch is a loiterer and in the dialect of Castro de'Volsci a thin, lively person. The existence of the verb sfringuellare, to babble, proves that like some other birds finch terms are used as synonyms for a chatterer or backbiter. Frusone is one of the expressions for a flirt. Relative to Cardello we have the Abruzzese saying sta cóme nu cardille, he is as healthy as a finch. Still other finch names are Migliarini, Miglierini,[96] and perhaps an occasional Montanelli (Lombard) and Machetti [97] (Bresciano), mountain finch; Crocioni [98] (Romano), common cross-bill; and possibly a few of the terms denoting a common

[90] Literally, breakiron. Could be a name applied to a bully.

[91] If from Parmigiano, Zigolo may be related to the word for onion. The three terms that follow could be traced to Germanic Verdo, (cf. Förstemann, op. cit. 1558) and to Berto. In Genoese a verdone is a blue shark.

[92] The font name Maggio (also meaning May) is a more likely source of the surname. In Tuscan-Veronese a maggiolino is a black beetle. We note in passing that Zei if Bergamascan may have some connection with green finch.

[93] A large number of font names in -cardo or -gardo (e.g. Riccardo, Edgardo) can develop into Cardello, etc. In Calabrese cardello is a grass, while cardiddu in Sicilian is a thorn thistle.

[94] Literally, sing-song, tiresome music.

[95] If Northern Italian, Canario could be from canario, i.e. cannaio, cane brake. In Tuscan it may refer to ribbon grass. On the other hand, a Calabrese canariu is a greedy person, a word which seems to be connected with cannaruto, greedy.

[96] Migliarini, Miglierini can be supplied through Emilio, or migliaro, millet patch.

[97] Montanelli is more logically linked with a highlander or the Saint, St. Montanus. For Machetti there are at least two other choices, macchia, thicket, and Germanic Macho (see Förstemann, op. cit. 1067).

[98] The relation between Crocione and croce, cross, is evident.

bunting—Ortolano, Cicerone (Neapolitan), Petazzo, Petasso [99] (both Venetian). Incidentally, the most common bird surname in both England and Germany is Finch, Fink.

Among the other song birds are the oriole represented by Rigogolo, Gogolo (Tuscan-Valdichiana), Vollaro, Volari, Galano [100] (Calabrese-Reggio Calabria), Ajolo [101] (Sicilian), Garbi, Garbino, Garbasso [102] (all Piedmontese). For the first of these names we have the set phrase giallo come il rigogolo, as yellow (pale) as an oriole.

The wren, often indicating a very small person or child, is represented by Regolo,[103] Rigillo (Calabrese rijillu). The creeper, a relative of the wren, gives the name Rampichini.[104] The linnet finds possible representation in Fanelli,[105] Montanelli [106] (Tuscan); the titmouse in Cinciarello, Capinera,[106] Parazzoli (Cremonese), Parussa, Parussolo, Parusolin [107] (Piedmontese), Parrella (Neapolitan), Parrillo [108] (Calabrese), and Codilunghi, Colunga,[109] long tailed titmouse; the wagtail in Boarini,[110] Civinini (Veronese), Rampinelli

---

[99] These bunting terms are obviously much weaker as surnominal sources than ortolano, gardener, Cicerone, dialectical for cicero, chickpea, Petazzo, Petasso, the pet forms of Benedetto, Elizabetta, and the word for trumpeter used in the Alto Adige. Cicerone, meaning tourist guide, is a dubious competitor in which sense it appears to have been introduced by Addison during the early part of the Eighteenth Century.

[100] Cf. galana, Venetian and Mirandolese for tortoise.

[101] But note aio, hence aiolo, a word for tutor.

[102] The names Garbi, etc., may also be or Germanic origin. Cf. Förstemann, op. cit. 600.

[103] Cf. the famous Latin name Regulus. Monacelli (little monk) is, if Sicilian, to be related to the word the islanders use for wren.

[104] Rampichino is often used as an expression for a restless child. Cf. the verb arrampicare, to climb.

[105] The font names Tofano, Cristofano, etc., have prior claims as surname sources. In Bergamascan a fanel is a nit-wit or fickle person; in Pavese a fanell a cunning and astute man.

[106] See Note 97.

[106] Literally, black head, black cap.

[107] Suggested by Bongioanni, op. cit. as names competing with Gaspare.

[108] Both Parrella and Parrillo could easily come from the dialectical form of Gaspare, Gasparro, hence Parrello, Parrillo. The Calabrese saying: Parca le cantau la parrilla, it appears that the titmouse has sung to him, refers to a person who is rich and fortunate.

[109] In his list of Florentines given by Pierfrancesco Giovanni in Sogno dell' Annebbiato is an Alessandro Codilunghi. Quoted by G. Frizzi in his Dizionario dei Frizzetti Fiorentini. Città di Castello, 1890, sub voce carnesecca.

[110] Boarini may allude to a bull herder or AlBOARO, a first name.

(Anconitano), Parrinello [111] (Sicilian), and Mazzacane, Massacane [112] (Piedmontese). The saying vispo come una quaglia codrettola, as lively as a water wagtail, explains that this bird term is applied to lively persons. Robin names have been assumed by Pettirosso,[113] Piccitto, Pincetti (both Milanese) and possibly the Romano Becci, Beccerini,[114] the Bassanese Betussi,[115] the Veronese Pitaro, the Venetian Pittarello [116] and the Bergamascan Piccialli (cf. picial).

Avire le gamme quantu nu ruvazzu, to have legs like a robin, is the Calabrese way of describing a spindly legged person, while the Bergamascan term just cited is an expression employed for a child. We have, finally, among the singing birds the stone chat, Cobianchi and Favularo.

Among the other figurative bird names are those for swallow—Rondone, Rondanina, Rondinelli, Rondinetti, Arondello, Rondello, Bargo and Bargoni (Piedmontese(?)). There is a common simile, grasso come un rondone, as fat as a swallow, pointing to a plump individual, but in the dialect of Ancona a rondone, coming from another source, is a dandy and in Calabrese a vagabond. Cf. English rounder. A noble family from Bologna is called Celidonii a Latin name for swallow.[117] Many of our readers know, incidentally, that the swallow has given rise to the most extensive literature that popular zoology can boast of. From ancient times to our own it has been the bearer of good news, the messenger of love and the horoscope for change of weather.

The woodpecker has the reputation of being a sneak, a meddler or a parasite as can be seen in the metaphorical meanings of Forabosco, and the Sicilian Pizzaferro, Pizzuferro. The same figure probably also applies to Picchi, Pighi, Pighetti, Pigotto, Pighini,[118] Pigoncelli, Pigozzo, Pigosso, Piccone, Picone, Pecci, Peccino [119] (the

[111] Parrinello is a poor competitior of parrino, priest, godfather. Another poor competitor, Umbrian Pastorella, also signifies wagtail.

[112] Homonyms are dog-killer, a stone or sluggard in Calabrese, a building stone and mason in Genoese.

[113] Literally, red breast.

[114] As the font name Opizzo, Obizzo re-appears in Lombard as Opessi, Obessi, Opezzi, Besso it is likely that Becci and Beccerini can be referred to this Lombard source. But compare peccia, chicken, peccio roman word for woodpecker, and peccio, paunch.

[115] More convincing claimants are Benedetto, Elisabetta.

[116] Another interpretation would be pittaro, pittarello, fritter seller.

[117] It is unlikely that the Albanian Sicilian Rondone has any ornithological connection.

[118] Some of these names can likewise derive from pica, magpie. But cf. Germanic Bicco, Picco, Förstemann, op. cit. 302. Pigott in Milanese is a rag doll.

[119] See Note 114.

last two Romano) and to Capitorto, Cavatorto,[120] wry-neck (which belongs to the same genus.) However, in Valsugana a pigozzo is an ignoramus. Individuals with long legs or long necks could easily be nicknamed after birds possessing one or both of these features. Some of them are the snipe, Beccadelli (Lombard), Falciglione (Tuscan), Pizzardo (Romano), Pizzicaro and Vizzicaro (Bolognese and Mantuan); the crane, La Grua, a rare name; the stork Cicogna,[121] Cicognini; the ostrich, Struzzo;[122] the heron, Arione [123] (= airone), Garzi, Garzoli, Carzolio, Scarzella, Scarsella [124] (both Piedmontese(?)), and the bittern, allied to the heron, which in Lombard is Fusella. As in English, let it be noted, that the various words for snipe can denote simplicity. With reference to the heron we know that it was used as a symbol of baseness. LaCurne de Saint Palaye in his *Flight of the Heron*, 1781, tells us that the exiled Robert d'Artois in trying to arouse Edward III against France presented him with a roasted heron on a silver platter exclaiming: "I offer the basest of birds to the legitimate heir of the crown of France, which he will never touch on account of his baseness." This bitter reproach so stirred Edward that it marked the beginning of the bloody One Hundred Years' War (1137).[125] Despite these possibilities, however, it is just as likely that any individual wearing an aigrette as a headdress might be called a heron.

The pellican feeding its young was taken as the symbol of Christ. Referring to John the Evangelist Dante writes in *Paradiso* XXV, 112-13:

> This man is he who lay upon the breast
> Of our pellican.[126]

The Italian Pellicano, Pallacano may, therefore, be a variant of such familiar names as Salvatore, Nazzareno, Emanuele, Agnello.

The fabled Phenix, Fenice,[127] is the symbol of Immortality. The

---

[120] A capitorto may actually have been a wry-necked person, or, figuratively, a hypocrite. Another wry-neck surname, Torcicollo, may or may not have anything to do with the bird.

[121] Cf. the sayings ha il collo lungo come la cicogna, come la grua, his neck is as long as a stork's, as a crane's.

[122] The Milanese say: deventà magher come on struzz, to become as lean as an ostrich. We could obtain Struzzo through CaSToRUZZO.

[123] Arione from IlARIONE is a more convincing source.

[124] The word for purse is scarsella.

[125] See G. Cairo, *Dizionario Ragionato dei Simboli*, Milano, Hoepli, n.d. p. 8.

[126] Cf. the original Italian
> Questi è colui che giacque sopra'l petto
> Del nostro pellicano . . .

[127] There is a small chance that as a spot name Fenice can be at times connected with fenice (Tuscan), reed bent grass.

word was also one of the commonplaces of Petrarchistic poetry, meaning a divinely beautiful and virtuous woman. It likewise refers to any extraordinary person.

Grifo, Grifone,[128] vulture, need no comment on their figurative significance. Another source of the name not at all connected with the bird is the Germanic given name Grifo.

The figurative meanings of hawk have already been taken up. In addition to Falcone and to Falco [129] and derivatives there are Girifalco,[130] Grifalcon, gerfalcon, Storino (unless it comes from CaSTORINO, Ristoro, Pastore), expressions for shrewd persons, Sparviere, Sproviere, Cestariello [131] (Neapolitan), Ieraci, Ciraci [132] (Calabrese), terms for sparrow-hawk betokening swiftness, as seen in a word sparvierato, as light and nimble as a hawk, or boldness, as evident in uomo sparvierato. Other kinds of hawks are the kite or buzzard, Nibbio, Nigliazzo, Adorno (if Calabrese), Buzzacca, Buzzacarini (cf. bozzago). Both in English and in Italian the word buzzard is applied to a dunce. The Pojani, too, point to a buzzard, which in the Piacentino dialect means a vagabond and in Metaurense a busybody.[133]

Last but not least is the eagle—Aquila, Aguglia, Agoli (Bergamascan), popular as a heraldic device and as a symbol of majesty. In the Calabrese an aquila is a beautiful woman of majestic bearing. The word also means a genius and a sharp sighted person (cf. occhi d'aquila, eagle eyes). Like Colomba it has been frequently given as a baptismal name. As we also have an aquila imperiale and an aquila reale, imperial, royal eagle, there is a remote chance that some of the Imperiali and Reali can trace their origin to this bird.

For a few bird names no figurative meaning has as yet been found nor can it be given on a hypothetical basis, but this does not imply that it does not exist. One of them is the bee eater,

---

[128] Some of the Griffoni may be namesakes of Grifone, son of Oliviero, a hero in Boiardo's *Orlando Innamorato* and Ariosto's *Orlando Furioso*. The imaginary griffin contributes another source of the cognomen through the realm of heraldry.

[129] Falco may also be a survival of the Germanic name Falco (cf. Förstemann, *op. cit.* 495).

[130] Girifalco as a Sicilian name is supposed to derive from the Castello di Girifalco.

[131] Another candidate for the name is unquestionably cestariello, little basket maker.

[132] Cf. Jerace, Gerace, a town in Calabria from which most of these names very likely come.

[133] Cf. also Romagnuolo pujanè, to ramble, lounge. A. Prati in "Spiegazioni di Nomi di Luogo del Friuli," *Revue de Linguistique Romane*, XII, 1936, hints that Pojana (place name) may come from Slovenian poljana, a meadow in the midst of a woods.

Paroli,[134] Parruli (from Neapolitan aparulo); another the fly-catcher Moscardi (also from the Neapolitan); and the red tail, allied to the fly-catcher, Corirossi, Caros(s)ini [135] (Bresciano); and still another is the hoopoe Pipitone [136] (Sicilian), Faloppa, Faloppio [137] (Umbrian). The giving of bird names to persons is a universal practice which is probably as old as the human race. In Hebrew Zypporah means bird and Jonah dove. The Trojan Paris goes back to an Illyrian Voltuparis, Assoparis, a hawk. Other Greek names are Penelope, wild duck, Perdiccas, partridge, Corax, raven, Glaucon, owl, Pelea, ring dove, but they appear as exceptional rather than as representative. Had they been frequent Aristophanes would un-doubtedly have made much of them in his *Birds*, which he does not. The Romans enjoyed conferring bird names upon their fellow men such as Titus, dove, Gaius, magpie, Gallus, rooster, Graccus, Gracculus, daw, Passer, sparrow, Corvus, Corvinus, raven, Aquila, Falco, Merula, eagle, hawk, blackbird, all of which were used by well known families. In English we have Fowle, Bird, Pigeon, Py, Pyatt (magpie), Coote, Finch, Goldfinch, Bullfinch, Pyefinch, Gander, Goose, Gosling, Daw, Dove, Crowe, Rooke, Lark, Nightin-gale, Hawke, Heron, Stork, Nottage (nuthatch), Titmass, Pocock, Poe, Powe (peacock), Spark, Sparhawk, Grew (French Grue), Starling, Speight, Spick, Pick (dialect names for woodpecker), Dunnock and Pinnock (dialect names for sparrow), Hearnshaw,

---

[134] Cf. also Germanic Paro (Förstemann, *op. cit.* 246). Gasparo plus the diminutive -olo, and the Cremonese and Modenese words for kettle and bucket, parol.

[135] A caroso (Southern Italian caruso) is a person with a clipped head. In Northern Italian carosa means carozza, carriage. But cf. PasCAROSA.

[136] A stone figure used by children as a target is called by the Sicilians a pipituni di petri. It may, therefore, refer to someone who is a butt or scapegoat.

[137] Faloppa in Tuscan means an unfinished cocoon and a braggart.

For the dialectical names of birds much aid has been derived from N. Camusso, *Manuale del Cacciatore*, Milano, 1887 and from Jaberg-Jud, *Sprach und Sachatlas Italiens und der Südschweiz, III*. A few names have been drawn from R. Riegler, "Italienische Vogelnamen," in *Archivum Romanicum*, VI, 1922, 167-74, and G. Bonelli, "I Nomi degli Uccelli nei Dialetti Lombardi," *Studi Romanzi*, IX, 1902, 370-467. Others have been gathered from numerous dialectical dictionaries.

A few more real or deceptive ornithological place names some of which have been borrowed as surnames are Allodola (Lombardy), Anatrella (Terra di Lavoro), Aquila (Abruzzi), Cajazzo (Campania), Cigno (Emilia), Cignoni (Cremona), Francolini (Tuscany), Frosolone (Molise), Gallo (Emilia, Pied-mont, Salerno), Gallodoro (Sicilian), Gazzola (Emilia), Malvizza (Irpino), Paparo (Messina), Tacchini (Novara), Taccola (Marche), Uccelli (Novara), Usignolo (Como). A. Amati, *op. cit.* and the *Guida Postelegrafonica*, New York, 1940, will undoubtedly supply more examples.

Wren, etc. The Germans possess Schwan, swan, Ente, duck, Gans, Gauss (low German), goose, Schneegans, white goose, Wildegans, wild goose, Adler, eagle, Tarbe, dove, Eule, owl, Fichter, cross bill, Krähe, crow, Rabe, raven, Amsel, blackbird, Sperling, sparrow, Strauss, ostrich, Drossel, thrush, Storck, stork, Fink, finch, Buchfink, chaffinch, Wachtel, quail, Schlundt, swallow, Rebhuhn, partridge, Hahn, rooster, Elster, magpie, Pfau, peacock, Specht, woodpecker, Nachtigall, nightingale, Habicht and Falke, hawk. Bird names exist in French and Spanish but apparently do not play a very heavy role in the onomasticon of these two languages. If it is true that there is a seemingly larger number of Italian bird names than can be found in other modern foreign languages this may in part be ascribed to the variety of the Italian climate which fluctuates from the frigidity of the Alps to the semi-torridness of Sicily, to the fertility of the Italian soil, to sharp differences in the geological configuration of the country, and to the fact that many of the dialects and sub-dialects have their own individual names for quite a number of the members of the bird world.

Chapter XI

ANIMAL NAMES

The chief sources of Italian animal surnames are the same as those for birds, namely nicknames, spot names, shop and inn signs, proprietorship. It should be clear that the last three of the main sources are always potentially present for most of the members of this series, though, as in the case of the birds, we shall here restrict our discussion to the nicknames and to a miscellaneous group of other possibilities. Heraldry, also an important source of animal surnames, is subject to the same observation.

Daily contact with domestic animals along with an intimate knowledge of their ways and habits have inevitably made their names favorites as sobriquets which later crystallized into cognomina.

The equines are represented in the Italian onomasticon by Cavallo, Cavallini, Cavallucci, Cavalletto, Cavalotti,[1] Cavallone, Cavallazzi, Callini (Bergamascan), Zaballi, Zavallone (Pragelato dialect in Piedmont); Equini, a Latinized form, Stallone,[2] stallion, Cortaldo,[3] a horse with clipped tail and ears, Mannarino, Mannerini[4] (Calabrese), Pagliaruolo[5] (Abruzzese), a horse born and raised in a stall; Bidetto, farm horse; Frisoni,[6] large draft horse; Baio, Baioni, bay; Storno,[7] black and white horse; Sauro,[8] sorrel; Rovani, roan;

---

[1] Perhaps some Cavallettos and Cavalottis go back to locust.

[2] If it be of Milanese origin stallone signifies cow stable.

[3] We suspect that Cortaldo is a variant of the font name Clotaldo.

[4] Besides horse mannarino can mean gelding, a sheepfold, an axe (Sicilian mannara). It can also refer to lupo mannaro, werewolf. But cf. Mannarino from Manna (St. Manna). Mannarino may also be a shortened version of Marianna plus suffix -arino.

[5] A pagliaruolo may also be a hosteler, a straw seller (Neapolitan), a deformed person (dialect of Sannio).

[6] A. Bongioanni, *Nomi e Cognomi* . . . Torino, 1928, gives Frisi as a derivative of Federico. If this is true Frisoni would also derive from the same. Otherwise, a frisone is a frisian, or, if Parmigiano (frison), a hawfinch. Frisians have been noted for their tall stature. Cf. Dante, *Inferno*, XXXI, 64-65. Hence, frisone might figuratively stand for a tall man.

[7] A storno is also a starling.

[8] Cf. St. Isauro, and sauro, horse mackerel.

Morello,[9] black horse; Leardi,[10] grey horse; Balzano,[11] a white footed horse; Barbaro,[12] barb; Corridori,[13] race horse; Destrieri, steed; Giumento, pack horse; Ronzini, Ronzone,[14] nag; Balassi,[15] (Bresciano), ugly, ill-tempered horse; Polledro, Poledrelli, Polera (Piedmontese), Stacca, Stacchetti, Stacchini,[16] (all Southern Italian), colt or mare; Mulo, Muletti, Mulas (Sardinian), Mulazzo,[17] mule; Asini, Bricchi, Bardotti,[18] Ciucci, Sommeri, Pucci [19] (if Agnonese), donkey.

A horse connotes a hard worker, in Calabrese (cavaddu) a restless person, but at times as in Sicilian and Reggio Calabrese, it can refer to an ignoramus, a meaning pretty generally implied by asino, ciucco, mulo, sommero. In the dialect of Teramo na femmene cavallone, a she horse, is a bold, talkative woman, and elsewhere in the Abruzzi parlare come nu cavalle, to talk like a horse, is to speak unrestrainedly and vivaciously. If Sicilian, asinu also means a boor. Mulo is often an illegitimate or a chronically stubborn person, Polledro and other words for colt refer to quick, adroit or eccentric people. In Neapolitan stacca applies to a young woman and in Calabrese to an attractive young woman.

The bovines supply us with Vacca, Vachetta, Vaccarella, Vaccariella, Baccaredda, Vaccarone,[20] Vaccini, the amusing Vaccarossa,

---

[9] Much more likely from the baptismal names Amore and Mauro, or moro, Moor, which, by extension means a dark-haired, dark-skinned individual. Cf. also morella, a designation for the bugle and heal-all plants.

[10] Leardi is traced to Adelardo by A. Bongioanni, *op. cit.*

[11] Balzano may be related to cervello balzano, a giddy-headed person.

[12] Barbaro is also barbarian, cruel and a masculine form of Barbara. A fleet-footed person might be called a barb. Cf. the phrase corre come un barbaro, he runs like a barb.

[13] Other meanings of corridore are runner, scout, a lark.

[14] The aphetic form of Oronzo plus suffixes can produce Ronzini, Ronzoni. One of the names for a hornet is ronzone.

[15] A balas in Bresciano is a rogue and in Pavese a niggard, while in Milanese a balas de badila is a digger. Balasso (balascio) is also a precious stone, ruby, and may even be derived from a dialectical form of palazzo, palace, mansion.

[16] It is possible to obtain Stacchetti and Stacchini from Eustachio.

[17] Mulazzo also stands for mulatto.

[18] On these two words and others from the asinine realm, see U. Rosa, Etimologie Asinine, Torino, 1879. Cf. Germanic Bricco from Germanic (E. Förstemann, *Altdeutsches Namebuch*. Erster Band. Personennamen. 2d ed. Bonn, 1900, 355) and the Parmigiano word for ram, bricch.

[19] The Agnonesi playfully apply the term pucce to children. However, most Puccis safely come from Jacopo, Giuseppe, Filippo.

[20] The relation of some of these words to vaccaro, cowherd, is of course, obvious. Vaccarella is also a Calabrese term for hawthorn, baccarel a Piacentino term for a club, while Vaccarone (Neapolitan), Vaccarella (Southern Italian) and Vachetta (Comasco-Veronese) mean bettle. Vaccaredda in Sicily (Butera) is a bird, martinaccio colorato.

terms for cow; Lo Bue, Bovio, Bovo, Bovetti, Bovelli, Bovone, Bovolini,[21] Bovicelli, Boasso, Boetti, bull or ox; del Toro, Tauro, Torello, bull; Bonasi (Tuscan), Trione (Tarantino), wild bull; Vitello, Vitellini, Boccini (Piedmontese), Bozzelli (Bresciano), Manzo,[22] Manzoli (Bolognese, Cremasco), Marucchi [23] (Ferrarese), Scottone [24] (Genoese), Veli, Belini (Piveronese dialect in Piedmont), Giovenco and Jenco, Gencarelli (Calabrese-Abruzzese), calf, heifer or bullock. The cow usually stands for corpulency, but may indicate laziness or slowness as implied in the Romagnuolo phrase fè la vaca, fare la vacca, to be a cow. The ox denotes fleshiness and in addition doltishness, and the bull, bigness and strength. The Bergamascan name for a lean cow is sterla, which may have produced the surname Sterlini, while an old ox in Calabrese is a mazzune, a slow-moving person, giving the surname to a few Mazzone, Mazzoni.[25] A manza (calf) may signify a young wench, a pretty lass, a meaning probably possessed by other calf words including vitello. In Abruzzese a vedellone (big calf) means a glutton or numbskull,[26] but in a certain section of the same province, Teramo, a vedellone is a tall, lean man. In Sicilian gridare comu un viteddu orfanu, to cry like a lonely calf, refers to one

[21] In Venetian a bovolino is a snail and in the Polesine a bovolo is a vortex or eddy.

[22] Manzo is also gentle, easy-going.

[23] Marucchi may come from the word for snail and with lesser frequency from the word for a jujube tree.

[24] Scottone may possibly come from Scotto, Scot, or Frascotto, Francescotto or Germanic Scot (Förstemann, op. cit. 1309). However, since the vogue of quite a few of the other bovine terms that have been mentioned has been reinforced by homographs from the patronymical field they may be discussed here as a group. Vacca, Bovo, Mazzoni, Bozzelli, Manzoni, Manzoli, del Toro, Torello, Vitello, Marucchi could be survival of Germanic names (see Förstemann, op. cit. 1487, 317, 1119, 330, 1094, 1467, 1563, 1102). Of these Mazzoni could also come from Dalmazzo, Giacomazzo, Genoese Mazzo from Maggio; Bozzelli from GiacoBOZZELLO, Torello from Ettore, Vittore, Salvatore, Amatore, and, along with Toro from Teodoro, and Cristoforo (Genoese). Baccini is a pet name for Bartolomeo or Genoese Baccio (Battista). Bocci is possibly a pet name from GiacoBOCCIO. Vitello may stem from Latin as well as Germanic tradition or from Vito or Agabito, Giovita, or Davitu (Calabrese for Davide), while Marucchi could derive from Aldemaro. As for Bovo there is little doubt that Bovo d'Antona, hero of a much read romance of chivalry had some influence in the diffusion of this name. Finally, there may be kinship between, Belini and Bello or IsaBELLA, IacoBELLO, etc.

[25] It is to be noted, too, that in the Como section a sterl is a calf or kid. But Sterlini is more logically connected with Ester, Esterlina. For Mazzone, cf. Note 24, the word for mullet and the word for club.

[26] Calf, veau in French and Kalb in German, also mean blockheads.

who weeps loudly. It is conceivable that if one's parents were nicknamed vacca or bove, etc., their children might facetiously be referred to as calves. Then, too, there is the Biblical fatted calf, but we are not sure that it can be connected with eke-name giving. The ovines give us Pecora, Pecorella, Pecorini, Pigorini, Piegora, Piecora, Bezza and Berini [27] (Milanese), Fea (Piedmontese), expressions for sheep; Agno, Agnello, Agnellini, lamb. Both imply innocence, timidity, stupidity. But aside from this there is no doubt that the Agnus Dei, Lamb of God, Symbol of Christ, has been a powerful incentive in giving Agno and its derivatives much of their currency. Names from ram are Montone,[28] Ariete, Arietti, Castrati, Bricchi, Bricchetti [29] (Parmigiano). Here, too, belong Bozzone [30] and Mannarino, Mannerini,[31] gelding. Like their relatives the rams belong to the category of simpletons. Cf. Montone.

The swine family offers Porci, Porcu, Porqueddu (Sardinian), Porcellotto, Porcellini, Purcelli,[32] Porcelletti, Maiale and della Scrofa,[33] meaning sow; Chirillo and Passature (both Calabrese), terms for little pigs. The figurative connotation of the animal is well known, e.g. gluttony, uncleanliness. Occasionally a snorer is designated by the name. Cf. Russa come un porco, he snores like a pig.[34]

Capra, Crapa, Cravetta, Cavaretta, Caproni, Caprino, Capretti, Crapulli, La Capruccia, Chiabra, Curci, Curcione, Corcione [35] (the three Abruzzese), Gullo (Calabrese), Bechi, Becchetti, Becchini,[36] Zappo (Castro de'Volsci), Lastrucci, Zoccoli [37] (Friulano zocul) are all surnames that go back to goat or kid, an animal that figura-

[27] Once again it is necessary to bring in a possible Germanic source—Bezo, Berin. See E. Förstemann, op. cit. 253-258.

[28] A large mound is a montone.

[29] See Note 18. Romagnuolo brichett is a one-edged sword. Brichet in Piedmontese is a match.

[30] Bozzone could conceivably come from Germanic Bozo (cf. Förstemann, op. cit. 331), GiacoBOZZONE, or Calabrese vozzune, a large goitre.

[31] See Note 4.

[32] Porci can be from Borci through Tiborcio (Tiburzio) while Porcellini, Purcelli may be namesakes of the famous Roman Porcelius.

[33] The name of a famous Paduan family also known as Scrovigni.

[34] The fairly common name Suini does not refer to pigs at all, but is very likely connected with the font name AnSUINO. Cf. also Friulano ssuin, squirrel.

[35] Cf. Curzio, Curtius.

[36] Bechi could be the Tuscan short form of Domenico or a word for earthworm, beco (also Tuscan). Becchino is a homograph signifying sexton, grave digger.

[37] Zoccolo could mean a mouse or rat in Calabrese, Lucanese, Tarantino, and, otherwise, a wooden shoe, a ninny, a clown.

tively betokens timidity or shamelessness. However, some capras may revert to capro emisario, espiatorio, scapegoat, and, by extension mean dullard. A caprone is a man with a long, unkempt beard or merely a bearded individual (cf. barbuto come un caprone, as bearded as a billy goat), while a cavrona in Romagnuolo denotes a tall, lean woman. Friulano zocul is a giddy-headed youngster. Another name, Castino, if it comes from the Calabrese castina, is a chestnut-haired goat.

The canines furnish the surnames Cane, Canello, Cagni, Cagnini, Cagnello, Cagnetti, Cagnazzo, Cagnassi, Cagnaccini, Cagnoni,[38] Cian [39] (Trentino), Grancagnolo (rare), Cacciarru (Sardinian) all meaning dog; Veltri, Livrieri, Leveroni, greyhound, Molossi, Mastini, Mastinelli, mastiff, Lo Bracco, Bracco, hunting dog; Caccione, Cacciune (Abruzzese), Cacciotto [40] (Calabrese), small dog. A dog is ordinarily a poor wretch or a heartless, avaricious creature, but other metaphorical meanings are also common, for example, that of a faithful follower or satellite as evidenced in the phrase fedele come un cane, as faithful as a dog, that of a hard working or overworked person as made clear by the Sicilian phrase travagghiari comu un cane, to work like a dog, that of a stubborn, tenacious person implied in the Genoese can and in the Spanish perro, that of a misbeliever, cane saraceno, Pagan dog, a phrase inherited from the romances of chivalry. Cagna, in Calabrese, fare la cagna, denotes a vain woman. In Romagnuolo, Ferrarese, a cagnon is a prevaricator. A cagnazzo regularly means a cruel or brutal human. A veltro is a fleet-footed person; a livriere a lounger; a bracco, a policeman or spy or, in Southern Italian-Greek, vraccu, a fat but short individual.

Feline names are frequent, Gatto, Lo Gatto, Gattini, Gattone, Gattullo, Gattarelli, Gattinelli,[41] Gattorna, Jatta (Tarantino), Mu-

---

[38] The variety of these names presupposes homographical accretions from font names like Gallicano, Africano and Ascanio. However, cagn, a wild daisy in Val Colla (Canton Ticino), might also contribute an occasional name.

[39] Gianni, Luciano, Marciano, Feliciano and other given names and perhaps ciano, fleur de lis, bachelor's button, could likewise account for Cian. We recall here the famous names Facino Cane, Cangrande della Scala, and Mastino della Scala.

[40] These may come from Caccia which used to be a common first name. Cf. also Brancaccio. Perhaps Cacchione instead of being a worm is only a variant of Caccione. Both Livrieri and Leveroni remind one of Oliviero.

[41] Gatto may be a Germanic proper name (cf. Förstemann, op. cit. 563). It could come from the dialectical form Catta for Caterina or, through the gemination of the internal consonant, from Agata or even Cato, Catone. In Calabrese the cat can change from a cat to a squirrel as we witness in Gattarella (jattaredda). Cf. also gattone, mumps.

scio and Muscini [42] (Modenese) and stand for a cunning, malicious
fellow, a nimble person, or a thief. If the phrase friand comme un
chat, as epicurean as a cat, has spread beyond the French boundaries,
then it is likely that some of the Gattos denote persons fond of
good eating. Gattamorta, a rare surname, literally signifies dead
cat and refers to an astute person pretending to be a simpleton. It
may also be a place name. Another rarity is Cattabianchi, probably
from gatta bianca, white cat.

Surnames drawn from European wild animals do not lag numerically much behind the domestic animal group. The bear,
standing for uncouthness, surliness, hirsuteness and sleepy-headedness
is represented in the onomasticon by Orsi, Orselli, d'Urso, Orsucci,
Orsatti, Orsini, Orsolini, Orsolone, Orsoni, Orzelli,[43] (Grossetano,
Aquilano), Arcudi, Arcuri (Calabrese), Licudi.[44] The wolf, denoting voraciousness and fraud, contributes Lupo,[45] Luppi (Genoese),
Lupicini, Luppino,[46] Lupoli, Lupoletti, Lupello, Luporini, Lovo,
Lovatelli, Lobetti, Luotto, Luffi (Novarese, luf), Lico [47] (Calabrese).
Cervera and perhaps Lincio,[48] lynx, allude to sharp-eyed persons as
revealed by the phrases occhio cerviero, occhi di lince. The cunning
fox is humanized in Volpi, Volpini, Volpicelli, Vulpetti, Volpone
and Raposa, a word of Spanish origin. The fleetness of the deer,
buck, chamois, doe and gazelle is exhibited in Cervo, Cervetto, Cer-
vini, Cervello, Cervellini,[49] de Caprio, de Capris, Caprioli, Craviotto,
Camoscio, Camozzi, Camusso, Camuzzo, Camosso, Daini, Dainelli,

[42] Muscio, Muscini are somewhat more convincing if related to Giacomo,
GiacoMUSCIO. In Calabrese musci, muscilla, means a rat, while muscio refers
to a slow-moving, lazy person.

[43] Cf. Saints Ursinus, Ursula.

[44] Arcudi is given by G. Rohlfs, *Dizionario Dialettale delle Tre Calabrie*,
Milano, 1932, I, 24, while the Venetian Licudi, also ultimately of Greek origin,
is noted by C. Poma in a review of A. Trauzzi, *Attraverso l'onomastica del
Medio Evo in Italia*, in *Archivio Glottologico Italiano*, XVIII, 1918, 389.

[45] Lupo can be either of Latin, Germanic or Spanish origin. Hispanic López
was Latinized into Lupus and Italianized into Lupo. This was the case of
Giovanni Lupo (López, Lupus) canon of Segovia, a writer on legal matters,
who acquired the name after many years of residence in Rome. See A. P.
Sereni, *The Italian Conception of International Law*, New York, 1943, 76.

[46] Cf. Saints Lupicinus and Lupinus.

[47] See Rohlfs, *op. cit.* 24.

[48] But Cervera may be a Spanish place name, and Lincio may be related to
the Latin name Lincius.

[49] Some possible non-animal sources of these cervo names are cervo, Venetian for oak and Calabrese for a non-poisonous snake, cerbo from acerbo, a
variety of grape, cervello and cervellino meaning queer, hair-brained persons.
Bongioanni, *op. cit.* derives Venetian Cervelli and Cervellini from Servilio.

Dainotti and Gazzelli.[50] Dal Buffalo and Bufalini are names that are derived from buffalo, wild ox, and usually refer to simpleton, but the famous Pistoiese family, Dal Buffalo, is said to have obtained its name from an ancestor who fought like a buffalo. The wild boar, Cignale, Cingale, Verri, may allude to individuals with large protruding teeth, grasping persons or irascible bullies. As the French put it: il est comme un verrat, he is like a boar. In Agnonese verro is guerre and perhaps accounts for a few of our Guerra names.[51]

Belonging to the list of dolts is the mole, Tarbi, Tarpini,[52] Talpone, Trapone (Piedmontese), Tampina (tampina, Val di Fiemme a Predazzo), Trappi [53] (Neapolitan). In Romagnuolo, besides meaning a dullard, the word also signifies a deaf person or one who feigns not to hear, as we can gather from the phrase sörd com'è una telp, as deaf as a mole. It may be that this idea of deafness is figuratively conveyed by the other dialectical mole surnames just mentioned. In Calabrese the term suricicuorvu, blind mouse, suggests its application to sightless or dim-sighted individuals. Even more commonly diffused is the phrase cieco come un pipistrello, bat blind. Whether because of this figure or for some other reason we meet with bat surnames like Nottoli, Barassi (Piedmontese), Faccidomo, Facciadomo (Neapolitan), perhaps Cordaro [54] (Reggio Calabrese) and a Pistelli here and there.[55]

As to the large family of the rodents, we find slyness connected with the mouse and rat surnames, Sorci, Sorcini, Zuricini, Soricelli, Sorcinelli, Sorachi (Calabrese), Sorica (Romano), Ratti,[56] Musone [57]

---

[50] Camoscio is also an expression for a flat nose and in the Greek background region of Southern Italy (Reggio Calabria) a term for a young beech tree, hamoscio, while Piedmontese camüss is a sort of cloak or cape. There may be a relationship between Camosso, Camusso and Giacomosso, Giacomusso. Dainelli might be a metathetical form for Danielli, while Gazzelli might derive from the given name Acacio and gazza meaning magpie.

[51] Verri may, however, be linked to a Germanic font name. Cf. E. Förstemann, op. cit. 1556. Guerra will immediately be recognized as the common word for war.

[52] A rather unlikely source of tarpina is a plant, monk's rhubarb.

[53] Trappu in Calabrese means a slow-moving person.

[54] A cordaro is also a rope maker. Any font name in n + vowel could give Nottoli.

[55] Used for vipistrello in I Nobili Fatti di Alessandro Magno. Bologna, 1872, 121, line 15. But it may be connected with the word for dry, white chestnut.

[56] In most instances Ratti may be considered a derivative of a number of Germanic names bearing the theme Rad, Rat, or a geological term meaning steep slope or precipice.

[57] A musone, from mouth, snout, is a pouter.

(Modena), Forchione [58] (Salernitano), Zoccoli, Zoccolillo [59] (Calabrese, Tarantino, Lucanese), Topo, Topino and the name for field mouse, Musaragni, owned by a noble Italian family. In Milanese a rat, ratton, may be a person leading a hermit-like existence. Lively restless people are denominated squirrels, Ciurla [60] (Abruzzese), Schiratti (Veronese), Taccarello, Taccarillo [61] (Calabrese), Ziroli [62] (Pragelato dialect of Piedmont, ezirol). The Abruzzese observe: è ccome la ciurla, and the French say c'est un écureil, il est vif comme un écureil, he is like a squirrel, as lively as a squirrel. To the weasel Donnola,[63] Dondolini (Romano), Bellorini (Milanese, Tuscan), Berlini [64] (Piacentino berla), mysterious and supernatural qualities have been attributed by tradition. According to the Romans it contained a powerful poison and even today in Sicily and Bergamo thin, emaciated persons are said to be sucked by weasels. Cf. Sicilian sucatu di la badottula and Bergamascan ssissit da la benola. By transference of meaning, then, the term could refer to individuals suspected of witchery or vampirism.[65] In English we have the compound, weasel-faced, meaning thin, a comparison suggested by the appearance of the animal. This metaphor has been passed on by the Italians to the polecat and has given rise to the surnames Faina, Martora and to the dialectical forms Favina (Romano), Mardenello (Trentino), Martorelli [66] (Northern Italian), Puzzone [67] (if Parmigiano), Schirru, Petosa (Calabrese pitusu). Contrasting figurative interpretations are faina, a screamer

[58] May mean a large den, cf. Calabrese forchia.

[59] Friulano zocul is a goat. See Note 37.

[60] Notice that ciurla can be a variant of chiurla, curlew.

[61] In Abruzzese the term taccarelle, which comes from a different source, is a garrulous man or woman, while in Tarantino a taccarello is a tanghero, a boor.

[62] Cf. Tarantino zirolu, large oval jar. Cf. also Zeroli from Lazzero.

[63] We may, perhaps, posit a possible Germanic origin here. Cf. Förstemann, op. cit. 418. Dondolini can be connected with dondolo, a slow-moving person.

[64] Cf. berlina, coach, gallows and the place name Berlin. Due to vigorous competition the surnames Cucci, Cuccia which seem to be linked with the Marchigiano word for weasel, cuccia, can all but be ruled out. Cf. FrancesCUCCIA, DomeniCUCCIA, etc., and cuccio (cucciolino), little dog, simpleton.

[65] In Lombardy the weasel epithet is used to denote a faithless woman.

[66] Matorell in Milanese coming from martor, martyr, means a wretched fellow. In the basso Milanese it can mean a squirrel and in the alto Milanese a polecat.

[67] A puzzone is also a fly, or a big well. Puzzoni can also come from Jacopo, Filippo, Giuseppe.

(cf. stride come una faina, he screams like a polecat), Vicentino martorelo, a nimble person, Calabrese marturella a busybody and pitusu an undersized youngster. Zibetto is the only name so far found relating to civet cat. The ermine, Armellini,[68] which is related to the weasel, is generally a symbol of purity. The marmot, Marmotta, a rather rare last name, signifies a nit-wit, an idler, a recluse, a sleepy head, in Mirandolese a slow-moving simpleton, or in the Romagnuolo dialect a mischievous urchin. Sicilian marmotta adds ugliness to doltishness.

The hare surnames, Lepri, Lepore, Leporini, Repulo (Calabrese riepulu), denote fleet-footed or keen-eyed, vigilant persons, or like rabbit Coniglio, Cuniglio, Coniglione, an individual who is pigeon-hearted.[69] The porcupine, Brocchi,[70] Spini, Spinosi [71] (Genoese), Strizzi (Parmigiano(?)), frequently indicates a sullen fellow. È un istrice, pare un istrice, he is or looks like a porcupine, is a popular expression which brings this out. Ingenuity is perhaps connected with the name Castore,[72] meaning beaver.

Both the dormouse (ghiro) and the badger (tasso), a non-rodent, are commonly used as epithets for sound sleepers. It will be interesting in this connection to quote from Ariosto's masterpiece, the *Orlando Furioso:*

> How oft of dormouse, badger or of bear,
> The heavy slumber would she fain partake!
> For she that time in sleep would waste and wear;
> Nor such prolonged repose desired to break.

Canto XXXII, 12

> No sooner he his head had rested there,
> Then with deep sleep opprest, he closed his eye;
> So heavily, no badgers in their lair,
> Or dormice, overcome with slumber lie.

Canto XVII, 109

---

[68] Coming from the Venetian section an Armellini might trace his name to apricot.

[69] Hase, the German word for hare, has this meaning.

[70] Cf. brocca, pitcher. Another meaning is shield. In Modenese is a bull's eye and, by extension, a fool.

[71] CriSPINO could give Spino. In Neapolitan spinuso, ommo spinuso, is a miser. Cf. also a Spanish surname, Espinosa.

[72] Cf. St. Castore.

Olimpia lay in slumber so profound
No sheltered bear or dormouse sleeps more sound.

Canto X, 18 [73]

But phrases like dormire come un ghiro, to sleep like a dormouse,
are current in most of the dialects; dormire come un tasso, to sleep
like a badger, somewhat less so. It is interesting to note that at
Bereguardo near Pavia and Coli near Piacenza the dormouse is
called durmuoela, durmioera, sleepy head. Cf. the etymology of
dormouse from French dormeuse. Tasso has given rise to Tasso,
Tassoni, Tassini,[74] and ghiro has given rise to Ghiron, Aglira (Calabrese aglire), Tirone [75] (also Calabrese), Galiero, Calero,[76] Callero
(all Neapolitan), and Lero, Lerone, Lira [77] (all Abruzzese). Young
dormice are called Cardaccio and Cardamone [78] in certain parts of
Calabria.

Exotic animals have found their way into the onomasticon espe-
cially through metaphors, heraldic devices and shop and inn signs.
The lion, symbolizing nobility and daring is represented by Leone,
Leonelli, Leoncini, Leonetti, della Leonessa, Aglioni (Romagnuolo);

[73] The translations come from W. S. Rose, *The Orlando Furioso*. The
Italian originals read as follows:

> Oh quante volte da invidiar le diero
> E gli orsi e i ghiri e i sonnacchiosi tassi!
> Che quel tempo voluto avrebbe intero
> Tutto dormir, che mai non si destassi.

> Non ebbe così tosto il capo basso,
> Che chiuse gli occhi, e fu dal sonno oppresso
> Così profondamente, che mai tasso
> Ne ghiro mai s'addormentò quanto esso.

> . . . . . ebbe Olimpia sì gran sonno
> che gli orsi e i ghiri aver maggior nol ponno.

[74] Tasso is also connected with the Germanic font name Tasso, see E.
Förstemann, *op. cit.* 405. It may be from Talassio through syncope (see
Talassio among the list of names given by E. Ferrari, *Vocabolario de'Nomi
Propri* . . . Bologna, 1827-28). A tasso is also a yew tree and in Sicilian a
velvet plant.

[75] In Sicilian a tiruni is a wild dove.

[76] If borne by a person with Spanish antecedents Calero means a lime
burner.

[77] Cf. lira, lyre, and lira, money, both rather poor possibilities.

[78] Given by G. Alessio in "Le Denominazioni del Ghiro e dello Scoiattolo
in Calabria," *Archivum Romanicum*, XX, 1936, 150, 152. Cardaccio may be
connected with Riccardo, Broccardo, caro, thistle, and several other terms.

the tiger denoting cruelty or irateness by Tigri, Tigrini;[79] the elephant indicating large stature by Elephant, Alifante, Linfante, Leofante, Elefantino;[80] the leopard and panther signifying cruelty and fierceness by Leopardi, Pardi,[81] Pantera; the giraffe alluding to long-necked, long-legged persons by Giraffi, Zirafi, Giaraffa. The camel, Cameli, Camelli, Cammelli [82] may refer to a hunchback, gobbo com'un cammello, as hunched as a camel), to a gluttonous person or to one who is tall and fat if the provenience is Calabrese. Scimia, monkey, exists as a surname, but it is quite rare. Mandrillo, may possibly come from mandrel, baboon.

Even imaginary animals are not neglected, for example Mannaro, Mannarino, Mannerino,[83] werewolf, which in the dialect of Arcevia (lupo manaro) indicates an epileptic; Drago, Dragoni, Dragotta, Dragonetti, dragon; Griffo, Griffone, Griffini,[84] griffin, both denoting fierceness and cruelty; the extremely rare Unicorno, unicorn, owned by a sixteenth century writer, and the curious combination Leoncavallo.[85]

These names seem to be spread over all sections of Italy, but it may be that by accident some of them are better known or more numerous in specific localities. A sixteenth century writer, Scipione Ammirato,[86] found that the Cavalli, Leoni and Mula of his time were predominantly from Venice and that the Asini and Vitellini of the epoch were largely restricted to Florence.[87]

---

[79] As a Tuscan name Tigrini is apt to be an alteration of Tegrimi from the Germanic Teudegrim.

[80] The noble Ravennate family of the Fantuzzi uses Elefantuzzi as a variant form. It appears that in Catanese an elefantu is a sort of lobster. See G. Alessio, "Note Etimologiche," *Italia Dialettale*, XII, 1926, 24.

[81] For Leopardi cf. the Germanic, Lephardt. Pardo may be an aphetic form of Leopardo or come from BernARDO.

[82] In Romagnuolo a camell means a lean horse, donkey or ox, a figure which may be extended to human beings. But compare Camel, Cremonese for Camillo, and Camelo, Cammello stemming from Giacamo = Giacomo.

[83] See Note 4 and cf. G. Crocioni, *Il Dialetto di Arcevia*, Roma, 1896, 45.

[84] Cf. Drago and Griffo also from the Germanic, Förstemann, *op. cit.* 420, 1462, 674. See also Bird Names.

[85] Since part of it contains an animal name, perhaps we should include here gatto mammone, bogeyman, which may survive in the surname Mammone.

[86] In his *Delle Famiglie Nobili Napoletane*, I, Fiorenza, 1580, 16.

[87] Some place names bearing names of animals or identically spelt terms are: Agnelli (Novara), Bellora (Tuscany), Bova (Calabria, Lombardy, Venetia), Cagno (Lombardy), Cagnoni (Alto Adige), Camele (Lombardy, Lucania), Camozza (Lombardy), Camuzzo (Emilia), Cavalla (Piedmont), Coniglio (Venetia), Cravetta (Piedmont), Dragone (Terra di Lavoro), Faina (Piedmont), Gatta (Lombardy, Piedmont), Gatto (Emilia, Venetia, Piedmont), Leone (Liguria), Leonessa (Abruzzi), Maiale (Piedmont), Verri (Ascoli Piceno), Volpe (Lucca, Brescia).

Looking at animal names historically and comparatively, we note that the Hebrews used them sparingly, for example, Rachel, lamb; Hamor, ass; Jael, mountain goat. The Greeks showed a preference for lion and horse names, Leonidas, Timoleon, Pantaleon, Hippocrates, strong horse, Xanthippus, yellow horse. The Romans frequently personified animals into human beings, Pecorius, Porcelius, Agnus, Asinij, Equitij, Suilij, Vitellius, Leporice, Ursus, Leo, Lupus. The Teutons employed a restricted number of such names, particularly the name of their forest king, the bear, Bera, and the mysterious wolf, Vulfo, one of the companions of Odin. A strong Germanic tradition in Northern Italy has caused the names of these two animals to appear frequently in Latin or Italian translation. Practically all the modern nations, in addition to Italy, also have their quota of animal names. The English, for instance, have Brock, Badger, Bull, Bullock, Calf, Catt, Colt, Fitch (polecat), Fox, Todd (fox), Lowrie (fox in Scotch), Oliphant (elephant); the French Labiche, Leboeuf, Lebouc, Ledain, Lachèvre, Lechien, Legoupil, Lelièvre, Leloup, Leloutre, Leveau, Cheval; the Spaniards, Caballo, del Toro, Becerra, Cordero, Ciervo, de la Cerda, Chivo, Raposa; and the Germans Bock, Bär, Dachs, Eber, Eichhorn, Fuchs, Voss (also meaning fox), Hase, Hirsch, Hund, Igel, Kalb, Katz, Kuh, Lamm, Löwe, Maus, Ochs, Stier, Ross, Schaf, Rappe (black horse), Schimmel (white or grey horse).

Chapter XII

FISH NAMES

Italian fish names as applied to person are to be found scattered most abundantly in those coastal areas that are largely devoted to fishery—Sicily, Taranto, Naples, Ancona, Venice, Istria, Genoa, the Italian lake region. In some instances, we know that they have figurative meanings. For example, the generic term fish, Pescio, Pescetti, Piscicello, Piscitello, usually denotes a good swimmer. Indeed, the most famous name in the natatorial annals is that of the legendery Nicola Pesce whose real surname, Pipe, has on this account been completely forgotten.[1] Expert swimmers might also be given an individual fish name. Such is said to be origin of the Venetian Delfini, dolphin, a branch of the Gradenigo family, one of whose founders was skilled in this diversion.[2] Pesce like agnello (agnus Dei) standing as it does for ΙΧΘΥΣ, Jesus Christus Filius Dei Salvator, may well have been used as one of the namesakes of Christ. Again, pesce like English fish, often denotes a simpleton along with Merluzzo, Baccalà, Baccalare, Mazzoni,[3] (Tarantino), Bertagnini (Bergamascan bertagni), cod; Chiozzi, Ghiozzi, Bottola (Lombard), Botta[4] (Piedmontese), Lardelli[5] (Trivigiano) and

[1] See B. Croce, *La Leggenda di Nicola Pesce*, Napoli, 1885. G. Pitrè, "La Leggenda di Nicola Pesce nella Letteratura Italiana e Tedesca." *Raccolta di Studi Critici dedicata ad Alessandro d'Ancona*, Firenze, 1901, 444-65. Schiller wrote *Der Taucher* based on the subject.

[2] See E. Salverte, *Les Noms d'Hommes, de Peuples et de Lieux*, Paris, 1824, 292. Another nobleman, Guy VIII, count of Vienna, was called the dolphin because he wore a dolphin on his helmet, a name which was transmitted to his descendants and to their holdings known as Dauphiné. Dolfin in Venetian also means a hunchback, but cf. Adolfino, Rodolfino, etc. We could easily obtain the name Delfino through del plus Fino from SeraFINO or any other name in -fo. In Neapolitan a dolfin is called Ferone, also a last name.

[3] But Mazzoni could also come from various other sources: DalMAZZO, GiacoMAZZO, Germanic Matzo, Genoese Mazzo = Maggio, mazzone, a big club. Mazzune in Calabrese means an old ox, a slow moving person. In his *Italian Dictionary* (Cambridge, 1925, 377) Hoare defines mazzone as mullet.

[4] Both bottola and botta can mean toad, but botta is usually tub, vat. GiacoBOTTO-OLA might also be a source for these words.

[5] It is clear that Belardo, Bilardo and other such names could give us the same results. Hence, fish-origin is weak.

Bosa [6] (Bergamascan), gudgeon. However, in Tarantino a merluzzo is a slow-moving individual, and in Sicilian a mirruzzu or facci di mirruzzu, cod face, is a pale, thin young man, while in Romagnuolo the phrase parer un bacalà, to look like a codfish, also denotes leanness. Thinness is likewise conveyed by Romagnuolo, Milanese, Cremonese Sardella, possibly Sardini, Sardoni, Sardonelli,[7] Calabrese Alice, Alicino, Salaghi, Saracchi (cf. Tuscan salacca) all meaning pilchard, herring. In Neapolitan an Anguilla, eel, is a thin but nimble woman. A Balena, whale, is, of course, a large, corpulent person.

We know that in the sea port of Grado (Istria), sobriquets of the ictiological type are very common.[8] Here they represent in a colorful manner the trade in which a large part of the villagers are engaged. If we were to extend the same procedure to other fishing localities, which seems logical, we can reach the fairly safe conclusion that many of the various fish names now in existence were originally synonymous with the word fisherman, Pescatore.[9] Among these are Aguglia, needle fish; Anguilla, Capitono, Cavedoni, Cerioli [10] (Anconitano, Castro de' Volsci), eel; Arata (Tarantino) gold fish or, possibly, mullet; Cefalo, Cefaro (Neapolitan), Capozza [11] (Tarantino), Triglia, Lustro, Praino (both Sicilian), Cavazzali (Como, Trentino), Cavasini, Cavaccini [12] (Lombard cavazzin), mullet; Puntaloro (Sicilian), smaris; Lissi (Triestino), Lizzi [13] (Venetian), mackerel; Rombello, Rombone,[14] turbot; Aluzzo, pickerel; Lampredi, Alampi (Sicilian), lamprey; Dentici, dentex; Varoli [15] (Anconitano), Paonissa [16] (Sicilian), wrasse;

---

[6] Bosa can be a first name. See E. Förstemann, *Altdeutsches Namenbuch*. Erster Band. Personennamen. 2d ed. Bonn, 1900, 329. A Buoso de' Donati and Buoso Donati are alluded to in Dante's *Inferno* XXV, 35, and *Inferno*, XXXI, 44. Yet, through the drop of the r, Bosa might come from AmBrOSA.

[7] In French there is a St. Sardon or Sardos to which these words may also be related. Sardo = Saldo from Ansaldo is another source.

[8] See R. M. Cossar, "Nomignoli Gradesi," *Falklore Italiano*, II, 1927, 453-54.

[9] Pescatore is also a surname, but it is not very common.

[10] Capitono may come from St. Capito. A Ceriola in Castro de' Volsci is a dissimulator. But if Ceriola hails from the Venetian sector it comes from Madona dela Ceriola, Madonna della Candela.

[11] Arata is also Southern Italian for plow. Cefalo is a Graeco-Italian word for head, while Capozza can likewise come from head and Reggio Emiliano can mean cabbage.

[12] Cavasini, Cavaccini may possibly stem from IaCAVA, variant of Iacobbo.

[13] Lissi, Lizzi may point back to Ulisse.

[14] There may be a connection between Rombello, Rombone and rombo, rumble.

[15] Varoli may be from AlVAROLA, or varola, small pox.

[16] Paonissa is normally a peahen.

Struzzo [17] (Sicilian), whiting; Mostellone (if from Sicilian mustedda), rocking or whimble fish; Persico,[18] Banderola [19] (Comasco bandirolo), Spinola,[20] perch, Spatula,[21] scabbard or frost fish; Zicarelli (Leccese), band fish; Bavuso [22] (Sicilian), blenny; Palumbo, Palombo,[23] dog fish, toad fish; Verdeschi (Sicilian), Verdone [24] (Genoese), blue shark; Razza,[25] Raia [26] (Neapolitan), Picarello [27] (Sicilian picara), Ragno,[28] Ragana, Racana,[29] weever or perch or pike (Baretti's dictionary); Carpo, Carpani, Carpanetti (Comasco, Pavese), Carpanelli [30] (Cremonese) carp; Cantarella [31] (Sicilian), sea bream; Coronedi (Sicilian), smelt; Fanfani [32] (Venetian), pilot fish; Scaro, Girola,[33] parrot fish; Tremoli, Trimoli,[34] torpedo or crawfish; Tenca, Tinca,[35] tench; Trotta, Trottolini [36] (Neapolitan), trout; Alosa (Sicilian), shad; Cerni

[17] Cf. struzzo, ostrich.

[18] Persico is also a peach.

[19] Banderola is likewise a plant, a flag, streamer, or figuratively a weathercock.

[20] Spinola might come from Crispino.

[21] Homographs of Spatula are a plant, a bird, a Southern Italian place name.

[22] A bavusu in Sicilian is a giddy-headed person or a braggart and in Calabrese a kind of mushroom.

[23] A Palombo may be a wood pigeon, ring dove.

[24] The same color identification is used for green finch. Cf. also Verdo from the Germanic (Förstemann, *op. cit.* 1558) and Bertone.

[25] Razza is also the name of several plants—charlock, rock cress (both Sicilian), dog rose (Modenese), blackberry (Cogorno, Liguria).

[26] Raia is sometimes a plant as well, a radish, smilax.

[27] A picarello in Anconitano is a goad.

[28] The common definition of ragno is spider.

[29] Ragana, Racana could be from Germanic Ragan (Förstemann, *op. cit.* 1221). Either word could also mean a frog.

[30] Carpo definitely calls PoliCARPO while Carpano, Carpanetti, Carpanelli should more logically be related to hornbeam.

[31] Other means of cantarella are frog, Spanish fly (Umbrian), mushroom, the chanterelle, and the Sicilian place name meaning bridge, from the Arabic qantrah. See C. Avolio, "Saggio di Toponomastica Siciliana. *Archivio Glottologico Italiano,* Supple. Sesta dispenza, 1898, 87. We may add that cantarella can also refer to a singer, and may even be from Germanic Ganthar if Northern Italian. Cf. Förstemann, *op. cit.* 596.

[32] We suggest a possible Fanfano from Cristofano as a competitive term.

[33] For Scaro and Girola cf. Germanic Scara (Förstemann, *op. cit.* 1304) and GIROLAmo.

[34] In the Sicilian toponomastica the word seems to mean swamp land.

[35] For a Germanic source of Tenca see Förstemann, *op. cit.* 1402.

[36] In Romagnuolo Trotta may be from Caterina and also means a stammerer. In Milanese trotta refers to a fast walker. Trottolino is normally defined as a romping little boy.

(Sicilian), spring headed perch; Sauro,[37] horse mackerel, Lamma (Genoese), a fish said to be related to the eel; Sarpi, gold line. We may add Stocco [38] standing possibly for pesce stocco, dogfish, shark. Scapecchi looks like a variant of Neapolitan scapece, pickled fish.[39]

The other well known temporary or permanent dwellers of the deep are for the most part all nicknames with established and wide-spread figurative meanings—Gambari, Gambaretti, Gambarini,[40] Ragosta,[41] lobster, and Grancini, Grancelli, Schillo [42] (Venetian), Cauro (Southern Italian), crab, all signifying tardy, hipshot persons. In Sicilian fari lu granciu, jucari lu granciu, to play the crab, is said of a petty thief. Gambaro has also been applied to drunkards with red faces and to German students who in Rome used to wear red gowns.[43]

Like the botanical group and other groups which conspicuously draw upon the dialects, this section is in need of special regional investigations to further clarify the picture.

[37] There is a St. Isaurus. Cf. also sauro, color, and sorrel horse.

[38] Friar Simon Stock, Carmelite, who lived in the seventeenth century used to sign many of his Italian letters. Fr. Simone Stocco. See "The Capuchin Prefecture of New England (1630-56)." *Franciscan Studies,* June, 1943. This serves as one of many examples that could be cited to show how easily it is possible to err in explaining names.

[39] In addition to the above, Naselli, may come from whiting; Trombetti (Nizzardo) and Trombino (Sicilian) from trumpet fish; Ciccinelli (Abruzzese and Neapolitan) from white fish, but other homonyms make their claims look rather remote.

[40] Cf. Langobard Gambara.

[41] Ragosta is also used for locust.

[42] Cf. FranceSCHILLO.

[43] Information on fish names has been chiefly obtained from G. Canestrini, *Fauna d'Italia: Pesci,* Milano, Vallardi, n.d. E. Sicher, "I Pesci e la Pesca nel Compartimento di Catania." *Atti dell'Accademia Gioenia di Scienze Naturali in Catania,* LXXV, 1898, Memoria V, 1-69; M. Monti, *Ittiologia della Provincia e Diocesi di Como.* Como, 1846. (*Estratto dall'Almanacco della Provincia di Como per l'anno 1846.*)

Chapter XIII

INSECT NAMES

It is quite likely that most of the insect surnames have gained the currency which they now enjoy through their use as nicknames. The bee, Dell'Api, Apicella, Apione, Lapini, Laponi [1] (Pisano), has everywhere symbolized diligence, industry. The hornet is represented by Calabrò (sometimes a drone), Scarfono [2] (Salernitano), and Ronzone [3] (Neapolitan and Tuscan). On occasion it means a lady's man. In Piedmontese a calabròn is a grumbler. The wasp, represented by Vespi, Vespri [4] (Tuscan-Romagnuolo), Vespoli, Vespucci, usually refers to a lively, witty or irritable individual. Compare the English term waspish. The fly denominated as Mosca, Mosconi,[5] Tafani, Tavano, Tavanelli, Puzzoni [6] (Anconitano) is customarily inclined to be an importunate person, but a moscon in Venetian and Romagnuolo may, like the hornet terms, be a lady's man, a tavan in Romagnuolo a nit-wit, a tavano in Romano and Marchigiano an uncouth fellow and a musca tavana in Sicilian an annoying gossip. Other importunates are indicated by the mosquito, Zanzara,[7] Sansale, Sansalone [8] (Lombard), Mo-

---

[1] Lapini and Lapone could easily be expanded forms of the pet name for Jacob, Lapo, or, if La be looked upon as an agglutinated article, Lapini might come from La Pina, that is, La GiusepPINA, La FilipPINA, La JacoPINA. In Calabrese a lapune is a wasp; in Campobasso the same word is used for a hornet, while a Laponi hailing from the Subiaco region might draw his name from a bur, a term which, by extension of meaning, indicates an importunate person.

[2] In Romagnuolo a scarafon, from a word synonymous with scarabocchio, a scrawl, alludes to an individual with an ugly face.

[3] Adding the augmentative -one to the aphetic form Oronzo leads to Ronzone. Ronzone is also a word for nag. The Calabrese word for hornet, Carbonaro (literally, charcoal burner) should not altogether be eliminated as a surnominal source.

[4] Vespro is also vespers. See Calendar Names in chapter on Miscellaneous Names.

[5] Mosca, Moscone are likewise words designating a kind of beard, imperial, or they may be from a Germanic Musco (cf. E. Förstemann, *Altdeutsches Namenbuch.* Erster Band. Personnennamen. 2d ed. Bonn, 1900, 1138. Dante places a Mosca de'Lamberti among the sowers of discord in *Inferno* XVIII.

[6] Preference should be given to other claimants, Puzzoni, coming from Jacopo, Filippo, Giuseppe, or puzzo, the word for well.

[7] It would be possible to reconstruct Zanzara from the compound Zan (Gian) plus Zara (Baltazara).

[8] A variant form for the term broker is sansale, but in Milanese a sansala is a sorrel, a plant of the buckwheat family.

schetti[9] and Fenaroli (Bolognese fnarol) which, incidentally, is also a lizard; by the gnat, Culicchia, Muscarelli, Moscarelli,[10] Mazzarelli[11] (Calabrese), Mussolini[12] (Veronese), Moscheni (Parmigiano), Moschino (Piedmontese); by the crab louse Piattoli,[13] Piattoni, Chiattone,[14] Chiattellini, Bacula[15] (Istriano-Friulano), Panaroni[16] (Polesine-Comasco), Scarfoni[17] (Caserta scarrafone), Babano (Piedmontese), Tecchi[18] (Romano, tecchia), Grisoni[19] (Friulano grisoon); by the flea, Pulci, Polci, Pulice, Polici, Policicchio, Puligheddu (Sardinian), Poci (dialect of Subiaco).[20] This list of bores can be possibly extended to the beetle Scarbini,[21] Scarabelli, Papaleo[22] (Sicilian), Panicola[23] (Biellese), Pisasale (Calabrese), to its relative the weevil, Gorgoglione, Barbolla (Genoese), Favarulo (Tarantino), and the Spanish fly Cantarella[24] (Umbrian), Cantrella (prov. di Lazio). One beetle not regarded as a pest is the

[9] Cf. moschetto, a word for musket, and the Germanic Mosca cited in Note 5. See section on Offensive Weapons and Defensive Armor under Object Names.

[10] Moscarello, Muscarello are Southern Italian words for muscatel grapes, while moscarello is a red clover in the Neapolitan region.

[11] Mazzarelli could come from GiacoMAZZO, DalMAZZO, Germanic Matzo, Genoese Mazzo = Maggio by the simple addition of the suffix -arello, as well as mazzarella, little club, or the Sicilian place name Mazzarelli.

[12] Mussolini may be tracked back to mussolina, a cloth, muslin. But P. Aebischer, "L'Origine et l'Air de Dispersion du Prénom Médiéval Italian Muntius," *Archivum Romanicum*, XVII, 1933, 279-88, argues for Muntius as the source of Mussolini.

[13] A piattola is also defined as a black beetle. A Venetian piatola is a slow, lazy man. Piattoli is also a place name in the prov. of Florence, and Piattola a place name in Piedmont. Cf. possible derivation from St. Plato = Piatto.

[14] The piatto, chiatto words could also mean plump. Cf. Calabrese chiattone.

[15] Bacula recalls Germanic Bag, Bacca (Förstemann, *op. cit.* 231).

[16] A panarone is likewise a large bread basket.

[17] See Note 2.

[18] Tecchi might come from tecchia, Lucchese for cliff.

[19] Additional candidates for this name are Grisoni, inhabitant of the Grison district in Switzerland, a grey-haired person or a plantain (Piedmontese grison).

[20] A person with very small eyes is said to have occhi di pulce. Cf. Pulci, place name near Siena.

[21] Cf. Scarbini with Scalabrini cited below.

[22] Another metaphorical meaning of papaleo, is the name given by Sicilian to policemen. But there is also competition from Papaleo, this is, Papaleone.

[23] In Calabrese panicula could mean corn. In Tuscan-Veronese a beetle is also called maggiolino, but the word has many other meanings. A Bergamascan beetle, balores, means simpleton.

[24] See Note 31 of Fish Names.

firefly which has given rise to the surnames Lucciola,[25] Lumini [26] (Lombard-Piedmontese), Panicucci, Cariola, Cairoli (if the three of them are Calabrese), Scalabrini (Pescantinese-scalabri) and Tasca(?).[27] Figuratively, it denotes a very thin person. Another beetle not looked upon as an annoyer is the lady bug which is known by various interesting dialectical names such as Marinella (Bellunese), Mariola (Anconitano-Umbro), Papucci, Papuzza (Calabrese-Sicilian), Pecorelli (Calabrese). It is easy for anyone to see that all of these lady-bug surname candidates face the competition of other homonyms which seem to have stronger source-claims than they do. But they have earned their right to be listed as possible cognomina by virtue of the existence of the many other insect surnames. Further bores are the earwig, Forcelli,[28] Forcellini (Umbrian), Forcina (Romagnuolo), Cugurra (Sardinian); the bed bug, Cimicini, Cimicioni; the woodworm, Tarli, Camola, Camulo (Sicilian); the animal-feeding insect, Magnabecchi; the insect infesting willows and poplars, Pontiroli (Parmigiano). The locusts, too, belong to the list of nuisances. They are represented by Locusto (rare), Ragosta,[29] Cavalletti, Cavalotti [30] (Veronese), Cavaretta,[31] Saltarelli,[32] Zuppetti [33] (Friulano), Capritti, Caprio [34] (Pesarese), Cravatta (Piedmontese). To the same category belongs the mole cricket supplying Zucarelli, Zuccarini [35] (Bolognese), Cipollaro [36] (Romano), Bagarozzo [37] (Abruzzese), Barbarotta [38] (Piedmontese). On the other hand, another relative, the grasshopper or

---

[25] It is conceivable that Lucciola through an accentual shift can come from Carluccia, Raffaeluccia, Lucio, Lucia, etc.

[26] The existence of the surname Bonalumi causes one to suspect that Lumini may be connected with a font name.

[27] A tasca can be a pouch, purse.

[28] A forcella may refer to the bifurcation of a river. Cf. Forcella, place name in Lombardy, Marche, Umbria.

[29] Ragosta is also a word for lobster. Cf. Calabrese ragusta.

[30] Cavalletti, Cavalotti suffer strong competition from cavallo, horse.

[31] Cavaretta can just as easily be translated goat.

[32] In some sections a saltarello is a dance. Cf. saltare jump, prance.

[33] The Friulani use a like word to describe an agile person.

[34] Capritti and Caprio also refer to the goat family.

[35] In this connection we also think of gourd, zucca, a gourd bed, zuccaro, zuccaio, and a gourd dealer, zuccaro, zuccaio.

[36] Cipollaro, meaning onion patch or onion seller has a stronger claim as the source of this name.

[37] In the dialect of Castro de'Volsci a bakarozze is a child or priest, so called on account of the black clothes they wear.

[38] If from the Valle Anzasca, barbarota is a series of peaks, giogaia.

cricket, Grillo,[39] Grilletti, Grelli [40] (Romagnuolo, Avellinese), Agrillo [41] (Salernitano), Arizzo (Messinese), Zangrilli, Pizzingrilli (both from the province of Lazio) refer to restless, eccentric or timid persons. Still another relative, the cicada, gives its name to chatterers. It can be found in the surnames Cicala, Cigalla, Cecala, Cigalini, Cicaroni, Cicalone, Cicalune, Cicarella and Cicatella (in Campobasso), Scorza, Scorcia (both Calabrese).[42]

Formichi, Formiconi, Formichelli, Formicola, ants, are popular designations for midgets.

If the figurative meaning of tignola, moth, is transferred to its other synonyms Falena,[43] Saraca (Catanzarese), these refer to scandal mongers. The butterfly Farfalla, Palombo, Palumbo,[44] Palomina (Romano), Parpagliola,[45] Passalacqua [46] (Calabrese), Pizzigallo (also Calabrese pizzingallu), La Morte [47] (Pugliese), Prampolini (Piedmontese prampöla), Farinelli [48] (Trentino) usually indicates a flighty frivolous fellow. Bachi, Vaco [49] (prov. di Macerata), Bigatti, Bagarelli (Umbrian-Metaurense), Bombici [50] may be surnames derived from the silk worm. A mal bigatto is a surly person while a buon bigatto is a discerning individual. In the highly doubtful bracket we may place Biancorosso [51] (Sicilian vrancarossa), lemon-eating insect.

---

[39] In some cases Grillo is a Germanic name. The Grillo family of Bovalino in Calabria traces its origin to Germany. Grilletti may, on the other hand, be a botanical name, quaking grass.

[40] AlleGRELLO could give us Grelli.

[41] Cf. agriddu, Otrantino for wild olive.

[42] In Tuscan a scorza is a plant of the chicory family. Incidentally, the cicala can also be an annoyer. Cf. the phrase tedioso come una cicala.

[43] Sometimes a falena is a lively person. Cf. CristoFALO plus dialectical diminutive -ENA.

[44] Dog fish and pigeon could be other meanings of Palombo.

[45] An old Lombard coin was called parpagliola.

[46] Literally, passwater. See Compound Names.

[47] Literally, death.

[48] See Botanical Names.

[49] Germanic Bago and Romagnuolo bach (in Imolese a club) with the meaning of a very fat person, compete with Bachi, Vaco.

[50] The pet form of Beatrice is Bice which in combination with buono could give Bombice, hence Bombici.

[51] Often Biancorosso is a term used to describe excellent health.

Chapter XIV

ARACHNID, WORM, REPTILE, AMPHIBIAN AND MOLLUSK NAMES

Most of the names in this group, too, can pretty safely be traced to nicknames. A few, perhaps, belong to heraldry.

ARACHNIDS

Among those drawn from the arachnids are Tarantola, Taranta,[1] Tirondola, Salanitro (Tarantino), Tignuso [2] (Palermitano) meaning tarantula and referring to restless, fidgety persons. The spider supplies Ragno and Ragnone.[3] In Neapolitan the term connotes a slightly-framed child. In Spanish araña (spider) alludes to a greedy fellow. Scorpio and Scorpione,[4] are both very rare.

WORMS

Worm names are seldom to be found. The lowly earth-worm can, however, probably claim the distinction of being used in the cognomen Scalici (Calabrese-Bovese). In addition, we have the leech, represented by Mignatto.[5] In the figurative sense it means a userer or a bore. One famous family is known as dal Verme, del Verme,[6] worm. We shall insert here a possible larva surname, Cacchione [7] (Calabrese), the worm of the bee.

---

[1] Through adjectivization in connection with a female font name the place name Taranto could become Taranta.

[2] Outside this restricted area a tignoso is apt to be a person afflicted with scurf. In other parts of Sicily a tignusu is an upstart or a small or unimportant fellow. In Calabrese a tignusu is an irascible individual.

[3] A ragno is also a fish or a plant, love in a mist.

[4] A Domenico Scorpione was a member of the Accademia dei Naviganti in Rossano (Calabria) in 1735. A scorpione is also a sea scorpion, cat o'nine tails, cross bow.

[5] The term could also refer to a leech-fisherman, a trade which, among other places, flourishes in the Canavese section in Piedmont (Chiusella and Dora Baltea). Cf. also St. Miniato and Erminio plus suffix -ato with Mignatto.

[6] Sometimes verme can mean a dragon, monster. Cf. Dante's *Inferno*, VI, 22, "Quando ci scorse Cerbero, il gran vermo." "When Cerberus the great monster beheld us." In the Como section a verm is a large snake.

[7] It is just as likely that Cacchione is a variant of caccione, cacciune, a dog, nit-wit.

REPTILES

Names taken from the snake are Scorsone, Corsonello, Viperi, Marasso [8] (Mantuan), Cervone,[9] Andrioni, Andriuni [10] (all three Southern Italian), Murena (Pugliese), Biscia, Biscioni, Bisciotti, Biscionini, the Northern Italian Bissa, Bissoli, Bissoni, Bissonetti, Bessi, Bessoni,[11] (Romagnuolo), Ortale [12] (Velletri), Serpe, Serpini, Serpenti and possibly Guardabasso [13] (Pugliese, Lucanese wardapass). This reptile usually stands for prudence, subtlety, slander, treachery. A scurzone in Neapolitan refers to a miser. In Milanese a bissa is a vixen. Vipera or lipara is a poisonous snake and, consequently, is related to an irascible or malicious individual. A cervone, large snake, denotes, on the other hand, a bold, courageous person. Cf. Abruzzese cervone.

The official terms for Italian lizard are lucertola, ramarro and orbettino. Lucertola commonly refers to the grey lizard and ramarro to the green variety, but both terms are often interchangeable. The orbettino is a blind lizard. Secco come una lucertola, as dried up as a lizard, alludes to a very thin person, while verde come un ramarro, as green as a lizard, indicates a pale and sickly-looking individual. Traseri n'cuorpu ad uno la licerta, to have a lizard in one, points to an impatient fellow in Calabrese. For lucertola we have the dialectical surnames Lacerda, Certa, Sarica, Saricone (both Pugliese), Tamarro [14] (Casertano), Caramusa and Carramusa (Neapolitan). For ramarro we have Certone (Neapolitan), Ligoretti (Vicentino, Romagnuolo), Ghezzi [15] (Milanese, Bergamasco), Ramallo and Verdone (Tuscan), and for the blind, inocuous orbettino Fenaroli [16] (Romano), Serinella (Umbrian). Basilisco, a rare last name, may be a lizard or a fabulous serpent or dragon whose breath and look were supposed to be fatal. Some

---

[8] Marasso can be related to Aldemaro, Maro plus the local suffix -asso.

[9] There is hardly any need to pointing out that cervone stands for big deer. Cf. also St. Cerbonius.

[10] The similarity between Andrioni, Andriuni and Andrea is also obvious.

[11] Biscia, Bissa, Bessa and their derivatives also have a close relation to Obizzio, Obizzo, Obesso.

[12] Ortale in Calabrese means a large garden inclosed by a wall.

[13] Literally, look down, a term applied to an astute person.

[14] Tamarro is popular Southern Italian for a rustic.

[15] Certone might have been listed under lucerta. Ghezzi can be from Germanic Sighezzo, a color, black, or a kind of crow.

[16] Verdone from Germanic Verdo (cf. E. Förstemann, *Altdeutsches Namenbuch.* Erster Band. Personennamen. 2d ed. Bonn, 1900, 1558), the Sicilian word for hawfinch verdune and the font name Bertone offer some competition. A fenarola is also a bird.

of the braggart soldiers of the Italian Commedia Erudita were called Basilisco as in the Renaissance plays *Altilia* by A. F. Rainieri and *Furiosa* by G. B. della Porta. In other plays we find a satiric association of the fierce-eyed coward with the serpent. It is synonymous with the term bully.[17]

The tortoise, Tartaruga, Cilona, Tartini [18] (Sienese), Scuzzari, Scozzari (Sicilian), Galana (Venetian, Mirandolese) is proverbial for its slowness, but for the Sicilians a turtle is a lazy or ugly and deformed individual.

AMPHIBIANS

Though small in numbers the amphibians furnish us with quite a few names.

The toad is represented by Rospi, Rosponi, Rosconi [19] (Veronese), Botta, Bottini, Bottolo [20] (Aretino), Babini [21] (Piedmontese), Baggio and Baggetta [22] (both Genoese), Satti [23] (Bresciano sat). It is customarily a symbol of irascibility and uncouthness, but in Calabrese it may imply a stubborn, misanthropic individual, in Romagnuolo a deformed woman, in Genoese a lean person, ruspo, in Neapolitan one who is both pale and obese, in Pitiglianese a miser. The frog gives us Rana,[24] Ragnini, Rajna [25] (Modenese, Genoese), Rainucci, Ranioli (Bardolino, Caprino), Buffa [26] (Reggio Calabrese, Sicilian), Cantarella,[27] Garganella,[28] Marabotto, Crotti[29] (Friulano), Scapocchio (Campobasso), and the green frog Ranocchio, Racano,

---

[17] See C. C. Boughner, "Sir Toby's Cockatrice," *Italica*, XX, 1943, 171-72.

[18] If from a font name, Tartini might come from GotTARDINO. Galano in Calabrese (Reggio) is an oriole. For a list of dialectical terms see L. Bonaparte, "Names of European Reptiles Living in Neo-Latin Languages," *Transactions of the Philological Society*, 1882, 4, 312-54, E. de Betta, *Fauna d'Italia; Rettili e Anfibi*. Milano, Vallardi, n.d. and the Jaberg-Jud linguistic atlas.

[19] Rosco is one of the names for holly.

[20] Botta, Bottini, Bottola means a barrel, hence a fat person, also a gudgeon, or they may come from GiacoBOTTO.

[21] Cf. babo, babbo, dad. Romagnuolo baben, child and Germanic Babin (Förstemann, *op. cit.* 224).

[22] Cf. baggeo, simpleton.

[23] Satti could be from OrSATTO.

[24] Cf. Germanic Rano, Förstemann, *op. cit.* 1245, and the font name GaleRANA.

[25] A rajna may be a carp. Rajna and with more certainty Rainucci could be connected with Saraina, Saracena, once common as a first name.

[26] Cf. buffo, clown, and buffa, hood of monk.

[27] See Note 28 of Fish Names.

[28] Garganella can point to throat, gullet.

[29] Cremasco crott is sickly, and, throughout Lombardy, beardless, the best source of the name.

Ragano, Racanelli, Raganelli [30] and Rago [31] (Roma, Velletri). This amphibian denotes pride, gonfio come una rana, as inflated as a frog, a croaking voice, gridare or cantare cuomo una rana (Calabrese), to shout or sing like a frog, a loquacious importunate, corpulency in Sicilian and Neapolitan, smallness or awkwardness in the dialect of Castro de' Volsci, shortness and fatness in Abruzzese (ranabotte) or merely smallness in Cremonese (ranabott). On the other hand, the salamander has been used less frequently for nickname purposes and offers only the surnames Salamandra, Salandra [32] (Barcio dialect of Venetia), Salamida, Salamita (Calabrese), and possibly Sestro (Genoese(?)). Piovani, if Piedmontese, competes with piovan, priest and piovana, bullfinch.

MOLLUSKS

A member of the mollusk family, the snail, reappears in nicknames such as Chiocciola with its dialectical equivalents Maruzza, Marozza,[33] Maruca, Marruca,[34] Giammaruchi (Southern Italian), Sulli (Calabrese), Izzo,[35] Scavuzzo (Sicilian(?)). Its sister, lumaca, also a snail, reappears as Lumachi, Bovoli, Bovolini [36] (Venetian), Maghin (Cremonese). Figurative meanings vary. A lumaca is defined as a grumbler, a sluggard, a sponger, a sly person who pretends to be a fool, a gull (cf. lumacone), a midget (Cremonese), a thin, tall child (Metaurense lumaghin). In Genoese fa comme e lumasone signifies to withdraw, to shut one's self in one's home. Dullards are indicated by the squibs: Calamaro,[37] Calamai, Totaro

---

[30] Cf. ragana, weever fish, sea dragon, and Ragana, Racana from the Germanic, Förstemann, *op. cit.* 1221.

[31] See Rago in Förstemann, *op. cit.* 1241.

[32] Salandra is also a place name. Incidentally, in Central Italy the salamander is often called a tarantola.

[33] Cf. Sicilian Maruzza a pet form for Marianna.

[34] A maruca is also a sort of jujube tree, a hawthorn.

[35] Izzu likewise means in Sicilian a holm oak. G. Deledda in her novel *Il Vecchio della Montagna* uses the phrase zitta come una chiocciola, as silent as a snail, which, if it is a popular saying, might indicate that taciturn persons might be referred to by the term.

[36] Both Bovoli and Bovolini might be connected with the font name Bovo and bovo, ox. In the Polesine a bovolo is a vortex or eddy. See A. Lorenzi, "Geonomastica Polesana," *Rivista Geografica Italiana*, XV, 1908. A. Prati in "Etimologie," *Archivio Glottologico Italiano*, XVII, 1910-13, 428n, cites in connection with Venetian snail terms a document dated 1394 containing a number of Bovolini from the town of Taseno.

[37] A calamaro is also a cane brake. Rings around the eyes are sometimes called calamari (Guastallese, Mantuan).

(Calabrese). Cozza [38] (Calabrese), Macagni (Venetian) and Cocciolone [39] (Neapolitan cocciola) are surnames for oyster.

CONCLUDING REMARKS ON ANIMAL NAMES

Looking upon the term animal as any living organism exclusive of plants we can now make some reflections relative to surnames that are applicable to this larger group.

The role that animal symbolism in religion has had in the vogue of names must be granted considerably more importance than has been apparent from the few references already made to it. Animals have been used in profusion to indicate qualities or virtues, to symbolize the Saviour and Christians in general. A verse in the XLII Psalm: "Like as the hart desireth the water brooks so longeth my soul after thee, O God," was interpreted as the image of the faithful Christians desirous of salvation. The writings of the early Fathers made the ox a figuration of Christ, the true sacrifice, a symbol of the prophets, apostles and saints, who suffered for Jesus' sake, and of the faithful who submitted to the yoke of Christ. In ecclesiastical architecture the lion is a common symbol of the Resurrection of Christ and of the general Resurrection. Pictorially and otherwise many of the saints have been traditionally associated with animals, for example, the lion is linked with St. Mark, the eagle with John the Evangelist, etc.[40] There is no doubt that religious zeal and mystical propensities may easily have led to the conferment upon individuals of these and other similar names.

The medieval bestiaries, too, must have left their mark on surnames just as they did on the intellectual life of the epoch. But their characterization of the animals is at many points the same as that which appears in the vast body of folklore tradition which makes it difficult if not impossible to give instances of indisputable influence. The many similes we have cited belong to the realm of popular lore. They represent only an infinitesimal fraction of the material available. Pertaining also to the same field are various calls imitating the throated noises of bipeds and quadrupeds. We are all familiar with the hog calling contests in the United States

---

[38] Any font name in -co could lead to Cozza, DomeniCOZZA, FrancesCOZZA.

[39] Cocciolone might likewise mean stubborn, from coccia, head. Several place name homographs may be noted here—Bissone (Canton Ticino), Marassi (Genoa), Ranocchio (Modena), Salandra (Lucania), Lumachi (Tuscany).

[40] See L. Turning, *Symbols and Emblems of Early and Mediaeval Christian Art*, London, 1885; E. P. Evans, *Animal Symbolism in Ecclesiastical Architecture and Art*, London, 1896.

and with the braying contest immortalized by Cervantes in his *Don Quixote*. Similarly, Italian hunters use rhymes in which attempts are made to imitate the calls of the birds.[41] It would be surprising, indeed, if, on occasion, the persons expertly indulging in this pastime should not be dubbed with the name of the creatures whose call they imitate.

Also belonging to folklore are thousands of animal nursery rhymes, *formulette infantili*, as they are called in Italian. They deal mostly with the smaller quadrupeds, birds and insects. Constant repetition of definite rhymes or insistence that they should be repeated has caused children to be jocularly named after some zoological creations. These names have clung to them throughout their lives and eventually have found their way into the repertoire of surnames. This seems to be one manner of explaining the great abundance of insect surnames.

But an even more fertile source of animal cognomina may be found in the custom of using as terms of endearment the names of young or small animals. Since the circumstances that have given rise to them have not changed materially through the ages we shall feel free to quote two passages from Plautus' *Asinaria*, which will serve as excellent illustrations of this point because of the long series furnished us by the author. In the first Leonidas says to Phillenium: "Call me, then, your little sparrow, chicken, quail, lamb, say that I am your kid or your calf." [42] In the second passage Leonidas again appeals to Phillenium as follows: "Call me your little duck, dove, or puppet, your swallow, jackdaw, little sparrow, mannikin." [43] Epithets of this nature have, of course, been used with reference to children far more frequently than any other class of persons.[44]

In a few words, the idea that we have primarily been trying to convey in our discussion of zoological surnames is that many of the nickname-surnames we have cited are metaphors. They are grains of pure poetic gold which when viewed singly or in small groups attract hardly any attention. Only when we assemble them in large quantities do we realize that the average human being, especially an Italian, is born with poetry in his soul, a poetry that he expresses undaunted by the struggle for existence which he is fated to carry on in a materialistic world. But we are not the only ones that have come to this conclusion. Others long before us have made similar observations, among them Giovanni Raiberti

---

[41] For the Province of Verona, see A. Garbini, *Antroponomie ed Omonime nel Campo della Zoologia Popolare*, Parte 2, Verona, 1925, 1121.

[42] Cf. line 666 ff.

[43] Cf. line 693 ff.

[44] An exhaustive discussion of these terms may be found in I. Pauli, *Enfant, Garçon, Fille dans les Langues Romanes*, Lund, 1919.

(1805-61) in a snatch of prose entitled "Men and Beasts." Quotation of this fragment will serve as a final summary of our lengthy discussion of the subject from this point of view. Raiberti comments: "From the epic similes to the proverbs of the common people comparisons between men and beasts appear in steady stream. If we are slow-witted we are called oxen; if untidy and corpulent, pigs; if rude and unsociable, bears; if ignorant, asses. He who repeats the talk of another is a parrot. He who imitates the actions of another is a monkey. And he who practices a little usury for the relief of the desperate is a leech. If you are absent-minded they call you an owl. If you are fickle they dub you chameleon. Are you cunning? Oh, what a fox! Are you voracious? Oh, what a wolf! Oh, what a mole, if you do not see things clearly! Oh, what a mule, if you are stubborn! Oh, what a barn owl if you shun the truth! An irate and vindictive woman is a viper; a fickle one is a butterfly; a flirt, a screech owl, and those who fall victims to her wiles, blackbirds. But only faults are dealt with here as someone will observe. Well, strength with generosity (and even without) has its eternal model in the lion. Faithfulness and friendship have as their exemplar the dog. . . . Tender lovers are called turtle doves; sublime intellects eagles; good poets swans. He whose mind's eye is acute a lynx; the gentle fellow is honored with the title of lamb; he who saves for future needs is said to be as provident as an ant; even the eclectic person is a bee that sucks honey from every flower. In short it is difficult to find a single individual who, good or bad, does not resemble three or four beasts at least." [45]

---

[45] Cf. "Uomini e Bestie," the Italian original:

Dalle similitudini dell'epopea sino ai proverbi della plebe è un continuo confrontare gli uomini alle bestie. Se siamo tardi d'ingegno ti chiamano buoi, se sudici e corpulenti, porci, se villani e selvatici orsi, se ignoranti asini. Chi ripete i discorsi altrui è un pappagallo. Chi riproduce le altrui azioni è una scimmia. E chi escercita un po' d'usura a sollievo dei disperati è una sanguisuga. Patite delle distrazioni vi danno dell'allocco. Siete uomo di tutti i colori vi dicono camaleonte. Siete astuto? O che volpe! Siete vorace? O che lupo! O che talpa se non vedete le cose più chiare! O che mulo se siete pertinace. O che gufo se abborrite la verità. La donna iraconda e vendicativa è una vipera, la volubile è farfalla, civetta la lusinghiera, e coloro che cascano sotto le sue smorfie si dicono merlotti.

Ma qui osserverà qualcuno non si tratta che di qualità viziose! O, la forza con generosità (e anche senza) ha l'eterno suo modello nel leone. La fedeltà e l'amistà hanno per tipo inevitable il cane . . . Gli amanti teneri si dicono colombi; gl'ingegni sublimi aquile, i buoni poeti cigni. Chi ha acuto l'occhio della mente vien paragonato alla lince, l'uomo mansueto s'onora col titolo d'agnello, chi fa risparmi per i futuri bisogni si chiama provvido come la formica, perfin l'eclettico è un'ape che succhia il miele da ogni fiore. Insomma stimo bravo chi mi sa trovare un individuo solo che in bene o in male non rassomigli a tre o quottro bestie almeno.

(Quoted from the phonetic script in Maître Phonétique,
Avril Juin, 1933, 42-43.)

Chapter XV

OCCUPATIVE NAMES

PUBLIC OFFICIALS

The varied and complicated set-up of Italian governmental bodies, participation in their administration on the part of military, ecclesiastical authorities, nobles, plebs and the arti, changes in the duties and functions of public officials in the course of the centuries, make it difficult to compile an accurate and complete list of surnames from this group. On this account, too, it is inevitable that some of the names mentioned here should also be registered in the sections dealing with other occupations.

A Podestà is a mayor, head of a commune, and in some places also a chatelain or bailiff. Because of the military functions that he often assumed he might be called a Capitano. Compare the title capitano del popolo, captain of the people. Consoli also goes back to mayor, but in Venice the term was applied to a kind of judge (console dei mercanti) and in Naples (cuonzolo) to a trade official consulted in disputes. From the original meaning of standard bearer, Confalonieri, the title came to be used for mayors of the Florentine Republic and other magistrates, gonfaloniere di giustizia, gonfaloniere della chiesa. Fourteenth and fifteenth century Rome had its Senatore, Sanatore,[1] a kind of mayor. In Mantua during the Middle Ages the podestà was called Massaro, a steward. Sindici (sindaco in the singular) might also be a mayor, but was more frequently a controller or inspector. Protospatario relates to a dignitary of the Byzantine court and was a title sometimes given to the doges of Venice. Governatore, governor, is a rare name. In the Venetian government a Rettore[2] was a civil governor who on occasion took on the title of Conte, count, and Bailo, bailiff, i.e. chief officer or magistrate. Elsewhere the term bailiff with this meaning is Baglivo, Vagliavello (Calabrese vagliviellu). Bailo, incidentally was also the title of the Venetian ambassador to Turkey. A Vicerè, Vincerè is a viceroy. In Venice he held the title of Duca, duke, with authority over the rettore. A Conestabile, Costabile, and the aphetism Stabile (which at times also comes from St. Stabilis) is a superior court or military officer, constable. Pro-

---

[1] From the calendar of the saints compare St. Senatore. A senatore, naturally, was often a member of the senato.

[2] The term can mean a president of a university, a prior or merely a director. Cf. Rettore dello Spedale di Santa Maria della Scala in Siena.

togiudice, del Giudice, Giudici, Iodice, de Pretoro, are judges; Delegato is a legate, delegate. A Cancellieri goes back to a chancellor, but often refers merely to a clerk; a Logoteta (Greek Southern Italian) points to a sort of controller. In Venice a camerlingo (surname Camerlinghi, Carmelenghi) usually a manager of a pontifical court, is a financial adviser. Compare one of the special meanings of chamberlain in English. Another ecclesiastical title, Inquisitore, inquisitor, has been applied there to a supervisor, inquisitore dell'acqua, delle arti. The Gastaldi, Gastaldini, Castaldi, Castoldi, normally signifying stewards, carried out civil orders by command of the doge. Vicedomini, Visdomini were supervisors of the Fondaco dei Tedeschi. Another kind of Venetian supervisor was the Savio, literally sage.[3] At Milan, a Vicario, vicar used to be in charge of provisions. Cf. vicario delle provvisioni. Logiurato, which looks like juryman, was probably a feudal revenue officer. Tesoriere, treasurer, is one of those terms that clearly speaks for itself. Locally elected government representatives of the commoners or the nobles or both are or were termed Consigliere, Conciglieri, Concilieri (councilor), Auditore, Anziani [4] (Tuscan), Bonomi and Buonomini [5] (Florentine, 12th century), Decurioni [6] (once current in Como, Milan, Pavia and Southern Italy), Priore,[7] Tribuno and perhaps Triumviri. As these administrative bodies were also designated by the number of the men that composed them, for. example, Senato dei Quarantotto (48), Magistrato or Consiglio dei Cinque (5), degli Otto (8), de'Nove (9), de'Dieci (10), the numeral was transferred to its officers with the equivance of Consigliero, senatore, etc. It is, therefore, quite conceivable that some of our figure surnames are survivals of this tradition.[8]

Among the lesser public officials we find Bargelli, Bargellini, sheriff; Carcerari, Custodi, Prepositi [9] (if related to Piedmontese pervöst), jailer; Secondini,[10] turnkey; Birri, bailiff; Agozzini, Gozzini, Guzzini, galley sergeant, convict keeper; Guardiano,

---

[3] A Venetian massaro could also be a mint official—massaro dell'argento, dell'oro. On government officials of this republic much interesting information can be gleaned from the Archivio di Stato di Venezia, I, II, Roma, 1937-40.

[4] Otherwise senior, elder.

[5] Cf. St. Omobono. Literally, good man.

[6] Curio, reduced form of MerCURIO plus an augmentative, -one, results in Curione. By prefixing the preposition de to it we can produce DeCurione.

[7] A priore is what it appears to be, a religious prior. Cf. St. Priore.

[8] See section on Number Names in Miscellaneous Names chapter.

[9] A preposito is also a dignitary of the metropolitan church.

[10] Secondino could be a first name indicating a second-born child. There are at least two saints by this name—Secondino and Secondina.

warden; Boia, Manigoldo,[11] hangman; Pisaturo [12] (Calabrese), public weigher; Curreri, Corriere, Corridore Staffetta, courier; Doganieri, Passaggiero, Garavani (Mantuan), Presentini (Anconitano), customs official; Procacci, Procaccini,[13] Pedone [14] (Genoese), postman, letter-carrier; Mazzacane,[15] Ferracane, official dog killer or catcher; Tromba,[16] herald or cryer; Dragomani, interpreter, originally an interpreter in an Oriental court.

MILITARY NAMES

The art of war has given us the general term Soldato, Soldatini, soldier, and the more picturesque Guerrieri, Guerrero, Armato, warrior; Battaglieri, battler; Campione, champion; Combattente, Pugnatore, fighter; Belligeranti, belligerant; Tornatore, jouster; Ventoliere (Calabrese) soldier of fortune; Vincitore, conqueror. Most of these words can likewise apply to a strong, brave or pugnacious individual including Guerra, Scaramuccia, Battaglia, war, skirmish, battle. Militare, service man, and perhaps Milite, soldier, seem to be surnames that have come into existence quite recently. Knighthood has furnished Cavaliere, Cavallero, Cavalliero, Civalieri,[17] knight, as well as Paladino, Palladino, Palatini, paladin, figuratively a strong or brave person; Scutieri, squire and possibly Crociato, crusader. Outmoded types of soldiery are represented by Galuppo,[18] baggage-carrying soldier; Albanese,[19] light cavalryman; Lanzi, Lanzoni,[20] mercenary German soldier; Dragone,[21] dragoon; Cappelletti,[22] Venetian cavalryman; Arcieri, Accieri,[23]

[11] Aguzzino, birro, boia, manigoldo figuratively mean rascal.

[12] In Neapolitan a pesaturo is a babe in swaddling clothes.

[13] But compare procace, petulant, arrogant.

[14] A pedone may also be a sentry, a person with large feet, anyone who travels on foot, a slow walker (Abruzzese).

[15] A mazzacane is also a wagtail, a building stone, a mason (Genoese), a sluggard (Calabrese).

[16] Literally, a trumpet. Also trumpeter.

[17] Cavaliere is likewise a title of nobility. More prosaic meanings are horse herder and draught horse guide.

[18] In Venetian a galuppo may be a sack maker. Other meanings of the word are despicable person, glutton (Piedmontese galup).

[19] These soldiers used to be Albanians, hence the name.

[20] Lanzilotto through its apocopated form could give Lanzi and Lanzoni.

[21] The word appears in Italian as early as 1611 in F. L. Melzo, *Regole Militari Sopra il Governo e Servitio Particolare della Cavalleria* with the meaning of a mounted harquebusser. See A. H. Gilbert, "The Etymology of Dragoon: Addendum." *Publications of the Modern Language Association*, LVIII, 1943, 580-81. Of course, dragone, dragon, is an alternative source.

[22] Also chaplet, little hat, children's game.

[23] In Sicilian an arceri is an industrious person.

Archieri, Arcari, archer; Balestrieri, Balestrari, Balestari, Balesterio, crossbowman; Lancieri, Lanciai, Lanciari, Lanzari, lancer; Manganaro, balistaman; Spadaro,[24] swordsman; Bombardieri, bombardier (i.e. one who is in charge of a bombarda). Araldi is a herald; Tamburo, Tamburino, Tamborra, a drummer boy; Tromba, Trombetta,[25] a trumpeter; Alfieri, Stendardo, Confalonieri, a standard bearer. A Catapano, Cattapani,[26] is a high Byzantine commander. In addition, there are Generale,[27] general; Colonelli,[28] colonel; Capitani, Cattani, Cattaneo, captain, a term also used for a commander or leader; Caporale,[29] corporal. Sargenti[30] refers to a foot soldier rather than a sergeant and so do Fante, Fantozzi, Fantucci,[31] Fantappiè and Pedone.[32] A Furiero, a Saccardo or a Saccomano is a quartermaster; a Piantone or a Fazione (Genoese) a sentinel; Levati (Piedmontese soldà d'levata) a conscript; La Guardia,[33] a guard and Artiglieri, Cannonieri, gunners.[34]

ARISTOCRATS AND THEIR RETAINERS AND SERVANTS

Names like Imperatore, Imperatrice, Re, Corona,[35] Regina, Reina, Soldano, Faraone, empress, king, queen, sultan, pharaoh,

---

[24] The archer, crossbow, lance, balista and sword terms may also refer to makers of these weapons. Perhaps an occasional spadaro can go back to a Byzantine imperial guard armed with a sword. Cf. also manganaro, mangle or calendar maker.

[25] Tamburo, Tromba and Stendardo are literally drum, trumpet, standard. In Old Italian a trombetta is a messenger. The term is also used for a spy and, in Bolognese, for a chatterer.

[26] But in Sicilian a catapano is a magistrate whose duty it is to settle market place disputes and, by extension, a bully; in the dialect of Reggio Calabria a head herdsman; in Neapolitan one who is in charge of a larder, and in Venetian a beggar, from accattapane.

[27] The word has the comic competition of generale dei porci, Pavese for pigherd.

[28] If the word hails from the Cadore section it means a strip of land. Cf. O. Marinelli, "Termini Geografici Dialettali Raccolti in Cadore." *Rivista Geografica*, VIII, 1901.

[29] Caporale in Calabrese is a herdsman, in Pavese a kitchen helper, in Cremonese (capoural), a bold or audacious person.

[30] Other meanings are servant, constable.

[31] These words have the competition of fante, child, servant.

[32] See Note 14.

[33] Also used as a place name, cf. La Guardia Piemontese in Calabria. La Guardia is common in Spain.

[34] For lack of a better place to put them we add here Ostaggi, hostage, and Graeco-Calabrese Mangalvite, armed with a club. The latter is also the name of a Calabrian town.

[35] The word corona, literally, crown, is an Old Italian equivalent of king. Cf. St. Corona.

can at once be attributed to roles played by individuals in various pageants and festivals. The same explanation partially applies to the names of the lower ranking nobles though the majority of them are likely to originate from actual possessors of these titles. We know that Contessa, countess, has been used as a first name, and this may be true of other appellatives of dignity. Metaphorical applications are, of course, as common as they are obvious.

Signore, Signorelli, lord; Patrizzi, patrician; Magnati, grandee; Gentilomo, gentleman; Corteggiani, Cortesani, courtier; Paggio, del Paggio, page; Vassallo, vassal; Valvassori, vassal in the second degree; are general terms which may refer to persons in any one of the rungs of the nobiliary ladder. More specifically, members of this class are Principe, Principini, Prenci, Princi, Principessa, prince, princess; del Duca, Lo Duca, duke; the rare Conteduca, count duke; Marchese, marquis; Conte, Contini, Contuzzi, Contarini, Contessa, Comiti, Comitini, count, countess; Visconti, Viceconte, Vissicome, viscount; Barone,[36] Baroncelli, baron; Cavaliere, Cavaglieri,[37] cavalier.

In the service of the aforementioned aristocrats were Castellano, chatelain; Scalco, Marescalco, Maniscalchi, Miniscalchi, Siniscalchi, superintendent of feasts and domestic ceremonies; Castaldo, Gastaldo, Gastaldini, Castoldi, steward; Fattore, Fattorini, Fattorelli, farm manager or steward; Camerlengo, Camerlongo, Ciambellani, Ciamberlini, Camerari, chamberlain; Dispenzieri, Spenzieri, spencer, butler; Catapano[38] (Neapolitan), Lardieri, person in charge of the larder; Falconieri, falconer; Cenario, Pranzataro, persons in charge of dinners; Lococo, Cuoco, cook; Guatteri, kitchen maid (guattera); Borsieri, Tesorieri, purser, treasurer; Giullari, jongleur; Staffieri, Valletti, lackey, footman; Battistrada, outrider, sometimes a servant on horseback attending a carriage; Portiero, Portinari, Portulano, doorkeeper, usher; Guardiano, keeper; La Guardia,[39] guard; Cocchiaro, coachman; a few Mozzo, Muzzo[40] (cf. Spanish mozo), stable boy. Different names for servant are Servo, Servente, Domestico (possibly reduced to Mestica), Garzoni, Garzonetti, Famigli, Famighetti, Famiglietti, Famigliari, Famigli, Meschino,

[36] A barone is often a rogue. Cf. Sicilian baruni, path.

[37] Also a general title, knight. Protonobilissimo is the name of a Tarantino family. For other examples, see Compound Names.

[38] See Note 26.

[39] Guardiano also belongs to the religious group of names while La Guardia belongs to the military group. Cf. La Guardia Piemontese, a Calabrese place name.

[40] Cf. Mozzo, Muzzo from GiacoMOZZO, GiacoMUZZO, and the same words signifying a handless or armless person.

Meschinelli [41] (archaic), Sargenti, Sargentilli,[42] Camerari, Camerieri, Camara, Camera,[43] Fante, Fantoni, Fantozzi,[44] Massera [45] (Reggio Emilia). Schiavo, Sclavo, Schiavetti, Schiavone are slave. All of these might be subject to a bourgeois masters, that is, a Padrone, Patrone, Patronelli, as well as a nobleman. Naturally, some of the names listed under other occupations can also belong to this group.[46]

ECCLESIASTICAL NAMES

From pope to sexton and altar boy all the names of the ecclesiastical hierarchy have become surnames. Persons bearing those of the higher clergy in some cases owe them, like the possessors of the name of the higher aristocracy, to ancestors who took such parts in church pageants or festivals, but an individual belonging to a churchman's household or who has been under his tutorship might just as easily assume the name of his master or tutor for purposes of identification. In Southern Italy functionaries of the Greek Catholic church (now probably extinct) were allowed to marry, so that some official church names indicate direct descent from former clergymen. This hierocracy is represented by Papi,[47] Lo Papa, pope; Cardinale, cardinal; Camerlingo, Camerlenghi,[48] manager of a pontifical court; Patriarca, patriarch; Protonotario, secretary of the patriarch of the Greek Church; Protopapa, another Greek Church dignitary; Primicerio, primate; Lo Prelato, Perlato, prelate; Prepositi, functionary of the metropolitan church; Arciepiscopo, archbishop; Vescovo, Visco, Scovetti,[49] Piscopo, Episcopo, bishop; Canonico, canon; Bonsignore, monsignor; Arciprete, Larciprete, archpriest; Chirico, Chirco, Crerico, Clerici,

---

[41] Possibly Guerin Meschino, hero of a famous romance of chivalry, has something to do with this name. Nowadays meschino means a wretched fellow.

[42] Also a constable, foot soldier.

[43] Cf. cameraro, chamberlain. Camara, camera, has come to mean servant through donna da camera, maid. However, S. Pieri, "Toponomastica delle Valli di Serchio e della Lima," *Archivio Glottologico Italiano*, Supplemento, 5a Dispenza, 1898, 174, gives the place name Camera and suggests its relationship to Low Latin camera, piece of land, and camera, charcoal or lime kiln.

[44] Fante and derivatives also mean child.

[45] Cf. Masera, a topografical name, and with schiavo, schiavone, slave, Schiavo, Schiavone, meaning Slav, Slavonian.

[46] Particularly agricultural occupations and arts and crafts.

[47] Cf. Papo Tuscan pet form for Jacopo, and Germanic Papo (see Förstemann, *op. cit.* 223).

[48] The reader will, of course, check back to the names of public officials and aristocrats for homonyms.

[49] A visco may also be a mistletoe, while a scovetto may be a broom patch.

Quirici, Quillici, Zago, Zagone [50] (Venetian), Servidio, Pastore,[51] clergyman, priest, choir boy; Prete, Lo Presto, Previti, Presbitero, Previtero, Previtomo, Lo Parrocco, Lo Parco, Parrino, Parrinello [52] (Calabro-Sicilian), Piovani, Piovanelli, Pivani, Plebani, Sacerdoti,[53] Curato, Curà, priest; Previtera, La Preta, Pappadia (Graeco-Italian), priest's wife; Rabbeno (Romagnuolo), rabbi; Confessore, confessor; Arcidiacono, archdeacon; Jacono, Diacono, Diagonetti, deacon; Jaconissa, deaconess; Decani, dean; del Vicario, Viccari, vicar; Cappellani, chaplain, almoner; Sacrestano, Sagrestano, Crestano, Campanaro, Becchini,[54] Picigotti (Venetian), sexton; Monaco, Moneghin, del Frate, Frati, Fratini, Frattini, Cappuccini,[55] Calogero (Graeco-Italian, a common Sicilian first name), a monk; La Monaca, nun; Lo Priore, Priolo (Sicilian, Venetian), Rettore, prior; Provinciale, district head of monks; Abbati, Abbatello, Abado, Abbatucci, Badini, Vatini, Labadini,[56] abbott, abbé; Labadessa, Abbadessa, abbess; Patrasso (Teramano), provincial superior; Guardiano, superior of a convent; Capoverde,[57] head of a convent; Romiti, Morabito (Arabic-Italian), Ermitani, hermit; perhaps Minimi,[58] monk of the order of Saint Francis of Paola; and the outmoded Leggitore, lister, Inquisitore, inquisitor. Porporati is either a cardinal or a wearer of a purple garb. A Palmiero, Parmiero, Parmieri, is nowadays one who carries the palm in processions, but if the word has descended from the Middle Ages, it means a pilgrim or cleric who distributed and sold indulgences. Romeo and Borromeo are other names meaning pilgrim. Cf. Pellegrino. Templare, templar, is the real or assumed name of a recent Italian writer. Picozzi [59]

[50] Zago, Zagone could also derive from Giacchino, Giacomo.

[51] Literally, shepherd, but frequently used for bishop as well as priest. Cf. St. Pastore.

[52] A wagtail is also called parrinello in Sicilian.

[53] In Piedmontese piovana can also be a bullfinch, salamander. Sacerdote is at times a rabbi.

[54] Campanaro is also belfry, bell ringer, bell maker. As to becchino it usually means a grave digger.

[55] Especially in the plural this and other names could be place names. Cf. vicino ai cappuccini, adjoining the capuchins.

[56] Frate is a widespread dialectical term for brother. Aphetic forms like Badini, Vatini could be from font names, cf. Genoese GaiBADO (Garibaldo), Monferrino Badin from Bernardo and Germanic Bado (see Förstemann, op. cit. 225). F.

[57] No need to indicate that guardiano is a watchman. Capoverde is sometimes a plover. If we searched among the place names we should also find a Capoverde, green cape.

[58] Conceivably also smallest or last born child.

[59] Cf. the terms for magpie and woodpecker.

(Abruzzese) is a layman of the order of the Capucins. To these we might add Paratore,[60] church upholsterer, decorator; Mazzaro, Mazzieri,[61] servant of a magistrate or prelate who precedes his masters carrying a mace as the sign of their authority; and Massaro,[62] which in Sicilian is a church porter. Several names in an associated category are Santaro, maker of saintly images; Santo, Santelli, Santarella,[63] Beati, Devoto, Di Votti,[64] Umili, saintly, devout person; Accattino, church beggar; Mendico, beggar; Bizzozero, bigot; Imprevidito, tainted by priestly influence. Profeta and Martire,[65] prophet and martyr have probably resulted from roles in church pageants. Other non-occupational names that we may mention at this point are Battezzati, Battiati, baptized, and Convertito, converted.

Some of the ecclesiastical cognomina have figurative meanings which have been productive of at least a few surnames from this group. Among those that have a fair degree of currency are papa, pope, denoting a vain, prosperous, or a fat and good-humored individual; patriarca, patriarch, an old and venerable man; canonico, canon, a sly fellow in Venetian, Vastese and perhaps other dialects; romito, hermit, a taciturn person or one who lives to himself. A patrasso, provincial superior, is in the dialect of Teramo a fat man, while in Romagnuolo he is a distinguished citizen. The abruzzese capeverde referring to a learned monk probably has by extension been applied to laymen as well. Profeta, prophet, speaks for itself.

THE LEARNED PROFESSIONS

From the learned professions come Dottore, del Dotto,[66] a learned man; Maestri, Maestroni, Maestrini, Magistro, Magistretti, Magistrelli,[67] Marro (Southern Italian), teacher; Prevosto,[68] rector; Ajolo, Lajolo, tutor; Studente, Scolari, Alunno, Discepoli, student; Baccellieri, bachelor; Licenziato, licentiate; Bardotti,[69] novice or ap-

---

[60] If Sicilian paratore could be also a place name, 'u paraturi, fulling mill. See C. Avolio, "Saggio di Toponomastica Siciliana," *Archivio Glottologico Italiano,* Supplemento, Sesta Dispensa, 1898, 100.

[61] A mazzaro, mazziero, is also a maker of clubs or maces.

[62] See Agricultural Occupations for the various meanings of this word.

[63] Santo is popular as a first name in Southern Italy.

[64] Cf. St. Beato, Beata. Both De Voto and Di Votti could come from IacoVOT(T)O or OliVOT(T)O.

[65] Cf. St. Martire.

[66] Dotto is also obtainable from GuiDOTTO. Formerly dottore was a lawyer as well.

[67] Maestro, Marro, can be applied to any tradesman, a band-master, a steward, maestro di casa.

[68] See Public Officials and Ecclesiastical Names.

[69] Another meaning of bardotto is mule.

prentice; Avvocati, Avogadro, Curiale, lawyer; Notari, de Notaris, Nodari,[70] notary; Scribante, Scrittore,[71] Poeta, poet; Scultore, Tagliapietra,[73] sculptor; Pentore, painter; Miniatori, miniature painter; Ingegneri, Ingigneri, engineer; Architetto, architect; Ragionieri, Faconti,[74] Contatore, accountant; Scrivano, scrivener; Astrologo, dello Strologo,[75] astrologer; Medici, dal Medico, doctor; Chiurco, surgeon; Speziali, Peziali, Speciale,[76] pharmacist; and several other names connected with the medical profession, though they may not be classed as learned, like Mammana, Mammanello, Bonadonna[77] (Genoese), Commare, Comari[78] (if Venetian, Friulano, Sicilian), midwife; Baila, nurse; Spitalieri, Spedalieri, hospital attendant.[79]

MUSIC ARTS NAMES

The followers of Euterpe are Musico,[80] Musicante, musician; perhaps Compositore, composer; Sampognaro, Ceramiraro,[81] Pivaro, Fistulario, bagpipe or flageolet player; Lautero[82] (Venetian), lutist; Piffero, Piffaro,[83] fifer; Cornaro,[84] horner; Trombetta,[85] Trombadore, trumpeter; Arpaia,[86] Arpaio, harpist; Tamburri, Tamburi, Tamborra, Tamburini,[87] drummer; Timpanaro, timbrel player; while the devotees of Terpsichore are Cantore, Cantatore, singer,

---

[70] See Chapter on Compound Names.

[71] Of course, scrittore could also be a writer, author.

[73] For example, Filippo Calendario, fourteenth century Venetian artist, was called tajapietra, stone-cutter.

[74] Faconti might well be from Facundo, a font name.

[75] An astrologo is often a shrewd or whimsical person.

[76] Also a dealer in spices.

[77] But compare the name Bonomi, good man.

[78] Comare is regularly god-mother, god daughter. Cf. DaGOMARA.

[79] Add Capoverde, Patrasso, for which see Ecclesiastical Names.

[80] A musico is sometimes a beardless or evirated fellow.

[81] Zampognaro carries the connotation of an idle prattler. Another meaning of the word ceramiraro is tiler.

[82] Cf. St. Lotharius.

[83] Also a fife, and in Mirandolese a big nose.

[84] A cornaro is also a chaplet maker, coronaro, or a rambling gossip (Abruzzese curunara).

[85] Other meanings of trombetta are trumpet, messenger, chatterer (Bolognese), spy and babbler (Friulano).

[86] There is a place name, Arpaia, Sicily.

[87] Other meanings for tamburro are drum, a sheriff, a fat man.

chanter; Canzoniere, ballad singer; Ballatore, Ballerini,[88] dancer. The names Soprani, Tenore, Basso [89] most probably have nothing to do with music. Incidentally, many fifers used to be Germans that went by the name of Tedeschi. Petazzi in the Alto Adige (Male) are trumpeters who play for the devout during the forty hour devotions. In Trento they are musicians who perform for students receiving school prizes.

AGRICULTURAL OCCUPATIONS

Agricultural callings are rich sources of cognomina. Names signifying farmers are Contadini, Contadinelli, Lavoratore (Southern Italian), Campagnaro, Campagnuolo, Forese, Loforese [90] (Tarantino furese), Villani, Villanelli,[91] Salani (Lucchese), and Agricola,[92] taken from the Latin. Fittaiolo, Fittante and Borgese, Burgisi (Sicilian) are tenant farmers. Mezzadroli, Mezzadrelli, Masciadri, Mezzari (Venetian), Menzieri (Calabrese) are sharecroppers. Annalora (Sicilian) is a farmer hired by the year. A Capoccia [93] is a farm overseer; a Torrieri a custodian of a rural holding. Massaro, Massaroli, Massai, Masseri [94] are subject to a number of different interpretations: in Neapolitan massaro is a tenant farmer or steward; in Reggio Calabrese massaru is a bull herder, and in Cosentino an owner of cattle; while a Bresciano, Mantuan and Pavese masser is a sharecropper. Among those that have special farming duties to perform are Seminatore, sower; Bifulco, Bifolco, Beolco, Biolchini, Aratori,[95] Gualano [96] (Southern Italian), ploughman; Falciai, Mietitori, reaper; Vaglieri, Cernitori, Ciarnatori, winnowers; Vignaro,

[88] In Bergamascan a ballerina is a frivolous woman. The term also means a wagtail. See Bird Names.

[89] Tenore can easily be related to AnTENORE and Basso to the word for short and JacoBASSO.

[90] Has been used as a first name, cf. the name of Dante's friend, Forese Donati. Often it means a foreigner. Calabrese furise is a shepherd.

[91] The word can mean a villager, a rude person, a country bumpkin.

[92] Cf. St. Agricola.

[93] A capoccia may be a ringleader or, if a variant of capocchio, a blockhead. Cf. also IaCAPOCCIA = Jacopoccia.

[94] Masser in Parmigiano and Romagnuolo is any kind of steward. In Sicilian massaru is a church worker, hard worker. Massaro in the Middle Ages (Mantua) was a podestà, mayor. (See *Statuti Senesi*, Bologna, 1877, 492.) In the case of the feminine Massera, which is more popular than the masculine form, the meaning might shift from farmer to servant. A Massara in Calabrese is a weaver. Moreover, Masera, ruined wall, and Massera are apt to be interchangeable terms. Finally a massarola may be a warbler, or in parts of Tuscany a wheatear.

[95] In Parmigiano an arador is a winnower. Cf. St. Arator.

[96] In Tarantino a vualano is a farmer and in Lucanese a cow herder.

Vitari, Vidari, keeper of a vineyard; Sapori (if from Milanese or Genoese sapoeur, sappeur), mower; Campari and possibly Macchiaroli, field custodians; Ortolano,[97] gardener; Boschiero, Boscaroli, Saltarini (Venetian), forester; Cacciatore, hunter; Oselladore, fowler; Mandriale, Pastore,[98] Pastoressa, Vergari, Caporale [99] (Calabrese), Guardiano,[100] Botteri (buttero), herdsman; Generale [101] (Pavese), pigherd; Cavalcante [102] (Calabrese), horse trainer. The other names which follow indicating herdsman, fowler, fruit growers and vegetable growers can refer not only to raiser-growers, but also to dealer-sellers as well as to zoological and ornithological stations,[103] fruit groves and vegetables patches. Frequently some of them imply a fancier, a hunter, or one who is unusually fond of eating a particular kind of meat, fruit or vegetable. Among such names are Cavallaro [104] referring to horses; Capraro, Cibrario, to goats; Pecoraro, to sheep; Porcaro, to pigs; Baccaro, Vaccarone, Vaccarelli,[105] to cows; Mulari, Mulattero, to mules; Asinari, to donkeys; Vitellaro, to calves; Boari, Boaretti,[106] Bovaro, Boveri, to oxen; Conigliaro, to rabbits; Bracaro, to hounds; Gallinaro, Pollari, Pollinari,[107] (Old Italian), to chickens; Occari, Papararo, to geese; Colomberi, Palombari,[108] to doves; Cignaro, to swans; Quagliere, to quails; Perniciaro, to partridges; Stornajoli, to starlings; Fasanaro, to pheasants, Falconaro, Falcheri, to falcons; Cornacchiari, Corviero,

---

[97] In rare instances an ortolano may be a bird, common bunting.

[98] Cf. St. Pastore. See Note 51.

[99] See Note 29.

[100] A guardiano is also a jailer, watchman, keeper, and, often a religious term.

[101] Also a military term.

[102] In Parmigiano a cavalcant is a hauler.

[103] See T. Zanardelli, *I Nomi di Animali nella Toponomastica Emiliana*. Bologna, 1907. This lists among other names Cicognara, Corvara, Asinare, Boare, Cavallare. Similar names can be added through consultation of A. Amati, *Dizionario Corografico dell'Italia*, Milano, Vallardi, n.d. 9 v.

[104] If Calabrese, a cavallaru is one who sells horses carved out of milk products, latticini.

[105] Vaccarone (Neapolitan) and Vaccarella (Southern Italian) are also beetles.

[106] A boarino is, at times, a wagtail, and a boaro (Bolognese), a bull pen. Cf. the given name Alboaro. In thirteenth century Sicily we find Matteo Iumentarius. See R. Starabba, "Miscellanea . . ." *Archivio Storico Siciliano*, n.s. anno XIII, 1888, 80.

[107] It should be noted that Pollinari from Apollinare is a more acceptable derivation.

[108] A palombaro is also a diver.

Croveri, Corbari,[109] to rooks and ravens; Melari and Pomari, to apples; Piraro, to pears; Prunera and Prunai,[110] to plums; Peschieri,[111] to peaches; Cerasaro, to cherries; Uvari to grapes; Morari (Parmigiano) to mulberries; Castagnaro, to chestnuts; Cedraro,[112] to citrons; Nosari, to nuts; Amendolara, Mandalari, to almonds; Iannaro,[113] to acorns; Olivari,[114] to olives; Verdaro, to greens; Granaro, Biadaroli, to grains; Ciciari,[115] to chickpeas; Fazzolari, Favaro and Fasolara, to beans; Finocchiaro, to fennel; Bruccoliri, to broccoli; Cipollaro,[116] to onions; Orziere, to barley; Pipari and Peponari, to peppers; Berzolari, to cabbage; Rabaioli, to turnips; Cominaro, Ciminaro, to cumin; Cardaro,[117] to cardoon thistles; Zuccaro, to pumpkins; Tartuferi,[118] to truffles; Fongaroli and Fungaroli, to mushrooms; Migliari and Migliarini,[119] Melegari (Lombard), to corn or millet; Melegari (if Mantuan) to buckwheat; and Sagginario to sorghum. Other names to be added are Curatolo [120] (Calabrese-Cosenza), maker of milk products; Casaro, Casiere, Facaccio, cheese maker and Perito (Parmigiano) field surveyor.

THE ARTS AND CRAFTS

We find corporations of skilled workers in the earliest days of the Venetian Republic. In the mediaeval communes these handicraftsmen gained great political power through their organizations. Whereas during the feudal period due to the restriction of commerce and industry within the corti of the great landowners it may be assumed that a carpenter or smith or tailor performed most of the various functions attached to their professions, now, with the rebirth of large urban centers and the widespread establishment of trade routes, the crafts were divided and subdivided

---

[109] In the dialect of Sannio a quagliera is a quail not an occupative or collective term. Corviero, Croveri, Corbari might refer to basket makers.

[110] Prunaio is also a common word for thorn bush.

[111] It will be recalled that Peschiera is the name of a town on Lake Garda, and peschiera a place where fish are kept.

[112] Another meaning is cedar grove.

[113] Possible variant of Gennaro. Witch in the dialect of Sannio.

[114] A probable variant of Oliviero.

[115] By shifting the accent cíciari we get the plant name.

[116] A cipollaro in the dialect of Amaseno is a mole cricket.

[117] A cardaro is also a carder, wool comber.

[118] Sometimes tartufaro has the meaning of simpleton.

[119] Could be a pet form of Emilio.

[120] In Sicilian a steward, and in Tarantino one who has charge of oil vats. Reggio Calabrese curatulu is defined as head herdsman.

with the offshoots attaining to the dignity of their own craft name. As late as 1762 the Venetian Corporazioni di Arti e Mestieri numbered one hundred and twelve arts and crafts. In the more populated centers shops and stalls were kept together in streets that were known by the name of the craft, for example, Via dei Balestrari, Crossbowman Street, etc.[121] Those who were masters of their trade received the title Maestro, Mastro, Magistro, Marro,[122] a title often used along with their baptismal names such as Mastrangelo, Mastronardi, Mastrovalerio. General terms for tradesmen are Artieri and the infrequent Lavorante, but unlike the master title they have had a small vogue. Craft specialization is liberally represented in surnames.

LEATHERGOODS TRADES

For example, we have in the leathergoods trades, in addition to the familiar shoemaker or cobbler, Calzolaio, Calzolari,[123] Scarpari, Ciabatteri, Ciabattini, Zavattini, such names as Conciatore, Consadore, Caligaio, Callegari, Calgari, tanner; Pellizzari, Pellettieri, furrier; Sellaio, Sellaro,[124] Sellaroli, saddler; Bastaro, pack saddle maker; Borsari, Borsieri,[125] Borzellieri, purse maker; Valisari, valise maker; Correggiari, strap maker; Guantieri, glover; Foderaro, sheath maker; and the rare Palminteri, parchment maker. Balzaro, Balzaretti also refer to strap makers but have strong competition in Baltazare which can give us the same names.

TEXTILE TRADES

Among those employed in the textile trades are Tessitore, Testore, Tessaro, Tessero, Tellarini, Massara [126] (Calabrese), weaver; Folladore (Milanese), fuller; Filadoro (filatore), spinner; Chiodarolo, master stretcher and dyer of cloth; Cimatore, Cimadoro, shearer; Lissario [127] (lizzarius), maker of thread for looms; Cavadore

---

[121] For further information see R. Vivaldi, "Toponomastica Romana," *Folklore Italiano*, III, 1928, 1-10. This raises the question as to whether some apparent craftnames can have started with craft-street names. If the Florentine del Garbo could assume their cognomen from Via del Garbo (See *Statuti Sanesi*, III, Bologna, 1877, 424-25) there is no valid reason why a Balestraro and his brother tradesmen should not, once in a while, have drawn names from Via de'Balestrari and other streets.

[122] Of course, these words can also refer to teacher, band master, steward.

[123] In the good old days calzolaio used to mean hosier.

[124] By shifting the accent, séllaro, we get the word for celery.

[125] Also bursar.

[126] Cf. Tellarino from AlberTELLO + ARINO. Another name, Tessarini, probably goes back to Contessa used as a given name. For Massara see Note 94.

[127] Derivation could be from the font name BeLISSARIO.

(Milanese), silk worker; Purgatorio,[128] possibly from Mantuan purgador, one who removes oil from woolens; Manganaro,[129] calendar; Mondadori (Venetian for emendatore di lana); Battilana, Cardaro,[130] wool comber; Lanari, wool man, laner; Tescaro (Venetian), Scartazzini (Parmigiano scartezzen), Ciompi,[131] wool carder; Cottonero, Cuttunaro, cotton mercer; Setaro, Setajoli, silk mercer or maker; Tintori, dyer and Linari, flaxman, unless it comes from ApolLINARE or Spanish Linares.

Sarto, Sartini, Sartori, tailor, are common but not nearly so numerous as the English Taylor. The dialectical synonym Custuliere (Calabrese), has some vogue, but Fapanni, Tagliatore and Cositori have a limited circulation. Specialized types of tailoring are represented by Capparo,[132] cape maker; Capucciaro,[133] hood maker; Mantellaro, Mantiero, cloak maker; Capellari, Capelliri, Cappellieri, hatter; Berrettari, Bertinari (Parmigiano), cap maker; Camisari, shirt maker; Traversari,[134] skirt maker; Sciallaro, shawl maker; Franzero (Bresciano), fringe maker. The more lowly textile trades furnish Saccaro,[135] Sacchiero, Galuppo [136] (Venetian) sack maker; Funaro, Funaioli and Cordaro, rope maker.

A by-product of this industry, old clothes mongering, gives Cenciarini, Pateri [137] (Parmigiano), Regattieri, Chiapusso [138] (Genoese ciapuss), Strazzari, Strazzeri, Pattarello and Pezzaroli (both Venetian), and the Calabrese Saponaro,[139] one who gives soap in exchange for old clothes.

---

[128] A purgatorio in the dialect of Amaseno is an ugly, deformed man and in Tarantino he is one who has suffered from any serious illness.

[129] Could be a ballista-man.

[130] Cardaro also means a cardoon thistle patch or cardoon seller.

[131] Also a coarse fellow, simpleton. With Maruffino (likewise a surname) he was an officer of the Arte della Lana.

[132] Placing the accent on the first syllable give cápparo, a word for caper.

[133] May also be a cabbage patch, or grower.

[134] Another meaning is cross-road dweller.

[135] A saccaru in Sicilian is an itinerant water seller. See G. de Gregorio, "Gruzzoletto di Voci Arabe Sicule," Zeitschrift für Romanische Philologie, XLIX, 1929, 530.

[136] A galuppo also used to be a baggage carrying soldier. Sometimes also a despicable fellow and, in Piedmontese, a glutton.

[137] May be a variant of pader, father. Cenciarini may come from Vincenzo.

[138] The word is also defined in Piedmontese as a bad artisan. But compare Old French chappuis, carpenter.

[139] Literally, soap maker. Also the name of a flower, bouncing Bet, and in Sicilian the name of a weed, Russian thistle.

METAL TRADES

The most common Italian equivalents of Smith are Ferraro, Ferreri, Ferrai, Fabbri, Fab(b)rone, Fabbrucci. Fucinari, Fusinieri, Forgiarini are more or less synonymous terms. Ferraioli (obsolete) and Magnano,[140] Magnini (Genoese) are locksmiths. A Fornacciari, Fornasari, is a workman in a furnace; he may or may not belong to the metal trades. In Tarantino, for instance, he is a maker of terra cotta articles, and in Romagnuolo a brick manufacturer. In this highly diversified industry we find Calderari, Calderai, Cardarelli,[141] cauldron maker; Catinari, chain maker; Chiavarini,[142] key maker; Cortellieri, Cultellaio, cutler; Falciai, Falceri, maker of scythes; Coltraro, maker of plough shares; Marraro, maker of hoes; Campanaro,[143] Campanato (Venetian), bell maker; Squillante, maker of cow-bells; Martellaro, hammer maker; Mazzolari,[144] maker of stone workers' hammers; Rotari, [145] wheelwright; Mannajuolo, axe maker; Fontanaro (Parmigiano), pump maker; Padellaro, pan maker; Perolaro (Modenese), bucket maker; Cerchieri, hoop maker; Spitaro, Spitero, spit maker; Lamieri, blade maker; Vaglieri, sieve maker; Agugliaro, specialist in making needles; Bussolari,[146] maker of compasses; Stagnaro, a worker in pewter, a tinker; Ottonieri, Ottonaio, a worker in brass; Piombanti,[147] a worker in lead. Orefici and the shortened form Rifici relate to a jeweler. Battiloro recalls the time-honored trade of gold beating. The silver smith is Argentieri or Argentaro. The makers of various types of military equipment are represented by Armieri, dell'Armaiolo, maker of weapons; Corazzieri,[148] Osberghieri, cuirass maker; Magliari, Magliero, nail maker; Spataro, sword maker; Lanzaro, Lanciari, Lancieri, lance maker; Scutari, shield maker; Cannonieri,[149] cannon maker; Bardari, maker of steel armor for horses.

[140] Nowadays the meaning of ferraiolo is cloak. The trade name magnano is extended to a maker of a number of small iron objects. In Pavese a magnan is a sly fellow. Magnano is also a place name near Novara and Udine.

[141] Cf. cardaro, wool comber, cardoon thistle patch or cardoon seller.

[142] Cf. the place name Chiavari and Abruzzese ciavarelle, a sort of bread soup, a flirtacious woman.

[143] Campanaro also means sacristan, bell ringer, belfry.

[144] A mazzolar in Milanese is a pork sausage maker.

[145] Rotari may come from the Lombard Hrotharit.

[146] A bussolaro could be a maker of sedan chairs.

[147] See B. Migliorini, "I Nomi Italiani del Tipo Bracciante," *Vox Romanica*, I, 1936, 64-85.

[148] Also royal guard.

[149] The last three occupations can also mean lancer, shield bearer, cannoneer.

CARPENTRY

In the realm of carpentry a limited number of individuals bear the trade names Carpenteri, Carpintieri, Marangoni [150] (Northern Italian), Chiapusso [151] (Piedmontese), Legnaiolo, Lignaroli,[152] Different ramifications of the craft produce Serraro,[153] Serratore, Secatore, Segantini, Seganti, sawyer; Tornatore, turner; Majellaro (Southern Italian), maker of kneading troughs; Fusaio, Fusaro,[154] Fuseri, spindle maker; Carradore, Carrieri, Carozzari, Carrozzieri, Carrante, cartwright; Cocchiaro,[155] maker of coaches; Bussolari,[156] maker of sedan chairs; Tavollaro, Tavolieri,[157] table maker; Seggiaro, chair maker; Quadraro,[158] frame maker; Secchieri, Sichirollo (Venetian), bucket maker; Bottai, Bottaro, Bottero, Barillari, Bigongiari, Mastellari, Concaro, Tencaro, Tencajoli, cask, barrel or vat makers; Bordonaro,[159] staff maker; Perticari,[160] Palieri,[161] perch or pole maker; Crivellari, Vaglieri, Tamisari (Venetian), sieve maker; Cazzaro, Meschieri (cf. Parmigiano mesch), ladle maker; Mazzari, Mazzieri,[162] mace maker; Scrignaro, jewel box maker; Coffaro, chest, casket maker; Casciaro, Cassaro, Cassettari, Scatolari, box maker; Pallaro, Boccieri,[163] ball or bocce maker. In the

[150] A marangone is also a bird, a human diver, and, in Sicilian, a jack of all trades.

[151] Chiapusso may have signified carpenter at one time. Cf. Old French chappuis and current surname Chappuis. Nowadays it has deteriorated into a poor artisan, or an old clothes man (Genoese).

[152] Another meaning is wood seller. Incidentally, the surname Resegotti derives from Milanese resegott, sawyer, an itinerant carpenter who comes into the Milanese region to spend the winter. Also campare resegot (Comascan), trouble-maker.

[153] It is possible that a serraro is a dweller of a serra, pass, defile, range.

[154] Fusari may at times go back to Low Latin fusaria, woods.

[155] The cartwright and coach maker terms may also refer to carter, coachman.

[156] Perhaps also maker of compasses.

[157] Cf. tavoliere, chess board.

[158] The surname is even more likely to derive from Southern Italian quatraro, young man. Because I have found Lettieri only in the possession of Southern Italians so far I should discard it in the meaning of bed maker. It seems to be more closely related to lettiera, litter.

[159] A muleteer in Calabrese.

[160] Also a plow or a measure of land.

[161] May be from pala which would make the term mean shovel maker.

[162] Also a mace carrying servant.

[163] Boccieri may likewise refer to a ball or boccie player or to a goblet maker. It is also possible that bocciero is related to Low Latin bucerius (cf. the Sicilian last name and place name Bucceri, and see C. Avolio, op. cit. 105) and to Boccieri, Buccieri, butcher.

allied field of basket making we have Panierari, Panerari, Cavagnaro (Romagnuolo), Cavagnini (Guastallese, Parmigiano), Cestaro, Canistaro, Corbari.[164]

MASONRY

In the restricted field of masonry we have Muratori, Murari, mason, and the rather infrequent synonyms Fabbricatore, Fabricante. In Genoese the word for a mason is massacan, from a building stone. It may have produced the surnames Massacane, Mazzacane.[165] Scarpellini recalls a stone chiseler; Stoccatore, a plasterer (stuccatore); Ceramiraro, a tiler; Pontari, Pontieri,[166] Pontarelli, Faciponti, a bridge builder; Molari, Molaioli, Moleta [167] (Bergamascan, Bresciano), a grinder or maker of mill stones. Tombari possibly refers to a maker of tomb stones.

GLASS AND POTTERY INDUSTRY

Pointing back to the glass and pottery industry are Bottiglieri, Boccieri,[168] Fiasconaro, flask maker; Boccaliero, Boccalari, Cannataro (Calabrese), jug or pitcher maker; Cupparo, Copperi, goblet, cup maker; Bicchierai, tumbler maker; Grastaro (Calabrese), flower pot maker; Scodellaro, Scotellaro, Scutellari, bowl or porringer maker; Lucernari, lamp maker; Coronaro,[169] Zuccalà (Otrantino and Bovese), chaplet maker; Pignataro, Coccari, potter. A Vetrarii is a glazer.

MILLING AND BAKING INDUSTRY

Once engaged in the milling and baking industry were most of our Molinari, Mugnaio, Monari, miller; Cernigliaro, sifter; Farinaro, flour man; Farinello [170] (Iesino), one who conveys flour from the mill to the home; Fogazzaro, Pistorio, Pistorino,[171] Panaro,[172]

---

[164] The word is also connected with rook, raven.

[165] See Note 15.

[166] A ceramiraro may be a bagpipe player, while Pontieri has been the regular Italian form of Poitiers.

[167] If Molari rises from one of the Northern Italian dialects it may stem from the word meaning spring or fire tong maker. Cf. molla, molli. Moleta, on the other hand, can be reproduced from any name ending in -mo, GiacoMOLETA?, RoMOLETA, GiroMOLETA.

[168] See Note 153.

[169] Cf. Abruzzese curunara, rambling gossip. Through anaptyxis coronaro may have developed from cornaro.

[170] See Note 21 of Botanical Names.

[171] Pistorino may come from a Latinized form meaning native of Pistoia.

[172] A panaro is also a bread basket.

Panettiere, Pananti,[173] Fapane, Prestinari (pestrinaro), Fornaro, Furnaro, Fornero; Pizzaioli and perhaps Pittaro, Pittarelli, Pittarini [174] (if Calabrese), pizza maker; Pasticceri, confectioner.

SEA NAMES

The sea has produced only a few occupative names—Marinaro, sailor; Pilotto, pilot; Comitini, sea captain; Barcaro, Barcai, Barcaroli, boatman; Rematore, rower; Pescatore, fisher; Piscianieri (Calabrese), fish monger; Calafate, Colafate, chaulker; Armatore, one who equips or freights mercantile vessels; Galeotto,[175] galley slave. Marangone, Palombaro,[176] diver, may or may not indicate occupation. Nauta seems to be a Latinized form of marinaro.

SHOPKEEPERS, VENDORS AND MISCELLANEOUS OCCUPATIONS

Since most items that are manufactured, raised or produced are saleable it will be easy for the reader to pick out possible shopkeepers, vendors and others from the long list of occupative names that have preceded. Others are Mercante, Marcatante, Merciaio, Traficante, Pegalotti (Bresciano), Drappieri, merchant; Firande (Sicilian), fair merchant;[177] Bottegari, Bottighieri, shopkeeper, apothecary; Macellaro, Beccaio, del Beccaro,[178] Boccieri, Buccieri [179] (Calabrese), Beccheri, Becheroni, Becherini [180] (cf. Mantuan bcher), Beghè (Piedmontese bechè), Carnaroli, Carnera (Northern Italian), Tagliacarne, Tagliabò, Tagliabue, Tagliavacche, butcher; Pizzicagnolo, pork butcher; Mazzolari [181] (if Milanese), pork sausage dealer; Cervellari, seller of brains; Lattari, Lattieri, milkman; Salari, Salaroli, salt seller; Oliari, oil merchant; Acquaro,[182] Acquaruolo, water seller; Barbieri, Barberio, barber; Barruccheri (parrucchieri) wig maker or hair dresser; Pettinari, comb seller; Cartaro, Cartolari, Cartuario, stationer; Antiquario, antiquary;

---

[173] See B. Migliorini, op. cit. 64-85.

[174] The names may be connected with the Venetian word for robin, pitar.

[175] Also means convict, and is the regular form of Galahad, hero of the Arthurian romances. Venetian galioto is a cunning man.

[176] Marangone is also a carpenter, a bird, and jack of all trades (Sicilian).

[177] The last name Fondacaro also means clothes seller as well as keeper of a warehouse.

[178] Beccaio, Beccaro could mean goatherder.

[179] See Note 153.

[180] The Tuscan pet form of Domenico, Beco, plus suffixes could give us Beccheroni and Becherini. Cf. the word for glass, tumbler.

[181] Also a hammer maker.

[182] Acquaro is frequently used for aqueduct.

Scupari,[183] broom merchant; Pignero, pawn broker; Carbonaro,[184] Carboneri, coal man; Vinattieri, Vinaj, Canevari [185] (Venetian), Canovaro, vintner or wine seller; Tavernaro, taverner; Ostellari, Positero, Pusateri (Sicilian from the Spanish posadero), Fondacaro [186] (also Sicilian), innkeeper; Ceraro, wax seller; Candelari, Candilaro,[187] Candelieri, chandler; Saponaro,[188] soap seller; Polverari (Calabrese), Fogaroli,[189] dealer in fire works; Mantegari, pomade seller; Gessaroli, chalk seller; Tappari, cork seller; Zondadore (from zendado), seller of fine silk stuffs; Pegolari, pitch seller; Pagliaruolo,[190] straw seller; Sassaiuoli, stoneman; Banchieri, banker; Cambiatore, Cozzone, Cuzzone,[191] Mezzanini,[192] Sensale, Sansale,[193] broker; Braccianti, Bracciale [194] (Calabrese), day laborer; Facchini, Facchinetti,[195] Spallino,[196] porter; Formentin (Venetian), grain loader and unloader; Cancello [197] (Sicilian canceddu) one who guides pack saddle horses; Mulettieri, Mollettiere, Bordonari [198] (Calabrese), muleteer; Postiglione, postillion; Vetturale, driver, cabman. A Caruso [199] in the Girgenti section of Sicily is a worker in the sulphur pits. Disguising its occupational connotation is the name Lombardo which if Sicilian means a shopkeeper due to the fact that a large number of persons from this province had set up shops there. A few occupational odds and ends are Pezzente,

---

[183] Also a broom patch.

[184] In rare instances a Carbonaro may hail from the Calabrese word meaning hornet.

[185] Can also mean a hemp field.

[186] See Note 167.

[187] The name may relate to the Madonna del Candelaio. A candeliere is also a chandelier.

[188] See Note 129.

[189] A fogarolo is also a red wing thrush.

[190] May be a hosteler; in the dialect of Sannio a deformed person, and in Abruzzese a horse born and raised in a stall.

[191] Cuzzone, Cozzone might come from any name in -co, Francesco, Domenico, etc., possibly Acuzio, cozzo, summit and cozza, oyster.

[192] Literally middling, go-between.

[193] Sensale is one of the words for mosquito. In Milanese sansal is a sorrel plant.

[194] Also breast armor, bracelet. ,

[195] Facchino in the sense of porter was imported from France in the fifteenth century. In Sicily it used to mean innkeeper. See A. Prati, in *Lingua Nostra*, I, August, 1939.

[196] Spallino also suggests a small river bank, an epaulet, a small shouldered person.

[197] The word also signifies gate.

[198] Might be also a pilgrim staff maker.

[199] Literally a clipped head and by extension a child. Most of the Carusos spring from nicknames with one of these two meanings.

Paltrinieri, Zarcone (Piacentino), beggar; Corsaro, Corsale,[200] pirate, corsair; Banditi, Brigante, bandit; Sicari, cut throat.

[200] Most of these terms can be taken figuratively as well as literally. We note that a Giuseppe Aromatarii, perfumer, lived in the seventeenth century. Object names are often the equivalents of occupational names. See Chapter on Object Names which follows immediately.

Chapter XVI

OBJECT NAMES

We have already called attention to the fact that either the name of an article made, raised or sold, or the name of a material or tool used in carrying on a trade might stand as the equivalent of an occupational name. It has further been noted that surnames could arise from objects employed as shop signs or from wares displayed or even cried. They are the most fertile sources of our cognomina. Some object names, however, must be the result of an accidental orthographical identity with other names. Others, probably many more than we are able to point out at this time, have become current through metaphorical usage. In any case the catalog of object names is an impressive one.

THE HOUSEHOLD

When we look into the cook room we discover that last names have been drawn from its larder in considerable profusion. Here, in addition to the possible originations just cited, it would be fair to state that an excessive fondness on the part of an individual for a particular viand might produce a nickname-surname in the guise of the favored food. Among them are Carne,[1] meat; Arrosto, roast; Lessi[2] boiled meat; Rognone,[3] kidney; Ventresca (Abruzzese), salt pork; Zarlenga, Zarlinga (Agnonese), a salted, sun-dried meat strip; Midolla, Medolla, Medulla, Merulla (Southern Italian), Miola, Cervelli, Cervellini, Carvello, Caravello,[4] brains; Milza, viscera; Coratella,[5] lights; Mazzarella[6] (Teramana), lamb lights; Sangui-

---

[1] Carne may represent a broken-up compound MalaCARNE, rogue. German Fleisch is usually connected with butcher.

[2] Lessi comes from Alessio in the great majority of cases.

[3] In Venetian a rugnon is a mumbler, and in Sicilian rugnuni, a sly person. Cf. Aviri li rugnuni.

[4] Cervello, midolla with their variants and derivatives are frequently applied to hair-brained, thoughtless humans, senza cervello, senza medollo. In Pavese a cervell is a stubborn person. Cervello can also mean young deer. Either Medolla, Medulla, Merulla can easily be obtained from a short form of Diomede, i.e. Mede plus the diminutive -olla, -ulla. In Southern Italian r replaces d. On the other hand Miola may be a variant with the suffix -ola or BartoloMEO, Amedeo, Matteo.

[5] If Abruzzese coratella points to a fierce, pitiless or courageous man. But Coratella may be an alteration of Corradella.

[6] Mazzarella could come from GiacoMAZZO, DalMAZZO, Germanic Matzo. It also means little club, and in Calabrese a gnat.

nacci, blood pudding; Prosciutto, Persutto, ham; Salami, Bondioli (Piedmontese), salame; Salsizza,[7] sausage; Vitello, veal, and other cuts of meat;[8] Minestra, Minestrina, soup; Insalata, Inzalata, Linsalata, Salata, salad; and other vegetables;[9] Baccalà, cod, and other kinds of fish.[10] Pane, Li Pani, Panetti, Pagnone, Pagnotta,[11] bread; Panebianco, white bread; Panegrosso, large bread; Pancaldi,[12] warm bread; Pancotto, pap; Buonpane,[13] good bread; Cuzzubbo (Calabrese cuzzuppu), bread with eggs inserted; Biscotti,[14] Biscottini, Biscuiti, biscuit; Fogaccia, Focacci, Fugassi (Genoese), Pizza, Pizzagrossa,[15] Pinza [16] (Tridentino, Ferrarese), Frittelli,[17] Frisella, Fresiella (both Southern Italian), Chizzola, Chizzolini [18] (Northern Italian) Ciampelli, Zambelli [19] (Mantuan), Tarallo (Southern Italian), Pattoni, cake, pancake; Polenta,[20] chestnut pudding; Panizza, Farinata, hasty pudding; Migliaccio,[21] black pudding; Buccellati,

---

[7] Prosciutto, salame, salciccia commonly refer to dullards. Bondioli should also be connected with Abbondio. We recall here salam, a Veronese word for cattail.

[8] See Animal Names.

[9] See Botanical Names.

[10] See Fish Names.

[11] A good source of Pagnone, Pagnotta is the font name Buoncompagno, reduced to Compagno, then to Pagno plus the suffixes -one, and -otta. Panetti and, in some instances, Pane, might be connected with Gaspano = Gaspare or Urbano. Cf. Bani, Banelli.

[12] Panebianco (Piacenza) is a flower, soapwort, bouncing Bet. If Calabrese, the name may be related to donna de pane jancu, a white bread woman, aristocrat. It is also a Calabrese place name. Pancaldo has strong earmarks of a Germanic name, i.e. the front theme Banc and the back theme hardu. But compare the French last names Painchaud, Paintendre. Nor must the botanical pancaldo (Piedmontese pan caud) meaning snake root be ruled out as a possibility.

[13] A pancotto in Anconitano is a simpleton, but a buon pane may be a kindly, docile person. Cf. buono come il pane, as good as bread.

[14] Cf. visco, vischio, mistletoe.

[15] Pizza and even Pizzagrossa could come from Opizza, Obizza.

[16] Cf. Germanic Binizo, Binzo. See E. Förstemann, *Altdeutsches Namenbuch*. Erster Band. Personennamen. 2d ed. Bonn, 1900, 306.

[17] The term is used to apply to a snub nose.

[18] The word also means an irascible person. Cf. Modenese chizza.

[19] Ciampelli could come from Gian Ampelle and Zambelli from Gian Bello. In Old Vicentino zambello is synonymous with zimbello, decoy bird, laughingstock.

[20] Pattone, polenta and, in addition, pane, pagnotta, may be considered decompounded forms of mangiapattoni, mangiapolenta, mangiapane, mangiapagnotta, designations for idlers. Polenta is also a place name. We recall here Sicco Polenton, the famous Renaissance author. Cf. polendone, sluggard.

[21] Could come quite easily from Emiliaccio.

cake made at Lucca; Torrone,[22] almond cake; Gnocchi, dumpling; Maccaroni, Maccheroni,[23] Lasagna, Maltagliati, Malfatti,[24] Vermicelli, Raviolo, Tagliarini,[25] Pasta, Pastacaldi (name of a fellow-exile of Garibaldi, in New York), Pastasciutta, macaroni; Caccio, Caso,[26] Casu (Sardinian), Formaggio, cheese; Ricotti,[27] Mascherpa (Northern Italian), buttermilk curd; Provolo [28] (Calabrese pruovola), cheese made of buffalo milk; Caglia, rennet; Soru (Sardinian), whey; della Torta, Tortelli,[29] Frangipane, Fracapane,[30] Chicca,[31] Marenga,[32] dessert sweets. Seasoning is not lacking in the form of dell'Olio, dall'Oglio, oil; Aceto,[33] vinegar; Sciroppa (sciroppo), syrup; Salsa, sauce. Then, too, there is Vino, Sciarappa [34] (Neapolitan), wine; Buonvino, good wine; Latte, milk; and even Zampaglione (Neapolitan), egg nog, zabaione.

Elsewhere in the room we might see the following kitchen utensil-names: Tavola, Deschino,[35] table, Tavolacci,[36] large bench; Arcadipane, Varcadipane, Arcabano, Scifo (Calabrese), bread trough; Scopa, broom; Cucchiaro, Cucciaro, Cucchiarone, Cocchiaro,[37] Cassola (Piedmontese), Mestola, spoon or ladle; Coltellini, Coltellacci, Cortelazzi,[38] Brotzu (Sardinian), knife; Trinciante,

---

[22] Also associated with torre, tower and Ettorre, Hector.

[23] A font name source for Maccaroni, Maccheroni is Macario. Cf. macarone (S. Bernardo, Liguria), bindweed.

[24] Malfatto and maltagliato also imply deformity.

[25] Italia and Italo are even now used as font names. Tagliarini may, therefore, be a pet form of Italia, Italiarina.

[26] Brancaccio, Pancrazio, Pascazio could give Caccio, Caso.

[27] Ricotti recalls EnRICOTTO ArRIGOTTO, AmeRICOTTO. Ricotta together with tarallo, lasagna, (cf. lasagnone), and maccherone may be added to the list of terms for nit-wit.

[28] A more likely claimant of the name is Probo, St. Probus. Venetian Provolo = Procolo.

[29] Torti can refer to gambetorte, bandy legs, occhitorto, squint eyes.

[30] Literally break-bread. See Compound Names.

[31] May be a variant of Cicca from Francesca.

[32] Cf. the place name Marengo.

[33] Aceto is a place name near Bari.

[34] Sciarappa in this sense is apparently an Arabic word. If Sicilian, sciarappa is connected with the plant, convolvulus jalapa. Vino could be the aphetic form of Salvino, Baldovino, Cherubino, etc.

[35] Possibly a clipped form of teDESCHINO or FranceSCHINO with prefix de.

[36] Also a wooden shield, plank bed.

[37] Cucchiaro, Cucciaro, Cocchiaro are likewise coachmen. A cucchiarone (Southern Italian) is also a bird, shoveller.

[38] Cortelazzo is also a term for bur-weed, hyacinth.

carving knife; Tagliere, trencher; Forca, Forcella, Forcellini [39] Forcone, Brocchi (Calabrese), fork; Coppa, Coppadoro,[40] cup; Piatti, dish; Scudella, soup plate; Biccheri, Beccheri, Becheroni,[41] glass; Fiaschi, Fiaschetti,[42] Ciasco (Sicilian), Bottiglioni, Penta (Parmigiano), La Boccetta, Ampolla, bottle, flask, phial; Brocchi, Brocchetti,[43] Cannatelli (Calabrese), Langello (Abruzzese), Urciuoli, Zola [44] (Barese), jug, pitcher; Boccali,[45] Boccalini, Petitti (Agnonese), Anfora, amphora; Pentola, Marmitta, Stagnetti (Marchigiano), Tiano [46] (Calabrese), pot or bowl; Parola [47] (Cremonese), kettle, (bucket in Modenese); Secchi,[48] bucket; Caldaro, Calderone, Calterone, Caldroni, Calderonello,[49] Callari (Castro de'Volsci), Pignatta, Pignatelli, boiler; Tinello,[50] tub, vat; Padella, Padelletti,[51] Pajella (Southern Italian), frying pan; Corbi, Corbelli, Corbetti, Corbino, Corbucci, Corbellini [52] Cesti, Cestoni,[53] Bozzi [54] (Modenese bozz), Casoli (Bresciano casöl), Canestra, Canestrini, Cavagna, Cavagnoli (Cremonese), Cerletti, Cerlini, Gerloni, Gavozzi,[55] Sportelli, Coffa (Sicilian, Calabrese), types of baskets some of which are naturally employed outside the kitchen precincts.

[39] Cf. also forcella, earwig, bifurcated piece of land; forcone, a pitch fork; forcina, a forked spear.

[40] Coppa is not impossible from IaCOP(P)A. Coppadoro, golden cup, seems to indicate an inn sign. Another surname, Tazzi, may be linked with tazza, cup, but more likely comes from AlberTAZZO.

[41] Plato (cf. St. Plato) could give Piatti, but the word may also be related to piatto, flat, fat. Through Tuscan Beco, pet form of Domenico, we can obtain Beccheroni. Mantuan bcher, butcher, could also furnish homonyms.

[42] In Pavese a fiascon is an annoyer.

[43] Also a term for hedge hog.

[44] Zola could come from any name in -zo, FranZOLA, RenZOLA, AnZOLA = Angela, etc.

[45] A boccale in the vernacular of Pisa is a person with a big mouth.

[46] Stagnetti might come from CaSTAGNETTO, and Tiano from SebasTIANO.

[47] Cf. GasPAROLA. Parola may also be connected with the bee eater, aparula.

[48] More often, dry, thin.

[49] One affected with catarrh is in Bolognese compared to a boiler, Pareir un caldron. Pare una Pentola conveys the same meaning. Cf. Spanish Calderón.

[50] Cf. Tinello from CostanTINELLO.

[51] We are reminded of Abatello, Abatelletto, abbot, abbé, and of Sabatello, Sabatelletto.

[52] Corbi, etc., recall corvo, raven. Corbello is usually defined as a simpleton but if Bresciano may mean something entirely different, corbel, sorb tree.

[53] The font name Alceste could lead to Cesti, Cestoni.

[54] Cf. Bozzo, Förstemann, op. cit. 330, and GiacoBOZZO.

[55] There is an apparent connection with Gaba, Förstemann, op. cit. 561. In the Alto Adige Gaba stands for Jacob.

An indispensable household article used to be Candela,[56] and Candeliere, candlestick, candelabrum.

Outside the kitchen there is little else that has furnished last names. We may cite Letto,[57] bed; Materazzo, Materassi, Matarazzo,[58] mattress; Lenzuolo,[59] sheet; Copertini,[60] cover; Cassoni,[61] trunk; Cantarano [62] (Tarantino), chest of drawers; perhaps Scavello (sgabello), stool; Testera,[63] tester, and there may be a few others.

ARTICLES OF CLOTHING

As costume has always been the subject of special attention it is natural to expect the various articles of clothing to be productive of quite a few surnames. Along with the other possible causes for their vogue we may surmise that John's inordinate talk and pride about his new hat, coat, cap, shoes at times led to his being dubbed hat, coat, cap, shoes by his friends. Even without the element of pride being injected into the picture an article of clothing that is worn might be conspicuous enough to cause it to be applied to the wearer through the use of synecdoche. This is the case of the name of the well-known comic character, Tabarrino, because of the short coat which set him apart from others on the stage.

Beginning, then, with the top of man's anatomy we can provide John and his family with Cap(p)elli, Cap(p)ellozzi, (Cap(p)elletti, Cap(p)elloni,[64] Cappiello, hat; Cervone,[65] traditional Calabrese headgear; Berretta, Baretti,[66] Bretti (Reggiano brett), Bertini [67]

[56] There is a Madonna della Candela. Cf. the first and last names Candelara, Candelora.

[57] Could even more easily and logically come from font names like Car-LETTO, DiLETTO, or any name in -lo.

[58] Obese persons are often called materazzi.

[59] Cf. Lenzo plus -olo deriving from Lorenzo.

[60] Copertini may be related to Colberto, Colbertino. Cf. the place name Copertino (Lecce).

[61] Cf. Cassio.

[62] A cantarana in Piedmontese is a toy used during Holy Week which makes a noise like a frog. In Sicilian a cantaranu is a seller of chambers.

[63] Testera regularly means head stall, head armor. Incidentally, a certain writer bears the name of Quinto Guanciali, pillow.

[64] The term cappella, chapel, can provide us with this and the three preceding names. Dialectical Iacapa (Jacob) could also supply them. A cappelletto is a Venetian cavalryman and a children's game.

[65] Cervone also means deer and, in Abruzzese, a snake.

[66] Baretti could derive from Alvaro.

[67] In most cases Bertini hails from ALBERTO.

(Piedmontese), Coppola,[68] cap; Cuffia, Coddazza [69] (Milanese), bonnet; Cappucci, Cappuzza, Copozzi (Romagnuolo), Cap(p)uccini,[70] hood; Pannelli (Ciocaria), Pezzotti [71] (Ligurian), shawl; Camicia, Cammisa,[72] shirt; Camisola (Southern Italian), waistcoat; Giachi, Giacchetti,[73] Sacconi,[74] jacket; Farsetti, Cossu (Sardinian), Saia,[75] doublet; Giubba, Giubbini,[76] Gipa (Piedmontese), dress coat, blouse; Cappa, Cappini, Capparelli,[77] Lo Manto, Mantello, Mantellini, Mantone,[78] Ferraioli,[79] Frajoli (Romagnuolo), Faldetta, cape, coat; Spolverini, travelling coat; Gabbano, large surtout; Tabbarri, Tabarrini, Tabarrelli, great coat; Cotta,[80] gown, long coat, mail coat; Pellicci, Pelliccione,[81] fur coat; Guarnaccia,[82] Pelanda (Milanese, Comascan), dressing gown; Calzoni, Pantaloni, Calza, Calzini, hose; Ghetti,[83] gaiter, hose; Gambale, legging; Cigna,[84] Cinti,[85]

---

[68] Coppola leads us back to JaCOPPOLA.

[69] Coddazza is also a godmother in Milanese. Iacapa again appears as a possible source of Capozzi and several other names in this group. Cf. also for Cappucci, the word for cabbage and for Capozzi, the word for head.

[70] The best known meaning of cappuccino is Capuchin monk.

[71] Cf. the font name Opezzo plus -otto for Pezzotti, and Sicilian Gaspaneddu for Pannelli. In Calabrese a pezzuottu is a piece of land.

[72] The dialectical Giacama plus -isa might explain Cammisa.

[73] Most frequently Giaco is a pet form of Giacomo.

[74] Sacconi may be from Isacco, or Germanic Sacco (Cf. Förstemann, *op. cit.* 1287).

[75] Cf. Isaia, Osaia. A Nicolò Saiabianca, white doublet, was a Venetian notary, 1361-1389.

[76] There is a chance that Giubbini can come from Giacobbino, Giacubbino, through syncope. Also through the substitution of bb for pp the name could be reproduced from a syncopated form of Giuseppino.

[77] Once more we are reminded of Iacapa by Capparelli and the two preceding names. A capparelle in Vastese is a mushroom, and is figuratively to allude to an untidy person with wax in his ears.

[78] The font name shortening of Amante, Bramante, Diamante plus suffixes could easily give us Mantello, Mantellini, Mantone.

[79] Also a locksmith, a word now apparently obsolete. Faldetta reminds us of MaFALDA and Germanic names with the theme Fardi (Förstemann, *op. cit.* 499). Cf. also BaruFALDO.

[80] Derivation of cotta may just as safely be from any name in -co, -go, DomeniCOTTA, ArriGOTTA = ArriCOTTA. Cf. the old Roman name Cotta.

[81] Pelliccioni is a place name in the Novarese. In Tuscan it means a mushroom of the lepiota group. Cf. also pellizzune (Calabrese) tatterdemalion.

[82] A guess at an alternative explanation would be Guar(i)naccia.

[83] Pantalone, Panteleone is a well known font name. Ghetti, like Cotta could derive from any name in -go, -co, Ughetti, Domenichetti = Domenighetti.

[84] Cigna could be from LiCINIA, Iginia, etc. It also means swan.

[85] Cinto from GiaCINTO would be a more acceptable source.

(Calabrese cinta), girdle, belt; Fascio, Fascia, Fascetta,[86] sash; Straccali,[87] suspenders; Gonella, Gonnella,[88] Traversa [89] (Milanese), skirt; Scarpa, Scarponi, Scarpazza, Scarpetti, Scarpelli,[90] Zavatta [91] (Northern Italian), shoe; Pianelli,[92] slipper; Papuzza,[93] toe slipper; Calandriello,[94] sandal; Zoccoli,[95] wooden shoe; Borzacchini, buskin; and Stivaletti, perhaps Stivala, boot. Compounds are not many but they are interesting—Mezzacappa,[96] half cape, Falzacappa, false cape, Cappadoro, golden cape, Cappinera,[97] Cappabianca, Cappapianca, black or white cape, Cappalonga, long cape, Calzelunghe, long hose, Calzibigi, grey hose, Bonicalzi, good hose, Calzanera, black hose, Bellipanni, Belpanno, fine clothes, Pannilunghi, long robes.

Adjuncts of costume, more or less, that may be listed here are Borsi, Borselli,[98] Portafoglio, Sacco,[99] Scarselli,[100] purse, pouch, Bisaccia, Bisaccione, Bezazza,[101] bag, knapsack, Balice,[102] valise; Guanti, gloves, Scolli [103] (if Calabrese), necktie, Zagaglia [104] (if Calabrese) garter, and various words for club, cane, Bastone, Canna,[105] Taccari (Southern Italian), Bordone,[106] pilgrim's staff, etc.

[86] A variant form of Bonifacio, BoniFASCIO, could supply all these names.

[87] In Calabrese a straccale is a halter.

[88] Cf. Ugonella.

[89] Traversa also means cross-road.

[90] Some competition comes from the Germanic Scarpa, Förstemann, *op. cit.* 1305, scarpa, scarp, scarpello, chisel. Big or small-footed individuals are referred to by such terms. In Venetian a scarpa is a disorderly person or thing.

[91] In Cremonese a zavatta is a big mouth.

[92] Cf. St. UlPIANO, as well as the word piano, plain.

[93] Other choices are Papuzza from Papo, short form of Jacopo and papuzza, Calabro-Sicilian for lady bug.

[94] Cf. calandriello from calendar lark.

[95] Zoccoli could mean goat if from the Friulano and mouse if from Southern Italian.

[96] Menzacappa is a term given by the Calabrese to a bourgeois.

[97] Cf. capinera, black cap, black head.

[98] Borso usually comes from Bonaccorso.

[99] See Note 74.

[100] If Piedmontese, scarsella may mean heron.

[101] Figuratively refers to a fat woman.

[102] Valice in Calabrese is a docile human being.

[103] Scolli through FranceSCOLLO is a possibility.

[104] We are almost ready to discard this meaning in favor in zagaglia, short javelin. See section on Offensive Weapons and Defensive Armor.

[105] Canna also signifies throat, gluttony; reed, bagpipe.

[106] Bordone may likewise be a variant of Boldone. Cf. Lombard Gariboldo. Club names frequently denote simpletons.

Among the ornamental adjuncts of costume that we are presented with are Pennacchio, Pennacchietti, plume; Campanelli, Barchetti [107] (Reggiano), ear-rings, Pettine, comb; Occhiali, Occhialini, glasses; Caramelli,[108] monocle; Frontali, Binda [109] (Milanese), head band; Catena (Milanese), Iannacca (Calabrese), necklace; Catena,[110] chain; Fibbia, Borchia (Pavese), clasp or buckle; Braccialetti, bracelet; Anelli, Aniello,[111] ring; Nastri, ribbon; Misurelli (Sicilian mizuredda), a ribbon which is blessed and which the devout wear around their necks to be cured of certain illnesses; dall'Orologio, Orioli, watch; Parasoli,[112] parasol, Bandettini [113] (Genoese bandeto), fan. Perhaps we should also list at this point the names of precious stones though they have been and are now used as first names, Gioia,[114] Zoja, Gioielli, Gemma, jewel; Diamante, diamond; Brillante, brilliant; Spinello [115] Balascio, Balasso,[116] Rubino,[117] ruby; Smeraldi, emerald; Topazio, Topazzini, topaz; Granato, garnet; Zaffiri, sapphire; Bellocchio,[118] white stone containing a spot gleaming like gold; the names Perla, Perlini, Perna (Calabrese), pearl, Cammeo, cameo, Corallo, coral, Avolio,[119] ivory. We also have Profumo, perfume, Gemmato, bejewelled, and Aurigemma.

Not exactly an adjunct but closely linked with costuming is color represented by the following surnames: Bianco, Candido,[120]

---

[107] Campanello is a little bell and various kinds of flowers. For Barchetti, cf. barchetta, boat.

[108] Cf. caramella, lozenge of candied sugar.

[109] Bindo is a common first name.

[110] If Romagnuolo Catena may be a syncopated form of Catarena, i.e. Caterina, but through substitution of a c for a g Catena could also come from Agatena, that is, Agatina.

[111] Frequently aniello represents agnello, lamb.

[112] Cf. Parussolo from Gasparo or the term for titmouse.

[113] Romagnuolo Bandetto is a variant form of Benedetto. Cf. also. Bando, Förstemann, op. cit. 245.

[114] The word also means joy.

[115] Other name candidates are Ospinello, Crispino.

[116] Cf. palasso dialectical for palazzo, palace.

[117] Cf. the aphetic form of CheRUBINO.

[118] See Anatomical Names.

[119] Avolio was one of the four sons of Duke Namo of Baviera. See Ariosto's Orlando Furioso, XV, 88.

[120] Of course, candido, usually means pure, spotless, but sometimes is synonymous with white. A Cardinal dei Marchesi di Monferrato was called Ottone Candido or Bianco. Some color names obviously refer to color of hair or complexion. See Anatomical Names.

white; Neri,[121] black; Bigi, Bisi,[122] Grigi, gray; Bruno, brown; Celesti, Celestra, Gilistro, Turchini, Azzurri, Violetti,[123] blue; Rossi, Russo, Purpura, Porpora, Vermigli, Vermigliolo, Scarlatti, Rubino, Cardinale, and the rare Cinabro and Coccimiglio, red; Castagna, chestnut; Olivo, olive; Olivastro, olivaceous; Baio, Baioni, bay; Giallo, yellow; Sauro, sorrel; Verdi, green; Moscato, dapple gray; Cedrone cedar colored. Color can, indeed indicate a suit or dress and, by extension, the wearer of clothing of a particular color.[124] In some cases the kind of textile worn, Lana, wool; Cottone, cotton; Tela, linen; della Seta, silk; Raso, Rasetti (Milanese), satin; Saia, serge; Sacco, sack cloth; Mussolini, muslin; Broccato, Brucato, brocade; Rosati, scarlet cloth, stammel; Zegrino, silk fabric; and Ciambellotto, camel's, goat's hair cloth, can perhaps be extended to the wearer also.

NAMES FROM CARPENTRY

Some tool surnames drawn chiefly from carpentry are Scuri, Accetta,[125] Mannara (Sicilian), Caccia [126] (if Calabrese gaccia), Piola (Piedmontese), axe, hatchet; Martelli,[127] hammer; della Sega, Serra, Sera (Northern Italian), saw; Trivellini, Tinivella [128] (Mil-

[121] Neri is a popular shortening of Raineri, Maineri.

[122] Bigio is a Milanese pet name for Luigi. As to Bisi, it may also be related to Ludovisi.

[123] Turchini recalls Turco, Turk, and the Germanic Turicco. The link between Violetti and the flower name, is obvious.

[124] Under bigio in the *Statuti Sanesi*, III, Bologna, 1877, 481, we read that as a substantive it means "un abito di quel colore," a suit or dress of that color, and that bigio dicesi anche chi porta l'abito di quel colore," the wearer of a suit (dress) of that color is also called grey. For other discussions of these words see Index. Rosati is listed elsewhere under Calendar Names, a subchapter of Miscellaneous Names. In the case of Porpora compare the surname Porporati, cardinal or wearer of purple robes. Obviously, several of our fabric names can in some instances be otherwise interpreted as font names—CataLANA, DomeniCOTTONE, AlberTELA, MoriSETA, Osaia, Isacco. Mussolini has been derived from Muntius and may be related to the Veronese word for gnat.

[125] Accetta from Bonaccetta should be favored as an explanation.

[126] A shift in the accentuation of mannara would make this Sicilian for cattle pen. See also Note 26 for additional light on Caccia.

[127] For Piola see Note 50 of Botanical Names. Martelli, of course, usually comes from Marta plus suffix or MARTinELLO.

[128] Serra is a mountain pass, defile. There are many such place names. The best source of Sera is the dialectical Baldisera. In the Venetian-Paduan dialects we find the saying: "se furbo Trivela, ma più furbo Trivelin," "if Trivela is cunning, Trivelin is more so," which indicates that Trivellini can apply to a sly individual. As to Tinivella the gimlet—claims are partially if not wholly cancelled by the Piedmontese jesting phrase Gian-tinivela, a good for nothing. Cf. the French Jean de Nivelle.

anese, Piedmontese), gimlet, augur; Scarpelli, Scarpellini,[129] chisel, Tenaglia,[130] pincers. A few vehicle products of the trade are Carri, Carretta,[131] Carroccio, Birocci, Biroccini, Barozzi [132] (Northern Italian), Carozzi, Carrozza,[133] Traini. We shall include at this point delle Chiavi, key; Chiodo, Chiodini,[134] nail; and Ruota,[135] wheel.

NAMES FROM FARM INSTRUMENTS

Cognomina from instruments that primarily pertain to the farm are Vommaro, Vomero, Arado, Arato [136] (Southern Italian), Dentale, Perticari,[137] plough; Falce, Falcetti, Falcione, Falciglia, Falzon (Bolognese), Ranza, and Ranzoli [138] (Bresciano), Seghezzi [139] (Milanese), Sessa [140] (Piedmontese), cythe or sickle, Zappa, Marazzi [141] (Northern Italian), Marra,[142] Marroncelli (Metaurense), hoe; La Vanga, spade; Rastelli,[143] rake; Forcina, Ronca, Ronchetti, bill hook; Forcone,[144] pitchfork; Tridente, three pronged fork; Picarello [145] (Metaurense, Anconitano), Pungitore, Pingitore (Cala-

---

[129] See Note 90. A scarpellino is often a stone-chiseler.

[130] In Calabrese a tenaglia is a miser.

[131] Carri, Carretta can be taken from the dialectical form of Carlo.

[132] Cf. Germanic Baro, Förstemann, *op. cit.* 246.

[133] This name, which is usually Sicilian, can be connected with the place names 'u Carrozzu, i Carrozzi meaning path, narrow pass. See C. Avolio, "Saggio di Toponomastica Siciliana." *Archivio Glottologico Italiano.* Supplemento, Sesta Dispensa, 1898, 96.

[134] Chiodo is a popular reduction from Melchiorre and in Tarantino refers to an amateur fisherman.

[135] Ruota may be a clipped form of Buonarrota.

[136] Cf. arata (Tarantino) gold fish or mullet.

[137] A perticaro is also a maker of pertiche, measuring rods. Latin writers on rural subjects had used pertica to refer to the land assigned to a colony. Compare Guardia Perticara in Lucania. See G. Racioppi, "Origini Storiche Investigate nei Nomi Geografici della Basilicata." *Archivio Storico per le Provincie Napoletane,* I, 1876.

[138] Ranza and possibly also the falce terms could mean land curving like a sickle. Cf. ranza, a word for orange and Germanic Ranzo (Förstemann, *op. cit.* 1246).

[139] Seghezzi could also be a Germanic font name.

[140] See Anatomical Names.

[141] Maro from AldeMARAZZO could be a source. Marrone is a chestnut tree. Cf. a variant name Marasso also related to a Mantuan word for snake.

[142] Marra is a Calabrese word for teacher.

[143] The font name Erasto has a stronger claim on Rastelli.

[144] See Note 39.

[145] Cf. Germanic Pico, (Bico) + suffix -arello, the words for magpie and woodpecker, and piccarello, Sicilian for skate or ray, likewise have claims on this name.

brese), goad; Vaglio, Crivelli, Crevelloni, Crivellucci, sieve, Stup-
piello (Southern Italian), dry measure. Gramola is a flax brake. Pico,
Picco, Picone, Piccone [146] may refer to pick.

MUSICAL INSTRUMENT NAMES

In the classical land of music and of song we should logically
expect to see the influence of musical instruments at work upon
surnames. The most common are Piva, Zampogna, Sampogna,
Canna,[147] Ceramella, Ciaramella, Cerebella (the three Southern
Italian), Ciufelli [148] and Totera (Abruzzese), bagpipe; Corno, horn,
Flauto, flute; Tromba, Trombone, Trombetti, Trombelli, Trom-
boncini,[149] trumpet; Cornetti,[150] Pistone,[151] cornet; Piffari,[152] fife;
Fagotto,[153] bassoon; Tamburi, Tambori, Tamborra, Tamborrini,[154]
drum; Timpano, Timpanelli, timbrel; Viola, viol; Violini,[155]
violin; Mandolini,[156] mandolin; Chitarrin, guitar; Cimbali, harpsi-
chord; Piano [157] and Pianforte, piano, which if genuine, are recently
acquired last names. Salterio, in Sicilian, is a musical instrument in
the form of a triangle.[158] Sufoletta, if from zufoletto, means whistle,
flageolet, spy. While on the subject of music we shall include here
Canzone, Canzonetti, song.

---

[146] Cf. preceding note.

[147] Also a word for cane, walking stick. In Milanese piva is a child, weeper,
hired mourner. The surnames Avena, Vena refer both to bagpipe and oats.

[148] A ciuffelle in the dialect of Castro de' Volsci is a spend-thrift.

[149] These words also mean trumpeter, messenger. A trombetta in Bolognese
connotes a chatterer. Trombete in Friulano is a spy and a babbler, while trom-
bon is an exaggerator. Sometimes a trombone is a blunderbuss, arquebuse. We
gain some insight into the formation of these last names from the knowledge
that Bartolomeo Tromboncino was so called because his father was a famous
virtuoso of the trombone.

[150] Cornet is a common Lombard word for bean.

[151] Pistone has several other meanings, a pestle, rammer, a blunderbuss,
a gun.

[152] A piffaro is also a fifer. In Mirandolese the term is used for a flat nose.

[153] A fagotto, cf. English fagot, may be a clumsy person, or in Romagnuolo,
a large misshapen and ill-dressed individual.

[154] A tamburro is likewise a drummer, a bargello or sheriff, a fat man, and
in Milanese and Cremonese tambor, tamburr, a simpleton.

[155] The flower name, violet, can of course be favored here.

[156] Cf. St. Amando plus suffixes.

[157] Cf. also St. ULPIANO, and the most likely source, piano, plain.

[158] A Lorenzo degli Organi, organ, was a fifteenth century Lucchese magistrate. See R. Archivio di Stato di Lucca, 1907. Cf. also the Florentine Francesco Landino, alias Francesco degli Organi. Naccari possibly refers to castanet.

OFFENSIVE WEAPONS AND DEFENSIVE ARMOR

For the most part surnames from offensive weapons and defensive armor are survivals of a rather remotely bygone day. They are apt to indicate makers-dealers or bearers. A few have the competition of homonyms and a few are subject to figurative interpretations. Weapons are represented by Spada,[159] Spadini, Spadoni, Spatoni, Spaducci, Spatuzza, Spadafina, sword; Bricchetti,[160] (Romagnuolo) a one-edged sword, perhaps an occasional Passetti,[161] fencing sword; Stocco,[162] rapier; Lanza, Lancetta,[163] Lanzanova, Lanzavecchia, Asta, lance; Bigordi, Zagaglia,[164] short lance; Forcina,[165] forked spear; Picchi,[166] pike; Balestra, Mangano, Manganella,[167] Bolzon (Old Vicentino) and Scorpione,[168] crossbow; Tromboni,[169] Pistone,[170] Trabucco, blunderbuss; Ariete, Montoni,[171] battering ram; Fucile, Schioppo, Battifuoco, Pistone (Parmigiano), Moschetti,[172] gun, rifle; Mazzagatti,[173] pistol; Terzetti,[174] possibly pocket pistol; Mascolo [175] (Neapolitan), fire arm used during celebrations; Pugnali, dagger; Cannone,[176] cannon; LaBombarda, Bombardi, Bombardini,[177] bombard; Falconetti,[178] a small cannon, falconet; Freccia, Frezza, Fileccia (Sicilian), Quadrello, Saitta,[179] arrow; Mitraglia, grapeshot; Palla, bullet, ball.

[159] Cf. spada referring to pesce spada.

[160] Cf. Germanic Bricco (Förstemann, op. cit. 355), bricco, donkey, bricchet, ram, brich, brichet Piedmontese for precipice and match.

[161] May be a variant of Bassetti.

[162] Cf. stocco referring to pesce stocco, swordfish.

[163] Lanza, Lancetta may be apocopated forms of Lancellotto.

[164] We add here a rather unlikely competitor zagaglia (Calabrese), garter.

[165] See Note 39.

[166] See Note 145.

[167] Mangano is also a mangle, calendar.

[168] Literally scorpion, but also sea-scorpion.

[169] See Note 149.

[170] Also pestle, rammer.

[171] Cf. the name montone for ram (animal), and montone, big hill.

[172] But a moschetto can be a mosquito.

[173] Literally kill cat.

[174] Literally third, i.e. third born.

[175] Literally male. Cf. surname Femmina.

[176] Figuratively a deaf person, in Milanese a person with a loud resounding voice, or in Sicilian a tall lean individual.

[177] More convincingly from buon Bardo, i.e. Bernardo, Berardo.

[178] The term falcon is to be favored as a name-candidate.

[179] Figuratively these arrow words denote a swift, agile fellow. Cremonese frezza is a haughtly irascible woman.

From the warriors' outfit come Scuto, Scudi,[180] Targhi, Targhini,[181] Brocchi, Brocchetti,[182] Brocchieri, La Rotella,[183] shield; Tavolacci,[184] wooden shield; Maglia,[185] coat of mail; Corazza, Corazzini,[186] cuirass, Corsaletti,[187] breast plate; Bracciali,[188] armlet; Cossali, cuisse; Gambale, greave, legging; Testera,[189] head armor; Cimera, degli Elmi [190] and possibly Galea,[191] helmet; Faretra, quiver; Fodera, Foderazzi, sheath; Staffa, stirrup, Zaino, knapsack; Tenda, tent; Stendardo,[192] Confalone, standard; Bandiera,[193] flag.

SEA OBJECT NAMES

The sea has not contributed as many object names as one might expect. Some of them are della Nave, Navilio, Barca, Barchetti, Barcelli (Cremonese), Battelli,[194] Burchi,[194] Paranza, Palazzoli [195] (Anconitano), Galea,[196] Galeri,[197] Gondola, Bergantini,[198] the extremely rare Piroscafo, indicating various kinds of boats, and perhaps Canevazzi, Cannavacciolo, canvas; Trinchitella, foremast; Bussola,[199] compass, and d'Ancora, anchor. Ancora is, of course, a well-known inn sign.

---

[180] Also a coin name, écu.

[181] Not impossible from a given name, cf. PluTARCO, ArisTARCO.

[182] Brocca, Brocco are terms for hedgehog, flask, fork (Calabrese).

[183] Another meaning is catherine wheel.

[184] Tavolaccio is also a large bench, plank bed.

[185] We could easily get Maglia from Amalia.

[186] Possible through syncope from Corradazzo.

[187] But compare corsale, corsair. Cossale might be a variant of this term.

[188] In Calabrese a bracciale is a day-laborer.

[189] Also tester, canopy over a bed.

[190] But Elmo is a common variant for Erasmo.

[191] Cf. the word for galley.

[192] A stendardo is also a standard bearer.

[193] Bandiera in Venetian is a flighty woman. An Orlandino della Piastra (piastra = armor) was a Lucchese magistrate in 1436. See R. Archivio di Stato di Lucca, 1907.

[194] Barcelli also recalls bargello, sheriff, Battelli, SabBATELLO, and abatello while burchio, if Pistoiese, means a child and is derived from puerculus. Cf. I. Pauli, Enfant, Garçon, Fille dans les Langues Romanes, Lund, 1919, 32.

[195] Palazzolo is a Sicilian place name while in Bolognese star li a far el palazol, refers to a person present but not taking part in anything that is said.

[196] A galea may also mean a helmet.

[197] Galera is still a common term for jail.

[198] Bergantini may come from bergante, a variant of brigante, brigand.

[199] Bussola could grow out of GiacoBUSSO. It is also a sedan chair.

MISCELLANEOUS OBJECT NAMES

Some of the tools and products of other crafts that have been borrowed for surname purposes are delli Quadri, frame, picture; Marrazzi,[200] (Tarantino), a sort of handaxe used by cask makers; Bernasconi (Milanese bernasc), fire shovel; Badile (Parmigiano), shovel; Pestelli,[201] Pistoni, pestle, rammer; Catena, Catinelli,[202] chain; Catenacci, bolt; Bilancia, Balanza, scale; Tagliola, trap; Campana, Campanelli,[203] bell; Baciocchi, Batacchi,[204] bell clapper; Gambetti,[205] fetters; Briglia, bridle; della Staffa, stirrup; Capestro,[206] halter; Sella, saddle; Bardella,[207] pack saddle; Barile, Botta, Mezzabotta, Botticelli, Bottini, Bottazzi,[208] barrel, cask; Vacili,[209] basin, tray; Specchio, mirror; Vetro, glass, Terracotti, terracotta ware; Funicello, rope; Bricchetti [210] (Piedmontese brichet), Zolfanella,[211] match; Ferone [212] (Tarantino), Carosello,[213] money box; Conocchia,[214] distaff; Fusella, Fusillo,[215] spindle; Mattassa, skein; Forbicini,[216] scissors; Ago, needle; Carta,[217] paper; Inchiostri, ink;

[200] See Note 141.

[201] A variant, Lucchese pistello, means a fat, heavy child. See I. Pauli, *op. cit.* 279.

[202] See Note 110.

[203] Figuratively campana refers to a deaf person. Campanella is a name for a number of flowers.

[204] Both baciocco and batacco can mean fool or child. For baciocco see I. Pauli, *op. cit.* 278.

[205] A gambetto likewise relates to a fellow with spindly legs.

[206] If changed from the Calabrese capizza, the word can mean a rascal.

[207] For Sella cf. PioSELLA, RoSELLA and Genoese MarSELLA (Marcella). The best explanation of Bardella is Bardo from Bernardo, Berardo plus the diminutive -ella.

[208] Barile, Botta figuratively mean fat. Botta is also derivable from Giaco-BOTTA and may mean a toad.

[209] Perhaps a variant of Basilio.

[210] See Note 160.

[211] In Bresciano a solfanel is an irascible woman.

[212] Neapolton is a dolphin.

[213] See Botanical Names.

[214] A conocchia in Neapolitan is a citadel on a height.

[215] Of a very erect person it is said that he is diritto come un fuso, as straight as a spindle. In Lombard a fusella is a bittern.

[216] Forbici are also defined as small insects infesting grapes, and as obstinate fellows.

[217] Usually this name is Sardinian in which case it may not be related to paper.

de' Porcellani, porcelain; Cuoio, leather; Gabbia, Gaggia[218] Caggiola, cage; della Sonaglia, bell, rattle; Figurelli, sacred image; and the rare Telescopio, telescope. Soffietti [219] looks as if it might come from the word for bellows. Metaphorically lavorare di soffietto, means to act as a spy.

[218] Cf. St. Gaggio and gaggia, magpie.

[219] However, Sofia, with a doubling of the f plus the suffix -etto can be put down as a very strong challenger.
Cf. the following place names with the object names already cited: Caggioli (Tuscany), Canna (Calabria), Chiodo (Piedmont), Medolla (Emilia), Piatta (Cuneo, Como), Piatte (Sondrio, Novara), Piatto (Piedmont), Nave (Lombardy), Scarpino (Lugano), Scudella (Messina), Spada (Alessandria, Bologna).

Chapter XVII

ANATOMICAL NAMES

Starting with the head we can gradually descend to the heel listing almost all of the important members of man's anatomy in the form of surnames. To mention first only the simple unmodified terms, we find head represented by Capo, Capoccia, Testa, La Testa, Cozza, Cuzza, Cefali (all three Calabrese), Coccia (Abruzzese, Marchigiano and Neapolitan), Conca (Sardinian), Coccaro (Otrantino coccalo); the hair by Capelli and Capei; the ear by Orecchio, Auricchio; the forehead by Fronte; the face by Faccia, Fazi (Bolognese faza), Visi, Cera, Ceffi; the eyebrow by Ciglio; the eye by Degli Occhi, Occi, Occhio; the cheek by Guanci, Guangi, Garzi (Abruzzese), Mascelli, Massilla, Massidda (Sardinian), Ganassa[1] (Romagnuolo and Lombard); the jaw by Gangale[2] (Calabrese); the nose by Naso, Nesi, Nescio (Romagnuolo neš); the mouth and lips by Muso, Musso; the mouth by Bocca; the tongue by Lingua; the teeth by Dente and Ganga[3] (Calabro-Cosentino and Sicilian); the chin by Mento, Mentone (Piedmontese-Genoese mentun), Bazza[4] (Tuscan), the beard and mustache by Barba,[5] Della Barba, Baffa,[6] Baffi, Mustacchio, Mostacchio, Mostacci,[7] Basetti and Pizzo (goatee), the throat by Gola, Gaula, Gorga, Canna, Strozzi, Cannarozzi; the neck by Colli; the shoulder and back by Spalla and Groppi; the chest by Busto, Bosti (Bolognese) and Petto; the breast and nipple by Menna (Lucanese and Pugliese), Minna (Sicilian and Calabrese), Tatti, Tetti (Bolognese), Poppi, Sessa (Abruzzese), Caparello (Romano, Tuscan), Caporello (Umbrian); the paunch by Pancia, Pansa, Panza, Pecci, Buzzo, Boggia,

---

[1] Throughout large areas of Central Italy ganassa means dente molare, molar. In Tuscany it means jaw. See K. Jaberg and J. Jud, *Sprach und Sachatlas Italiens und der Südschweiz,* I. Zofingen, 1928, Karte 115.

[2] In Sicilian gangali is defined as a jawbone of any animal.

[3] In some parts of Calabria ganga has the meaning of cheek. On the various meanings of cheek see an exhaustive discussion by H. R. Kahane, "Designation of the Cheek in the Italian Dialects," *Language,* XVII, 1941, 212-22.

[4] So in Jaberg-Jud, *op. cit.* Karte 115. However, the dictionaries define the word as mento sporgente, projecting chin.

Barba along with its suffixes also means chin in Northern Italian.

[6] In Lazio baffa means donna baffuta; in Guastalese a bafa is a double chin.

[7] In Lombardy, especially, mostaccio is synonymous with cheek, but mustazzo in Venetian is a depreciative term for face.

Ventre, Trippa, Matta (Sardinian); the buttocks by Chiappa, Pacchi (Abruzzese pacca); the arms by Bracci; the hand by Mano; the fingers by Dito, Dedo, Dido; the ribs by Costa; the haunch by Coscia, Coscione, Cosi (Bolognese cosa), Cossa (Abruzzese, Marchigiano, Venetian), Fianco; the leg by Gamba, Zanca, Comba (Italian-Swiss); the knee by Genocchi, Ginocchi; the ankle by Cavigli, Caviglia and perhaps Garrone (if Calabrese, garrune); the foot by Piedi, Pedi, and perhaps Pei; the heel by Calcagno, Carcagno and Tallone.

The length of these simple terms is somewhat surprising since we are all aware that anatomical nicknames are nowadays usually given to call attention to some distinctive or striking feature through the compounding of these nouns with adjectives or modifying suffixes. A similar catalog, though perhaps not quite as complete as in Italian, could be compiled for other languages. As samples compare Head (English), Haupt, Kopf (German), Hofft, Kop (Dutch), Teste (French), Cabo, Cabeza(s) (Spanish), Glova (Polish), Golova (Russian). Capito, Naso and Pedo, Labeo, Fronto are frequent in Latin inscriptions. The most obvious explanation of this phenomenon is that the majority of these simple forms actually do, by implication, call attention to distinctive or striking features of the human anatomy.[8] In such cases they have an augmentative force: Head, Naso, Pedo signifying big head, big nose, big foot. It is also likely that the paired members of the physical structure if made single or maimed by accident or disease can also explain some of the simple terms. Orecchio, Occhio, Braccio, Mano, Gamba, Pede would then mean one-eyed,[9] one-eared, etc., while Dente could, of course, refer to a one-toothed individual or one born with a single bony appendage.[10]

[8] E. Weekley in *The Romance of Surnames*, London, 1914, 199, writes: "Names like Beard, Chinn, Tooth were conferred because of some prominent features." The same opinion is expressed in his *Surnames*, London, 1936, 125n. "Such names when genuine undoubtedly indicate something conspicuous or abnormal in the feature selected. Such a name as Foot would have been conferred on a man afflicted with a club foot." A similar view is shared by E. Schröder in his *Deutschen Namenkunde*, Göttingen, 1938, 107. Al M (Alberto Manzi) writing in the *Enciclopedia Italiana*, XVI, 360, on Alberto Naselli, famous Renaissance Commedia dell'arte manager, opines that the nickname, Ganassa, came to him on account of the size of his cheek or appetite "la proporzione o della sua mascella o del suo appetito."

[9] Dante in his *Divine Comedy*, *Inf.* XVIII, 46-48, recalls il Vecchio da Verrucchio, Malatesta da Rimini, and his son, called Dell'Occhio because of the fact that he was minus one eye. Cf. the nickname Cocles, one-eyed, owned by Horatius who in the war with Porsenna defended the bridge alone.

[10] E. Schröder, *op. cit.* 107, makes this suggestion in connection with the German surname Zahn.

Important, too, in accounting for the existence of the simple terms is the fact that in many an instance they represent clipped forms in which the adjective or the modifying suffix of the original has been eliminated. Thus Head may once have been Longhead, Broadhead; Foot, Barefoot, Lightfoot, etc. It is common knowledge that in Italian there has been a widespread tendency towards shortening both first and last names [11] often including the reduction of a compound to its simple noun form: cf. Ventura, Bonaventura, Pace, Bonapace, Giunta, Bonagiunta. This procedure has affected names of the anatomical variety—Bocca for Malabocca, Branca for Malabranca [12] and very likely others.

Since heraldry made use of the human form and its parts, especially heads, hands, arms and legs, it, too, can be allowed as a source of not a few of these surnames.[13]

In trying to show that the simple anatomical terms can be taken more or less literally, we have so far dealt only with the positive side of the picture. Unfortunately, there is a negative approach through which it becomes clear that we are faced with a double or even a multiple origin of these names, the literal anatomical source, and one or more different sources. This is due to the existence of homonymical terms or to the figurative employment of a body region to denote mental or moral qualities, personal habits, rank, etc. Thus Capo and Testa at times hark back to some kind of leader or chief. In many instances, however, Testa is a short Northern Italian form from Battista = Batesta = Testa. Capoccia regularly means the head of a peasant household, Cefalo is also a fish. It is possible to obtain Capelli [14] from Northern Italian capelo, hat, or

---

[11] See chapters on Pet and Compound Names. Also cf. M. Orlando, "Raccorciature di Nomi e Cognomi," *Italia Dialettale*, VIII, IX, 1932-33, 1-54, 65-135.

[12] See also G. Piccolo, "Vezzeggiativi Italiani di Persona," *Zeitschrift für Romanische Philologie*, L, 1930, 553-56. It may be added that the son of the famous condottiero Oddo Fortebracci was known as Braccio da Montone. In these names the prevailing bisyllabic forms are either apocopate or aphetic, usually in relation to the most important part of the compound. Names that might influence psychic reaction such as scorn or shame are, naturally, subject to change, and when this type is not completely replaced by a less offensive name, it is logical to think that it might, particularly in the case of a compound name, be altered or amputated so as to remove the stigmatic portion. See chapter on Given Names and C. P. Oberndorf, "Re-Action to Personal Names," *Psychoanalytic Review*, V, 1918, 47-52.

[13] Consult G. C. Rothberg, *ABC of Heraldry*, Philadelphia, G. W. Jacobs, n.d.

[14] Capello was the name of one of the early Venetian families of Paduan origin who moved to the Rialto section in 810. It is even conceivable that Capelli might go back to gabella through the interchange of g and b or c and p. Cf. Romagnuolo gabella, awkward, useless person.

capela, chapel or * Iacapello (= Iacopo). In some cases it may be an attempt at a translation of the Spanish Cabello. In Old Italian and Latin a capella is a she-goat. The humanist Galeazzo Capra Latinized his name to Galeacius Capella. Faccia, Fazi, can be recognized as short forms of Bonifacio, Bonifazio. In Pavese faza means faggio, ash, also capable of producing a surname.[15] Visi is a regional abbreviation from Ludoviso (Ludovico). Cera could be a pet form of any name in -cera or g(i)era, GliCERA, RugG(i)-ERA, CaloGERA. It has, besides, the common meaning of wax and in Northern Italy means a beech. Ciglio may be a phonetic variant of giglio, lily, refer to an embankment or grassy rampart or turn out to be no more than a shortened pet form of Virgilio, Pacilio, (Gillio) or the Germanic names beginning with Lilio-, Liliopinctus, Lilodunus.[16] Degli Occhi may be a masculine pluralization of Dell'Oca, goose, or from Germanic Oki, Occo,[17] while Occi may be related to ocio, turkey,[18] or a Roman dialect word for maple, occia. Guanci recalls the Germanic Wantia, Wancio,[19] and Garzi the garza, white heron. Ganassa is used figuratively to denote voraciousness. Nasi could stem from Germanic Naso,[20] but it is more likely that it is connected with the familiar reduction of Atanasio or Ignasio = Ignazio. It also exists as a Sicilian place name and as a Veronese plant name, (nas, yew tree). As for the two names Nesi and Nescio, the former could come from Ginesio, AgNESE, and the latter from Nescio meaning ignoramus.[21] Musso calls to mind GiacoMUSSO and the medieval Italian Muntius. Bocca may stem from Burcardo (Boccardo), Burchardt.[22] Dente is also an abbreviated version of the font names DefenDENTE, PruDENTE, ReDENTE, while Lingua is obviously a curtailment

---

[15] Cf. the surname Faggi. But for this, too, the source may be Bonifacio through Bonifaggio.

[16] See E. Bianchi, "La Declinazione dei Nomi di Luogo della Toscana," *Archivio Glottologico Italiano*, X, 1886-88, 376.

[17] Cf. Förstemann, *Altdeutsches Namenbuch*. Erster Band. Personennamen. 2d ed. Bonn, 1900, 1174.

[18] See N. Caix, *Studi di Etimologia Italiana e Romanza*, Firenze, 1878, 129.

[19] Cf. Förstemann, *op. cit.* 1525-26.

[20] Cf. Förstemann, *op. cit.* 1153.

[21] Necio is a common Spanish word for simpleton.

[22] A. Bongioanni, *Nomi e Cognomi* . . . Torino, 1928, notes sub voce Burcardo . . . "La tendenza del toscano ad abbreviature e contrazioni ardite consente di classificare sotto Burcardo, Boccardo, anche Bocca, Boccaccio, Boccaccini, Bocconi." "The tendency of Tuscan towards bold abbreviations and contractions permits us to classify under Burcardo, Boccardo, also Bocco, etc." See also Bianchi, *op. cit.* 330-31. A Bocca degli Abati is mentioned in Dante's *Inferno*, XXXII, 105.

of the surname Malalingua.[23] Mento is most often a short form
of Clemento, dialectical variant of Clemente. Mentone could also
be an augmentative of Clemente, a plant, or a place name.[24] Bazza
may lead back to the Germanic Bazzo [25] and to GiacoBAZZO. A
popular Northern Italian term for uncle is Barba,[26] which, in
Milanese, also signifies innkeeper. It is likewise a variant of Balbo
(cf. Latin Balbus) and is related to Germanic Barbo.[27] Mostaccio
in Milanese can mean strong, courageous, and in Modenese chubby-
cheeked, while Basetti could be a short form of Gervasio through
GerBASSETTI. Many of the Pizzos can trace their names back
to an Obizzo, Opizzo and a few to pizzo meaning peak. Cf. Pizzo
di Calabria. With Ganga we may compare the Germanic Kanko,
Kanka,[28] but it is also connected with gluttony, means a prairie hen,
and is the name of a place in Val da Serchio.[29] Gangale survives because of its figurative meaning—chubby-cheeked, miser, brazen-
faced. Like Ganga, the terms Gola, Gaula, Canna, Strozzi and Cannarozzi Southern Italian), are all associated with gluttony, but Gola
could likewise come from ArriGOLA, UGOLA, PaGOLA (Paola)
and perhaps NiCOLA, AgriCOLA, and golo, a Casentino, Valdi-
chiana and Sienese word for wren.[30] Canna means cane, reed, and
is a commune in Calabria. Colli immediately recalls the word for hill
and a variant of Cola from Nicola.[31] Besides meaning a river bank
Spalla suggests a phrase like fare spalla a uno, to support, and, by
extension, a protector. Groppo indicating a land elevation is a place
name in Val di Magra in Tuscany. Busti can be related to Robusto,
possibly a given name, or at any rate, a reduction of Robustiano.
Spanish Busto and Germanic Busto [32] are also competitors. Petto

---

[23] An early Malalingua, Uberto, lived in the thirteenth century. See E.
Monaci, *Crestomazia Italiana dei Primi Secoli*, II, 2d ed. Città di Castello, 1912,
352. Incidentally, the noble family of the Denti from Forli actually has three
teeth on its coat of arms.

[24] Cf. the Romano term for applemint and Mentone in the Province of
Nice, France.

[25] Cf. Förstemann, *op. cit.* 253.

[26] Surnames referring to relationship are, of course, many, cf. Lo Zio,
Cugino, Nepote, Cognato, Nonno, etc.

[27] Cf. Förstemann, *op. cit.* 247.

[28] Cf. Förstemann, *op. cit.* 597. Ganga can also be found among the Spanish
sunames.

[29] See S. Pieri, "Toponomastica delle Valli del Serchio e della Lima,"
Archivio Glottologico Italiano, Quinta dispensa, 1898, 206.

[30] See R. Riegler, "Perol im Italienischen-Osterreiches Dial. Gugler and
Verwandtes," *Archivum Romanicum*, IX, 1925, 67-68.

[31] The double l may result from the gemination of the internal consonant
which is a common phenomena in pet names. Cf. Catte from Caterina, Toffano
from Cristofano. There is a town called Colli in the province of Aquila, and
a Tuscan place name, Colle.

[32] Cf Förstemann, *op. cit.* 353.

is sometimes a short form of JacoPETTO, FiliPETTO, etc., and, through the replacement of a p for a b a short form of BenedETTO and ElisaBETTA, or it may be of Germanic origin.[33] Besides a St. Menna, and Menno [34] from Domenico we have Menno and Minno from the Germanic.[35] Furthermore, due to the gemination of internal consonants particularly in Central and Southern Italian these names could come from Filomena, Giacomina, Gelsomina, etc. Tatti can be from Germanic Tatto [36] and is or was the name of a fortress in Val di Bruna in Maremma.[37] For Tetti compare Ber-TETTI and tëto, Piedmontese for child. Poppi may be from a saint's name, Poppo; possibly one of the many forms of Jacopo (cf. Peppe from Giuseppe) and is also a comune in the province of Arezzo. In the dialect of Sannio Sessa is from ossessa, obsessed; in Piedmontese it is a sickle, but it is evident that most of the Sessas have received their surnames from Sessa Aurunca, province of Caserta, and Sessa Cilento, province of Salerno. Capitelli may come from a Val di Chiana word meaning bulrush, or from a term in the dialect of Comelico and Venice meaning little chapel or tabernacle. Zizza could easily come from the Sicilian zizzu, dandy. Panza appears in part to be a lingering of Lombard-Germanic Panzo, while most instances of Buzzo can be traced to IacoBUZZO, and the majority of Boggios to AmBrOGIO. However, in a few cases Buzzo may point back to Germanic Buzo.[38] Dito may be from the Germanic root Theuda-Dito,[39] a variant of Tito, or a short form of the font names ArDITO, CanDITO (Sicilian Canditu.) For Chiappa, Ciappa there are several alternative explanations: chiappo (Neapolitan) meaning a wicked man; chiappe (Abzruzzese) meaning a rope; ciapo (Genoese) meaning slate [40] or fishery; and ciappa (Reggio Emiliano) meaning a constable. All of these terms assume a secondary role when faced with the competition of Ciapo from

[33] Cf. Förstemann, op. cit. 225, and Bianchi, op. cit. 369.

[34] Menno from Menico = Domenico, is Lucchese. In the same dialect it also means a simpleton.

[35] Cf. Bianchi, op. cit. 381, and Förstemann, op. cit. 1090. N. Caix, op. cit. 34-35 tells us that menno, "dal significato di manchevole, diffettoso, passò a quello di privo di facoltà virile, di mente, etc." "From the meaning wanting, defective, passed to that of lacking virile, mental faculty," etc.

[36] Cf. Bianchi, op. cit. Archivio Glottologico Italiano, IX, 1886, and Förstemann, op. cit. 387.

[37] Cf. Förstemann, op. cit. 246.

[38] See M. Orlando, op. cit. for Boggio = (Am)brogio, and Förstemann, op. cit. 331 for Buzo.

[39] Cf. Förstemann, op. cit. 1411.

[40] A synonym, Lavagna, slate, exists as a surname. It is also a town near Genoa noted for its slate deposits. Cf. also the surnames Lastri, Lastrucci.

Jacob. In Pacchi we may also have an appellative of Germanic origin.[41] Gamba, and especially, Gambi, could result from Buoncambio or Gámbara, and reminds us of stare in gamba, to be vigilant. Costa at once recalls costa, coast, shore or hillock, the short forms of Costanza, Costantino and the common Portuguese surname Da Costa. The famous Neapolitan family Coscia, Cossa draws its name from Coza, Greek name for the island of Ischia. Cossa and sometimes Coscia [42] are also short forms of Buonacossa. The former appears in the Piedmontese words for gourd and corn-cockle, while Cosi is usually from NiColOSO or COSimO, or less often, from Coso, misshapen. The ending -occhi in Genocchi, Ginocchi seems to indicate Celtic origin, possibly an ending added to the Germanic Genno.[43] Caviglia may be a bolt maker, quel delle caviglie, or a pretext-finder. Pedo like Petto is linked with a Germanic personal name.[44] We have also found pedo meaning child in the Otrantino dialect, which gives us another possibility. Pei, on the other hand, may come from PomPEO, the Genoese form of Pietro, or the Genoese and Piedmontese name for pear. Calcagno may be interpreted as the outgrowth of a phrasal voltar le calcagna, aver sempre uno alle calcagna, to turn one's heels, to have someone always at one's heels, or a name deriving from a playful contrast with capo, head. We could also obtain Calcagno, Carcagno through a starred form Galganio, Garganio [45] from Galgani and Gargani. An attempt to imitate the Latin gens names in -ius would produce the same results. Tallone also means cavolo, cabbage. Figuratively it is a term used to denote a simpleton. But the word can likewise be related to the Piedmontese Tallone from Pantaleone,[46] to Catallo and Clotallo from Cataldo and Clotaldo and perhaps to other first names.

But it is when the compound forms already mentioned appear in full dress with their descriptive adjectives or modifying suffixes, augmentatives, diminutives and pejoratives (which make them com-

---

[41] Cf. Förstemann, op. cit. 231, and Bianchi, op. cit. 371.

[42] Under Gambara, Bongioanni, op. cit., suggests Gamba, Gambetta, Gambini as derivatives. As to Coscia it was used as a given name in Pisa. Choscia di Stefano and Nicolaio di Ser Coscia are listed by I. M. Bencini, "Sulla Guerra e l'Acquisto di Pisa (1404-1406)," Archivio Storico Italiano, XVIII, 1896, 239.

[43] Cf. Förstemann, op. cit. 627. The existence of Ginocchietti definitely points away from the anatomy towards some font name.

[44] Cf. Förstemann, op. cit. 226.

[45] Bianchi, op. cit. 316, 405-06, notes that in Tuscan the morphological epithesis of -o is common. Ex. Boni, Bonio, Bosi, Bosio, Peri, Perio. Cf. also Galvano, Galvagno. Some names whose endings seem to be made to resemble the Latin gens name in -ius are Barberio, Ferrario, Rizzio. See Evolution of Surnames.

[46] Given by Bongioanni under Pantaleone. See op. cit.

pound in meaning if not in form) that they become really interesting. We have collected the following names which are grouped under the simple forms *a capite ad calcem*.[47]

In addition to their *a la lettre* value many of the head-names are capable of a figurative interpretation indicating stubbornness and blockheadness. They are Capone, Caponetta, Caputo, Capasso, Capaccio, Capuzzi, Capini, Cavina, Capinetti, Testoni, Testolini, Testena (Romagnuolo), Cocciolone,[48] Capogrosso, Testagrossa, Grossatesta, big head or little head; Capograsso, fat head (also a place name in the province of Salerno); Capopiccoli, little head; Capolungo, long head; Capotondi, round head; Capuzucca, pumpkin head; Capitorto, Cavatorta, twisted head, wry neck; Mezzacapo,[49] Mezzatesta, half head. The rare Capomagro and Testasecca, lean head, dry head, look like humorous contrasts to capogrosso, testagrossa. Contrast may also be responsible for the infrequent Bonatesta as opposed to the popular Malatesta. Cappuzzelli, Capuzziello almost invariably connote headstrong individuals as do Capotosto [50] (frequently shortened to Tosto, Tosti) and the rare Capaduro, hard head. Capodiferro, Codiferri are ironhead.[51] Capodivacca,[52] cow head, may be an outcropping of a fancied similarity between two zoological specimens. It exists in Spanish as a personal

[47] For interior parts of the anatomy like Cervello, Carvello, Caravello, Midolla, Medolla, Medula, Miola, brain; Milza, spleen; Coratella, pluck, liver, see sub-chapter on Household goods under Object Names.

[48] Names bearing modifying suffixes, -uto excepted, often indicate differentiation of members of the same family, relatives or others claiming the identical surname as to age, size, appearance and character. An old or big person of the Capo group might be called Capone, while younger or smaller members might be dubbed Capino, Capuzzo, etc. Likewise an ugly or churlish Capo might be called Capaccio, Capasso. This should be kept in mind not only with reference to these and other anatomical terms but also in connection with most Italian names with suffixes. Torquato Tasso used to be called Tassino to distinguish him from his father, Bernardo; Malatesta da Verucchio's son was called Malatestino, while the grandson of the artist Pesello (Giuliano d'Arrigo) was called Pesellino. But see chapter on Pet Names.

We note here that some capo-names are possible from Jacapo variant of Jacopo. Capone can also mean capon, and, by extension, a person with a hoarse voice. Northern Italian capa = cappa, hooded cloak offers another possible explanation for some capo-names. Capo can likewise mean cape, promontory. Weaker competitors for Capozzi and Capuzzi are Northern Italian dialectical names for cauliflower. Testoni, Testolini, Testena are also regular formations from the dialectical Battesta for Battista. Metaphorically, capotorto means a hypocrite. It is also a bird of the woodpecker family.

[49] Compare this with the fairly common Mezzacappa, half cape.

[50] In Naples a capatosta may be an alder buckthorn.

[51] This name was also borne by a famous sixteenth century inlayer.

[52] This happens to be the name of a contemporary writer who uses the pseudonym Giancapo.

and as a place name.[53] Rare, too, are Codagnello [54] (capo d'agnello), lamb head, Codebò (capo di bove), bull head, Capitegalli,[55] rooster head, and Capurso, bear head, but Capilupo, wolf head, is fairly widely diffused. It may well go back in a few cases to the time when beggars used to show the head of a wolf as a justification for their begging. Among the more localized head-terms we have Venetian Ciaffone,[56] Otrantino Coccoluto, Calabrese Cuzzale, all meaning big head. Heraldry is a good source for these animal-head names.

As to the colors connected with Capo or Testa it is obvious that they refer to the hair rather than to the head—Capobianco, Cavobianco, white head; Caporossi, Caporusso, Testarossa, red head; Caponigro, Caponera, Testanera, black head. Among these Capo-nera, if Milanese, may mean a capon-basket or the maker of such an object, while due to the dropping of the *g* before an *r* in Southern Italian Caporosso and Testarossi might well be the same as Capogrossi, Testagrossi. Capalbo, Capialbi [57] may be a Latin-ized form of capobianco. Capoverde and Testaverde, green head, are anatomical only insofar as birds are concerned, but it should be noticed that in Abruzzese capeverde denotes a monk who is out-standing by reason of rank or learning, a term that could easily be transferred so as to apply to the laity. A Caporaso is a cropped head and a Caporizzo, a curly-head.

Capello has given rise to only the debatable derivative Capellini, which can be duplicated from capa = cappa and capella = cappella plus a diminutive,[58] the Tuscan botanical terms for marsh or skull

---

[53] Cf. the name of the famous Spanish explorer, Cabeza de Vaca. There are two such place names in Spain, one near Badajoz and the other in the province of Orense.

[54] Codagnello (Caputagni) was also the name of a chronicler and notary of the Trecento. Cf. capotagno, Old Vicentino for capitano. These zoological head-names could also trace their beginnings to shop signs or coats of arms. A dweller of the Capo di Bove castle on the Appian Way, so called because of its ornamental bull-head cornice work, might, quite naturally be called Giovanni (di) Capo di Bove. This is an additional example showing how difficult it is to be absolutely certain of the source of a surname.

[55] The name of a noble Rome family. Giovanni Capo di Gallo, rooster head, was bishop of Belluno between 1398 and 1402. In Tuscan the term refers to chanterelle, mushroom. Similarly, Capoccelli, bird head, may derive from the Neapolitan capa d'auciello, unicorn plant.

[56] In Abruzzese ciaffone means a cheat, while in Lucchese ciaffo = ciaffone (from ceffo) means a disfigured face.

[57] Capalbio is the name of a fortress in Val di Fiora in Maremma. See Bianchi, *op. cit.* 404n. The surname may also be related to caparbio, stubborn.

[58] The derivation of Capelletti from either capa or capella is even more positive than Capellini. It may be a variant of Cappelletti, Venetian cavalrymen.

cap and red top, capellina, obsolete for a small she-goat, and Iaca-pella = Iacobella. Its place is taken by pelo, also meaning hair, as in Pelinero, black haired; Peliroccia, red haired; Pelrizzio, curly-haired. Malpelo is, of course, figurative — a rogue. We have, in addition, the infrequent Bellatreccia, beautiful tresses; Bellachioma and Belcavello, beautiful hair. Compare Fairfax.

The beard can likewise be described by its color — Barbanera, Barbanegra, black beard; Barbarossa, red beard; Barbadoro, golden (blond) beard; Barbabianca, white beard (metaphorically a decrepit old man). Add to these, Barbariccia, curly beard; Barbalonga, long beard; Barbapiccola,[59] little beard; Barbalarga, large, broad beard; Barbatosta, bristly beard; Barbaliscia, smooth beard; Barbagelata,[60] frozen beard. Malabarba, bad beard (possibly a variant of Malpelo), is the name of a Milanese family, while the Mezzabarbas, half beard, hail from Pavia. Suffixes joined to barba give Barbetti, Barbacci, Barbarone, little beard, big beard, and Barbato, bearded.[61] A part of the beard, pizzo, goatee, furnishes several cognomina, Pizzetti, Pizzolorusso, little red goatee; Pizzorusso, red goatee; Pizzoferrato, ironized goatee. But the first two names could easily be traced back to the Germanic Obizzo, Opizzo, while Pizzoferrato is an Abruzzese place name. Auspizio (a saint's name) might also account for Pizzetti.

The mostachios through baffo supply Baffuto, Baffato, Baffone and Baffetti. One of these terms, baffuto, means chubby-cheeked in Neapolitan; another, baffone, means a braggart in Abruzzese.

From orecchio come Orecchiuto, Ricchiuti, Orecchione, Riccioni and Riccitelli. The large-ear terms, due to comparison with a well known quadruped, tend to indicate ignoramuses. Riccioni, which, incidentally, is a word for mumps, can with Riccitelli, refer to the hair, riccio, curl, and possibly even to Morigi, Maurici. One of the many designations for bat is orecchione.

Both Frontealta, high forehead, and Malafronte, bad (deformed) forehead, may be taken literally or figuratively. Frontini (i.e. fron-tino) means an impudent fellow; it is a font name of Greek origin; in Genoese frontin) it is a wig. It is also the namesake of Rug-giero's famous steed in the Orlando Furioso, which, by transference

---

[59] Barbapiccola is a rare surname. A Giuseppe Barbapiccola was a member of one of the numerous Neapolitan accademies in the eighteenth century. See C. Minieri-Ricci, Archivio Storico per le Provincie Napoletane, IV, 1879, 381.

[60] Cf. the identical Ligurian place name.

[61] It should not be forgotten that barba also means chin and in Northern Italian uncle and that Barba may be a variant of Balbo. Barbarone could come from Barbara. For Barbato compare St. Barbato.

of the appellation of the horse to its owner is capable of becoming a surname.[62] Fronticelli is a rarity.

Occhio has regaled us with Occioni, Occhiuto, Occhiuzzi, Occhietti, Occhini, Occhelli. But Occioni is also a short form of Ugoccione; can mean a keen-eyed, prying person,[63] or be a morphological variant of ocio, turkey. Occhini and Occhelli can, moreover, originate from the Germanic patronymic Okki, Occo, and perhaps also from oca, goose. In addition to these terms we have Occhigrossi, large eyes, Occhineri, black eyes, Occhibianco, clear eyes.[64] Malocchi recalls defective eyesight or the evil eye. Perhaps it has something to do with a place name, mala loca,[65] maloca, a Leccese word for a black beetle, malocchi, a Monferrino word for a bundle of rags, or Maloc, a Biblical name. It should be paired with Bellocchio despite the fact that some of the persons bearing it may trace it back to belloccio (from bello), Isabelloccia, a possible place name bellus locus, bella loca),[66] the Provençal Belloc,[67] or bellocchio, a white stone with a gleaming gold spot in it. Occhiboi can be translated as ox-eyed.

Ciglione, Cigliuto, Gigliudo, beetle-browed, come from ciglio, but the first of the series can also be connected with the word meaning slope, embankment or with several personal names,[68] and the last two with a figurative meaning, cunning.

Like Viso, Visone, Viselli, Visetti as well as Belviso, Belvisotti and Bonviso usually hark back to Ludoviso. The last three names may also be grouped with Visibelli, Bonsembiante, Cerabona and Bellacera, beautiful face. There is a Madonna del Belviso, French Beauvoir. Faccione, Faccetta, Faccini, Faccinetti, Faccioli may be connected with Bonifacio as in the case of Faccia. Faccione is Southern Italian for owl. Another faccia derivative is Facciuta, chubby-faced. Ceroni, Cironi,[69] and perhaps Visaggi imply ugliness

---

[62] Cf. the surname Brigliadoro from another famous horse in the *Orlando Furioso*. See Romances of Chivalry a sub-chapter under Miscellaneous Names.

[63] Cf. Romagnuolo ucion.

[64] Nicola Occhiobianco was the name of a member of the eighteenth century accademy of Spioni e Speculatori of Lecce. See *Archivio Storico per le Provincie Napoletane*, III, 1879, 152. Occhilupo, wolf-eye, is a rarity.

[65] See Pieri, *op. cit.* 129.

[66] See Pieri, *op. cit.* 120. However, cf. German Feinaigle (feinäuglein), pretty eyes.

[67] See F. Mistral, *Lou Tresor du Felibrige.* Avignon-Paris, n.d. Vol. I, 260. Provençal origin may be the explanation for any Genoese and Piedmontese Bellocchi.

[68] See Note 16.

[69] Cerone could also be derived from Gero, Ruggero, Calogero, etc., while Ciro, Cyrus, also appears as an important competitor.

and bruttishness as well as chubbiness and so does Cefone. In Bresciano a ceron is one who is habitually sullen, and in Venetian the word means a wax gatherer. Cerini is short for Ruggiero, Berlingiero, Gerini = Cerini, and if the name is drawn from the Pavese dialect it signifies a jovial person.

The much maligned nose contributes Nasuto, Nasino, Nassini, Naselli, Nasetta, Nasolini, all of which, except Nasuto could at the same time be pet forms of Atanasio and Ignasio. Naselli (from nasella) is also to be listed among the fish names. Figurative meanings should, however, not be forgotten, for example, Nasino, one who does not talk clearly (Abruzzese nasine); Nasuto, a busy-body in Anconitano and Pitiglianese; and nasetta, a disdainful person. Nasca, an augmentative, belongs here. It enjoys a famous classical Latin precedent in the name of Cornelius Scipiones Nasica. In Sicilian a nasca is a pug-nose and in Calabrese a persuna de nasca fina, and parrare ccu le nasche refer to an astute person and to one who speaks with a nasal tang. From nasca come Nascone and Nascarella. Nor should we neglect Napioni from Bergamascan napio, large nose, despite competition from the telescoped form of Napoleone.

Few names stem from guancia and ganassa among them Guancione and Ganassini. From lingua comes Linguadivacca cow tongue, the name of a noble Paduan family, but in this case the source may well be linguadivacca (Belluno), dick sorrel.

Muso (Musso) is more prolific with Musini, Mussoni, Mussini, Mussetti, Mussettini, Muselli, Musulillo, Mussigrosso. Musso, the short form of Giacomo, GiacoMUSSO has a good claim on the terms with -ss. Mussoni may be connected with the dialectical word for mosquito. A musone is defined as a sullen person, an implication which, in addition to the idea of deformity, is contained in Malmusi. But in Modenese a muson is nothing more than a field mouse.

The bocca-word family supplies at least one famous member, Boccaccio. Others are Bocconi, Boccaccini, Bocchini, Bochetta, Boccuzza, Boccuto, Boccabella, Bellabocca. Several of these are, naturally, just as easily derivable from Boccardo.[70] Some may derive from bocco, simpleton.[71] In addition, a boccaccio may come from boccaccia, a foul-mouthed person. Boccadoro, golden mouth, is a translation of Chrysostomus.[72] It also means a loquacious fellow

---

[70] See Note 22.

[71] See N. Caix, *Studi di Etimologia Italiana e Romanza*, Firenze, 1878, 85.

[72] St. John Chrysostomus is called Giovanni Boccadoro in the poem: *Historia di Santo Giovanni Boccadoro*, Messina, 1599.

and, in Sicilian (vucca d'oru), a liar and scandal monger.[73] Boc-
caurati, a name in the possession of a Sanseverinate family, is a
probable variant. The Boccapecori, sheep mouth, hail from Rome.[74]
A Boccadifuoco, fire mouth, is a shooting piece. Other names like
Boccabianca (white mouth), Boccanera (black mouth), Boccarusso,
Boccarossa (red mouth), Boccadiferro (iron mouth), Boccafusco
(dark mouth), Boccafurni (oven mouth), Boccalupi (wolf mouth),
are probably spot names.

Dente and Ganga have remained virtually sterile, Dente producing Dentono, Dentone (also possible from DefenDENTE, Re-
DENTE, PruDENTE), Dentuti, big teeth and Maldenti, bad teeth,
and ganga the rare Gangarotta, broken tooth.

Mento, chin, takes second place in comparison to Mento from
Clemento = Clemente as the provider of our Mentones and Men-
tinis. In like manner, Tuscan bazza, chin, has a formidable rival in
JacoBAZZO in connection with Bazzoni and Bazzetti, while two
Bolognese possibilities gageina, a woman with a slightly protruding
chin but otherwise pretty and attractive, and gagiot, compete with
gaggio (acacia) as the source of Gaggini and Gaggiotti.[75]

Golini, the only apparent derivative of gola, is very likely from
Ugolino, Pagolino (Paolo) and Niccolino and Marcolino, in the last
two instances due to the substitution of a g or a c. It should also
be recalled that gola can also mean a greedy person or a defile.
Malagola, which looks as if it might refer to a person with a
defective neck, is a common place name in the Trentino section,
probably meaning dangerous defile.

Colle, hill, collo, mountain top, and Collo, a variant of Cola
from Nicola, rather than collo, neck, are much more likely to give
us Collino, Collaci, Colluccio, Colletto. One of these, Collaci, may
also be from Vulgar Latin frater collacteus, which is collazo in
Spanish.[76] Coltorto, Collitorto mean wry neck, sly fellow, hypocrite.

Linked to spalla, shoulder, back, are Spallone, Spallacci, Spallazzi,
Spallino, Spalletti, Spalluto. Besides their face value significance we
must bear in mind that all except Spalluto can come from spalla,

---

[73] See G. Pitrè: *Medicina Popolare Siciliana*, Torino, Palermo, 189, 82.

[74] Probably extinct are the names Boccadivacca, cow mouth; Boccapesci,
fish mouth; Boccatorta, wry mouth. A Sandeo Boccadivacca is listed in the
Bandi Lucchesi dal 1331 al 1356, Bologna, 1863, 323; the unofficial name of the
anti-Pope, Celestine (1119-24), was Tebaldo Boccapesci. A Guido Boccatorta,
wry-mouth, lived in the twelfth century.

[75] This word is a common noun in the Lombard-Venetian territory and in
Tuscany a place name meaning terrain à bain. See P. Aebischer, "Les Derivés
Italiens du Langobard Gahagi et Leur Répartition d'Après les Chartes Médié-
vales," *Zeitschrift für Romanische Philologie*, LVIII, 1938, 51-62.

[76] See A. J. Carnoy, "Adjectival Nouns in Vulgar Latin and Early Romance," *Romanic Review*, VIII, 1917, 169.

a river bank. Moreover, a spalon in Romagnuolo is a porter; a spallazzu in Calabrese is a bully; a spallino is both an epaulet and (in Tuscan) a porter; while a spalletta is a parapet or (in Friulano) a hunchback, all terms capable of furnishing surnames. From groppa we have Groppetti, Grupposo, Gruppuso, but the first of this series has the competition of groppa, hill.

The patronymics, Benedetto, Berto, Perto, Elizabetta, Filippo, Jacopo, Giuseppe, etc., could supply Pettoni and Pettini.[77] In addition to these we find Pettigrosso, big chest; Pettinigro, Pettinero, black chest (also a plover), and Pettoruto, pigeon-breasted, haughty. Cf. the Calabrese name Pettoruto. Bustini may go back to Busto from Robusto.

Deriving from words meaning breast and nipple are perhaps Sissini from Abruzzese sisa; Southern Italian Mennella, Minnella, and Romagnuolo Titone, Tittoni, Tettoni, from titon meaning poppatore. Nevertheless, Titoni, etc., are regular results of Battista and Tito, while Mennella, Minnella, as in the case of Menna, Minna, represent Central and Southern Italian gemination of internal consonants and could come from GuglielMINELLO, FiloMENELLA, CarMINELLA, GelsoMINELLA.[78]

The derivatives that braccio furnishes us — Braccioni, Braccini, Bracciolini, Braccialini — may be accepted as literal. Bracciolarga, long arm, implies also a person with a propensity for taking things. Bracci(o)forte and Fortebraccio denote strong men (cf. Armstrong). Fierabraccio is, finally, a revival of a name from the epic romances.

Almost all of the mano-terms have double origins, anatomical and patronymical (Germano, Alamanno, Ormanno, etc.) giving Manoni, Manini, Manetti, Manussi, Manuzzi. Manini is also related to Manin, little Magdalen, if it comes from the Monferrino dialect, while Manetti can derive from the word meaning manacles. Biancamano, white hand (cf. French Blanchemain) comes to us from the Middle-Ages, and Bonamano, unless bona means big, from a word signifying tip.

Ventre supplies us with Bonventre (bon = big) and with Ventrone which in Calabrese also means a glutton. But cf. BonaVENTuRONE. The Panza progeny is more abundant with Panzone,[79] Pancini, Panzuti, Pansuti, but the first three of the group of four can also stem from a German patronymic or the font name

---

[77] See Note 33.

[78] We should also include St. Menna as a source of Mennella, and, for Minella, the Sicilian place name I Minnelli. See A. Avolio, "Saggio di Toponomastica Siciliana," *Archivio Glottologico Italiano*, Supple. VI, 1898, 102.

[79] In Calabrese panzune (like ventrune) means glutton.

Avanzo.[80] Buzzo gives Buzzoni, Bozzone, Buzzini [81] all of which are likewise explainable from Buzzo from JacoBUZZO. Tripputi and Trippetti and the only derivatives of trippa.

It may be that Fianchino is related to fianco, but we are not sure, and are somewhat puzzled about Fiancobono — does bono mean big here, too?

Coscioni, Coscietti, Coscino, Coselli, Cosetti are linked with coscia, but coscino (with a shift of the accent to the first syllable) signifies hunch as well as haunch, while Coselli, Cosetti may be from Nicoloso, Coso, Cosimo, or coso, deformed, or derive from gos, Bolognese for goitre. Anca is restricted to Malanca, hip shot, and its false opposite Bellanca which seems to be really related to Spanish Blanca.

Chiappa supplies Chiappone, Chiappini, Chiapparelli, Chiapelli, Chiapuzzi, Chiapusso, Ciapponi, Ciaputo, Ciap(p)etta. However, Chiappini in Sicilian denotes a slow-moving person, and in Calabrese a rogue. Chiapparelli in the dialect of Ancona means April fool, and Chiapusso means an old clothes seller or, in Piedmontese, a poor artisan, boor. A ciappetta in Southern Italian is a brooch. Chiappuni in Sicilian, like chiappini, may allude to a slow-moving, lazy person. But despite all these possibilities, it is safe to say that the greatest percentage of the ciappa names are due to Ciapo, one of the numerous short forms of Jacopo.

To be grouped under gamba are Gambino, Gambetta, Gambone, Gambuti, Gambudi, Gambassi,[82] Gambaccini, Gambarotta, broken; Gambacorta, short leg; Gambatesa,[83] stiff leg; Gambalonga, Gambalarga, long leg; Bonagamba, Bellagambi, perhaps shapely leg. Some of these names can be obtained from Cambio (Boncambio) and from Gámbara.[84] In addition, gambette are fetters; Milanese gambin [85] means a sickly person, and gambon, in the same dialect, a tall man with long legs; but a Piedmontese gambon refers to a person with short and thick or swollen legs. For more light on Bellagambi we can turn to the phrase fare il or la bellagamba, to be an idler. We may suppose that Gambadoro, golden leg, once

[80] Cf. Germanic Panza, (Förstemann, op. cit. 1411). Panzarella, Calabrese for pancia di maiale, pig stomach, is also a common surname.

[81] Buzzini is also possible from Boezio (Boetius) through Boezuccio, giving Buccio and Buzzo. See B. Capasso, Le Fonti della storia delle Provincie Napoletane dal 568 al 1500, Napoli, 1902, 122.

[82] Gambassi is a place name in Val d'Elsa, Tuscany. It derives from campus bassus.

[83] Cf. also Gambatesa, an Abruzzese place name.

[84] See Note 42. S. Pieri, op. cit. 90, gives as last names from gamba, Gambarini and Gambarucci. But cf. gambero, gambaro, crab.

[85] Gambino d'Arezzo was a fifteenth century imitator of Dante.

came from a gilded shop sign indicating a bootery. Gambarossa, red leg, may have a similar origin or it may stand for gambagrossa, just as caporosso stands for capogrosso. Northern Italian gambagrossa (Sarzana, Mondovi, Bordighiera) is a grass of the buckwheat family or pellitory of the nettle family. The Vicentino Gambadecane can be translated literally into dog leg. A Sgambati presumably was once a legless or crippled person or one weary from too much walking.

Through piede we are provided with Pedone, Peduzzi, Peduto, Southern Italian Perullo, and Malpede, Malapedi, Malipedi, cripple foot. By transference of meaning pedone is a sentry or foot soldier, a postman, or anyone who journeys on foot. In Abruzzese it denotes a slow walker.[86] Pedeferro, iron foot, is the name of a noble Paduan family. Other rarities are Pedilepore, rabbit foot (cf. German Hasenfuss), a Siracusan family; Pedigallo, rooster foot or leg, a Bergamascan family, and Pedocca which looks like goosefoot.[87]

Finally, we have Calcagnino and Calcagnadoro, the only derivatives from Calcagno as yet found. The first may possibly come from Galgano through Galganio, or from a Marchigiano term meaning grappling-iron;[88] the second seems to refer to golden spurs.

In addition to the wealth of anatomical terms already cited, the most striking feature of this study so far as the homonymical forms which constitute a fairly complete catalog of orthographically identical words that can be placed alongside them. Undoubtedly, thorough search will uncover more of them. While the meanings of some of these latter words are clearly discernible, the meanings of others have been dimmed or erased by time and circumstance. They have all remained as labels which the common folk have usually interpreted in the light of what they most obviously seem to refer to, the human anatomy.

The fact that there are many surnames that are intimately connected with the foregoing in so far as they descriptively point to man's anatomy without specifically naming the body or any part of it demonstrates that our subject is not yet exhausted.

Among these terms that portray an attractive physique are

[86] See Note 44.

[87] In Piacentino a pedocca is a plant, and in Venetian a starfish. A Pedeboi, ox foot, lived in Ferrara in the thirteenth century. See E. Lorenzi, "Osservazioni Etimologiche sui Cognomi Ladini," *Archivio per l'Alto Adige,* II, 1907, 367. Also compare the French Piedeleu (leu = Old French for wolf), Pied-de-Lièvre, and English Pettifer (pied de fer), Pettigrew (pied de grue), Crowfoot and the German Ochsenbein.

[88] See G. Fiorentino, "Note Lessicali ad 'Maqre Dardesquè," *Archivio Glottologico Italiano,* XXIX, 1937, 141. For some anatomical names involving numbers see chapter on Compound Names.

Bello,[89] Lo Bello, Bellino, Bellincino, Belluccio, Belluzzo, Bellissimo,[90] most beautiful; Bonaspetti, good looking; Bellomo, Belluomini, fair man; Belladonna,[91] fair woman; Belgiovine, Belfante, Belfiglio, fair youth, fair child; Bellofatto, well formed; Belliboni, beautiful and good; Bellagrande, beautiful and large; Vezzosa, Atraente, Piacente and Leggiadro, comely. A personal touch is added to such names as Colabella, Ottobello, Petrobelli, Bellantonio. In contrast, names denoting ugliness are few: Lo Brutto, Brutto,[92] and Malfatto, Maltagliati, deformed. Aged appearance is indicated by Vecchi, La Vecchia, Vecchietti, Vecchiotto, Veccherelli, Vecchione, Vegeti, Vecchiato, Bonvecchiata, Vetrani, Veterani (Friulano); youthfulness by Giovani, Giovanelli,[93] Quadraro (Southern Italian); by Fanciulli, Bimbo, Bimboni, Citti, and many other terms meaning child.[94]

Tallness is evidenced by Longo, Del Lungo, Lunghetti, Grande, Macri (Graeco-Calabrese), and Altadonna,[95] tall woman, while its opposite is designated by Basso,[96] Lo Basso, Vascio, Bassetti, Corti, Lo Curto, Curcio, Curtis, Scurti, Piccoli, Piccoletti, Piccirilli (Southern Italian), Piccini, Piccinni, Picinnini, Piccinotti, Petitto, Citti, Citelli (Abruzzese), Cinino (Ferrarese), Piccitto (Sicilian), Meninno (Abruzzese), Tantillo (Calabrese), Micò (Graeco-Calabrese).

A squat person is designated as Tozzo,[97] Tozzetti, Tozzini, Tozzoni and perhaps Torselli.[98]

Fleshiness gives us Pacchioni, Pacchierotti, Grasso, Lo Grasso,

---

[89] Bella, a short form of Isabella, has contributed to the bello-group. Gabriello can also be reduced to Bello. See E. Ferrari, *Vocabolario de'Nomi Propri* . . . Bologna, 1827, 92.

[90] G. D. Serra in "Per la Storia del Cognome Italiano . . .," *Dacoromania*, III, 1922-23, 523-48, deals briefly with names formed from superlative adjectives. They continue a Latin tradition. In Chicago we find Attivissimo, most active.

[91] Cf. the plant name, belladonna.

[92] The Latin Brutus may have influenced the diffusion of this name.

[93] Giovani = Giovanni is a Northern Italian competitor.

[94] See Names of Kinship.

[95] Cf. Altadona, a Marchigiano place name.

[96] The name of St. Bassus may be recalled in this connection. Cf. also GiacoBASSO, and basso, lowland.

[97] We can arrive at Tozzo and derivatives through AlberTOZZO or any font name ending in -to. Cf. also Förstemann, *op. cit.* 414-15, and Sicilian Tuzzo = Petruzzu.

[98] Of Torselli, Bianchi, *op. cit.* 316n. says, "puo essere stato sopranome di uomo bassotto e grosso," "it may have been a nickname of a short, thick-set man."

Grassotti, Grassini,[99] Grasselli,[100] Tondo, Rotondo, Rotunda, Rotunno,[101] Chiatto, Grosso, Carnazza [102] (fleshy). This condition is offset by surnames relating to leanness, slenderness—Magri, Magrini, Magroni, Lo Magro,[103] Scarnati, Secco, Sicco,[104] Carnesecchi, Sottili, Asciutto, Sciutto, Lusciutto, Lento (Calabrese lientu).

Dark complexion is brought out by Fusco,[105] Ferrigno,[106] Fregni (Modenese), Pellinegro, Pellabruno. On the other hand, the texture of the skin as well as the tint of the hair and beard is referred to in the colors: Bianco, white; Biondo, Oro,[107] Diorato, Fulvio, Flavio, blond; Rosso, Russo, Ruju (Sardinian), Rubbio, Lo Rubbio, red; Bruno, brown; Olivo, Olivastro, olive and olivaceous; Negri, Nigro, Neri [108] and derivatives,[109] Nieddu (Sardinian), black; and Bronzini, Bronzetti, bronze; Castagno,[110] chestnut. Notable are the rare Biancorosso,[111] and Bianbianco (quite light, blond). Rodinò is a Greek survival in Reggio Calabria meaning red hair. Descendants

---

[99] Some of the Grassini are or were originally Jewish Gersciom. See C. Poma, "Fallaci Apparenze in Cognomi Italiani." *Archivio Glottologico Italiano*, XVIII, 1918, 357.

[100] Grasso, etc., can also come from Pancrazio. For grasselli meaning big-lobed ears, see below, and for a possible Germanic origin of the name, cf. Förstemann, *op. cit.* 666. In Bresciano grassel is an edible herb.

[101] Tondo, Rotondo can mean a simpleton. Cf. also rotonda, a circular building.

[102] The word also refers to a sluggard. In its literal meaning it comes close to our slangish "fat stuff."

[103] The vogue of these words has been increased by the existence of saints names—Macra, Macrina, Macrinus.

[104] It may be that Secco and Sicco can be traced back in a few instances to FranSECCO, FranSICCO.

[105] Fusco (Fuscus) was a first name used by both Romans and Germans. See Förstemann, *op. cit.* 562.

[106] Ferrignu in Calabrese means a robust, tireless worker. It should be remembered that fregna (Romagnuolo) may likewise refer to an importunate, intractible man.

[107] Oro can come from TeodORO, IsidORO, etc.

[108] For Bruno add St. Bruno as a source. Neri can also be easily traced to Raineri, Guarinieri, Arnieri, etc.

[109] When suffixes are attached to these and other color words we get the idea or age or size as well as color.

[110] Castagno like Olivo may, of course, be a botanical name, chestnut.

[111] Some of these compounds and many another may well be agglutinations of two last names. For example Francesco Trivellini's translation of Antonio de Trueba's *I Dobloni. Il Meglio delle Fanciulle*, Bassano, Roberti, 1870, was done "Per Nozze Bianco-Rossi," Bianco-Rossi nuptials. But compare here Sicilian Vrancarussa (biancarossa) insect which attacks lemons. See A. de Gregorio, "Aggiunte ai Lessici Siciliani," in *Studi Glottologici*, VIII, 1928.

of gray haired individuals are recognized by Griggi, Grisi,[112] Grisoni,[113] Grisini, Bigi,[114] Bixio, Cano (Sardinian), Canuto,[115] and possibly Argento, silver. Wavy or curly hair is represented by an abundance of Riccio, Rizzo, Ricciuto, Rizzuto, Rizzitiello, Rezzo, Rezzuto, Rizzini, Ricciotto,[116] Crespi,[117] and the Greek term Sgrò, Sgroi. Long hanging hair, once worn by men, has given rise to Zazzara, Zazzera, Zazzaretti, Zazzarone. Paucity or lack or hair is indicated by Calvo,[118] and the Graeco-Italian Spano.[119] Sbarbato and Crotti [120] (if Cremonese) mean beardless. Clipped heads are variously called Raso, Caruso, Carusatti, Carosi, Toso, Tosetti, Tosone, Tosato,[121] Tonso.

A hirsute state is represented by Peloso, Peluso, Pelosini,[122] Piludu (Sardinian), and the obsolete Capelluto.

Coming to the characterization of other members of the anatomy, we have for the ears: Sordi, Lo Surdo, Sortino [123] (Lombard), indicating deafness; for the eyes: Cecati, Cecatelli, Cicatello, Segati, Borgni, Orbuti, denoting blindness, and Loschi, Lusco, Guercio, Lo Guercio, Guercini, Guerzoni, Cicaglione (Neapolitan) pointing

---

[112] Grisi is possible from short forms of Cristotomo and Crisologo. See also Förstemann, *op. cit.* 674.

[113] Cf. Grisone, an inhabitant of the Grison section of Switzerland. In Parmigiano a grison is a partly grayed individual, in Piedmontese a weed of the plaintain family, and in Friulano (grisoon) a crab-louse.

[114] Bigio is also a Milanese pet name for Luigi. As to Bisi compare Visi from Ludovisi.

[115] Add as a source the name of St. Canuto (Knut).

[116] Many Rizzi, Ricci, etc., undoubtedly come from Maurizio, Mauricio, and a few from German Rizo (cf. Förstemann, *op. cit.* 1280), and perhaps riccio, hedgehog. Cincinnatus is a Latin parallel.

[117] Crespi is the name of a Sicilian family hailing originally from Valencia, Spain. In Spanish crespo means curly, too.

[118] Cf. the Latin personal name Calvus and the Corsican place name Calvi.

[119] In Greek spano means beardless, in Otrantino and other Southern Italian dialects it is bald and in Sicilian half-bald.

[120] Crott also means sickly in Cremasco, but in Friulano an identical word means a frog.

[121] Carusu in Sicilian and tosin, tosett in Milanese mean a child, while carosa in Northern Italian is the same as carrozza, carriage. Fruttuoso and even Artusio (Arthur) can, through their pet forms, supply Toso and derivatives. In the Girgenti section of Sicily a carusu is a worker in the sulphur pits. Finally, Carosi might be possible from PasCAROSA, Whitsunday.

[122] Peloso in the Romagnuolo dialect is a speckled alder, while pelosino is a hawkwood plant of the composite family.

[123] Note that Sortino is the name of a Sicilian town.

to strabismus. Pellini [124] (if from the Abruzzese pelline) and the Sicilian Ciuffia both refer to dim-sightedness.

The face is alluded to in Grinzuto, Grinzato, wrinkled, and the tongue in Tartaglia, Tartaglione, Trotta, Trottolini,[125] Balbo,[126] stammerer, while Muto, Lo Muto, Mutaccio allude to mutes.

Camozzi, Camozzini, Camuso, Camuscio,[127] Schizzi (Friulano), are snub-nosed individuals. Neck and throat defects furnish Gozzi,[128] Gosetti (Bolognese gos), Vozza [129] (Calabrese) and Gavotti, Gavozzi [130] from the Piedmontese meaning goitre.

Spinal deformity has resulted in Gobbo,[131] Lo Gobbo, Sgobbo, Gobbato.

Monco, Zonchi, Gionchetti, Mozzo, Muzzo and derivatives mean one-armed, one-handed persons.

Left-handedness has left its mark on a host of names — Manco, Mango, Manconi, Mancini, Mancini,[132] Mancuso, Moncuso, Mancinelli, Mancinforte (strong left hander); Sinistri, Ciampi (if from the Friulano ciamp); Zerbi (if from the Graeco-Calabrese).

Lame individuals have supplied Zoppo, Zoppetti, Zoppelli,[133] Cioppo, Genoese Rango, Monferrino Ranghetti and Venetian Ranconi, Rangoni, and the bowlegged Storti,[134] Torti, Ciampo, Ciampoli, Ciampolini, Ciampelli.[135] Belzoppi is, literally, a handsome lame man. Bilenchi probably also alludes to a bow-legged person.

---

[124] Good competitors are Tuscan Ampelle, Apelle. Cf. also any name ending in -po, -pe, FilipPELLINO, GiusepPELLINO.

[125] In Bolognese Trotta is a short form of Caterina. Cf. also PeTROTTA. The same word also means trout.

[126] See Notes 26 and 27.

[127] See Animal Names.

[128] Ugo, Arrigo, Domenico, Francesco, etc. could give Gozzi as pet forms. In Tuscan gozzo may be the double chin of a fat person.

[129] Cf. Vozza from GiacoVOZZA.

[130] Both Gavotti and Gavozzi are listed as derivatives of Agapito by Bongioanni, op. cit. Gavotta, a dance, and gavotta, a dossier, basket, are also possibilities. Cf. IaCAVOTTO = Iacobotto.

[131] But compare Gobbo coming from GiaCOBBO. Not very likely as a source is gobbo, artichoke. We recall here that the gobbo, hunchback, and the zoppo, lame man, are common Italian carnival figures and as such good explanations of the origin of these names.

[132] In Calabrese a mancinu is an untrustworthy person. As to terms immediately preceding cf. Muzzo, Mozzo from GiacoMUZZO, GiacoMozzo and mozzo, stable boy.

[133] Bongioanni, op. cit. lists Zoppelli as a derivative of Giuseppe.

[134] In Calabrese stuortu is a quarrelsome individual, and in Venetian, quel dai storti, a seller of cinnamon sticks. Storto is also used to refer to cross-eyes.

[135] Cf. the Latin name Varrus. The above terms can also indicate persons with one crooked leg. Yet Gian Paolo can give us Ciampoli, Ciampolini, and Gian Ampelle Ciampelli. Orlando, op. cit. derives Ciampoli from Luciano plus Paolo.

Finally, it is curious to see how some of these descriptive terms combine with first names giving us such odd cognomina as Giampiccoli, Giallongo, Zangrandi, Pietrogrande, Pergrossi, Colagrosso, Giangrasso, Giambianco, Vanbianchi, Jannigro, Giarrosi, Gianrossi, Iarussi, Colanero, Colarussi, Giarizzo, Giammanco, Colasurdo, Ciccocioppi.[136]

The figurative employment of the anatomical terms discussed in the first three sections of this chapter has tended to draw our attention away from the terms themselves to abstract mental and moral peculiarities possessed by an individual. Other figures starting with a fancied similarity between them and the human frame carry us back to the concrete pictorial realities of the body or body regions. Through them the particular features of the physique are given vividness and precision, and, at times, an exaggerated or comic connotation. Often they designate two physical characteristics at once or a physical and a character trait. The metaphors are of miscellaneous origin.

Large stature is denoted by Gigante, Giagante,[137] Ziganto, giant; Toro, bull; Gaglione (Tuscan) rooster; possible Elefante, Alifante, Linfante, elephant; and occasionally by Alcide, Ercole, Hercules; Sansone, Samson (cf. Bergamascan Sansù), and Colossi,[138] colossus. Balena, whale, and Camello (if Calabrese) refer to an excessively large and corpulent individual.[139] Fagotti,[140] fagot, Romagnuolo fagott, is a large misshapen and ill-dressed person. The usual meaning of Baracca, Barracca,[141] is hut or hovel, but in Sicilian it may also indicate a tall fat woman. Colascione, a lute-like instrument, has come to signify a large and somewhat stupid man. Marcantonio, Mark Anthony, is in Bolognese, a large man or woman, but it may also, as in Pavese, allude to a blockhead.[142] In Mantuan Gramola, flax brake, is a big man or woman.

Tallness combined with thinness stands out in Pertica, Perticone, Batacchi,[143] Stangarone (Abruzzese stangalone), Pau (Sardinian), all meaning pole; Bacchetti (Bolognese bachet), stick; Pioppi,

---

[136] Piccolo is small; longo, long; grande, large; grosso, grasso, fat; bianco, white; negro, nigro, black; rosso, roso, russo, red; rizzo, curly; manco, left-handed; surdo, deaf; cioppo, lame. See also Compound Names.

[137] In Castro de'Volsci a gigante is a bully or lady's man.

[138] NiCOLOSSO is, of course, a strong rival.

[139] See Animal Names.

[140] A fagotto is also a musical instrument.

[141] In some dialects—Cremasco baraca, Romagnuolo, baracon,—the word means good-timer.

[142] See Evolution of Italian Surnames.

[143] Also a bell-lapper.

Chioppo, poplar; Lasagna,[144] Maccaroni,[145] Paglialunga (Milanese pajalonga), literally, long straw, Campanaro, belfry (cf. Calabrese campanaru); Calendario [146] (Abruzzese calennarije), alamanac. Slenderness, without emphasizing the idea of height, is expressed by Luccioli, fire-fly, and the rare Ficosecchi, dried fig, very thin persons. Franguele, Fraguele, chaffinch, bullfinch, is, in the dialect of Castro de'Volsci, a thin, lively individual. Rubini, Robini (Milanese robin from roba), meaning small thing or dress, is applied especially to thin girls and women.[147] A Cuaresima, Lent, drawn from the realm of folklore, is a very thin old woman.[148] Leanness associated with sickness can be seen in Merluzzo,[149] codfish (cf. Sicilian merruzzu), and Pochini (Milanese pochin from poco). Though it enjoys the competition of Silvestrino we can add here Strinati, singed, and, by extension, very lean. The rare Sucato seems to mean a very thin person. Cf. Calabrese sucatu de nu lampu, sucked by lightning and Sicilian sucatu di la baddotula, sucked by a weasel.

Obesity finds expression in things — Matarazzo, Materassi,[150] mattress, Botta,[151] Bottazzi, Barile, cask barrel; Mazzino [152] (Sannio), Pistone [153] (Parmigiano-piston), pestle-club; Rigoli [154] (Cremonese

[144] Both pioppo and lasagna can mean simpleton. Lasagnone in this sense is in common use.

[145] Like the above a common term for simpleton. But perhaps some Maccaroni can be traced to Maccario plus an augmentative.

[146] Finamore in his *Vocabolario dell'Uso Abruzzese*. Lanciano, 1880, p. 61, after citing the phrases è nu calennarije, è cchiù lònghe de lu —, he is an alamanac, longer than an alamanac, defines the word as a tall slow-acting person, and adds: "The calendar or alamanac lasts a year; the length of time for that of space (stature)." There is a chance that the term has to do with an alamanac maker or seller, quello del calendario.

[147] However, Rubini, Robini, in nine cases out of ten, are apt to be from CheRUBINO, or the word for ruby.

[148] A person born during the Lenten season might likewise be called Cuaresima.

[149] In the dialect of Teramo, a slow-moving person.

[150] Inasmuch as almost any object that is made or sold can refer back to its maker or seller, so in Materazzi, Barile, Botta, Bisaccia, etc., we may have terms for tradesmen; quello dei materazzi, quello dei barili, quello delle botte, quello delle bisaccie.

[151] The painter, Botticelli, is said to have got his name from the nickname of his brother, who was "as round as a little barrel." But in Venetian the term means an ignoramus. Botta, toad, means in Romagnuolo an ill-shaped woman. For a Germanic source of Botta, cf. Förstemann, *op. cit.* 319-21.

[152] Possible from DalMAZZO, Germanic Mazo (Förstemann, *op. cit.* 1119), and Genoese Mazzo = Maggio.

[153] Another meaning of the word is blunderbuss.

[154] Cf. ArRIGO plus -OLO and Germanic Richulus cited by Bianchi, *op. cit.* 385.

rigol), roller; Mazzocchi [155] (Venetian), butt-end of a club; Strummolo (Calabrese), top; Tamburro, drum; Bisaccia, Besazza,[156] bag, wallet, meaning a fat, uncleanly woman; Chiancone (Sicilian chiancuni), a fat stupid sluggard; Traversa,[157] from traversa, a cross-bar; Caccavella (Neapolitan), pot, describing a fat and short woman; Barca (Bergamascan), a big, fat woman; Spampinato, stripped of leaves, lopped off, that is, disproportioned. It finds expression in animals, Buasso (Bergamascan) and very likely Bove, Boi (Sardinian), Lo Bue, Vacca,[158] Vitello,[159] ox, cow, calf, all of which carry the connotation of obesity in English. Maiale, pig, usually means a fat and dirty fellow as do Porco, Porci, Porcelli,[160] especially in those parts of Italy where porco replaces maiale as a dialect word. Fowl names furnish some surnames of this type: Dell'Oca, Papara,[161] Paparazzo, goose, in addition to fleshiness refer to awkwardness and dullness, but Quaglia, La Quaglia, quail, if Southern Italian, means a stout but comely young woman. Beccafigo,[162] Mangiafico, fig-pecker, seem to refer to fatness without any other implication. Even the batrachians are asked to contribute with Rospo,[163] toad, which, if of Neapolitan provenience, is an uncouth, fleshy fellow. Vegetables contribute Cicerone (Irpino), chick pea. Monastic life may have furnished two plump-surnames —Badiale,[164] pertaining to an abbey, and Abate, Abbate, abbott.[165] Popular lore gives us a horde of Carnevali, Carnevalini, Carnavale, Carnovale, commonly a fat, awkward, stupid fellow, but sometimes, as in Bolognese, a corpulent, gay-faced individual, or as in the dialect of Teramo, merely a simpleton. Another popular character, pagliaccio, a clown, has given Pagliacci, Pagliasso, Pagliazzo, Palaccio (Amaseno-palacce), a fat, ill-dressed man. A Badalone from badare, to look agape, is a loiterer, a ninny, or a big, fat person.

---

[155] Mazzoca (Venetian) means head, and mazzocchio, endive, chicory, wheat.

[156] Cf. Germanic Bessa and Biso plus suffix -accia (Förstemann, *op. cit.* 298, 308.)

[157] In Milanese a traversa is a skirt, in Vicentino an apron and in Calabrese a path.

[158] Cf. Romagnuolo grass com' è una vacca, as fat as a cow.

[159] See Animal Names.

[160] Porcelli may be related to the Latin name Porcellius.

[161] In Ancona papara means a rather unkempt woman.

[162] Cf. Metaurense grass com un becafich. As fat as a figpecker.

[163] Rospo may also designate a surly, irritable person. See chapter XIV.

[164] Most common in the phrase naso badiale, large nose.

[165] Cf. the phrase parere un padre abate, to look like an abbott, i.e. very fat.

One of the oddest of the obese-metaphors is Pavese Masciotta,[166] a stoutish woman, a word derived from maschio, male.

Formica, Formichelli,[167] ant, is a widely diffused term for a little person. If he is small and young he is a Grillo [168] or a Saltarello, grasshopper. Baciocchi,[169] a rod, bell-clapper, knocker, if of Bergamascan origin is a smallish individual or child. Neapolitan Muzzone, Mozzone,[170] stump, stub, is used to denote a pigmy. Cinquepalmi, five spans, unless it is a spot name, also refers to a diminutive fellow.

Hirsuteness is indicated by Lanuto, wooly, and perhaps by Velli, Vellotti, Velluti,[171] Veludo, from vello, fleece. Nazzareno, Nazarite, may in a few instances point to a man with long hair.

Turning to the individual features viewed metaphorically we find the head humorously referred to as Zucca, Zoca, Cocozza, Cucuzza, Cocozella, pumpkin, and as Cipolla, Cipolletti, Cipollini, onion.[172] These are also terms for simpleton. If very large the head may be described as a Mascarone, Mascarò (Cremonese mascaroun), mask.

Jaberg and Jud give in their atlas [173] quite a variety of terms for a lock or tuft of hair. Although the etymology of some of them is obscure the meaning they imply is that of a mass, a bunch or a fringe. Among the surnames derived from them are Ciuffii [174] Ciufetti, Tupputo, Ciocchi,[175] Ciocchetti,[176] Cerro,[177] Cerruto, Cer-

---

[166] In its Parmigiano meaning of lively girl the term approaches our tomboy.

[167] In Parmigiano a formica is a sly old soldier, and in the dialect of Castro de'Volsci, a thin, little person or an irascible woman.

[168] The word also means a scatterbrain, and in the dialect of Amaseno, rile, a thin agile fellow. Cf. the Romagnuolo saying parer un grell, to look like a grasshopper.

[169] The usual meaning of Baciocchi is simpleton. In Genoese it signifies a dandy, and in Romagnuolo baciocch is the same as batocc, an urchin. In Milanese baciocch is also a term for child.

[170] Giacomo or any name in -mo could lead to Muzzone, Mozzone.

[171] Vello from OliVELLO JacoVELLO and vello, velluto, velludo meaning satin must also be considered as probable sources.

[172] Coccia, vase (cf. etymology of testa) is a regular designation for capo in some parts of Italy, as is Conca, shell in Sardinian. Cicogna (from stork?) is Calabrese for a large head. These are all surnames.

[173] Sprach und Sachatlas Italiens und des Südschweiz, I, Zoffingen, 1928.

[174] Another apparent derivative of ciuffo is Ciuffelli which in Abruzzese (ciuffele) means a bagpipe.

[175] Ciocch in Northern Italian means a drunkard. Ciocco likewise means stump and hence a blockhead.

[176] In Venetian the word is a violet, viola odorata.

[177] Cerro can also be connected with cerro, bitter oak.

rato, Mazzi,[178] Mazzocchi,[179] Pugno, knot, fist. Other possible names are Fezzi, Frezzi,[180] and Lembi. Here belongs Zignoni [181] from cigno, a swan, a Romagnuolo term for an artificial tuft or curl, and Biscioni, from biscia, snake, Piedmontese for a lock of hair. In contrast, Spinnato, deplumed, Pilato,[182] plucked and Luna (Sicilian) and Mezzaluna (Calabrese menzaluna), moon, half moon, denote baldness. In Melone, melon, we have a choice between a clipped head, a simpleton and a short form plus augmentative of a first name such as Carmelo-CarMELONE.

Though most of the Mori, Morelli, Moretti, Morittu (Sardinian), etc., can be traced to Mauro and Amore a few instances may well go back to the term Moro, Moor, meaning a negro or a person with very dark hair and complexion. The Moors of Barbary were, on the other hand, designated as Ghezzi, also a nickname-surname.[183] Ghignoni from ghigna, sneer, grin, is by extension, an ugly face. The condition of the complexion resulting from illness is referred to in Cerini,[184] Ceruti, wax color. A pocked-face due to small pox, vaiolo, is described by the disease — Varoli, Veroli,[185] or by its effect, Pizzolato, pecked; Bollati (Milanese boláá) blistered; Mascarella (in the Teramo dialect mascarille), mask; and the Southern Italian rare but uncomplimentary Grattacaso, cheese grater.[186]

Freckles are portrayed by Lenticchia, lentil, the literary name for these spots, perhaps by Lenti, Lentini,[187] and Semmoli, Simili from semola, bran. The peace-loving propensities of a fat person

---

[178] Again Giacomo or any name in -mo could give Mazzo. Cf. also Germanic Mazo, Förstemann, *op. cit.* 1119, Genoese Mazzo = Maggio.

[179] See Note 155.

[180] Fezzi and especially Frezzi could be pet dialectical forms of Federico. The latter is given by Bongioanni, sub voce Federico.

[181] Compare cignone, large girth.

[182] A possible source is also Pilato, Pilate.

[183] Ghezzi could stem from Ugo, Arrigo, Domenico and Seghezzo. The first three possibilities are given by Bongioanni, *op. cit.* under Domenico. Ghezz is likewise a Milanese term for lizard.

[184] See Note 69. Cf. also the dialectical ger, dormouse.

[185] Veroli is a place name in Lazio and Verolo in Piedmont. A verola in Neapolitan is a widow as well as a roasted chestnut. Cf. also Varo, Verro, Vera, Förstemann, *op. cit.* 1533, 1555-56. Alvaro plus -ola easily gives Varola.

[186] The Provençal place name Grato—cats should not be totally counted out as a source. See F. Mistral, *op. cit.* 89. On Provençal colonies in Southern Italy see A. da Salvio, "Relics of Franco-Provençal in Southern Italy." *Publications of the Modern Language Association of America*, XXII, 1908, 45-79.

[187] Lenti is also connected with lento, slow and leanness (Calabrese). It may derive from BuontaLENTO, while Lentini may refer to a Sicilian place name and VaLENTINO.

have caused the term Pacioni [188] (Romagnuolo pacion), to be transferred to chubby cheeks. Possibly the word faccia, face, has influenced this meaning. Rossetti, Russetto,[189] a word for rouge is used
to refer to persons whose cheeks are naturally ruddy. The name
Musico (perhaps also Musica), composer, player, also betokens a
beardless individual. It was formerly applied to evirated male
sopranos. Mascheroni, big, ugly mask, sometimes denotes a man
with a disfigured face. Even the dimples are not neglected as can
be seen in the names Pozzetti, Fossetti, Fossarelli, literally, pits and
hollows.[190]

Grasselli [191] from grasso, fat, refers to big-lobed ears. The
hard of hearing are sometimes called Cannone, cannon, and Campana, bell.

Occhi di pulce, flea-eyes, that is, very small eyes, may have
given us some of our Pulci, Pollice, Pulice.[192]

Anent the nose we have Scacciato, Cacciato,[193] Cazzato, Schizzi
(Friulano schizz), crushed, decompounded forms of naso scacciato. Frittelli,[194] if from the Parmigiano section may be related
to frittela fritter, a designation for a flat nose. Boccia,[195] goblet,
is often used to allude to a big nose, and so is Carcioffo, artichoke
(in Teramano). A vrogna in Calabrese is a horn used by pigherds
to call pigs, and, by transference of meaning signifies an oversized
smeller, too. It may have given rise to some of our La Vorgnas
and perhaps Borgnas and Brognis.[196] A few of the Griffi, Griffoni,
Griffoli [197] may originate from grifo, snout.

Mosca, Moscone,[198] fly, describes an imperial.

---

[188] Another source is Pacione from Acquistapace, a font name.

[189] Most of the Rossetti, Russetto are from rosso, red, red haired, ruddy-
cheeked.

[190] Cf. fossette, dimple, in English, which may well be the source of our
Fawcetts, Fossetts. Under Alfonso, Bongioanni, op. cit. points out that some
Italian surnames take on the Provençal form Anfos in Anfossi. From Anfosso,
therefore, we can obtain both Fossetti and Fossarelli.

[191] See Note 100.

[192] Some of the Pulci may hail from a town near Florence. In Neapolitan,
police, applies to a small, agile person.

[193] Scacciato, Cacciato also mean expelled, outlawed. In the dialect of
Avellino Scacciato also indicates a cisposo, blear-eyed.

[194] In Tuscan a frittella is a frivolous person as well as a prickly pear.

[195] Cf. IacoBOCCIA.

[196] However, the Brognis are more likely to come from Tuscan, Romagnuolo plum or blackthorn.

[197] The Griffin (fabulous animal and vulture) are good sources of Griffo,
etc. Griffo and Grifo are likewise common Germanic names, cf. Förstemann,
op. cit. 674.

[198] Also means a petulant, boresome individual.

The Cremonese word for old shoe, zavatta, surname Zavatta,[199] has, through some fantastic comparison, come to mean big mouth. Becco, beak, is sometimes used for mouth and may be related to Becchi, Becchini.[200]

The popular designations: tusks, fangs for teeth, big teeth are in Italian zanna, whence Zannuto, Zanudo, Sannuto, Sanudo (Venetian), Zannoni.[201] Claws and paws for hands and feet are represented by Branca, Zampa,[202] and their derivatives.

The haunch is not infrequently referred to as a prosciutto, ham, perhaps giving on occasion the last name Presutti.

Finally, to end the list of this type of metaphor, which is suggestive rather than exhaustive, Scarponi, Scarpetti,[203] Scarpelli, from scarpa, shoe, may allude to persons with large or with small feet.

The role that anatomical names play in the Italian onomasticon is, as can be seen, a very important one. Their number and variety make up a vast gallery of word-portraits painted by a people endowed with a strong sense of realism which appears to be a heritage left to them by their Roman ancestors, past masters in the art of the extreme humanization of portraiture.[204]

---

[199] Zavatta is also a Valsuganese term for a good-for-nothing.

[200] Becco is also a billy-goat, and becchino a gravedigger. Then, too, Beco is one of the pet forms of Domenico.

[201] Zannoni could come from Giovanni = Zanni or zanni, a clown.

[202] Zampetti, Zampitti, if they come from a word in the Amaseno or allied sections mean peasant, while Zampelli may be related to the Bolognese zampell, decoy. Zampino in Tuscan is spruce tree. Abbreviated combinations of Zan (Gian) plus any name in -po could easily produce any of these names. Italian Branca might doubtless come from Spanish Blanca. Brancadoro, gold claws, and Brancacci are greedy old gripers.

[203] But cf. Förstemann, *op. cit.* 1305, for the Germanic origin of these names. Scarpetta in the Lunigiana region is an ailanthus glandulosa. Dantists will remember Scarpetta degli Ordelaffi of Forlì who was Dante's host during his exile.

A few place name homographs offering competition to anatomical names as sources of cognomina have already been cited. For further reference we now mention the following: Bianco, Bianchi (Calabria), Bracci (Lombardy), Comba (Piedmont), Curti (prov. of Caserta), Gambetta (Piedmont), Gambino (Venetia and Piedmont), Magri (prov. of Rome), Muso (prov. of Bergamo), Musone (prov. of Ancona), Nasino (prov. of Firenze), Rossi (Tuscany, Piedmont and Genoa), Sordio (Lombardy), Testa (prov. of Modena), Testoni (prov. of Milano), Trezza (prov. of Milano).

[204] Cf. R. Burn, *Roman Literature in Relation to Roman Art,* London, New York, 1888, 41-67.

Chapter XVIII

MISCELLANEOUS TYPES OF NAMES

CALENDAR NAMES

Latin inscriptions show that with the single exception of August the names of the months had a fairly wide currency as cognomina among the early Christians.[1] Their appearance, indicating the period of birth, was doubtless a natural one, but their popularity must also have been measurably increased by the power of association. For example, Junius and Julius are gens names and Junius and Martius survivals of deity names, Juno, Mars. January is linked with St. Januarius, Gennaro, the patron saint of Naples, whose cult was started as early as the fifth century. April has always been connected in the poetry of all nations with the concept of youth, joy, new life. In Calabria there is still in existence the old Roman and Greek tradition (now taking place on the day of the Ascension) celebrating the return of May with majumae feasts. Furthermore, in all Catholicism May is also the mese mariano, the month of Mary. August not only harks back to Caesar Augustus, but is also connected with the famous St. Augustine, who is honored on the 29th of August, the Madonna di Agosto or Mezz'Agosto, and has, moreover, an easily understandable and attractive meaning, august. Lacking strong associative ties are February, September, October, November and December.

All the months of the year, without any exception, appear in Italian font names and through them in surnames such as de Gennaro, Gennari, Nari (its short form), Zennari, Zonari, Febraro, Fibbraio, di Marzo, Marzino, Marzetti, Marzitelli, Marzoli, Marzolino,[2] Aprile, Aprilante, Maggi, di (de) Maggio, Maggini, Maggioli, Maggiolini,[3] Maio; Giugni, Lugli, Lui (Mantuan); Agosti, Agostini and the pet forms Gustini, Ostarello, Osterello; Settembre, Settembrini and Sembrini, a short form; Ottobre, Ottobrino, Novembre, Decembre, Decembrio. Of these by far the most common names are Gennaro, Maggio, Agosto and their derivatives due to their strong religious implications.

---

[1] This is borne out by an examination of the *Corpus Inscriptionum Latinorum.* Berlin, 1863 ff.

[2] Could on rare occasions refer to a magpie, pica marzola.

[3] Maggiolini may (with less likelihood than the above) go back to maggiolino, green finch, black beetle.

Also alluding to time of birth, we have a number of first names and, subsequently, last names, drawn from days of the week — Lunedei, Lunarino, Lunetta,[4] Monday; Marti, Martini, Tuesday; Mercuri, Mercorino, Mercolino, Wednesday; Iovino, Giovetto, Giovarelli, Thursday; Venneri, Veneri, Friday; Sabato, Sabatino, Sabadino, with the pet forms Badini, Battelli,[5] Saturday; Domenica, Sunday. Since early inscriptions reveal no established tradition on this score it is likely that they are the product of the Middle Ages and later times. Again association accounts for part of the small vogue which these names possess: the names of the gods Mars, Mercury, Jove, Venus, resurrected by Humanism along with other pagan dieties — Diana, Minerva, Ercole and others,[6] the names of saints — Martha, Martin, Mercurius, Jovinus, Venerus and Dominic. Sabato and derivatives are usually given to persons born on Holy Saturday. Unmistakable as to their provenience and more popular than their Italian parallels are the German Sontag, Montag, Dienstag, Mittwoch, Donnerstag, Freitag, Samtag. French Dimanche and Spanish Domingo mean both Sunday and Dominic, but the occasional French Vendredi seems clear enough.

Both month and day appellations often re-appear indirectly in a number of religious names, due to the fact that an unofficial ecclesiastical calendar has taken a deep, century-old root in folk tradition. According to it January is the month of the Epiphany; March the month of the Annunciation; June the month of St. John; July the month of the Madonna del Carmine and the month of Mary Magdalen; October the month of the Rosary; November the month of St. Martin; December the Christmas month.[7] From this type of name spring some of our Epifani, Bifano, Befani, Pasquetti, Lucenti (a possible translation of Epiphany), Annunziati, Nunziati, Annunzio, Nunzio; de (di) Giovanni; Carmine; Rosari; Martini; Natale, Nadalini. Several of these names could also have come from the custom of giving a festival name to a child born on a great church holiday. Others are Pasquale, Pascale, Pasqua, Paschini, Pascotti, Pascaletto, Pascalino with the short forms, Scala, Scaletti, Scalini, Quarelli (from PasQUARELLO,) referring to

---

[4] Possible also from luna, moon, which could become a last name through use as an inn sign or heraldic device. Cf. lunetta, lunette window.

[5] Badini could go back to Abate, abbé, or to a dialectical form of Bernardo (Monferrino). A battello is also a boat.

[6] The vogue of the names of pagan gods is betrayed by the fact that as late as 1614 the *Rituale Romanum* enjoins the priests to see that unbecoming names of deities of the godless pagans are not given in baptism.

[7] See C. Merlo, *I Nomi Romanzi delle Stagioni e dei Mesi*, Torino, 1904.

Easter; Pasquarosa,[8] Rosato (from Pasqua rosata), Spirito (from Spirito Santo), Fiori, Fiorita[9] (possibly from Pasqua dei Fiori, Pasqua Fiorita), Alba (cf. dominica in albis), referring to Pentecost or Whitsunday; Ognisanti, to all Saint's Day (cf. French Toussaint); Palma, to Palm Sunday; Candelori, Candelari, Ceriola [10] (Venetian), to the feast of the Purification of the Virgin on the 2d of February; and Passioni, very likely given to one born during the Passion Week.[11] One of the very few holidays from a non-religious source to be honored by a surname is New Year through Bonanno, Capodanno, Capadanno.

Nothing is more natural than the use of the word Primavera, spring, as a first name to indicate the joy that comes to the parents of a new-born child. It may have come into the world at Springtide, but on such occasions it is always Spring no matter what the season. More definite is Bellario, fair weather (cf. English Fayrweather), and possibly also Bontempo, Bontempelli, Bontemponi, Tempobono.[12] Estate, summer, is rare, and so is Invernio, Verni,[13] winter. The winter name is also found in the compound Malinverno and is implied in Maltempo. Bisesti, Besesti points pretty clearly to a leap year child. The carnival and lenten season, Carnevale, Carnovale, Carnesale (old Vicentino), rather than relating to the time of birth and hence season are nicknames referring to people who have acted these roles in popular performances. A fat, gluttonous person, a dullard, a clown, is often dubbed carnevale, while an old and very thin person is termed cuaresima, interpretations that have grown out of these performances.

Bongiorno and its reduction Giorno, as well as Bondì,[14] mean good day, an allusion to an auspicious event, often the arrival of an heir. Reminiscence of parts of the day when birth occurred

[8] See C. Merlo, "I Nomi della Pentecoste nei Dialetti Italiani," *Italia Dialettale*, II, 1926, 238-50. Perhaps Carosi from PasCAROSA should be added to the list.

[9] Naturally, fiore, flower, is a good source of Fiori. For Fiorita (usually Calabrese) cf. the variant Jurita. For Alba see Note 15.

[10] In Anconitano ceriola means eel. A candelario is also a candle maker, candle seller.

[11] Cf. English Noel, Yule, Easter, Pascall, Pascoe, Pancoast, Tiffany, and see E. Weekley, *Romance of Names*, London, 1914, 79, for further information. With some hesitation we add here a possible calendar name Casconi, Cascucci, probably deriving from Abruzzese casca, fruit picking season.

[12] These terms, esp. Bontemponi, also mean good timers.

[13] Could come from Berni, Bernardo. Cf. Inverno, place name in the province of Pavia.

[14] Perhaps a weak competitor of Abbondio, through (Ab)Bondi(no).

seem to lurk in Alba,[15] Laurora, Mattina, La Mattina,[16] morning; Meriggi,[17] noon; Sera,[18] eve; Vespri,[19] vespers; Tramonti,[20] sunset; Notti,[21] night; Mezzanotte,[22] midnight; Malanotte,[23] bad night; Buonasera, Buonanotte, good evening, good night; are congratulatory like Bongiorno and Bondí as well as common greetings. We also have Notturno, Nottorno, nocturnal and Tenebrini, darkness.

Zodiac names do not appear to be a part of the folk tradition. They can, of course, be supplied as, for example, Toro (Taurus), Gemini, Verginelli (Virgo), Scorpione (Scorpio), Acquaro (Aquarius), Pesce (Pisces), Ariete (Aries), Leone (Leo), Cancro (Cancer), but all of them can pretty definitely be traced back to other sources.

THE SKY AND THE WEATHER

Taken from the sky are Sole,[24] sun, Luna, moon, Stella,[25] star, terms that are among the most common inn signs and heraldic devices. All of them, especially Stella, are still used in their literal sense as personal names. There are, in addition, Nuvoli, Nuvolini, Nuvoloni, cloud, Neglia, Calabrese for cloud and fog, perhaps a nickname alluding to dim-sightedness. Compare avire na neglia all'uocchi, to have a cloud or fog in one's eyes. Nebbia,[26] fog, may refer to the same defect. Neve, Della Neve, snow, could apply to a very light complexioned person. Tempesta, Tempestini, hurri-

---

[15] Cf. Alba Pompeia in the province of Cuneo.

[16] Matto means crazy, eccentric. Cf. also Mattina from Matteo.

[17] Possibly also from Americo.

[18] Sera can easily be obtained from BaldiSERA, and is a saw or mountain in Northern Italian.

[19] Vespro may be a Tuscan-Romagnuolo term for wasp.

[20] Tramonte likewise means a place between mountains. Cf. English Tremont.

[21] Notti can be derived from any font name in -no, na, MarciaNOTTO, LuciaNOTTO, GiovanNOTTO, etc.

[22] Cf. German Mitternacht and Abend. Vormittag, has no parallel in Italian. Buonanotte exists as a place name (prov. of Chieti).

[23] The term may hide the mystery of some tragic happening, but if Venetian it is merely a form of Madalena, Malena, Malanotte.

[24] Sole may have gained some of its currency as a font name as a translation of the Greek Elios. Cf. St. Elio.

[25] Stella is also a common reduction of BattisSTELLA.

[26] The cloud terms cited may be place names indicating lowlands as suggested by S. Pieri, "Toponomastica delle Valli del Serchio e della Lima." *Archivio Glottologico Italiano*, Supplemento, Quinta Dispensa, 1898, 184. Nebbione means a dunce, and Sienese nebbio for ebbio means a dwarf elder. The pagan king, Nuvolone, appears in *Uggero il Danese*, a chivalric romance. Cf. Neglia from CorNELIA.

cane, hail-storm, is often used in speaking of quick-tempered or destructive creatures. Besides flood, rain storm, Dilluvio can mean great quantity, great eater. Borrasca is a variant term. Bagliore is lightning, a fast moving or acting person. Troni, Southern Italian for thunder might be nothing more than a shortening of PeTRO-NIO, but Neapolitan Tronolone is a clearer case. It may apply to a noisy person. A tron in Old Vicentino is a strong, robust individual.[27] Vento, wind, is figuratively linked with vanity, but it may be a deceptive form, possibly from Venturino or Bentivoglio. Levante, Levantini,[28] Orienti, Orientale, east, point to emigrants from the Levant. Tramontani refers to north or to a person coming from beyond the mountains, and Mistrali to the northwest wind. The poetical L'Occaso [29] and the literary Occidentale mean west and westerner. Scirocchi and Cirocchi are local for south. These direction-names are all very infrequent in contrast to the great profusion of English North, South, East and West. A rare but interesting surname is d'Ecclisso, eclipse, possibly alluding to birth taking place during this phenomenon.

NUMBER NAMES

The Romans frequently employed ordinals to indicate the numerical position of the birth of a child as compared to that of his brothers and sisters. Famous men who have owned this type of name include Sextilius and Quintilian, Roman consuls. Between the first and fifth centuries ordinal number names of saints from Primus to Octavius make their appearance indicating a fairly widespread vogue in the early Christian period. Italians, especially in the North, have carried on the tradition with Primo, Primanta, Secondo; della Terza, Terzo, Lotierzo, Terzetti;[30] Quarto, Quartino, Quartucci, Quartarelli, Quarticelli; Quinzio, Quintino, Quintilla, Cinquini, Cinquetti; Siesto, Sesto, Sestini, Sestile; Settino, Settoni, Settimio, Settano, Setticelli; Ottavio, Ottaviano, Ottolonino; Nono and Decio, Decimo, ordinals from first to tenth. In Sicily Settimo, the seventh-born child, is considered to have such extraordinary virtue that all persons suffering from intermittent fever need to do is to catch one individual bearing this name by surprise and say:

[27] But Venetian Tron is supposed to come from Tribunus, a political office. See C. Poma, "I Cognomi Monosillabici in Italia." *Archivio Glottologico Italiano*, XVII, 1910-13, 416.

[28] In Neapolitan a levantino is an early riser.

[29] The only L'Occaso met with so far is Carlo Maria L'Occaso, author, born in Castrovillari, Calabria.

[30] Not altogether improbable from terzetto, pocket pistol.

Maria's Septimus, oh pray,
Do cause my chills to pass away.[31]

Most of these, as we have implied, have crystallized as surnames through first names. But in some instances their source can be traced to spot names indicating kilometric road markers which give the distance to large centers of population, or stop-station names, military or otherwise.[32]

The same explanation probably holds true for some of the cardinal number surnames like Di Quattro, four; Cinque, five; Sei,[33] six; Setti,[34] seven; Nove, nine; Dieci, ten; Dodici, twelve; Venti,[35] Vigenti, twenty; Ventiquattro, twenty-four; Venticinque, twenty-five; Delvintisette, twenty-seven; Ventinove, twenty-nine; Trenta, Trenda, thirty; Trentadue, thirty-two; Trentacinque, thirty-five; Trentanove, thirty-nine; Quaranta, Quarantelli,[36] forty; Quarantotto, forty-eight; Cinquanti, fifty; Cento, one hundred; Mille,[37] one thousand, Millanto,[38] thousands. Trenta, for example, is the designation of a town near Caserta and one near Cosenza; Quattordio is near Alessandria, Quaranti is in the province of Acqui; Cento in the province of Ferrara. There is also a possibility that some of these numbers may indicate the families once residing at

---

[31] The Sicilian words

> Settimu di Maria
> Fammi passari lu friddu a mia . . .

are quoted from G. Pitrè, *Novelle e Racconti Popolari Siciliani.* I, Palermo, 1875, 193n.

[32] In the Upper Rhine Valley, near Wallendstadt, we find at regular intervals the villages of Seguns, Tertzen, Quarten, Quinten and Sewes which were once Roman stations derived from numerals. See I. Taylor, *Words and Places.* New York, Dutton, n.d. 398. For some Italian number place names see S. Pieri, *op. cit.* 185.

[33] Sei might be a variant of zei, Romagnuolo for lily.

[34] Other possibilities might be MoriSETTO, PariSETTO.

[35] Venti could have an alternative derivation from Ventivoglio from Bentivoglio. We add here the peculiar Diecidue, twelve(?).

[36] Of course, one could be called Quaranta in honor of the feast of the Forty Martyrs.

[37] Cento may be obtained from ViCENTO, variant of Vincenzo. With regard to Mille we think of the short form of CaMILLA, or Milla, Tarantino for Emilia.

[38] Note that millantare means to boast. We have also seen the surnames Millioni and Migliardi which look like million and billion in translation, but Millioni probably comes from Emilione and and Migliardi from a combination of Emilio and Leonardo. For other number names we refer the reader to C. Poma, "Numeri come Cognomi." *Archivio Glottologico Italiano,* XVIII, 1918, 345-52.

given places.[39] But it is even more likely that some represent posts held by progenitors of the owners in provincial or city administrations. Thus in Florence there used to be a Magistrato dei Cinque, de' Nove, de' Dieci; a Magistrato dei Sedici Gonfalonieri; i Venti Cittadini; a Senato de' Quarantotto; a Consiglio dei Settanta.[40] These administrative names could be reduced and, in fact, were reduced, to the numeral, which came to be synonymous with the office and the individual occupying it. Weekley in his *Surnames* (London, 3rd ed. 1936, 179) cites the mediaeval name of Andre Sixantwenti alias Vinte-sis-deners which suggests that a few number names can likewise be abbreviated versions of coin names.[41]

COINS

During the Middle Ages quite a number of coin names were in existence.[42] Many have disappeared, but those that are left together with the new ones that have come into being since that time are abundant enough to attract some notice. Among them are the general terms Danaro, Denari, Moneta, Soldi, Boragni (Neapolitan), and the specific terms Baiocchi, Bigattini (Venetian bagatin), Bolognini, Bisanti, Carrino, Cianfrone, Cianferone, Ducati, Fiorini, Lira, Parpagliolo, Patacca, Reali, Scillengo, Tari, Tornisi, Tornesella, Zecchino, Zecchinello. As bagattino, baiocco and patacca are terms used to refer to worthless fellows we may presume that the same meaning has been extended to the other base coins like parpagliolo, tornese, carlino (= carrino). Unfortunately, we cannot insist too strongly on the connection between these names and the coin terms because of the appearance of homographs which give them stiff competition.[43] However, their claim as genuine products

---

[39] See S. Pieri, *op. cit.* 184.

[40] Among the other localities Siena had its Nove Priori, Trieste its Dodici Famiglie Tribunizie, Ferrara its Magistrato di Dodici Savi, Milan its Dodici di Provvisione, Venice its Consiglio dei Dieci, Bologna its Quaranta Famiglie del Senato, Teramo its Quarantotto Famiglie Patrizie, etc. Cf. also the Spanish veinticuatro de Sevilla, alderman of Seville.

[41] See the section on Coin Names immediately following.

[42] See C. Poma, "Numeri come Cognomi," *op. cit.*

[43] For example, Danaro, Denari can be interpreted as de Gennaro; Moneta as a reduction of SiMONET(T)A; Soldi as a reduction of Lombard AnSOLDO; Bigattini as a silk worm; Bisanti as a place name; Bolognini as a place name; Carrino as Southern for Carlino (Charles); Ducati as duchy; Fiorini as a flower; Lira as a musical instrument; Patacca as an aquatic worm (Valle Anzasca); Reali as areale, arealis, a topographical name; Scillengo as the Germanic Schilling; Tarì as a short form of Autarino; Zecchino as Calabrese zichini, zichiniellu, meaning a little bit, hence a midget. As to cianfrone, cf. Milanese cianfer, an inept person, and Parmigiano cianfer, a midget.

of the mints is strengthened by compound coin names about which there can be no doubt such as Sansoldi, penniless and Tresoldi, Quattrosoldi, Cinquesoldi, Cinquegrana, Settesoldi, Setteducati, Settegrani, Centoducati, Centolivre, Centolire, Millefiorini, Millelire, Milletari [44] representing denominations ranging from three to one thousand.

AMUSEMENTS

Surnames from amusements appear to be few, but if we dig beneath the surface a little it is easy to unearth a considerable number. Italians have always been great lovers of pageants of all kinds. Frequent religious festivals have given them the opportunity to dramatize episodes from the Old and New Testament and the lives of the saints, performances which occasionally have caused the individual participants to receive as a nickname the role which they enacted. It may be one of the many saint names or appellatives like Caino [45] (Cain), Sgarioto (Judas Iscariot), Faraone (Pharaoh), Pilato [46] (Pilate), Soldano (sultan), Turco, Saraceno, Pagano, Moro (Turk, Saracen, Pagan, Moor); devil names like Lucifero, Maligno; ecclesiastical designations like Papa (pope), Vescovo (bishop), Prete (priest), Romito (hermit), or Barbaruto (Sicilian), a person disguised as a monk with sack and hood who marches in religious processions; titular names like Imperatore, emperor, Re, king, Regina, queen, Cesare, Caesar, Duca, duke; Cavaliere, knight; officials like Giudice, judge, Avvocato, lawyer, Notaro, notary. Some of these re-appear in the popular rappresentazioni carnevalesche along with other characters like Carnevale, Carnevalini, Cuaresima,[47] Carneval and Lent; Dottore, doctor; Magnano, smith; Zoppo, lame man; Gobbo, hunchback; Pecoraro, shepherd; Cacciatore, hunter; Vecchia, old woman; Urso,[48] bear, etc. The joust and the tourna-

[44] Giovan Battista Buondenari, a Modenese, lived in the seventeenth century. Some of our coin names are cited in the above article by Poma. We add here the nickname-surname Caparra, earnest money.

[45] Caino is, figuratively, a perverse individual.

[46] Pilato is also plucked, bald.

[47] Carnevale and Cuaresima may likewise relate to appearance and time of birth.

[48] For an interesting discussion of pageantry names see E. Weekley, *Surnames*, 3rd ed. London, 1936, 198-224, and for descriptions of feste carnevalesche consult G. Pitrè, "Mastro di Campo. Rappresentazione Carnevalesca in Mezzoiuso." In *La Famiglia, la Casa, la Vita del Popolo Siciliano*. Palermo, 1913, 266-78, and G. Giannini, "Il Carnevale nel Contado Lucchese." *Archivio per lo Studio delle Tradizioni Popolari*, VII, 1888, 307-22. It should be noted, incidentally, that in the Middle Ages saraceno was a term regularly applied to people from the Near East.

ment have, on their part, added the devices of the fighters. Children's playing at war has undoubtedly resulted in the transmittance of quite a few of the names of the heroes of the Carolingian and Arthurian cycles.[49] Perhaps some of our Fantinos go back to fantino, jockey. Biped and quadruped names have been applied to hunters;[50] fish names to swimmers.[51] Applied to humans are botanical names as the result of their use in the universally popular ditties, the fiori and stornelli,[52] and various zoological names as the result of their use in nursery rhymes.[53] Music contributes names of musical instruments conferred upon the players of the same.[54] While all such surnames obviously have to contend against strong rivals from other sources it, nevertheless, remains clear that as diversions they have contributed a substantial quota to the onomasticon.

More specifically alluding to amusements are dance names — Ballarino, Ballerini,[55] Danza,[56] Saltarelli [57] (Abruzzese), Tarantelli, Gavotta,[58] Cicconi [59] (if Pavese), Scarpetta [60] (if Metaurense), Pavana, Correnti (if Milanese), Viglione,[61] Gagliardi [62] and Furlanetti, which is more often to be related to the name of Friuli. There are also playing card names — Tarocchi, Bagatti (if Cremonese, Parmigiano or Piedmontese), Bagatella (if Milanese), the first of the tarocchi; Pizzichini, from an Anconitano word for the tressette; Venticinque,[63] the two and three, one of the strongest combinations

[49] See names under section Romances of Chivalry.
[50] See chapters on Animal and Bird Names.
[51] See chapter on Fish Names.
[52] See chapter on Botanical Names.
[53] See remarks on p. 75.
[54] See section on Musical Instruments in chapter on Object Names.
[55] Other meanings of ballerino are frivolous woman, wagtail, quagmire (Pavese).
[56] Danza might also very logically come from a font name AbbonDANZA, Lattanzia.
[57] A saltarello (from salto, jump) is also a lively person or a grasshopper. In Rome the tarantella is called saltarello.
[58] Gavotta might come from the name for a sea fish. Cf. Gavotta from Agapita.
[59] In the majority of cases Cicconi should be related to Cicco, short form of Francesco.
[60] Scarpetta can also be a Germanic first name. The current face value of the word is slipper.
[61] Viglione (veglione) is likewise a waker and a derivative of Amabilia.
[62] A common meaning of gagliardo is strong, brave. Spanish Gallardo is a good source of the name.
[63] Besides referring to the playing card Piedmontese bagatt means a clown. The current meaning of bagatella is a trifle, worthless fellow. For Venticinque see section on Number Names.

in this game; Tribastune, three of clubs. The ball game may have supplied Boccieri, Pallaro, ball players, Boccia,[64] Palla, Pallone, ball, and Trocchi,[65] a sort of Romagnuolo ball game. Morra, Murra, Mora, Mura [66] may relate to the ancient but still popular mora; Sassetti,[67] if Milanese, to a game played with pebbles and coins; Boschetti,[68] if Bergamascan, to one played with twigs; Troccoli,[69] if Neapolitan, to a rattle used during Holy Week. Sicilian Pipituni, Pipitone,[70] is a figure made of stones which serves as a target; Strummolo [71] (Calabrese) and Busnelli [72] (Venetian) are tops; Cuccagni [73] points to albero della cuccagna, greasy pole; a Frugolo [74] is a rocket, a La Rotella [75] a catherine wheel; Capitummino and Capriola,[76] both Southern Italian, refer to somersault; Cappelletti [77] to a children's game; Cerabottani, Cerebottani,[78] to a pea shooter; Parapatta (Calabrese) is a tie in any kind of game, and de'Scacchi may relate to chess.

ROMANCES OF CHIVALRY

In his *Bibliografia dei Romanzi di Cavalleria in Versi e in Prosa Italiani* [79] Melzi lists an astonishing number of French romances of chivalry which have been more or less adapted by Italian writers from the Middle Ages to our times. In the early period of their vogue many a romance was recited by hordes of wandering minstrels in the courts and in the market places. In the South both Arthurian and Carolingian legends had been introduced by

---

[64] Bocciero and pallaro are also makers of balls. In addition, bocciero and boccia are connected with the word for goblet. Cf. also bocciero, butcher.

[65] Trocchi could point to PeTROCCO.

[66] A mora is also mulberry, blackberry, heap of stones, Moor, while mura recalls walls. Cf. also the given name Amore.

[67] Sassetti could be a Germanic name, or sassetto, heap of stones.

[68] Usually in the sense of woodland.

[69] PeTROCCOLO could claim Troccoli.

[70] Cf. the name of the hoopoe bird.

[71] Metaphorically, a strummulu is a short fat person. Abruzzese strommele has the same meaning.

[72] A busnello could also mean a voluble individual.

[73] Cuccagna can, by extension of meaning, refer to abundance, happiness, comfort.

[74] Metaphorically, a frugolo is a lively child.

[75] A rotella is also a kind of shield.

[76] Capriola may be connected with the word for deer.

[77] Other meanings are chaplet, little hat, Venetian cavalryman.

[78] Also ear-trumpet.

[79] Riformata ed ampliata da P. A. Tosi, Milano, 1865.

the Normans.[80] The Quattrocento court of Este at Ferrara was well stocked with manuscripts in the French original, and so enthusiastic were members of this noble family about these stories that two of the sisters of Borso were given the names of Isolda (Iseult) and Ginevra (Guenevere), two brothers the names Meliaduse and Gurone, and a daughter the name of Isotta.[81] It was this atmosphere of enthusiasm that produced Boiardo's *Orlando Innamorato*, Ariosto's *Orlando Furioso* and Tasso's *Gerusalemme Liberata*, three great masterpieces in the genre. Prosifications like *I Paladini di Francia, I Reali di Francia, I Cavalieri della Tavola Rotonda, Guerino detto il Meschino* have long been and still are the most popular reading of the common folk, who have never ceased to be charmed by the marvellous and supernatural elements in the stories. Some of the tales formed part of the repertoire of the Improvised Comedy or Commedia dell'Arte. They are also popular subjects in the marionette theatres of Naples and especially in Sicily. The most common and oft-repeated scenes on the highly colorful Sicilian carts are drawn from the Carolingian romances.[82] Children on the island continue to play the Jocu di li paladini, the game of the paladins, in which groups representing the Christian and Pagan factions fight each other.[83]

Such a great and prolonged vogue was bound to manifest itself in a very striking way in the Italian onomasticon first by the borrowing of the names of these fictional characters as personal names and through them as surnames. They were already in wide circulation in the twelfth and thirteenth centuries and continued to grow from the new sources until at least the seventeenth century.

Thus, out of the pages of the Breton cycle have sauntered Arturi, Artusi (Arthur), Tristani, Lancillotto, Lanzarotti, Isoldi, Isotti and its short forms Sotti,[84] Soldi,[85] Ginevri, Cinefra, Percivalle, Galassi,[86] Galeotti [87] (Gallahad), Galvano, Gavino (Gauwain), Recchi, Rec-

---

[80] Consult G. Paris, "La Sicile dans la Litérature Française du Moyen Age," *Romania*, V, 1876, 108-13.

[81] See G. Bertoni, *L'Orlando Furioso e la Rinascenza a Ferrara*, Modena, 1919, 91-95, 316-17.

[82] See C. Capitò, *Il Carretto Siciliano*, Milano, 1923. The book has been translated in mimeograph form for the United States Army under the title *The Sicilian Cart*, Palermo, 1944.

[83] See G. Pitrè, "Le Tradizioni Cavalleresche Popolari in Sicilia," *Romania*, XIII, 1884, 315-98.

[84] Competes with DioniSOTTO.

[85] Soldo also means penny and could derive from Lombard AnSOLDO.

[86] Also an augmentative form of gallo, rooster.

[87] Other meanings are galley-slave and jail bird.

chini,[88] (possibly from Erec, Erecco), Brunori, Storino [89] (possibly from Estore), Lionello,[90] Ghezzi [91] (possibly from Kex), Merlino,[92] Ivani, Vani,[93] Bramante, Fieramonte, Marcabruno, Governale, with its short form Vernale, Palamidessi, Scalabrino, Morgana and perhaps others, among them Perciabosco, who may be none other than a namesake of Perceforest, a hero of the Arthurian romance that bears his name.

The Carolingian cycle and its Renaissance continuations have furnished Carlomagno, Carlomano, Carmano, a possible reduction, Mainetto,[94] Fioravanti, Fiorelli, Riccieri, Rizzieri, Torpini,[95] Spinello [96] (from Ospinello), Marfisa, Avino, Avolio,[97] Malagese (same as Malagigi), Pinamonti, Passamonte, Galerano, Brandimarte, Marsilio, Agramante, Sacripante, Ferraguti,[98] Zerbino, Argalia, Mambrino, Medoro. Danese [99] might refer to Uggero il Danese, while Meschini, Meschinelli [100] may go back to Guerino detto il Meschino and Furiosi [101] to Orlando il Furioso. Despite preference for the Christian heroes there were apparently no serious scruples against the adoption of pagan names. Names that had existed previously gained re-newed diffusion due to their being employed as warrior appellatives in these stories — Carlo, Rolando, Orlando and the aphetic forms Lando, Landini, Landucci, Landozzi, Rinaldo and the aphetic forms Naldi, Naldini, Naldoni, Nallini,[102] Bovo,[103] Ber-

[88] Cf. the aphetic forms of orecchio, ear, and orecchini, ear-rings.

[89] Just as likely from Astorino, Ristorino and Castorino.

[90] The connection of this name with lion is, of course, clear.

[91] For competition from Ugo, Arrigo, Domenico, see Bongioanni, *op. cit.* Also cf. SeGHEZZO, ghezzo, dark complexion, black crow, and Milanese ghezz, lizard.

[92] Cf. Merlo, blackbird.

[93] GioVAN(N)I, VAN(N)I is a much more prolific source of the name.

[94] Through apocope Maineri can become Maino and then Mainetto.

[95] Cf. the English surname Turpin.

[96] Also possible from CriSPINO.

[97] Another meaning of Avolio is ivory. "Berlinghieri e Avolio e Avino e Ottone" were the four inseparable sons of Duke Namo of Baviera. See *Orlando Furioso*, XV, 88.

[98] The Ferraguti family of Ferrara very plausibly derives its name from Ferragut Castle in Scotland.

[99] Nese is short for AgNESE. Therefore, Danese may be nothing more than de Nese, D'Anese, Danese.

[100] A meschino is also a miserable, wretched individual.

[101] Furioso, of course, regularly means furious, mad.

[102] ArNALDO and other names could produce these shortenings.

[103] Also an animal name, ox. See chapter on Animal Names.

lingieri, Uggeri with its reduction Geri,[104] Aimone, Olivieri with its reductions Vieri, Verini, Guerino, Tancredi with its reduction Credi, Dodone, Pipino, Viviano and its abbreviated form Viano,[105] Angelica, etc.[106]

Even the great horses of the most famous knights seem to have given rise to surnames, Rinaldo's horse giving Baiardo and Boiardo, Orlando's horse giving Brigliadoro, Bovo d'Antona's horse giving Rondello, and Ruggiero's horse giving Frontino.[107]

Quite a few names in the romances have the termination -ante, Agramante, Aquilante, Agolante, Atalante, Sacripante, all of which have furnished last names except Atalante. These were destined to serve as models along with Greek Patronymics in -antis for names like Armenante, Grisante, Massante, Mazzante, Olivanta, Rodante, Rigante, Zaccante, etc. When Cervantes named Don Quijote's Rocinante he may have been unconsciously influenced by this name-type which he has found so frequently in the course of his reading of the books of chivalry that he satirizes in his masterpiece.

Several of the names of the warriors have, in time, suffered depersonization. The exploits and behavior of Rinaldo, that saucy chieftain of rebellion against his feudal overlord, had so endeared him to the democratic-loving populace, that the minstrels were forced to give him the lion's share in their recitals. This was done so often and for so long that in Neapolitan and other dialects Rinaldo and street minstrel became a synonymous terms.[108] Sacripante is used as a substitute for bully; a Zerbino is a dandy; a Marfisa in Romagnuolo is a doltish woman. Occasionally, these new meanings gained enough strength to install themselves as surnames.

[104] Geri might be from Ruggiero, another well known name in the romances of chivalry. Cf. gera, gravel.

[105] Cf. Viano from OttaVIANO.

[106] Most of these are mentioned in P. Rajna's informative study: "Contributi alla Storia dell'Epopea e del Romanzo Medievale," *Romania*, XVII, 1888, 161-85, 355-65, XVIII, 1889, 1-69. See also P. Rajna: "Le Origini delle Famiglie Padovane e Gli Eroi dei Romanzi Cavallerschi," *Romania*, IV, 1875, 161-83. L. Natali in "Le Tradizioni Cavalleresche in Sicilia," *Folklore Italiano*, II, 1927, adds nothing new to the subject.

[107] Baiardo, Boiardo and Rondello are cited by Rajna, "Contributi . . ." *op cit.* However, A. Bongioanni, *Nomi e Cognomi* . . . Torino, 1928, plausibly gives Abelardo, Abailardo as the source of the first two. For Rondello cf. rondello, swallow. Brigliadoro is a place name in Calabria. Frontino is a small forehead; figuratively an impudent fellow; in Genoese (frontin) a wig, and a font name of Greek origin. The case for these horse names is weak, but see Animal Names.

[108] See P. Rajna, "I Rinaldi o Cantastorie di Napoli," *Nuova Antologia*, XLII, 1878, 557-79.

BABES IN THE WOODS

In 1928 a law was passed in Italy forbidding the imposition upon foundlings or illegitimates of names and surnames that might cast reflection on their origin. The law has probably stopped the increase of such names, but has hardly affected those already in existence.

The most diffused of the deserted child names are Esposito, Sposito, Esposto, Esposuto, Esposi, usually Neapolitan; Ventura, Venturini, if from the Ancona section; Innocenti, Innocentini, Nocenti, Nocentini, if from Tuscany; and Colombini, if from Pavia. Others are dell'Orfano, Arfanetti, orphan; D'Ignoto, Ignotis, Incerto, Incognito, unknown; Trovato, Trovatello, Ritrovato, foundling. (Compare German Findling, Fündel); Fortuna, della Fortuna, della Stella, Stella, Stellato, child of fate; Proietti, exposed; Amandonada, abandoned. Those who have read the *Confessions* of St. Augustine know that he called his illegitimate son Adeodatus, a name that appears to have been adopted in some quarters for children born out of wedlock. Mastro Don Gesualdo in Verga's famous novel thus philosophizes in the presence of his servant Diodata: "You see, every one comes into the world under the influence of the stars. Have you yourself perchance had a father or mother to help you? You have come into the world by yourself, as God sends the grass and the plants which nobody has sown. You have come into the world as indicated by your name . . . Diodata! That means that you have been claimed by no one." [109] The last name Diodati and its reduction Dati is fairly common.

Somewhat cruder names for other illegitimates are Bastardo,[110] Mulo, Spurio (cf. Latin Spurius); D'Amore, Amore, Dell'Amore, child of love; della Gioia, del Gaudio, child of pleasure; della Donna, della Femmina, child of woman; de Alteriis, another's child; and perhaps Naturale, natural son. There are also Cavicchioni (Pavese caviggion), and Bardotti (Aretino). Of course, some of the names given — Ventura, Innocenti, Colombini, Fortuna, Stella, Trovato, Mulo, Amore, Gioia, del Gaudio, Bardotti, and even della

---

[109] From *Mastro Don Gesualdo*, Chapter IV, Part I. Cf. the original: "Vedi, ciascuno viene al mondo colla sua stella . . . Tu stessa hai forse avuto il padre o la madre ad aiutarti? Sei venuta al mondo da te, come Dio manda l'erba e le piante che nessuno ha seminato. Sei venuta al mondo come dice il tuo nome . . . Diodata! Vuol dire *di nessuno!*"

[110] But compare Bastardo a place name in both the province of Arezzo and Spoleto.

Donna and della Femmina [111] can just as easily come from other sources, and in most cases they actually do.

[111] Consult Index for further discussions of these names. Besides coming from bentrovato, welcome, trovato may mean troubadour. Cf. "Siccom'io Jacopo di Tieri cantore o *trovato*," "as I Jacopo di Tieri, singer or troubadour." See *Storia di Ajolfo di Barbicone*, I, Bologna, 1863, xxii.

We take occasion to mention here that the role of foundling asylums in the history of last names would, if investigated, yield very interesting data on the formation of last names. For example, the last name, Gemito, of the famous sculptor, Vincenzo Gemito, is supposed to be due to the fact that when, as a babe, he was deposited at an asylum a nurse found him moaning, and fearing that he might die immediately had him baptised calling him Vincenzo because it was St. Vincent's day and Gemito to indicate the condition that had given her so much alarm. See *La Piccola Illustrazione Italiana*, no. 1, Oct. 1947, p. 14.

Chapter XIX

THE ANGLICIZATION OF ITALIAN SURNAMES IN THE UNITED STATES [1]

There are thousands of anglicized Italian surnames in the United States. That this should be the case need not cause any surprise. The new environment which is so profoundly transforming Old World customs and habits through community living, education and intermarriage also extends its influence to such minute and apparently inconsequential details as the identification tags which we use as last names.

What are some of these changed names? How are the many modifications they undergo to be explained? The answers to these questions can, I believe, most conveniently be given under six headings — translations, dropping of final vowels, analogical changes, French influences, decompounded and other clipped forms and phonetic respellings. By means of them it will be possible to explain the vast majority of those Italian surnames which we find in anglicized form.

TRANSLATIONS

Under the influence of a large number of translated names from other languages, notably German, which transforms Mueller into Miller, Schmidt into Smith, Pfeifer into Piper, Stein into Stone, and the like, the average non-Italian might assume that this is the most common form of the anglicized Italian name. Translations are, indeed, numerous. Because many surnames that derive from baptismal names have equivalents in English, it is natural to expect them to be translated. Thus it is that Bonfazio, Lorenzi, Martini and Olivieri become Boniface, Lawrence, Martin and Oliver. Some of these names discard the preposition di, de or the article la when the change is made, but, in general, where these particles are a part of the original they are usually retained intact, as in De George, De John, De Mark, De Mary, Di Caesar, La Frank, La Mark. At times, in addition to the translation, this type take on an s in imitation of the possessive ending so common in English and German patronymics, as in De Clements, de Michaels, De Peters for De

[1] This chapter is reproduced with some modifications from an article published in *American Speech* for February 1943. Thanks are due to Columbia University Press for permission to reprint.

Clemente, De Michele, De Pietro, and Alberts, Richards, Roberts for Alberti, Riccardi, Roberti. In contrast, surnames that derive from sanctuaries are apt to translate both elements if the name is translated at all: St. Angel, St. John, St. Marie, St. Peter, etc.[2] A few compounded names, such as Mastropaolo, Mastrogiulio and Mastroberto, likewise translate both elements: Masterpaul, Masterjulius, Masterbert.

Other translated surnames are from nicknames Bevilacqua, Drinkwater, Bianco, White, Piccolo, Little, Scaramuccia, Scaramouche, Vinciguerra, Winwar; from occupations: Barbieri, Barber, Mercante, Merchant, Molinari, Miller, Lo Prete, Priest; from geographical areas; Napoli, Naples, Spagna, Spain, Francese, French; from dwellings: Chiesa, Church, Casalegni, Woodhouse, Palazzo, Palace. Translations from these groups are, however, relatively infrequent.

Occasionally one comes upon freak aliases which look like translations but which do not have the remotest connection with their originals except in spelling or sound such as Artery for Artieri tradesman; La Liberty for La Liberta (a font name); Monopoly for Monopoli (a place name), Peptone for Pepitone, Pipituni (a bird name); Special or Speziale (dealer in spices), Change from Ciancio, a pet-name form of Vincenzo.[3]

DROPPING OF FINAL VOWELS

There are, nevertheless, other types of anglicized Italian surnames which are even more common than translations. One of them consists of those names whose final vowel has been dropped, such as Bacigalup for Bacigalupo, Dirienz for Dirienzi, De Bias for De Biasi, De Gustanz for De Gustanzi, Occhigross for Occhigrossi, and hundreds of others. This is in accordance with one of the most characteristic word features of the English language, the consonantal ending. In this case the English themselves long ago set up models by their treatment of the names of the great Italian cities — Milan, Turin, Venice, the names of great Italian writers, Petrarch, Machiavel, Guicciardin, and names which were long ago transplanted on English soil, such as Jessup and Tolliver which derive from Giuseppe and Tagliaferro. Some names with consonantal endings, like Battistell, Bertell, Borrell, Capparell, Lucarel for

[2] Translations of only the second element are extremely rare: San George, San Thomas, Santalucy. The unique San Angelo for Sant'Angelo and San Antonio for Sant'Antonio may be the result of Spanish influence. There is also the possibility that the latter name has been influenced by the name of the Texas city.

[3] L. Adamic. *What's Your Name?* New York, 1942, 48, cites Buckeye and Neareye, comical transliterations of Bucci and Neri.

Battistelli, Bertelli, Borrelli; etc., tend, in addition, to follow the model furnished by a group of English names in -ell, -el, such as Bartell, Bartel, Pennell, Purcell, Terrell, Terrel. The addition of a consonant to a name ending in a vowel is extremely rare; I have found it in only three instances, Grecol for Greco, Matrangol for Matrango, and Garofolow for Garofolo. Something of a freak is Johngrass, the first part of which is a translation and the second drops its final vowel. Not so long ago this cognomen was Giangrasso.

ANALOGICAL CHANGES

Following the model of Cady, Gary, Murphy, Perry and the French Bonamy, Fresny, Livry, etc., the i-ending of a number of Italian names becomes y, as in Arditty, Bovery, Cipully, Ferrandy, Guerry, and Spellacy. Other names terminating in i change their i to e on the basis of models like Milne, Mabbe and the pronunciation of the final e in names of German origin like Janke, Heine, Ratke. Among these are Alegrette, Centanne, Dagostine, Garofale, Leonette, Vassalle. It is just as common, however, not to sound the final e at all, in which case we may posit the influence of French pronunciation Chapelle, Lalanne, Lasalle, Brisette, Racine, or models furnished by a miscellaneous group of English names like Erskine, Cooke, Greene, etc. In addition to the influence of these non-Italian types of surnames we should not overlook the heavy role which the endings of certain everyday words have had in bringing about the change of the i, for instance, words like beauty, glory, library; brunette novelette, rosette; marine, nicotine, routine.

When the i is changed to ie it echoes the type Beattie, Christie, Petrie, etc., as in Alessie, Cangelosie, de Giovannie, Fiorie, Lombardie. There are a few cases where the type Barney, Casey, Finley is copied, causing the i to become ey, as in Caldroney, Contey, Dolcey. Finally, a few names in o assume a final e, as in Spagnoloe, Fuscoe, due perhaps to the analogy of Doe, Roe, Briscoe, and the like. Carusoe, however, distinctly recalls the well-known fictional character, Crusoe.

Where there are two names (an Italian and a non-Italian) that closely approximate one another in pronunciation, the former will not infrequently be completely changed into the latter. Thus a Bonfiglio will become a Bonfield, a Camilli, Campbell, a Canadeo, Kennedy, a Cestaro, Chester, a Cosenza, Cousins, a Crecchia, Craig, a Melone, Malone, a Manino, Manning, a Marsala, Marshall, a Zicaro, Seeger, etc.[4] Sometimes the analogical metamorphosis is

---

[4] We note here that some of the well known Quigleys may have been Quaglias. See G. B. Watts, *The Waldensians in the New World*. Durham, N. C., 1941, 173.

effected by the mere similarity of the fore parts of two such names, no matter how different the rear parts happen to be. In this way Baratta becomes Barry, Campolongo, Campon, Carsella, Carsey, Nicotera, Nickels, Parrella, Parry, Pitucco, Pitt, Ridarelli, Ridell, Roselini, Russell, Rossignuolo, Ross, Scalzitti, Scully, Triusciuzzi, Tracey, etc.[5] Very rarely do we find end-part similarities playing a role in the analogical change such as Elmore for Guglielmo, and the queer Youngo for Capobianco. If the fore part of a name already bears a strong resemblance to a current monosyllabic English name, there is no need for further development, as in the case of Del Judd for Del Giudice, Mack for Maccarone, Mann for Mangiarulo, Quint for Quintieri, etc.[6] Here belongs the strange transformation of Del Tufo into Dell. Some of the Calarcos have quite naturally allowed Clark to usurp the place of their original surname.

FRENCH INFLUENCES

Everyone knows that there is a great mass of Italian surnames which begin with a preposition (da, de, di, d') or an article (li, lo, la). The universal rule in Italian is that the preposition or article be separated from the principal part of the name, as da Dario, de Luca, di Matteo, d'Amato, La Rocca, Li Sacchi, Lo Verde. Probably less than five per cent of this type of name show any deviation from this practice. But when these cognomina are introduced into the United States it is quite usual for them to be merged with their particles, as Dadario, Deluca, Dimatteo, Damato, Larocca, Lisacchi, Loverde. The merging is particularly frequent in names like Desaria, Detalis, and Dichele, that is, in surnames built up of shortened or pet forms of personal names — De Rosaria, De Natalis, Di Michele.

In Italy it is almost unheard of to combine in one unit a surname consisting of preposition plus article plus noun. But in the United States the combination is very common, as for example in Delsanto, Delgenio, Dellorto, and Dellaquila. Such forms may be due to the spelling of names orally without specifying capital letters or apostrophes. However, it is more plausible to explain them as an imitation of the practice followed in French names, which are, of course, very numerous in this country, such as Defontaine, Laforest, and Lemoyne. This theory of French influence will make it easy to explain such odd forms from the Italian

[5] C. Schettler in "Does your Name Identify You?" *Social Forces*, XXI, 1941, 172, adds Mandell from Mandarella. Another name that the author lists, Medal for Medaglia, is a direct translation.

[6] Knapp for Napoli, given by H. L. Mencken, *The American Language*. (4th ed., New York, 1937), 493, obviously belongs to this category.

point of view as De Larosa, De Larocca, De Larco, De Lorto, etc., in which the preposition is separated from the main word, but the article is linked with it. Compare French De Lamar, De Latour, De Laval.

In the case of some Italian surnames ending in i we have already observed a tendency to give them a gallicized appearance by changing the i to a mute e. French influence is also directly or indirectly at work in the change of a and o to e in an even more sizeable group — Bellome, Campagne, Esposite, Marine, Melograne, Passalacque, Quarante, Raguse, Serritelle, etc. However, a parallel influence must here be given considerable weight — the tendency in some of the Southern Italian dialects to turn a final vowel into an indefinite [ə].

In addition to the models which the American environment abundantly offers, the disposition to choose French or French-sounding names is strengthened by the fact that many of our Italian immigrants have come to us after undergoing a period of partial assimilation (including modification of their surnames) in France, the French African colonies or French Canada. Moreover, those who have enjoyed the benefits of a higher education in Italy, which normally involves training in French, are naturally well aware of the way Italian names are adapted in this language (cf. Arioste, Boccace, Tasse, Metastase, etc.), and some of them succumb to the temptation of gallicizing their own surnames. On the whole, it would seem that French endings and French patterns have been used as a sort of compromise approach to anglicization.[7]

DECOMPOUNDED AND OTHER CLIPPED FORMS

Through the application of the law of minimum effort it has always been customary to shorten long names, both first and last. If a surname is a compound it is logical to reduce it to one of the two elements that compose it. For example, the great humanist Poliziano took his name from Monte Pulciano. In the United States we can see a continuation of this process in the rather frequent occurrence of the surname Maestro, which in nine cases out of ten goes back to an original Mastrofrancesco, Mastronicola, etc. Less often Mastro is eliminated in favor of the second element, as in Valerio for Mastrovalerio. Other names which have retained the first element are Notar for Notarpasquale, Papa for Papandrea, Presto for Prestogiacomo, Santo for Santochirico, Trenta for Trentadue, Passo for Passalacqua. Similar reductions appear even in translation in the case of White for Panebianco and Cross for

[7] For some interesting hispanizations of Italian surnames, see B. Roselli, *The Italians in Colonial Florida (1513-1822)*. Jacksonville, 1940.

Trecroci.[8] These reduced versions are, of course, due to the rarity or nonexistence of any current equivalents in English. If patronymics and other names containing diminutive or augmentative suffixes are translated it would be done in terms of compound words — Filippella, Iacobucci, Matteucci, Petruzzi, Ciavolini, Tomasone giving Little Philippa, Little Jacob, Little Matthew, Little Peter, Little Crow, Big Thomas — but as in the case of Panebianco and Trecroci, the lack of current equivalents causes the expulsion of the modifying word, resulting in Philips, Jacobs, Matthew, Peters, Crow, Thomas.[9] Some names suffer a partial decompounding, in which the second element does not wholly disappear but remains in an almost unrecognizable abbreviated form. This accounts for the odd Arcide from Arcidiacono, for Bombast coming from Bombastiano, for Fiorda and Fiordi coming from Fiordaliso and Fiordiliso, and Scari, which goes back to Scaricaciottoli.[10] Noncompounded surnames consisting of three or more syllables are also subject to clipping, as in Agrig for Agrignola, Balis for Balistriero, Felish for Feliciacchia, Patri for Patriglia, Pelle for Pellegrini, Zinga for Inzinga, but the number of these is comparatively small.

PHONETIC RESPELLINGS

In order to preserve the pronunciation of Italian ch, the ch may be replaced by k, as in Baldakini, Marketti, Markesi, etc., but more often the c is retained and k substituted for the h, as in Giackino, Luckino, Quattrocki, Scarnavack (Scornavacco), etc. On the other hand, the soft c before e or i is transformed to ch, as in Ameche from Amici, Checko from Cecco, Cherry from Cerri, De Chesaro from De Cesaro. The change of c to ch in Christofaro, De Christini, Christello the numerous Christiano, Christiani is, of course, to be analogically related to Christopher, Christ, Christian, etc. To avoid cacophony in names containing gl which is apt to be given two sounds by those who do not know Italian, some of their owners have eliminated the g, as in Lulio for Luglio, Palia for Paglia, Pulio for Puglio, Pulise for Puglise. A few names which have sci change the combination to sh: Barrashano, Locashio, Pashotte, Shortino. Double z is sometimes changed to tz in order to preserve the affiricate, as in Matzolo for Mazzolo and Pitzaferro for Pizzaferro. The form Ritzo for Rizzo plainly shows the influ-

---

[8] If both elements had been translated the result would have been Whitebread, Three Crosses.

[9] Mencken, *op. cit.* p. 495, gives the name of a Tomasini which is anglicized into Thomas. Partial translations like Philippone from Filippone are rare.

[10] Ardiacono means archdeacon, Fiordaliso, Fiordiliso, fleur-de-lis, Scaricaciottoli, unloader of stones.

ence of Ritz. Since American short o is a close approximation of Italian a, it replaces this letter in a few names like Konopa, Conopa from Canapa, Caccomo from Caccamo, Giocomo from Giacomo, De Stefono from De Stefano. In the termination -ese, in Albanese, Calabrese, Maltese, Marchese, etc., the Italian sound of the first e is preserved while the final vowel is muted. Hence the spellings Albanase, Albanace, Calabrase, Calabrace, Calabraise, Maltase, Markase. The dialectal equivalent of -ese, which is -ise, is affected in the same way: names like Albanise, Apuglise and Calabrise are spelled Albaneese, Apugleese, Calabrees. The i of the initial diphthong ia is transformed into y in many instances — Yacobone, Yacullo, Yanuzzi, etc.

There are a number of Italian surnames containing double consonants which in America reduce the two consonants to one. The reduction occurs most often in the names made up of preposition plus article plus noun, as in Delaquila, Delapietra, Del Arena, etc. Other simplifications (which occur very sporadically) of double consonants can be illustrated by the following examples: Ricardo, Tadei, Gofreda, Di Magio, Tominello, San Giovani, Sorentino, Di Piaza. While a few spellings of this type can be traced back to dialectical peculiarities in Italian, most of them have unquestionably come into being in the United States. Inasmuch as Italian double consonants are not equivalent in their sound values to English double consonants, we may say that simplifying them represents an effort to adopt them to anglicized pronounciation.[11]

CONCLUSION

Anglicization of Italian surnames is achieved by the drive of two strong forces converging upon their goal from opposite directions. One force (the most powerful of the two) represents the non-Italians—neighbors, employers, foremen, fellow-workers, etc., who, consciously or unconsciously in speech or in writing, make Italians names conform to English linguistic patterns, spelling, or individual names or types of names with which they happen to be acquainted. The other force represents the people of Italian origin who deliberately change their names or tolerate modifications made by outsiders as a concession to their new environment. There are,

[11] If considered from the standpoint of spoken rather than written change it is at once obvious that practically all Italian names are Anglicized in so far as they are made to conform to the rules of English pronunciation, syllabification and accentuation. Incidentally, the names cited in this chapter have been largely drawn from cases personally known to me or reported to me by friends and relatives. They are supplemented by examples found in city and telephone directories, marriage license lists and obituary notices appearing in the newspapers, the *Italian-American Who's Who*, New York, 1939, and U. M. Pesaturo, *Italo-Americans of Rhode Island*, Providence, 1940.

of course, some who feel that an anglicized name will remove the barrier of prejudice that they might have to encounter in their social or business relations, and some who mistakenly think that an anglicized name will make them better Americans. Though there are rare examples in which a Di Giovanni has become a Brown, a Faltera a Smith, a Pizzichini a Moore, etc., the evidence overwhelmingly shows that neither on the score of non-Italians nor on the score of the people of Italian descent has there been any systematic attempt to deliberately hide the Italian character of a surname which, as has already been shown, almost never totally disappears even in its anglicized dress.

How much this tendency to anglicize surnames will keep growing cannot easily be gauged. National pride and the cultural, political and social rise of the Italians in the United States have slowed down the process at least temporarily, but the environmental conditions that have brought it into existence are still the same, and these will be aided by the breaking up of the so-called Italian colonies, the virtual stoppage of immigration from Italy, and the disappearance of the Italian language from home life.[12]

---

[12] We shall not break our objective consideration of these altered surnames at this point by a discussion of the pros and cons involved in the change of a name. It is a delicate matter and much more important than many of us realize. No one should miss reading the one book on the subject—*What's your Name?*—by Adamic.

DICTIONARIES, VOCABULARIES, WORD-LISTS AND GRAMMARS USED IN THE PRESENT STUDY

Accattatis, L. *Vocabolario del Dialetto Calabrese*. Parte I. Castro-villari, 1895.

Aebischer, P. "Le Derivées Italiens du Longobard Gahagi et leur Répartition d'après les Chartres Médiévales." *Zeitschrift für Romanische Philologie*, LVIII, 1938.

―――― "L'Origine et l'Aire de Dispersion du Prénom Médiéval Muntius." *Archivum Romanicum*, XVII, 1933.

―――― "Un Mot d'Origine Normande dans les Dialects des Pouilles: Sire, Père." *Archivum Romanicum*, XXII, 1938.

Alessio, G. "Le Denominazioni del Ghiro e dello Scoiattolo in Calabria." *Archivum Romanicum*, XX, 1936.

―――― "Note Etimologiche." *Italia Dialettale*, XII, 1936.

―――― *Saggio di Toponomastica Calabrese*. Firenze, 1939.

Amati, A. *Dizionario Corografico dell'Italia*. Milano, Vallardi, n.d.

Angiolini, F. *Vocabolario Milanese Italiano*. Torino, 1897.

Avolio, C. "Di Alcuni Sostantivi Locali del Siciliano." *Archivio Storico Siciliano*, n.s. anno XIII, 1888.

―――― *Introduzione allo Studio del Dialetto Siciliano*. Noto, 1892.

―――― "Saggio di Toponomastica Siciliana." *Archivio Glottologico Italiano*. Supplemento, Sesta Dispensa, 1898.

Azzolini, G. B. *Vocabolario Vernacolo Italiano pei Distretti Rove-retano e Trentino*. Venezia, 1856.

Belèze, A. *Dictionnaire des Noms de Baptême*. Paris, 1863.

Bertoni, G. *Italia Dialettale*. Milano, 1916.

―――― "Per la Storia del Dialetto di Modena." *Archivio Glotto-logico Italiano*, XVII, 1910-13.

Bianchi, B. "La Declinazione de' Nomi di Luogo della Toscana." *Archivio Glottologico Italiano*, X, 1886-88.

Biundi, G. *Dizionario Siciliano Italiano*. Palermo, 1857.

Blanc, L. G. *Grammatik der Italienischen Sprache*. Halle, 1844.

Boerio, G. *Dizionario del Dialetto Veneziano*. Venezia, 1856. 2d ed.

Bonaparte, L. "Names of European Reptiles in Living Neo-Latin Languages." *Transactions of the Philological Society*, 1882, 4.

Bonelli, G. "I Nomi degli Uccelli nei Dialetti Lombardi." *Studi Romanzi*, IX, 1902.

Bongioanni, A. *Nomi e Cognomi*. Saggio di Ricerche Etimologiche e Storiche. Torino, 1928.

B. P. F. *Vocabolario Tascabile Genovese Italiano per il Popolo*. Genova, 1873.

Bortolan, D. *Vocabolario del Dialetto Antico Vicentino*. Vicenza, 1893.

Caix, N. *Studi di Etimologia Italiana e Romanza*. Firenze, 1878.

Camusso, N. *Manuale del Cacciatore*. Milano, 1887.

Canestrini, G. *Pesci*. In *La Fauna d'Italia*. Milano, Vallardi, n.d.

Carnoy, A. J. "Adjectival Nouns in Vulgar Latin and Early Romance." *Romanic Review*, VIII, 1917.

Casaccia, G. *Vocabolario Genovese Italiano*. Genova, 1851.

Cherubini, F. *Vocabolario Milanese Italiano*. Milano, 1839. 3 vols.

Chiappelli, L. "I Nomi di Donna in Pistoia dall'Alto Medioevo al Secolo XIII." *Bullettino Storico Pistoiese*, XXII, 1920.

Contarini, P. *Dizionario Tascabile delle Voci e Frasi Particolari del Dialetto Veneziano*. Venezia, 1850.

Conti, E. *Vocabolario Metaurense*. Cagli, 1902.

Cornalia, E. *Catalogo Descrittivo dei Mammiferi*. In *Fauna d'Italia*. Milano, Vallardi, n.d.

Coronedi-Berti, C. *Dizionario Bolognese Italiano*. Bologna, 1869-74. 2 vols.

Corpus Inscriptionum Latinorum. Berlin, 1863 ff.

Cremonese, G. *Vocabolario del Dialetto Agnonese*. Agnone, 1898.

Crocioni, G. "Il Dialetto di Velletri." *Studi Romanzi*, V, 1907.

——— *Il Dialetto di Arcevia*. Roma, 1896.

——— "Lessico." In *La Poesia Dialettale Marchigiana*, II. Fabriano, 1936.

Crollalanza, G. B. *Dizionario Storico Blasonico delle Famiglie Nobili e Notabili Italiane*. Pisa, 1886-88. 2 vols.

d'Ambra, R. *Vocabolario Napoletano*. Napoli, 1873.

Dean, L. H. *A Study of the Cognomina of Soldiers in the Roman Legions*. Princeton, 1916.

de Betta, E. *Rettili ed Anfibi*. In *Fauna d'Italia*. Milano, Vallardi, n.d.

de Gregorio, G. "Gruzzoletto di Voci Arabe Sicule." *Zeitschrift für Romanische Philologie*, XLIX, 1929.

de Salvio, A. "Relics of Franco-Provençal Colonies in Southern Italy." *Publications of the Modern Language Association of America*, XXXIII, 1908.

Ferrari, E. *Vocabolario de' Nomi Propri Sustantivi.* Bologna, 1827-28. 2 vols.

Ferraro, G. *Glossario Monferrino.* Torino, 1889.

Festa, O. F. "Il Dialetto Irpino di Montella." *Italia Dialettale,* V, 1929.

Finamore, G. *Vocabolario dell'Uso Abruzzese.* Lanciano, 1880.

Fiorentino, G. "Note Lessicali ad 'Maqre, Dardequè.'" *Archivio Glottologico Italiano,* XXIX, 1937.

Flechia, G. "Di Alcuni Criteri per l'Originazzione de' Cognomi Italiani." *Atti della R. Accademia dei Lincei,* Serie terza Vol. II, 1877-78.

—— *Di Alcune Forme de' Nomi Locali dell'Italia Superiore.* Torino, 1871.

—— "Lessico Piveronese." *Archivio Glottologico Italiano,* XVIII, 1918.

—— "Nomi Locali d'Italia Derivati dal Nome delle Piante." *Atti della R. Accademia delle Scienze di Torino,* XV, 1879-80.

Florio, J., and Torriano, G. *Dictionary: Italian and English.* London, 1659.

Förstemann, E. *Altdeutsches Namenbuch.* Erster Band. Personennamen. Bonn, 1900. 2d ed.

Foresti, L. *Vocabolario Piacentino Italiano.* Piacenza, 1836.

Frezzi, G. *Dizionario dei Frizzetti Fiorentini.* Città di Castello, 1890.

Fumagalli, G. *Piccolo Dizionario dei Nomi Propri di Persona.* Genova, 1901.

Galiani, F. *Vocabolario delle Parole del Dialetto Napoletano che più si Scostano dal Dialetto Toscano.* Napoli, 1789.

Galvani, G. *Saggio di un Glossario Modenese.* Modena, 1868.

Garbini, A. *Antroponomie ed Omonime nel Campo della Zoologia Popolare.* Verona, 1925-29. 2 vols.

Gatti, R. "Piccolo Vocabolario Iesino." *Archivum Romanicum,* IV, 1920.

Gavuzzi, G. *Vocabolario Piemontese Italiano.* Torino, Streglio, n.d.

G. G. "Nomi di Luogo Friulani Derivati da Piante." *Ce Fastu,* XV, 1929.

Gould's Medical Dictionary. 2d ed. rev. and enl. Philadelphia, 1928.

Grassi-Previtera, G. B. "Nomi Propri e Loro Vezzeggiativi Usati a Partinico." *Studi Glottologici Italiani,* VIII, 1928.

Gualzata, M. "Di Alcuni Nomi Locali del Bellinzonese e Locarnese." *Studi di Dialettologia Celto-Italiana.* Genève, 1924.

Guastalla, A. *Dal Dialetto Guastallese alla Lingua Nazionale.* Guastalla, 1929.

Gysling, F. "Contributo alla Conoscenza del Dialetto della Valle Anzasca." *Archivum Romanicum,* XVIII, 1929.

Hoare, A. *An Italian Dictionary.* Cambridge, 1925.

Holybin's Dictionary of Terms Used in Medicine and the Collateral Sciences. 15th ed. London, 1912.

Holweck, F. G. *A Biographical Dictionary of the Saints.* St. Louis, 1924.

Jaberg, K. u. Jud, J. *Sprach und Sachatlas Italiens und des Südschweiz.* Zoffingen, 1928-

Kahane, H. R. "Designation of the Cheek in the Italian Dialects." *Language,* XVII, 1941.

Lautberg, H. *Die Mundarten Südlukanien.* In Beihefte 90 of *Zeitschrift für Romanische Philologie,* 1939.

Lazzarini, A. *Vocabolario Scolastico Friulano Italiano.* Udine, 1930.

Longa, G. "Vocabolario Bormino." *Studi Romanzi,* IX, 1912.

Lorenzi, A. "Genonomastica Polesana." *Rivista Geografica Italiana,* XV, 1908.

Lorenzi, E. "Dizionario Toponomastico Tridentino." *Archivio per l'Alto Adige,* XIX, XX, XXI, XXII, XXIV, 1924-29.

——— "Osservazioni Etimologiche sui Cognomi Ladini." *Archivio per l'Alto Adige,* II, III, 1907-08.

Luciani, V. "Augmentatives, Diminutives and Pejoratives in Italian." *Italica,* XX, 1943.

Malagoli, G. *Vocabolarietto del Dialetto Pisano.* Pisa, 1937.

Malaspina, G. *Vocabolario Parmigiano Italiano.* Parma, 1858. 3 vols.

Manfredi, R. *Dizionario Pavese Italiano.* Pavia, 1874.

Marinelli, O. "Termini Geografici Dialettali Raccolti in Cadore." *Rivista Geografica Italiana,* XIII, 1901.

Menagio, E. *Le Origini della Lingua Italiana.* Geneva, 1685.

Merlo, C. "I Nomi della Pentecoste nei Dialetti Italiani." *Italia Dialettale,* II, 1926.

——— *I Nomi Romanzi delle Stagioni e dei Mesi.* Torino, 1904.

Meschieri, E. *Vocabolario Mirandolese-Italiano.* Bologna, 1876.

Migliorini, B. "I Nomi Italiani del Tipo Bracciante." *Vox Romanica,* I, 1936.

Mistral, F. *Lou Tresor du Felibrige.* Avignon-Paris, n.d. Vol. I.

Monaci, E. *Crestomazia Italiana dei Primi Secoli,* II. 2d ed. Città di Castello, 1912.

Monti, M. *Ittiologia della Provincia e Diocesi di Como.* Como, 1846.

Morisani, G. *Vocabolarietto del Dialetto di Reggio Calabria.* Reggio Calabria, 1886.

Morri, A. *Vocabolario Romagnuolo Italiano.* Faenza, 1840.

Mortillaro, V. *Nuovo Dizionario Siciliano Italiano.* Palermo, 1881.

Mowat, R. "Les Noms Familiers chez les Romains." *Mémoires de la Societé de Linguistique de Paris,* 1871.

Musoni, F. "Nomi Locali e l'Elemento Slavo in Friuli." *Rivista Geografica Italiana,* IV, 1897.

Nannini, F. *Vocabolario Portatile Ferrarese Italiano.* Ferrara, 1895.

Nazari, G. *Dizionario Vicentino-Italiano.* Oderzo, 1876.

Nittoli, S. *Vocabolario di Vari Dialetti del Sannio.* Napoli, 1872.

Nuovissimo Dizionario Postelegrafonico. New York, 1940.

Olivieri, D. *Cognomi della Venezia Euganea.* Genève, 1923.

Orlando, M. "Raccorciature dei Nomi e Cognomi." *Italia Dialettale,* VIII, IX, 1932-33.

Paoletti, E. *Dizionario Tascabile Veneziano.* Venezia, 1851.

Paoli, I. *Enfant, Garçon, Fille dans les Langues Romanes.* Lund, 1919.

Pasquali, P. S. "Note di Onomastica Lunigianese. Nomi Personali Maschili da Nomi di Terre e Paesi di Lunigiana." *Memorie della Accademia Lunigianese di Scienze Giovanni Capellini,* XVI, 1935.

Pei, M. A. *The Italian Language.* New York, 1941.

Pellegrini, A. "Nuovi Saggi Romaici di Terra d'Otranto." *Archivio Glottologico Italiano,* Supplemento, Terza dispensa, 1895.

Penzig, O. *Flora Popolare Italiana.* Genova, 1924.

Perez, G. *Vocabolario Siciliano Italiano.* Palermo, 1870.

Peri, A. *Vocabolario Cremonese Italiano.* Cremona, 1847.

Petrocchi, P. *Nuovo Dizionario Universale della Lingua Italiana.* Milano, 1902.

Pianigiani, O. *Vocabolario Etimologico della Lingua Italiana.* Milano, 1938. 2 vols.

Piccolo, G. "Vezzeggiativi Italiani di Persona." *Zeitschrift für Romanische Philologie,* L, 1930.

Pieri, S. "Toponomastica delle Valli del Serchio e della Lima." *Archivio Glottologico Italiano,* Supplemento, Quinta Dispensa, 1898.

Pitré, G. "Grammatica delle Parlate e del Dialetto Siciliano." In *Fiabe, Novelle e Racconti Popolari Siciliani,* I, Palermo, 1885.

Poma, C. "Fallaci Apparenze in Cognomi Italiani." *Archivio Glottologico Italiano*, XVIII, 1918.

―――― "Numeri come Cognomi." *Archivio Glottologico Italiano*, XVIII, 1918.

Prati, A. "Etimologie." *Archivio Glottologico Italiano*, XVII, 1910-13.

―――― "Facchino." *Lingua Nostra*, 1939.

―――― "Nomi e Sopranomi di Genti Indicanti Qualità e Mestieri." *Archivum Romanicum*, XX, 1936.

―――― "Spiegazioni di Nomi di Luogo nel Friuli." *Revue de Linguistique Romane*, XII, 1936.

Puoti, B. *Vocabolario Domestico Napoletano e Toscano.* Napoli, 1850.

Raccioppi, G. "Origini Storiche Investigate nei Nomi Geografici della Basilicata." *Archivio Storico per le Provincie Napoletane*, I, 1876.

Raccolta di Voci Romane e Marchiane. Osimo, 1769.

Raccuglia, S. "Saggio di uno Studio sui Nomi di Persona usati in Sicilia." *Archivio per la Tradizioni Popolari*, XVIII, 1899.

Ratti, A. "A Milano nel 1266." *Memorie del R. Istituto Lombardo di Scienze.* Classe di Lettere e Scienze Morali, Serie 3, vol. XXI, 1899-1907.

Richter, E. "Das Altitalienische Tabacco." *Archivum Romanicum*, XI, 1922.

Riegler, R. "Italienische Vogelnamen." *Archivum Romanicum*, XI, 1927.

―――― "Perol im Italienischen." *Archivum Romanicum*, IX, 1925.

Rohlfs, R. *Dizionario Dialettale delle Tre Calabrie*, I-II. Milano, 1932-39.

Rosa, G. *Vocabolario Bresciano Italiano.* Brescia, 1877.

Samarani, B. *Vocabolario Cremasco Italiano.* Crema, 1852.

Savani, G. *La Grammatica e il Lessico del Dialetto Teramano.* Torino, 1881.

Scala, G. *Piccolo Vocabolario Domestico Friulano Italiano.* Pordenone, 1870.

Scerbo, F. *Sul Dialetto Calabro.* Firenze, 1886.

Schröder, E. *Deutsche Namenkunde.* Göttingen, 1938.

Serra, G. D. "Nomi Personali Femminili Piemontesi da Nomi di Paesi e Città Famose del Medioevo." *Rivista Filologica* (Cernauti), I, 1927.

—— "Per la Storia del Cognome Italiano. Cognomi Canavesi di Forma Collettiva in -aglia, -ata, -ato." *Dacoromania*, III, 1922-23.

Sicher, E. "I Pesci e la Pesca nel Compartimento di Catania." *Atti della Accademia Gioenia di Scienze Naturali in Catania*, anno LXXV, 1898, Memoria, V.

Skok, P. "Die Verbalkomposition in der Romanischen Toponomastik." Beihefte zur *Zeitschrift für Romanische Philologie*, 1911.

Spano, G. *Vocabolario Sardo Italiano*. Cagliari, 1851.

Spotti, L. *Vocabolario Anconitano Italiano*. Genève, 1929.

Tagliavini, C. "Il Dialetto di Comelico." *Archivum Romanicum*, X, 1926.

Talmon, A. Saggio del Dialetto di Pragelato." *Archivio Glottologico Italiano*, XVIII, 1918.

Taylor, I. *Words and Places*. New York, Dutton. n.d.

Tiraboschi, A. *Vocabolario dei Dialetti Bergamaschi Antichi e Moderni*. Bergamo, 1873.

Toschi, L. *Dizionario Anconitano Italiano*. Parte I. Castelflamio, 1889.

Ungarelli, G. *Vocabolario del Dialetto Bolognese*. Bologna, 1901.

Vignola, C. *Lessico del Dialetto di Amaseno*. Roma, 1926.

—— "Il Vernacolo di Castro dei Volsci." *Studi Romanzi*, VII, 1911.

Vivaldi, R. "Toponomastica Romana." *Folklore Italiano*, III, 1928.

Vocabolario degli Accademici della Crusca. Firenze, 1739-38.

Volpi, G. "D'un uso Antico della Parola Tabacco." *Archivio Storico Italiano*, Anno LXXI, 1913.

Weekley, E. *Jack and Jill*. London, 1939.

—— *The Romance of Names*. 2d ed. London, 1914.

—— *Surnames*. London, 1936.

Woolf, H. B. *The Old Germanic Principles of Name Giving*. Baltimore, 1939.

Zalli, C. *Dizionario Piemontese Italiano, Latino e Francese*. Carmagnola, 1830.

Zanardelli, T. *I Nomi di Animali nella Toponomastica Emiliana*. Bologna, 1907.

—— "I Nomi Etnici nella Toponomastica." *Atti della Società Romana di Antropologia*, XII, 1901-02.[1]

---

[1] We omit here hundreds of telephone and city directories covering all sections of the United States and Italy, annuari, calendari, almanacchi, author lists, etc., etc., from which we have gathered the great bulk of our surnames.

OTHER BOOKS OR ARTICLES CITED

Adamic, L. *What's Your Name?* New York, 1942.

Alberti, G. B. *Opere Volgari*, II. Firenze, 1844.

Ammirato, S. *Delle Famiglie Nobili Napoletane.* Firenze, 1640.

Angelini, L. "Insegne d'osterie Bergamasche." *Rivista di Bergamo*, IX, 1931.

Anon. "Maria to the Fore." *Scribner's Magazine*, LIX, 1913.

—— "Super-Twins." *Life.* March 6, 1944.

Archivio di Stato di Venezia, I-II, 1937-40.

Ariosto. *Orlando Furioso.*

—— *Satira Settima.*

Aristophanes. *The Birds.*

Avery, D. "The Man Who Dared Call Himself Percy." *Chicago Sunday Tribune*, March 12, 1944.

Bandello. *Novelle.*

Bandi Lucchesi dal 1331 al 1356. Bologna, 1863.

Bencini, I. M. "Sulla Guerra e l'Acquisto di Pisa (1404-1406). *Archivio Storico Italiano*, XVIII, 1896.

Benussi, B. D. *Storia Documentata di Rovigo.* Trieste, 1888.

Bertoni, G. *L'Orlando Furioso e la Rinascenza a Ferrara.* Modena, 1919.

Boccaccio. *Decameron.*

Bonfigli, L. "Un Mazzetto di Stornelli Genzanesi." *Archivio per la Storia delle Tradizioni Popolari*, XXII, 1906-07.

Borghini, R. *Amante Furioso.* Firenze, 1583.

Boughner, D. C. "Sir Toby's Cockatrice." *Italica*, XX, 1943.

Bradley, H. *The Story of the Goths from the Earliest Times to the End of the Gothic Dominions in Spain.* New York, London, 1888.

Britton, R. L. and Brown, A. *Illustrated Flora of the United States, Canada and British Possessions.* New York, 1898. 3 vols.

Brown, T. G. "Names Can Hurt Me." *Wilson Library Bulletin*, April, 1943.

Burn, R. *Roman Literature in Relation to Roman Art.* London, New York, 1868.

Cairo, G. *Dizionario Ragionato dei Simboli.* Milano, Hoepli, n.d.

Calmo, A. *La Spagnola.* Venetia, 1555.

Capasso, B. *Le Fonti della Storia della Provincie Napoletane dal 568 al 1500.* Napoli, 1902.

Capitò, G. *Il Carretto Siciliano.* Milano, 1923.

Cecchi, G. M. *Martello.* Venetia, 1585.

Celesia, E. *The Conspiracy of Gianluigi Fieschi.* London, 1866.

Cibrario, L. "Dell'Origine dei Cognomi." *Opuscoli Storici e Letterari.* Milano, 1835.

Cossar, R. M. "Nomignoli Gradesi." *Folklore Italiano*, II, 1927.

Croce, B. *La Leggenda di Nicola Pesce.* Napoli, 1885.

Croce, G. C. *Bertoldo, Bertoldino e Caccasenno.*

Dante. *Divina Commedia.*

——— *Vita Nuova.*

Dauzat, A. *Les Noms de Personnes.* Paris, 1928.

de Bartolomeis, V. "Aimeric de Peguilhan." *Studi Romanzi*, VI-VIII, 1909.

de Gregorio G. "La Grecità del Dialetto Calabrese." *Zeitschrift für Romanische Philologie*, XLIX, 1929.

Deledda. *Il Vecchio della Montagna.*

di Giovanni, V. "Etnografia della Popolazione di Palermo." *Archivio Storico Siciliano*, n.s. XIII, 1888.

Dudan, B. *Il Dominio Veneziano di Levante.* Bologna, 1938.

Enciclopedia Italiana.

Evans, E. P. *Animal Symbolism in Ecclesiastical Art.* London, 1896.

Gabotto, F. "L'Elemento Storico nelle Chansons de Geste e la Questione delle loro Origini." *Bollettino Storico Bibliografico Subalpino*, XXVI, 1924.

Gamillscheg, E. "Romania Germanica." *Grundriss der Germanischen Philologie*, 11/2, 1935.

Gaudenzi, G. "Storia del Cognome a Bologna nel Secolo XIII." *Bullettino dell'Istituto Storico Italiano*, No. 19, 1888.

Giannini, G. "Il Carnevale nel Contado Lucchese." *Archivio per lo Studio delle Tradizioni Popolari*, VII, 1888.

Gilbert, A. H. "The Etymology of the Dragoon. Addentum." *Publications of the Modern Language Association of America*, LVIII, 1943.

Giusti, G. *Raccolta di Proverbi Toscani.* Firenze, 1871.

Gracián, L. *Il Criticón* (Cattaneo version). Venezia, 1720.

Manzoni. *I Promessi Sposi.*

Marucchi, O. *Epigrafia Cristiana.* Milano, 1910.

Melzi, G. B. *Bibliografia dei Romanzi di Cavalleria in Verso e in Prosa Italiani.* Riformata ed Ampliata da P. A. Tosi. Milano, 1865.

Mencken, H. L. *The American Language.* 4th ed. New York, 1937.

Migliorini, B. *Dal Nome Proprio al Nome Comune.* Genève, 1927.

Minieri-Ricci, C. "Cenno Storico delle Accademie Fiorite nella Città di Napoli . . ." *Archivio Storico per le Provincie Napoletane,* IV-V, 1879-80.

———— "Memorie della Guerra di Sicilia negli Anni 1282-1283-1284." *Archivio Storico per le Provincie Napoletane,* I, 1876.

Nazioni Unite (N.Y.), June 1, 1945.

Neri, F. *Gli Animali nelle Opere di Virgilio.* Pisa, 1896.

Oberndorf, C. P. "Re-Action to Personal Names." *Psychoanalytical Review,* V, 1918.

Paris, G. "La Sicile dans la Litérature Française du Moyen Age," *Romania,* V, 1876, 108-13.

Pasqualigo, L. *Fedele.* Venetia, 1576.

Pitrè, G. *La Famiglia, la Casa, la Vita del Popolo Siciliano.* Palermo, 1913.

———— "La Leggenda di Nicola Pesce nella Letteratura Italiana e Tedesca." *Raccolta di Studi Critici Dedicata ad Alessandro d'Ancona.* Firenze, 1901.

———— *Medicina Popolare Siciliana.* Torino, Palermo, 1896.

———— "Le Tradizioni Cavalleresche Popolari in Sicilia." *Romania,* XIII, 1884.

———— *Usi e Costumi, Credenze e Pregiudizi del Popolo Siciliano.* Palermo, 1889.

Pucci, A. *Contrasto delle Donne* (ed. A. Pace). Menasha, Wis., 1944.

Rajna, P. "Contributi alla Storia dell'Epopea e del Romanzo Medievale." *Romania,* XVII-XVIII, 1888-89.

———— "Le Origini delle Famiglie Padovane e gli Eroi dei Romanzi Cavallereschi," *Romania,* IV, 1875.

———— "I Rinaldi o Cantastorie di Napoli." *Nuova Antologia,* XLII, 1878.

Reggio Archivio di Stato di Lucca, 1907.

Roselli, B. *The Italians in Colonial Florida (1513-1822).* Jacksonville, 1940.

Rothery, G. C. *A B C of Heraldry.* Philadelphia, Jacobs, n.d.

Ruffini, M. "Onomastica Lunigianese. Cognomi Spezzini fra il 1558 e il 1650." *Memoria dell'Accademia Lunigianese di Scienze, Giovanni Capellini*, XVI, 1935.

Salvatorelli, L. *A Concise History of Italy*. New York, 1940.

Salverte, E. *Les Noms d'Hommes de Peuples et de Lieux*, I-II. Paris, 1824.

Sandys, J. E. *Latin Epigraphy*. Cambridge, 1919.

Schettler, C. "Does Your Name Identify You?" *Social Forces*, XXI, 1941.

Schlesinger, A. R. "Patriotism Names the Baby." *New England Quarterly*, XIV, 1941.

Sereni, A. P. *The Italian Conception of International Law*. New York, 1944.

Sforza, C. *The Real Italians*. New York, 1942.

Starabba, R. "Miscellanea. Catalogo ragionato di un Protocollo del Notaio Adamo di Citella dell'Anno XII d'Indizione 1298-99." *Archivio Storico Siciliano*, n.s. anno XIII, 1888.

Statuti Senesi Scritti in Volgare ne' Secoli XIII e XIV. Vol. III. Bologna, 1877.

Turning, L. *Symbols and Emblems of Early and Mediaeval Christian Art*. London, 1885.

Varchi, B. *Storia Fiorentina*. I. Firenze, 1843.

Verga, G. *Mastro don Gesualdo*.

Villani, G. *Chronicle* (trans. R. E. Selfe). London, 1906.

Volpi, G. "Uno Sguardo all'Onomastica Fiorentina." *Rivista d'Italia*, VI, 2, 1903.

Watts, G. B. *The Waldensians in the New World*. Durham, N. C., 1941.

INDEX

NOTE

The Reader can enlarge this list by prefixing di, de, de', del della, La, Lo, Li to many of the names that follow or by tacking diminutives and augmentatives on to them. See chapter on Pet Names. In order to save space we have made use of root words in a considerable number of instances. They are those that appear in italics. The italicized name, then, points to other names that are derived from it.

A

Abate 165, 216
Abatecola 62
Abatemarco 62
Abateminnici 62
Abatescianni 62
Abba 21
Abbadessa 165
Abbado 165
Abbate-i 165, 216
Abbruscato 88
Abele 22
Abello 22
Abetti 91
Abisso 99
Abrami 22
Abruzzese 106
Abruzzi 106
Abruzzini 106
Accattino 166
Accavallo 65
Accetta 187
Accieri 161
Accoramboni 56
Accorimboni 56
Accorinti 114
Accoroni 56
Acerbi 88
Aceto 181
Achillini 20
Acicaferro 56
Acierno 89
Acinello 89
Acione 86
Acqua 101
Acquafredda 64

Acquaro 176, 224
Acquaruolo 176
Acquistapace 55
Acuto 29, 68
Adami 22
Adamol(l)o 22
Adimari 21, 28
Adorno 129
Adorato 69
Affatato 72
Affaticati 72
Afflitto 72
Affranti 72
Africano 109
Agabiti 20
Agamenone 20
Aggarbati 67
Agelli 102
Agilufo 21
Agli 83
Agliè 32
Aglietti 83
Aglione 83, 141
Agnello-i 53, 135
Agnese 197
Agnisio 18
Agno 135
Agnolillo 135
Agnusdei 65
Ago 192
Agolante 233
Agoli 129
Agosti 221
Agostini 20, 221
Agozzino 160
Agramante 232, 233
Agresti 88

Agricola 168
Agrig 241
Agrignola 241
Agrillo 151
Agro 102
Aguglia 129, 145
Agugliaro 173
Aimone 233
Aiutamicristo 55
Ajolo 126, 166
Alamanno 21, 111
Alampi 145
Alano 89
Alaro 108
Alba 223, 224
Albanace 242
Albanase 242
Albaneese 242
Albanese 110, 161, 242
Albanise 110, 242
Albarella 91
Alberghini 104
Alberico 35
Albertanti 18
Alberto 21
Alberts 237
Albicocchi 87
Albizi 21, 28
Alcide 214
Alcionis 121
Aldana 89
Aldobrandini 28
Alegrette 238
Alessandri 20, 28
Alessich 18
Alessie 238
Alessio 20, 238

Alemagna, 51

Corrao 101
Correggiari 171
Correnti 229
Corridori 123, 133, 161
Corrieri 161
Corsale 178
Corsaletti 191
Corsaro 178
Corso 36
Corsonello 153
Cortaldo 132
Corte 104
Corteggiani 163
Cortelassi 77
Cortelazzo 77, 93, 181
Cortellieri 173
Cortes 109
Cortese 67
Cortesani 163
Corti 102, 210
Cortina 102
Cortopasso 63
Corvaia 93
Corvi 119
Corviero 169
Cosa 35, 36
Coscia 29, 195, 208
Coscino 208
Coselli 36, 208
Cosentino 106
Cosenza 238
Cosetti 208
Cosi 28, 195
Cosimo 20
Cosini 36
Cositori 172
Cosmati 17
Cossa 29, 80, 195
Cossali 191
Cos(s)azza 36
Cossu 184
Costabile 159
Costa 99, 195
Costetti 80, 99
Coticone 73
Cotta-i 38, 40, 46, 184
Cottone 40, 96, 187
Cottonero 172
Cotugno 87, 97
Cousins 238
Covazzi 44
Covello 44, 108
Coverelli 44
Coviello 44
Covino 45

Covolini 45
Covone 45
Covotti 45
Cozza-i-o 38, 40, 99, 156, 185, 194
Cozzone 40, 177
Craig 238
Crapulli 135
Cravatta 150
Craviotto 137
Creatura 53
Crecchia 238
Credi 233
Credico 164
Credidio 55
Creonti 20
Crescimbeni 55
Crescioli 95
Crescioni 77
Crespi 212
Cresta 99
Crestano 165
Creta 98
Cretaro 98
Cretinelli 71
Crevelloni 189
Crisanti 76
Crispi 212
Cristiano 60, 68
Crivellari 174
Crivelli 189
Croatti 110
Crobu 119
Croce 105
Crocetta 24
Crociato 161
Crocioni 125
Crollalanza 57
Cross 240
Crotti 154, 212
Crovaia 93
Crovelli 119
Croveri 170
Crow 241
Crudeli 69
Crudo 69
Crugnale 90
Cuaresima 215, 223, 228
Cuba 44
Cubito 44
Cuccagni 230
Cuccetta 38, 40
Cucchetti 78, 121
Cucchi 99, 121
Cucchiari 96, 181

Cucchiarone 122, 181
Cucci(o) 38, 40, 46
Cucciardo 123
Cucciari 96, 181
Cuccioli 40
Cuccoli 78, 99, 121
Cuccovillo 120
Cucuzza 80, 217
Cuffia 184
Cugino 53
Cugurra 150
Culicchia 149
Cultellaio 173
Cumella 41
Cumo 41
Cuneo 107
Cuniberti 21
Cuniglio 140
Cuoco 163
Cuonsolo 159
Cuoio 193
Cuorvo 119
Cupparo 175
Curà 165
Curato 165
Curatolo 170
Curci(o) 135, 210
Curcione 135
Curiale 167
Curreri 161
Currao 101
Curti 102
Curtis 210
Cusman(n)o 21, 109
Custodi 160
Custuliere 172
Cuttone-i 97
Cuttunaro 172
Cuzza 194
Cuzzale 202
Cuzzi 38, 40, 46
Cuzzone 38, 40, 46, 177
Cuzzubbo 180

D

da Bari 107
d'Addamio 18
Dadario 239
Dagomari 167
Dagostine 238
Dainelli 137
Daini 137
d'Albergo 104
dal Buffalo 138
dal Foco 70